PHILIP GARIGUE

A BIBLIOGRAPHICAL INTRODUCTION TO THE STUDY OF FRENCH CANADA

GREENWOOD PRESS, PUBLISHERS
WESTPORT, CONNECTICUT

Library of Congress Cataloging in Publication Data

Garigue, Philippe, 1917-
    A bibliographical introduction to the study of French Canada.

    Reprint of the 1956 ed. published by the Dept. of Sociology and Anthropology, McGill University, Montreal.
    1. French-Canadians—Bibliography. 2. Quebec (Province)—Bibliography. I. Title.
[Z1377.F8G29 1977] [F1027] 016.9714   77-11621
ISBN 0-8371-9807-0

All rights reserved.

Originally published in 1956 by Department of Sociology and Anthropology, McGill University, Montreal

Reprinted with the permission of Philippe Garigue

Reprinted in 1977 by Greenwood Press, Inc.

Library of Congress Catalog Card Number 77-11621

ISBN 0-8371-9807-0

Printed in the United States of America

INTRODUCTION

Social studies demand the same type of critical thinking as is found in all scientific research. However, the greater complexity of social and cultural facts makes it impossible to open most books reporting the findings of a research without coming upon sentences which can be shown to be related to doubtful empirical evidence. Statements which are not scientific in any sense stand side by side with obviously well proven findings. Certain fields of the social sciences, and certain types of studies, are more prone than others to these contradictions. This has been the fate of French Canadian studies. For a long time its history has been that of a polemical struggle for or against the acceptance of particular theses. This, because statements about French Canada involved its status in North America. This is one of the reasons for the slow growth of accurate research, especially when social scientists themselves became involved in the fight and even used pseudo-scientific arguments to bolster the aspirations of specific groups.

It would be wrong, however, to reject all the evidence and generalizations to be found in past research. These writings often contain a great deal of valuable information and may be viewed as historical documents representing some of the social thought which existed at the time. This is not to say that an increasing number of more and more accurate studies are not being produced. Such studies as are now coming from young social scientists in the Universities of Montreal, Laval, McGill, or the National Museum in Ottawa, have reached a high degree of scientific procedure. Unfortunately, this cannot be said for the major part of the writings about French Canada.

French Canada has been, on the whole, very imperfectly studied. While much has been written, most of it is descriptive and far too little analytical. From the point of view of present empirical research many of the statements which have been made are too speculative to be reliable. A reassessment is necessary. The first requirement is an evaluation of the multiple meanings which have been given to the words *French Canada*. There seem to be as many opinions as there are writers. Precise definitions are lacking, and the opinions themselves are not very clear. So far most usages have implied a definition rather than made one explicit. For instance, until recently some writers viewed French Canadians as persons who could trace their descent to 17th century French migrants, were Catholic, spoke French, lived in the Province of Quebec, followed certain traditions and held "nationalistic" views. Others have implied that without these characteristics a person was not a "true" French Canadian, while a community in which these were not dominant was either in a state of disintegration or marginal to French Canada. There are certain historical reasons why these criteria do describe some features of French Canada. However, it would be wrong to accept these as the only valid criteria, or their sum total as the means of measuring change in French Canada. Since French Canada has never been a national state, and presents itself today as an ethnic distribution in North America with a concentration in one Canadian Province, an element of arbitrariness always enters into its description. It is in the selection and appraisal of the factors which have contributed to its maintenance as a separate entity that most authors have followed their own inclinations rather than scientific procedure.

It is suggested here that the only satisfactory approach to research is the selection of criteria in terms of observational data. This proposed change is more than a replacing of one definition by another. It demands a reassessment of what has been said about French Canada according to research findings, and a non-acceptance of statements until confirmed by empirical research. It is also the recognition that research must take into account all the social and cultural dimensions which are relevant to the lives of French Canadians, however far removed these seem from any preconceived notion of what is French Canada. Lastly, it is also a critical awareness of what is being assumed in research, so that subjective evaluation will not be taken for reality. Thus, previously, many social scientists have studied rural French Canada on the assumption that it was more significant than its urban areas to an understanding of its total culture. This arbitrary assumption had a prejudicial effect on research, and resulted in the creation of a number of fallacies. For instance, according to these authors the most isolated rural communities were the most representative of traditional French Canada — although actually New France had originated as a highly urbanized settlement. Other writers have also held that French Canadian culture not only came from rural communities, but that its "ethos" was similar to that of 17th century peasant France. As a logical step in inference another fallacy was produced. It was shown that the presence in French Canada of non-17th century French peasant cultural traits, or of urban cultural traits, was the result of the social and cultural disintegration which took place after the conquest of 1760, or the sign of its assimilation by English-speaking North America. These opinions, which recent research has shown to be mistaken inferences, were the results not only of the arbitrary selection of criteria which had chanelled research towards certain conclusions, but also of the making of mistaken assumptions as to the present and past of French Canada.

A BIBLIOGRAPHICAL INTRODUCTION...

If a minimum definition of French Canada is given, for the purpose of initiating research, as the totality of persons claiming to be French Canadian, irrespective of the reasons for these claims, the recurrence of the above and other mistakes can be prevented. It can be shown that the core of French Canada consist of a number of frequencies between the claims and the reasons for making them. A scale of these frequencies represents the importance of each symbol in the identification of French Canada by French Canadians. The investigation of the economic, political, religious, family, and other activities of these persons can then show its structure as a social unit and the functional interrelationship between its social institutions. The present situation can then be seen against the past by taking into consideration the history of each symbol or social institution. Lastly, what non-French Canadians think of French Canada can be added to indicate its status in North American society. This approach would eliminate the making of unwarranted assumptions. It would also prevent assuming that French Canada is simply an extension of 17th century France, or isolated from the general history of North America. It would most definitly prevent the misuse of the word "americanization" as if French Canadians were not North Americans, or as if North Americans must, of necessity, be English-speaking. Indirectly, it would allow for the making of a comparative study of the similarities and differences between French Canadians and members of other North American ethnic groups on the basis of their actual rather than their assumed characteristics.

This view of French Canada as something fundamentally different from the rest of North America, to be explained by the presence of special laws of survival, is not an isolated instance of misguided opinion. It cannot be separated from slogans, political and otherwise, which have been effectively used to gain support for leaders and movements. This opinion belongs to a period in the history of French Canada when it was held what was peculiar to it was the unwavering allegiance of French Canadians to their language, religion and laws. Here again, recent research has shown that this came about as the result of a type of evaluation which can be called myth-making. This is not to say that preference for the speaking of French, membership of the Catholic Church, and the possession of a special Code of laws, have not influenced events, but rather that these were not the only, or even the main factors which contributed to the maintenance of a French Canadian group. A separation must be made here between what the French Canadians created as the symbols of their integration, and the reality. The "mythology" of symbols fails to explain, for instance, the present position of Catholicism in Canada as no longer restricted to French Canadians. Neither can it explain why the Civil Code of the Province of Quebec is not

A BIBLIOGRAPHICAL INTRODUCTION...

an unchanging "traditional" Code, but the result of influences which have adapted as well as created laws during the fast changing political history of Canada. Lastly, it fails to explain why many persons who claim to be French Canadians speak no French or use it as a secondary language. Most important, the "mythology" ignores the sociological implications of the political, economic, geographic, demographic, and other factors. Historical evidence does show that at one time all French Canadians spoke French, were Catholics and obeyed the "Coutumier de Paris" as interpreted by the administration of New France. However, it does not mean that because New France once existed, French Canada is to be forever analysed according to what existed then, as if the conquest of 1760, the opening of new trade routes, the timber trade, the industrialization of Canada and North America, as well as other major transformations, had not taken place. Just as the "mythology" came into existence to explain the position of French Canadians in North America according to an "ad hoc" evaluation, the use of a past situation as a limiting factor in the study of the present is another form of myth-making as dangerous as the assuming that rural French Canada represents its "true" nature. Present day research demands some degree of sophistication in the handling of these myth-making propensities, as well as an awareness of their existence in the thoughts of French Canadians and others. There is no doubt that authors who write of the disintegration of present-day French Canada or of the existence of a crisis situation, often assume the existence of a mythical "Golden Age" when all was well. This seems to be the idea behind the often made contention that French Canada ceased to exist as a social unit when New France disappeared, and that its "true" existence can only be achieved in the present by a separation from the rest of Canada. This argument is not sociologically valid for at least two reasons. Firstly, while there were important changes in political and other institutions, the conquest of 1760 did not mean the loss of political sovereignty by the French Canadians, since they did not have it, but the passing from one situation of political dependency to another. Secondly, to imply the non-existence of present-day French Canada on no more grounds that it is not the same as New France, seems simply to say that it does not exist as the person making that denial wants it to exist. Acceptance of this would go far to permit a more critical perception of what does exist, which, together with a cautious use of such words as survival, tradition, assimilation, disintegration, americanization, nationalism, etc., could settle the argument as to the social and cultural reality of French Canada.

Finally, another important source of error in research has been the ignorance by many social scientists of the details of French Canadian history. This seems to be due to a reluctance to investigate and accept the importance of historical causation. This reluctance is especially strong among those sociologists and anthropologists who have looked upon French Canada as a sort of "Folk Society". Because of their lack of historical knowledge these social scientists have identified French Canada with the so-called under-developed areas of the world, and used in its description and analysis the concepts elaborated in the study of societies without written history. There is little need here to show how mistaken this is. The present bibliographical introduction is offered as a corrective for this and other biases. Its aim is to give an adequate, not an exhaustive listing, of the writings on various topics by French and English speaking historians, geographers, economists, sociologists, anthropologists, as well as others. These topics, which form the bibliographical classification, have been chosen because they are thought to be of major importance to an understanding of French Canada. The bibliography is, however, to be considered more as a contribution to research planning than as a final product in classification. To include as many references as possible, as well as lower the cost of production, some of the niceties of bibliographical information have been left out and only enough included to allow for their location.

The bibliographical research was carried out in Montreal and most items are known to be available in the libraries of that city, or obtainable through inter-library loans. The author wishes to acknowledge the award of a grant from the Faculty of Graduate Studies and Research, McGill University, which made publication possible. He also wishes to thank the many persons who helped in his reseach, especially Miss Renée Caron, who was his research assistant for some months.

TABLE OF CONTENTS

	PAGES
Introduction	5
Table of contents	10
Abbreviations	12

Bibliography

1. General Historical studies 13
   a) General Historical introduction 13
   b) The History of New France 14

2. The Human Geography of French Canada 18
   a) General geographical studies 18
   b) Land settlement and colonization 19
   c) Gaspesia 21
   d) Saguenay, Lake St. John and North Coast 22
   e) The Quebec Region 23
   f) Quebec City 24
   g) Lake St. Peter and the Central Region 26
   h) The Eastern Townships 27
   i) The Montreal Region 28
   j) Montreal City 29
   k) The Ottawa-Abitibi-Temiscamingue Region 32

3. The Social Institutions of French Canada 33
   a) Demography 33
   b) Kinship and the Family 34
   c) The Economic Organization 37
      I) Economic History 37
      II) Agriculture 40
      III) Forest and Fishing 43
      IV) Mining and Industries 44
      V) Cooperative Movement 46
      VI) Labour Problems and Trade Unionism 48
   d) The Political Organization 52
      I) Political History 52
      II) Government 57
      III) Political Ideologies and Parties 59
      IV) Nationalism 61
      V) The "St. Jean Baptiste" Society 64
      VI) Laws and the Legal System 65
   e) The Religious Organization 67
      I) History of the Catholic Church in Quebec 67
      II) Religious Orders 71
      III) Missionary Activities 73
      IV) Social Catholicism 74
      V) Parish Organization 76
      VI) Non-Catholic Religious Organizations in Quebec . 77
      VII) Anti-Clericalism 78

A BIBLIOGRAPHICAL INTRODUCTION...

	PAGES
4. French-Speaking Groups outside the Province of Quebec	80
a) Acadians	80
b) Other Groups in Canada	81
c) Metis	84
d) French-speaking Groups in the United States	85
5. Social Changes and Social Problems	88
a) Migration to the United States	88
b) Rural-Urban Migration and Urbanization	88
c) Social Stratification	89
d) Status of Women	90
e) Relationship with other ethnic groups	92
I) French-English relationships	92
II) Other Ethnic Groups	94
f) Social Problems	96
g) Social Work and Social Legislation	97
6. Cultural Characteristics	101
a) Folklore and Traditions	101
b) Linguistics and Language problems	103
c) Bilingualism	105
d) Journalism, Radio, TV and Public Spectacles	106
e) Literature	108
f) Arts and Music	112
g) Cultural values	114
h) The influence of the United States	118
i) The influence of France	118
7. The Educational System	120
a) History of Education	120
b) Elementary Education	123
c) *Collège classique* and Secondary Schools	124
d) Technical Education	126
e) University Education	126
8. Special problems in the study of French Canada	128
a) Historical Interpretation and "Historicism"	128
b) Theories and Methods of Social Research	129
9. Bibliographies	132

ABBREVIATIONS

AE	L'Actualité Economique
AdF	Archives de Folklore
AF	L'Action Française
AJS	The American Journal of Sociology
AN	L'Action Nationale
ASR	The American Sociological Review
AU	L'Action Universitaire
BESC	Bien-Etre Social Canadien
BRH	Bull. des Recherches Historiques
CAC	Cahiers d'Action Catholique
CESH	Contributions à l'Etudes des Sciences de l'Homme
CF	Le Canada Français
CG	The Canadian Geographer
CGJ	The Canadian Geographical Journal
CHAR	The Canadian Historical Association Report
CHR	The Canadian Historical Review
CJEPS	The Canadian Journal of Economics and Political Science
CL	Cité Libre
CV	Carnets Viatoriens
ES	Enseignement Secondaire au Canada
ESP	Ecole Sociale Populaire
ISP	Institut Social Populaire
JAF	The Journal of American Folklore
NRC	La Nouvelle Revue Canadienne
OT	L'Oeuvre des Tracts
PO	Pédagogie et Orientation
RB	La Revue du Barreau
RC	La Revue Canadienne
RCG	Revue Canadienne de Géographie
RD	Revue Dominicaine
RdD	Revue du Droit
RHAF	Revue d'Histoire de l'Amérique Française
RI	Relations Industrielles
RTC	Revue Trimestrielle Canadienne
RUL	Revue de l'Université Laval
RUO	Revue de l'Université d'Ottawa
SCHEC	Société Canadienne d'Histoire de l'Eglise Catholique
SS	Service Social
TRSC	Transactions of the Royal Society of Canada
VF	La Vie Française

BIBLIOGRAPHY

1. GENERAL HISTORICAL STUDIES

a) *General Historical Introduction*

1. **Arnould, Louis**
    1913 *Nos amis les Canadiens*, Oudin, Paris, 364.
2. **Bovey, Wilfrid**
    1933 *Canadien*, Dent, Toronto, 293.
3. 1938 *The French Canadians Today*, Dent, Toronto, 362.
4. **Bracq, Jean-Charlemagne**
    1924 *The Evolution of French Canada*, Macmillan, Toronto, 467.
5. **Bruchési, Jean**
    1933-1940 *Histoire du Canada pour tous*, Lévesque, Montréal, 2 v.
6. 1948 *Canada : Réalités d'hier et d'aujourd'hui*, Variétés, Montréal, 403.
7. 1950 *A History of Canada*, Clarke Irwin, Toronto, 338.
8. **Brunet, Michel and others**
    1952 *L'Histoire du Canada par les textes*, Fides, Montréal, 297.
9. **Buies, Arthur**
    1900 *La Province de Québec*, n. e., Québec, 252.
10. **Call, Frank Oliver**
    1926 *The Spell of French Canada*, Page, Boston, 272.
11. **Chapin, Miriam**
    1955 *Quebec Now*, Ryerson, Toronto, 185.
12. **De Bie, Pierre**
    1948 Le fait Canadien-français, *Bull. de Recherches économiques et sociales de l'Université de Louvain*, 13, 7, 695-741.
13. **De Caze, Paul**
    1880 *Notes sur le Canada*, Darveau, Québec, 232.
14. **Desrosiers, A. et Fournet**
    1911 *La Race française en Amérique*, Beauchemin, Montréal, 306.
15. **Esprit**
    1952 Numéro spécial sur le Canada français, *Esprit*, août-sept., 20, 193-4, 169-293.
16. **Falardeau, Jean-Charles**
    1951 *French Canada, past and present*, Cyclostyled MS, 25.
17. 1953 *Essays on Contemporary Quebec*, (éd.), Presses Universitaires Laval, Québec, 260.
18. **Forbin, Victor**
    1935 *La Grande Passion d'un petit peuple*, Beaudinière, Paris, 255.
19. **Garneau, F.-X.**
    1946 *Histoire du Canada*, (8th edition), L'Arbre, Montréal, 9 v.
20. **Girard, Alex**
    1905 *La Province de Québec*, Dusseault et Proulx, Québec, 318.
21. **Groulx, Lionel**
    1950-1952 *Histoire du Canada français*, L'Action Nationale, Montréal, 4 v.
22. **Hopkins and Castell**
    1898 *Canada, an Encyclopedia of the Country*, Linscott, Toronto, 5 v.

A BIBLIOGRAPHICAL INTRODUCTION...

23. **Hopkins, J. C.**
    1913 *French Canada and the Saint Lawrence,* Philadelphia, 431.
24. **Lanctot, Gustave**
    1935 *Le Canada d'hier et d'aujourd'hui,* Lévesque, Montréal, 315.
25. **Langlois, Gilles**
    1944 *Le Type social du Canadien français,* M. A. Thesis, University of Ottawa.
26. **Le Jeune, L.**
    1931 *Dictionnaire Général du Canada,* Université d'Ottawa, Ottawa, 2 v.
27. **Loir, Adrien**
    1908 *Canada et Canadiens,* Guilmoto, Paris, 371.
28. **Maheux, Arthur**
    1942 *French Canada and Britain,* Ryerson, Toronto, 121.
29. **McInnis, Edgar**
    1947 *Canada. A Political and Social History,* Rinehart, New York, 574.
30. **Marquis, C.-E.**
    1923 *The French Canadians in the Province of Quebec, The Annals,* 107, 1-12.
31. **Minville, Esdras** (éd.)
    1946 *Notre Milieu,* Fides, 443.
32. **Nicholson, Byron**
    1902 *The French Canadians,* Bryant, Toronto, 132.
33. **Province of Quebec**
    1913-1954 *Statistical Year Book,* King's Printer, Quebec, 38 v.
34. **Rameau de Saint-Pierre, Edme**
    1859 *La France aux Colonies. Acadiens et Canadiens,* Jouby, Paris, 335.
35. **Ryerson, Stanley B.**
    1944 *French Canada, a study in canadian democracy,* Progress Books, Toronto, 237.
36. **Rumilly, Robert**
    1952 *Histoire du Canada,* Fides, Montréal, 456.
37. 1943-56 *Histoire de la Province de Québec,* various editors, Montréal, 29 v.
38. **Short, Adam** (ed.)
    1914-17 *Canada and its Provinces. A history of the Canadian people and their institutions by one hundred associates,* Glasgow Brook, Toronto, 23 v.
39. **Stewart, Wallace W.**
    1935-37 *Encyclopedia of Canada,* University Associate of Canada, Toronto, 6 v.
40. **Sulte, Benjamin**
    1882-84 *Histoire des Canadiens français, 1608-1880,* Wilson, Montréal, 8 v.
41. 1908 *A History of Quebec, its resources and people,* Canadian History Co., Montreal, 2 v.
42. **Taurines, Guilly de**
    1894 *La Nation Canadienne. Etude historique sur les populations françaises du Nord de l'Amérique,* Plon, Paris, 338.
43. **Wade, Mason**
    1946 *The French Canadian Outlook,* Viking Press, New York, 182.
44. 1955 *The French Canadians, 1760-1945,* Macmillan, Toronto, 1136.
45. **Wood, W. C. H.**
    1931-32 *The Storied Province of Quebec,* Dominion Publishing Co., n. p., 4 v.

b) *The History of New France*

46. **Adair, E. R.**
    1944 France and the beginning of New France, CHR, 25, 3, 246-278.
47. 1947 Anglo-French Rivalry in the fur trade during the 18th century, *Culture,* 8, 434-455.

A BIBLIOGRAPHICAL INTRODUCTION...

48. 1954 The French Canadian Seigneury, CHR, 35, 3, 187-207.
49. **Biggar, H. P.**
    1901 *The Early trading companies of New France*, University of Toronto Press, Toronto, 308.
50. **Boucher, Pierre**
    1664 *Histoire véritable et naturelle des mœurs et productions du pays de la Nouvelle-France, vulgairement dite le Canada*, Lambert, Paris, 164.
51. **Boucault, N.-G.**
    1763 Etat présent du Canada, *Province of Quebec Archives*, 1920-21, 11-59.
52. **Bougainville, Louis-Antoine de**
    1861 *Mémoires sur l'état de la Nouvelle-France à l'époque de la guerre de sept ans (1757)*, Ministère de la Marine, Paris, 609.
53. **Bonnault, Claude de**
    1950 *Histoire du Canada français (1534-1763)*, Presses Universitaires de France, Paris, 348.
54. **Burt, A. L.**
    1940 *The Frontier in the history of New France*, CHAR, 93-99.
55. **Chapais, Thomas**
    1904 *Jean Talon, intendant de la Nouvelle-France (1665-1672)*, Demers, Québec, 540.
56. **Colby, C. W.**
    1908 *Canadian Types of the Old Regime*, Holt, New York, 366.
57. **Charleroix, Pierre-François-Xavier de**
    1744 *Histoire et description générale de la Nouvelle-France*, Nyon, Paris, 3 v.
58. **Delalande, J.**
    1927 *Le Conseil souverain de la Nouvelle-France*, Proulx, Québec, 358.
59. **Douglas, James**
    1905 *Old France in the New World*, Burrows, Cleveland, 597.
60. 1913 *New England and New France*, Putman, New York, 560.
61. **Eastman, M.**
    1915 *Church and State in early Canada*, Constable, Edinburgh, 31.
62. **Fauteux, Joseph-Noël**
    1927 *Essai sur l'Industrie au Canada sous le Régime français*, Proulx, Québec, 2 v.
63. **Ferland, Jean-Baptiste-Antoine**
    1861-65 *Cours d'histoire du Canada*, Côté, Québec, 2 v.
64. 1929 *La France dans l'Amérique du Nord, 1497-1760*, Granger, Montréal, 2 v.
65. **Filteau, Gérald**
    1937 *La Naissance d'une Nation. Tableau du Canada en 1755*, A. C. F., Montréal, 2 v.
66. **Fiske, John**
    1902 *New France and New England*, Houghton, Boston, 378.
67. **Frégault, Guy**
    1944 *Iberville le Conquérant*, Pascal, Montréal, 418.
68. 1944 *La Civilisation de la Nouvelle-France*, Pascal, Montréal, 288.
69. 1945 L'Absolutisme en Nouvelle-France, *Amérique Française*, mars, 4-20.
70. 1945 Pierre Boucher, *Le Devoir*, 34, 171, 21 juillet, 1 and 2.
71. 1948 *François Bigot, administrateur français*, Fides, Montréal, 2 v.
72. 1952 *Le Grand Marquis, Pierre de Vaudreuil et de Louisiane*, Fides, Montréal, 483.
73. 1954 *La Société Canadienne sous le Régime français*, Société Historique du Canada, Ottawa, 16.
74. 1955 *La Guerre de la Conquête*, Fides, Montréal, 514.
75. **Gérin, Léon**
    1946 *Aux Sources de notre Histoire*, Fides, Montréal, 274.

A BIBLIOGRAPHICAL INTRODUCTION...

76. **Glazebrook, de T. G.**
    1934 Roads in New France and the policy of expansion, CHAR, 48-56.
77. **Groulx, Lionel**
    1919 *La Naissance d'une Race*, L'Action Française, Montréal, 294.
78. **Heneker, Dorothy A.**
    1927 *The Seignorial Regime in Canada*, Proulx, Québec, 447.
79. **Kalm, Per**
    1937 *The America of 1750. Peter Kalm's Travels in North America*, Wilson-Erickson, New York, 2 v.
80. **La Hontan, Louis-Armand de L. d'Arc**
    1703 *Nouveaux voyages de M. le baron de La Hontan dans l'Amérique Septentrionale*, Honoré, La Haye, 2 v.
81. **Lanctot, Gustave**
    1929 *L'Administration de la Nouvelle-France*, Champion, Paris, 169.
82.   1929 La participation du peuple dans le Gouvernement de la Nouvelle-France, RTC, 15.
83.   1929 La Nouvelle-France et sa survivance, TRSC, 3rd series, 23, 71-84.
84.   1936 Quelques rectifications de notre histoire, TRSC, 30, 29-37.
85.   1948 Le Régime Municipal en Nouvelle-France, *Culture*, 255-283.
86.   1951 *Réalisations françaises de Cartier à Montcalm*, Chantecler, Montréal, 204.
87.   1952 *Filles de Joie ou Filles du Roi*, Chantecler, Montréal, 230.
88. **La Potherie, Claude-Charles le Roy de**
    1722 *Histoire de l'Amérique Septentrionale*, Nion et Didot, Paris, 4 v.
89. **Lemieux, Rodolphe**
    1913 Le Régime Seigneurial au Canada, TRSC, 7, 151-68.
90. **Lescarbot, Marc**
    1609 *Histoire de la Nouvelle-France*, Paris, 888.
91. **Lorin, Henri**
    1895 *Le Comte de Frontenac*, Colin, Paris, 502.
92. **Lunn, A.-Jean-E.**
    1934 *Economic developments in French Canada, 1740-1760*, M. A. Thesis, McGill University.
93.   1942 *Economic developments in New France, 1713-1760*, Ph. D. Thesis, McGill University.
94. **Mcouat, Donald Frazer**
    1947 *Military Policy and Organization in New France*, M. A. Thesis, McGill University.
95. **Munroe, D. C.**
    1938 *The Fur Trade in New France*, M. A. Thesis, McGill University.
96. **Munroe, W. B.**
    1907 *The Seignorial System in Canada*, Longman, New York, 296.
97. **Parkman, F.**
    1902 *The Old Regime in Canada*, Little, Boston, 559.
98.   1903 *A half-century of conflict. France and England in North America*, Brown, Boston, 2 v.
99. **Reid, A. G.**
    1951 The Nature of Quebec Society during the French Regime, CHAR, 26-35.
100. **Renaud, Paul-Emile**
    1928 *Les Origines Economiques du Canada*, Enault, Namur, 488.
101. **Roy, Antoine**
    1930 *Les lettres, les sciences et les arts au Canada sous le régime français*, Jouve, Paris, 292.
102. **Roy, Pierre-Georges**
    1921 *Nouvelle-France, Conseil Supérieur de Québec*, L'Eclaireur, Beauceville, 325.

103.   1940 *Nouvelle-France, Conseil Supérieur de Québec*, Archives de la Province, Québec, 287.
104. **Sainte-Marie, Pierre**
            1948 Le développement industriel de la Nouvelle-France, AE, juillet, 298-311.
105. **Salone, E.**
            467 *La Colonisation de la Nouvelle-France*, Guilmoto, Paris, 467.
106. **Séguin, Maurice**
            1947-8 Le régime Seigneurial au pays de Québec, RHAF, 382-402 ; 519-32.
107. **Séguin, Robert-Lionel**
            1953 L'habitant, AN, 41, 321-44 ; 395-421.
108. **Twaites, R. G.** (ed.)
            1896-1901 *The Jesuit Relations and Allied Documents, 1610-1791*, Burrows Brothers Co., Cleveland, 73 v.
109.   1905 *France in America, 1497-1763*, Harper, New York, 320.
110. **Wallace, W. S.**
            1939 An unwritten chapter of the fur-trade, TRSC, 33, 1, 1-8.
111. **Wurtele, F. C.**
            1886 Historical record of the St. Maurice Forges, TRSC, IV, 2, 77-90.

2. THE HUMAN GEOGRAPHY OF FRENCH CANADA

a) *General geographical studies*

112. **Barette, Gérard**
  1952 Contribution de l'arpenteur-géomètre à la géographie du Québec, CG, 2, 67-71.
113. **Blanchard, Raoul**
  1935 *L'Est du Canada français*, Beauchemin, Montréal, 2 v.
114. 1946 *Géographie Générale*, vol. II, Beauchemin, Montréal, 157-219.
115. 1948 *Le Centre du Canada français*, Beauchemin, Montréal, 577.
116. 1952 *Le Québec par l'image*, Beauchemin, Montréal, 138.
117. 1952 *Les traits géographiques d'ensemble de la Province de Québec*, Cahiers de Géographie, Université Laval, Québec, 15.
118. 1953 *L'Ouest du Canada français, Montréal et sa région*, Beauchemin, Montréal, 399.
119. 1954 *L'Ouest du Canada français, Les pays de l'Ottawa, l'Abitibi, Témiscamingue*, Beauchemin, Montréal, 334.
120. **Bouchette, Joseph**
  1815 *Topographical description of Lower Canada*, Fadem, London, 664.
121. 1832 *The British Dominions in North America*, Longman, London, 2 v.
122. 1832 *A Topographical dictionary of the Province of Lower Canada*, Longman, London, 276.
123. **Brouillette, Benoît**
  1939 *La pénétration du continent Américain par les Canadiens français*, Granger, Montréal, 242.
123a. 1941 Les régions géographiques de la Province de Québec, AE, 16, 451-461.
124. 1946 *Le Canada par l'image*, Beauchemin, Montréal, 134.
125. 1952 The Province of Quebec, in *The Regions of Canada*, (Putman, D. F., ed.), Crowell, New York, 123-212.
126. 1953 Les régions géographiques de la Province de Québec, CG, 3, 85-88.
127. **Desfontaines, Pierre**
  1953 *Le rang, Type de peuplement rural du Canada français*, Presses Universitaires Laval, Québec, 32.
128. **Joubert, L.**
  1935 Les groupements canadiens-français au Canada, *Etudes Economiques*, 75-118.
129. **Leclaire, Alphonse**
  n. d. *Historical, legendary and topographical guide along the St. Lawrence*, Reynolds, Montreal, 248.
130. **Lefèvre, J.-J.**
  1945 Deux descriptions ethnographiques des Canadiens, BRH, 75.
131. **Le Moine, J.-M.**
  1892 Etude ethnographique des éléments qui constituent la population de la Province de Québec, TRSC, 10, 17-28.
132. 1902 Etude ethnographique des éléments qui constituent la population canadienne, les Loyalistes, TRSC, 15, 23.
133. **Lewis, H. H.**
  1940 Population of Quebec Province: its distribution and national origin, *Economic Geography*, 16, 1, 59-68.
134. **Miller, Emile**
  1924 *Terres et Peuples du Canada*, Beauchemin, Montréal, 122.

A BIBLIOGRAPHICAL INTRODUCTION...

135. **Morissette, Emilien**
 1948 *Le régionalisme économique*, Thesis, Laval University.
136. **Rouillard, Aug.**
 1914 *Dictionnaire des Rivières et des Lacs de la Province de Québec*, Dépt. des Terres et Forêts, Québec, 432.
137. **Sutherland, John C.**
 1931 *The Province of Quebec, Geographical and Social Studies*, Nelson, Toronto, 126.
138. **Thibault, Marc**
 1949 *Etude du concept de région économique et description de la région du bas Saint-Laurent*, Thesis, Laval University.
139. **Thomas, R. B. and Clegg, A.**
 1952 Ways about Quebec, CGJ, 24, 1, 22-37.
140. **Thompson, Zadoc**
 1835 *Geography and History of Lower Canada*, Walton and Gaylord, Montréal, 116.

b) *Land settlement and colonization*

141. **A. C. J. C.**
 1920 *Le Problème de la Colonisation au Canada français*, Bureau de l'ACJC, Montréal, 300.
142. **Anonymous**
 1912 *Monographies paroissiales, esquisses de quelques paroisses de colonisation*, Dépt. de la Colonisation, Québec, 169.
143. **Auclair, E.-J.**
 1930 *Le Curé Labelle*, Beauchemin, Montréal, 271.
144. **Bilodeau, Georges-Marie**
 1931 *Le vrai remède, étude sur la crise actuelle*, L'Action Sociale, Québec, 170.
145. **Caron, Ivanhoe**
 1916. *La Colonisation du Canada sous la Domination française*, n. e., Québec, 90.
146. 1923 *La Colonisation de la Province de Québec, Débuts du Régime Anglais, 1760-1797*, n. e., Québec, 333.
147. 1927 *La Colonisation de la Province de Québec, de 1791 à 1815, Les Cantons de l'Est*, n. e., Québec, 350.
148. **Commission on Seigneurial Tenure**
 1844 *Rapport des Commissaires nommés pour s'enquérir de l'état des lois et autres circonstances qui se rattachent à la Tenure Seigneuriale dans le Bas-Canada*, Imp. de la Reine, Montréal, 311.
149. **De Montigny, Testard**
 1895 *La Colonisation, Le Nord de Montréal et la Région Labelle*, Beauchemin, Montréal, 346.
150. **Drapeau, Stanislas**
 1863 *Etudes sur les développements de la colonisation du Bas-Canada, 1851-1861*, Brousseau, Québec, 528.
151. **Dugré, Alexandre**
 1917 *Vers les terres neuves*, Messager, Montréal, 67.
152. 1951 *Où beaucoup n'est pas assez*, Relations, 131, 295-298.
153. 1953 *La Terre qui sauve*, ISP, nu. 466-7, Montréal, 64.
154. **Ecole Sociale Populaire**
 1945 *La Colonisation dans la Province de Québec*, ESP, 32.
155. **Frégault, Guy**
 1944 *Le Régime Seigneurial et l'expansion de la colonisation dans le Bassin du Saint-Laurent au dix-septième siècle*, CHAR, 61-73.

19

156. **Frémont, Donatien**
    1951 Un apôtre de la colonisation française dans l'Ouest canadien, l'abbé Jean Gaire, TRSC, 45, 9-14.
157. **Gagné, Eugène**
    1941 La Colonisation : Oeuvre sociale, CF, 28, 9, 915-922.
158. **Garon, J.-E.**
    1940 *Historique de la Colonisation dans la Province de Québec de 1825 à 1940*, Québec, 137.
159. **Gavreau, Georges**
    1942 *Essai sur l'histoire du droit des terres tenues en franc et commun soccage dans la Province de Québec*, M. A. Thesis, McGill University.
160. **Hamelin, Louis-Edmond**
    1951 *La marche du peuplement à l'intérieur du Diocèse de Joliette*, n. e., Joliette, 13.
161. **Harvey, D. C.**
    1936 *The colonization of Canada*, Clarke, Irwin, Toronto, 154.
162. **Laforce, Ernest**
    1946 *Bâtisseurs de Pays, Religieux et Laïques*, Garand, Montréal, 356.
163. **Lamarche, Gustave**
    n. d. *Les principes de la colonisation française sous l'ancien régime*, Thesis, University of Montreal.
164. **Lecompte, Henri**
    n. d. *L'Oeuvre du Curé Labelle*, OT, nu. 64, Montréal, 16.
165. **Magnan, Hormisdas**
    1927 *Le guide du Colon, Province de Québec*, Ministère de la Colonisation, Québec, 101.
166. **Minville, Esdras**
    1933 L'Oeuvre de la Colonisation, *Le problème de la Terre*, Semaines Sociales du Canada, ESP, Montréal.
167. 1943 La Colonisation, *L'Agriculture*, (éd. Minville, E.), Fides, Montréal, 275-346.
168. **Noiseux, Donat**
    1943 *Dix années de colonisation à Sainte-Anne de Roquemaure, 1933-1943*, Ministère de la Colonisation, Québec, 79.
169. **Pelland, Joseph-Alfred**
    1910 *La colonisation dans la Province de Québec*, Québec, 106.
170. **Pelletier, Joseph**
    1944 *Quinze jours chez les Colons du Nord*, Imp. Populaire, Montréal, 126.
171. **Plante, Albert**
    1950 Connaissez-vous l'Etablissement Rural ?, *Relations*, 110, 44-47.
172. **Proulx, Gérard**
    1942 *Etude sur l'agriculture, la colonisation et le repeuplement dans la Province de Québec*, M. A. Thesis, University of Ottawa.
173. **Rouillard, Eugène**
    1899 *La colonisation dans les comtés de Témiscouata, Rimouski, Matane, Bonaventure, Gaspé*, Ministère de la Colonisation, Québec, 150.
174. 1901 *La colonisation dans les comtés de Dorchester, Bellechasse, Montmagny, L'Islet, Kamouraska*, Ministère de la Colonisation, Québec, 80.
175. **Savard, Félix-Antoine**
    1939 Conférence sur la Colonisation, *Le Devoir*, 30, 43-44-45.
176. **Semaines Sociales du Canada**
    1944 *Congrès de la Colonisation*, ESP, Montréal, 156.
177. **Société Générale de Colonisation**
    1900 *Rapport du Congrès de la colonisation*, La Patrie, Montréal, 386.
178. **Vattier, Georges**
    1928 *Esquisse Historique de la colonisation de la Province de Québec, 1608-1925*, Champion, Paris, 128.

c) *Gaspesia*

179. **Barbeau, C.-Marius**
    1931   Gaspé Peninsula, CGJ, 3, 2, 79-92.
180. **Béchard, Auguste**
    1918   *La Gaspésie en 1888*, Imp. Nationale, Québec, 130.
181. **Bernard, Antoine**
    1925   *La Gaspésie au Soleil*, Clercs de Saint-Viateur, Montréal, 332.
182. **Bérubé, Louis**
    1937   La Gaspésie Ethnique, CF, 24, 10, 968-979.
183. **Boisseau, Lionel**
    1939   *La mer qui meurt*, Ed. du Zodiaque, Montréal, 200.
184. **Boucher, Jean**
    1941   On devient maître chez-soi en Gaspésie, *Ensemble*, novembre, 6-18.
185. **Buies, Arthur**
    1895   *La Vallée de la Matapédia*, Brousseau, Québec, 52.
186. **Coleman, A. P.**
    1921   The Gaspé Peninsula, TRSC, 15, 39-55.
187. **Dugré, Alexandre**
    1946   La spoliation du bas de Québec, *Relations*, 68, 232-234.
188.   1954   La Gaspésie de la mer, *Relations*, 162, 173-175 ; 163, 195-197 ; 164, 229-231.
189. **Ferland, J.-B.-A.**
    1897   *La Gaspésie*, Côté, Québec, 300.
190. **Gagnon, Antoine**
    1945   *Monographie de Matane*. Imp. Générale, Rimouski, 370.
191. **Guay, Ch.**
    1902   *Lettres sur l'Ile d'Anticosti*, Beauchemin, Montréal, 315.
192. **Guérette, Fernand**
    1944   *Causapscal, Monographie d'une municipalité rurale*, Thesis, Ecole des Hautes Etudes Commerciales.
193.   1945   *Monographie économique de la municipalité de Causapscal*, AE, Février, 340-364.
194. **Guite, Gérard**
    1941   *Le Milieu Gaspésien*, M. A. Thesis, Laval University.
195. **Hubert, Paul**
    1926   *Les Iles de la Madeleine et les Madelinots*, Imp. Générale, Rimouski, 252.
196. **Lafontaine, Georges**
    1940   *Le coopératisme et l'organisation économique de la Gaspésie*, Valiquette, Montréal, 120.
197. **Marie-Victorin, Fr.**
    1921   *Chez les Madelinots*, Frères des Ecoles Chrétiennes, Montréal, 161.
198. **Pelland, A.**
    1914   *La Gaspésie, Esquisse historique*, Ministère de la Colonisation, Québec, 272.
199.   1910   *La Témiscouata*, Ministère de la Colonisation, Québec, 95.
200.   1912   *La Région Matane-Matapédia*, Ministère de la Colonisation, Québec, 138.
201. **Péninsulaire**
    1928   *La Gaspésie Intérieure*, ESP, nu. 174, Montréal, 36.
202. **Rumilly, Robert**
    1951   *Les Iles de la Madeleine*, Chantecler, Montréal, 258.
203. **Schmitt, Joseph**
    1904   *Monographie de l'Ile d'Anticosti*, Hermann, Paris, 368.

d) The Saguenay, Lake St. John and the North Coast

204. **Anonymous**
    1879 Le Saguenay et le Lac Saint-Jean, Dépt. de l'Agriculture, Ottawa, 54.
205. **Barbeau, Marius**
    1938 Saguenay, CGJ, 16, 6, 285-292.
206. **Bélanger, René**
    1946 Les Escoumains, Société Historique du Saguenay, Chicoutimi, 58.
207. **Brouillard, E.**
    1908 La Côte Nord du Saint-Laurent et le Labrador Canadien, Laflamme et Proulx, Québec, 188.
208. **Brouillette, Benoît**
    1947 La Côte Nord du Saint-Laurent, Revue Canadienne de Géographie, Vol. 1, 1, 3-30 ; 4, 3-16.
209.   1947 L'habitat et la population au Saguenay, AE, Janvier, 646-71.
210. **Brunet, Edmond**
    1949 Le Labrador et le Nouveau Québec, Payot, Paris, 344.
211. **Buis, Arthur**
    1896 Le Saguenay et le Bassin du Lac Saint-Jean, Côté, Québec, 420.
212. **Cormeau, N.-A.**
    1953 Life and Sport on the north coast of the lower St. Lawrence, Québec, 372.
213. **Dugré, Alexandre**
    1950 La Côte-nord, sa richesse et sa vie, Relations, 110, 47-49.
214. **Garry, Robert**
    1955 Chibougamau, ville minière, RCG, 9, 1, 47-52.
215. **Gosselin, Mgr A.-E.**
    1917 A Chicoutimi et au Lac Saint-Jean, RTSC, 11, 113-36.
216. **Hamelin, Louis-Edmond**
    1953 Le fer et le chemin de fer du Québec-Labrador, RUL, 7, 753-63.
217. **Hare, Kenneth**
    1952 The Labrador Frontier, Geographical Review, 42, 405-24.
218. **Johnston, C. M.**
    1950 The historical geography of the Saguenay valley, M. A. Thesis, McGill University.
219. **Junek, Oscar Waldemar**
    1937 Isolated communities, a Labrador fishing village, American Book, New York, 130.
220. **Knott, Leonard L.**
    1938 A city in the wilderness, Editorial Ass., Montreal, 40.
221. **Labrie, Mgr C.-J.-M.**
    1949 La Côte-nord et l'industrie sidérurgique, ESP, no 422, Montréal, 32.
222. **Lacasse, Fulard**
    1937 La Côte-nord du Saint-Laurent, n. e., Montréal, 134.
223. **McGuire, B.-J. and Freeman, H. E.**
    1947 How the Saguenay River serves Canada, CGJ, 35, 5, 200-25.
224. **Ouellet, M.-F.**
    1951 Evolution et fonction urbaines de Chicoutimi, CG, 1, 25-30.
225. **Potvin, Damase**
    1920 Le tour du Saguenay, n. e., Québec, 168.
226.   1953 Trois petits clochers, n. e., Québec, 93.
227. **Rochette, Edgar**
    1926 Notes sur la Côte-Nord, Le Soleil, Québec, 120.
228. **Rouillard, Eugène**
    1908 La Côte-Nord du bas Saint-Laurent, Laflamme et Proulx, Québec, 188.

A BIBLIOGRAPHICAL INTRODUCTION...

229. **Roy, Roger**
   1945 *Monographie économique du Comté de Mégantic*, Thesis, Ecole des Hautes Etudes Commerciales.
230. **Simard, H.**
   1917 La Côte-Nord, *Bull. de la Soc. de Géographie de Québec*, 11, 202-16.
231. **Taylor, Griffith**
   1945 Town pattern on the Gulf of St. Lawrence, *CGJ*, 30, 6, 254-275.
232. **Tremblay, V.**
   1938 *Histoire du Saguenay depuis l'origine jusqu'à 1870*, Société Historique du Saguenay, Chicoutimi, 331.
233. **Vien, Rossel**
   1955 *Histoire de Roberval*, Société Historique du Saguenay, Chicoutimi, 369.

e) *The Quebec Region*

234. **Banks, M. B.**
   1944 *The Isle of Orleans*, M. A. Thesis, Clark University.
236. **Benoist, Emile**
   1945 *Rimouski et les pays d'en bas*, Le Devoir, Montréal, 193.
237. **Blachet, Gaston**
   1945 *Etude de la communauté de Lorette*, M. A. Thesis, Laval University.
238. **Bois, L.-E.**
   1895 *L'île d'Orléans*, Côté, Québec, 150.
239. **Boivin, Léonce**
   1941 *Dans nos Montagnes*, n. e., Les Eboulements, 254.
240. **Casault, F.-E.-J.**
   1906 *Notes historiques sur la paroisse de Saint-Thomas-de-Montmagny*, Dussault, Québec, 447.
241. **Casgrain, Henri-Raymond**
   1880 *Une Paroisse canadienne au XVIIe siècle*, Brousseau, Québec, 213.
242.   1902 *Histoire de la paroisse de l'Ange-Gardien*, Dussault, Québec, 374.
243. **Chapais, Thomas**
   1952 *Monographie du Comté de Kamouraska*, Thesis, Laval University.
244. **Cimon, Jean**
   1947 *Une île d'Adon (Monographie de l'Ile-aux-Coudres)*, Thesis, Laval University.
245. **Croteau, René**
   1946 *Saint-Antoine-de-Tilly, analyse sociale*, Thesis, Laval University.
246. **Dawson, Nora**
   1954 *La vie matérielle de la paroisse de Saint-Pierre de l'île d'Orléans*, Ph. D. Thesis, Laval University.
247. **Dionne, N.-E.**
   1910 *Sainte-Anne-de-la-Pocatière (1672-1910) et l'Ile-aux-Coudres (1646-1910)*, Laflamme, Québec, 219.
248. **Doré, Gillen**
   1942 *Monographie économique du Comté de Portneuf*, Thesis, Ecole des Hautes Etudes Commerciales.
249. **Guay, Ch.**
   1873-74 *Chronique de Rimouski*, Délisle, Québec, 2 v.
250. **Harrington, Richard**
   1951 Ile-aux-Coudres, *CGJ*, 43, 2, 50-57.
251. **Laberge, Lionel**
   1948 *L'habitant de la Côte de Beaupré*, Thesis, Laval University.
252. **Mailloux, Alexis**
   1879 *Histoire de l'Ile-aux-Coudres*, Burland-Desbarats, Montréal, 130.

A BIBLIOGRAPHICAL INTRODUCTION...

253. **Michaud, J.-D.**
    1925 *Le Bic, les étapes d'une paroisse*, Tremblay, Québec, 2 v.
254. **Michaud, Joseph-Désiré**
    1922 *Notes historiques sur la Vallée de la Matapédia*, Voix du Lac, Val-Vullant, 241.
255. **Michaud, Philippe**
    1950 *Développement économique de la rive sud du Saint-Laurent, de Rivière-du-Loup à Matane*, Thesis, Ecole des Hautes Etudes Commerciales.
256. **Miner, Horave**
    1938 Changes in Rural French Canadian culture, AJS, 44, 365-78.
257. 1939 *St. Denis, a French Canadian Parish*, University of Chicago Press, Chicago, 283.
258. 1950 A new epoch in rural Quebec, AJS, 56, 1-10.
259. **Paradis, Alexandre**
    1948 *Kamouraska, 1674-1948*, n. e., Québec, 305.
260. **Pattie, Roderick**
    1921 The problem of communication in the lower Saint Lawrence Valley, *Journal of Geography*, 20, 1-12.
262. **Rioux, Marcel**
    1953 Sociabilité et typologie sociale, CESH, 2, 6-73.
263. 1953 Sur le sens de l'évolution socio-culturelle de l'Ile-Verte, *Rapport annuel du Musée National*, Ottawa, 128.
264. 1954 *Description de la culture de l'Ile-Verte*, Ministère du Nord Canadien, Ottawa, 98.
265. **Routhier, A.-B.**
    1900 *Québec et Lévis*, n. e., Montréal, 355.
266. **Roy, Edmond**
    1887-1904 *Histoire de la Seigneurie de Lauzon*, Lévis, 5 v.
267. **Roy, Jean-Paul**
    1943 *Regards sur la région de Lévis*, Chambre de Commerce, Lévis, 47.
268. **Roy, P.-G.**
    1928 *L'Ile-d'Orléans*, Proulx, Québec, 505.
269. **Tremblay, Antoine**
    1948 *Sur le Plateau Laurentien, Analyse sociale d'une communauté rurale : N.-D. de l'Assomption-des-Eboulements*, Thesis, Laval University.
269-a. **Saint-Pierre, J.-C.**
    1949 *L'économie du Comté de Charlevoix*, Thesis, Ecole des Hautes Etudes Commerciales.
270. **Tremblay, Jean-Paul**
    1948 *La Baie Saint-Paul et ses Pionniers*, n. e., Chicoutimi, 69.
270-a. **Trudel, Henri-Paul**
    1950 *Monographie de Saint-Adolphe*, Thesis, Laval University.
271. **Turcotte, L.-P.**
    1867 *L'histoire de l'Ile-d'Orléans*, Le Canadien, Québec, 186.
272. **Wrong, George McKinnon**
    1908 *A Canadian Manor and its seigneurs (1761-1861)*, Macmillan, Toronto, 295.

f) *Quebec City*

273. **Beaudet, Colette**
    1947 *Banlieue réelle et ville de Québec*, Thesis, Laval University.
274. **Brown, W. C.**
    1952 *Québec, Croissance d'une Ville*, Presses Universitaires Laval, Québec, 76.
275. **Burpee, Lawrence J.**
    1924 Quebec in Books, TRSC, 18, 75-85.

A BIBLIOGRAPHICAL INTRODUCTION...

276. **Comité des Fêtes Jubilaires**
  1911 Les Fêtes du troisième Centenaire de Québec, (1608-1908), Laflamme et Proulx, Québec, 630.
277. **Dallaire, Bernadette**
  1952 Le Foyer Sainte-Geneviève de Québec, Thesis, Laval University.
278. **Doughty, A. G. and Dionne, N.-E.**
  1903 Quebec under two flags. A brief history of the city, Quebec News, Quebec, 424.
279. **Doughty, A. G.**
  1908 The Cradle of New France, Cambride Co., Montréal, 315.
280. **Falardeau, Jean-Charles**
  1944 Evolution et Métabolisme contemporain de la Ville de Québec, Culture, 5, 121-131.
281.   1944 La crise du logement à Québec, (with others), Ed. du Cap Diamant, Québec, 45.
282.   1951 Délimitation d'une banlieue de Grande-Ville, Community Planning Review, 1, 1, 16-22.
283. **Gamache, J.-Ch.**
  1929 Histoire de Saint-Roch de Québec et ses institutions, 1829-1929, Charrier et Dugal, Québec, 836.
284. **Gaudreau, Stanislas**
  1942 Québec à l'aurore du vingt et unième siècle, CF, 29-8, 676-91.
285. **Jobin, Albert**
  1948 La petite histoire de Québec, Inst. Saint-Jean-Bosco, Québec, 353.
286. **Juchereau, Mère J.-F. et Duplessis, Mère M.-A.**
  1939 Les Annales de l'Hôtel-Dieu de Québec, 1636-1716, Québec, 444.
287. **LeMoine, J.-M.**
  1882 Picturesque Québec, Dawson, Montréal, 521.
288. **Lamontagne, Maurice**
  1947 Les problèmes économiques de Québec, Chambre de Commerce, Québec.
289. **Lamontagne, P.-A. (rédigé par Rumilly, R.)**
  1952 L'Histoire de Sillery, (1630-1950), n. e., n. p., 117.
290. **Marier, Georges**
  1954 Développements urbains dans Québec, Community Planning Review, 4, 41-44.
291. **Morisset, Gérard**
  1952 Québec et son évolution, Soc. Historique de Québec, Québec, 31.
292. **Reid, Allana Gertrude**
  1945 The importance of the town of Quebec, 1608-1703, M. A. Thesis, McGill University.
293.   1950 The development and importance of the town of Quebec, 1608-1760, Ph. D. Thesis, McGill University.
294. **Rochette, Fernand**
  1952 Monographie du Quartier de Saint-Sauveur, Thesis, Laval University.
295. **Rosa, Narcisse**
  1897 La construction des navires à Québec et ses environs. Brousseau, Québec, 202.
296. **Roy, Jean-Marie**
  1952 Québec, esquisse de géographie urbaine, CG, 2, 83-98.
297. **Roy, Pierre-Georges**
  1930 La Ville de Québec sous le Régime français, Imp. du Roi, Québec, 2 v.
298. **Têtu, H.**
  1899 Résumé historique de l'industrie et du commerce de Québec de 1775 à 1900, n. e., Québec, 29.

A BIBLIOGRAPHICAL INTRODUCTION...

g) *Lac Saint-Pierre and the Central Region*

299. **Anonymous**
     1917   *Histoire de Saint-Gabriel-de-Brandon*, Ducharme, Montréal, 236.
300. **Bellemare, Joseph-Elzéar**
     1911   *Histoire de la Baie Saint-Antoine, 1883-1911*, La Patrie, Montréal, 681.
301.   1924   *Histoire de Nicolet*, Imp. d'Arthabaska, Arthabaska, 410.
301-a. **Bellemare, R.**
     1901   *Les bases de l'histoire d'Yamachiche, 1703-1903*, Beauchemin, Montréal, 448.
302. **Blanchard, Raoul**
     1950   *La Mauricie*, Bien Public, Trois-Rivières, 158.
303. **Brouillette, Benoît**
     1932   *Le développement industriel de la vallée du Saint-Maurice*, Bien Public, Trois-Rivières, 54.
304. **Camu, Pierre**
     1951   Le port et l'arrière-pays de Trois-Rivières, *Geographical Bulletin*, 1, 1, 30-56.
305. **Caron, N.**
     1900   *Deux voyages sur le Saint-Maurice*, Ayotte, Trois-Rivières, 322.
306. **Charland, T.-M.**
     1942   *Histoire de Saint-François-du-Lac*, Collège Dominicain, Ottawa, 364.
307. **Cloutier, Prosper**
     1915   *Histoire de la Paroisse de Champlain*, Bien Public, Trois-Rivières, 2 v.
308. **Cloutier, Saint-Georges**
     1939   Trois-Rivières, AE, 15, 1, 2, 147-67.
309. **Cotret, René de**
     1949   *Monographie industrielle de la ville de Trois-Rivières*, Thesis, Ecoles des Haute Etudes Commerciales.
310. **Couillard-Després, A.**
     1926   *Histoire de Sorel*, n. e., Montréal, 323.
311. **Dugré, Alexandre**
     1953   Comté rural en baisse (Yamaska), *Relations*, 146, 37-39 ; 147, 64-67 ; 148, 92-95 ; 149, 124-127 ; 150, 155-157 ; 151, 190-192.
312. **Durand, Louis-D.**
     1955   *Paresseux, Ignorants, Arriérés*, Bien-Public, Trois-Rivières, 296.
313. **Forget, Marcel**
     1947   *Monographie de Saint-Sylvère*, Thesis, University of Montreal.
313-a. **Garigue, Philip**
     1956   Saint Justin. A case-study in French Canadian rural organization, CJEPS, 22, 3, 301-18.
314. **Gérin, Léon**
     1934   La paroisse canadienne-française sur la rive nord du lac Saint-Pierre, RTC, 20, Sept.
315.   1898   L'habitant de Saint-Justin, TRSC, 5, 139-216.
316. **Hamelin, Louis-Edmond**
     1953   Le rang à Saint-Didace-de-Maskinongé, *Notes de Géographie*, Université Laval, Québec, 8.
317. **Hubert, Jean-Louis**
     1947   *Etude économique du Comté de Gatineau*, Thesis, Ecole des Hautes Etudes Commerciales.
318. **Létourneau, Firmin**
     1946   *Le Comté de Nicolet, enquête économique et sociale*, Fides, Montréal, 200.
319. **Mailhot, Ch.-E.**
     1925   *Les Bois-Francs*, Imp. d'Arthabaska, Arthabaska, 4 v.

321. **McGuire, B.-J.**
    1950   A river in harness, Saint Maurice, CGJ, 40, 210-231.
322. **Norbert, Prosper**
    1951   *Monographie économique du Cap-de-la-Madeleine*, Thesis, Ecole des Hautes Etudes Commerciales.
324. **Plante, Hermann**
    1937   *Saint-Justin*, Bien Public, Trois-Rivières, 162.
326. **Salvail, Narcisse**
    1945   *Monographie économique de la ville de Sorel*, Thesis, Ecole des Hautes Etudes Commerciales.
327. **Sainte-Marie, Joseph**
    1940   La région Vaudreuil-Soulanges, AE, 301-31 ; 428-51.
328. **Thériault, Yvon**
    1954   *Trois-Rivières*, Bien Public, Trois-Rivières, 126.
329. **Uren, Philip Ernest**
    1949   *A historical geography of the Saint Maurice Valley with a special reference to urban occupance*, M. A. Thesis, McGill University.
330. **Weston, D. R.**
    1955   Sorel, Past and Present, CGJ, 51, 2, 84-89.

h) *Eastern Townships*

331. **Adams, C.**
    1929   *Thetford-Mines*, Lac Mégantic, Thetford-Mines, 315.
332. **Anonymous**
    1956   Sherbrooke, reine des Cantons de l'Est, *La Famille*, 20, 1, 28-39.
333. **Bailey, P. J. M.**
    1956   The geography of settlement in Stanstead Township, Province of Quebec, *Geography*, 191, 39-48.
334. **Benoît-Marie, Fr.**
    1939   Le milieu physique et humain de la Beauce canadienne, AE, août-sept., 317-51.
335.   1939   La mise en valeur agricole de la Beauce canadienne, AE, oct., 337-58.
336.   1939   L'industrie, les transports et le tourisme en Beauce, AE, nov., 54-68.
337. **Bernard, C.-A.**
    1926   *Le Comté de Rouville*, Grisé, Saint-Césaire, 23.
338. **Catelier, M.-Hubert**
    1955   *Le problème géographique de l'hiver dans les Cantons de l'Est*, Faculté de Commerce, Cité Universitaire, Sainte-Foy, Québec, 176.
339. **Dresser, John A.**
    1935   The eastern townships of Quebec, a study in human geography, TRSC, 29, 89-100.
340. **Dugré, Alexandre**
    1945   Pas de place aux Cantons de l'Est, *Relations*, 58, 255-58.
341. **Gauthier, Claude**
    1948   *Belleville, Communauté rurale des Cantons de l'Est*, Thesis, Laval University.
342. **Gravel, Albert**
    1921   *Sainte-Praxède-de-Brampton (Bromptonville), 50 ans de vie paroissiale dans les Cantons de l'Est*, Progrès de l'Est, Sherbrooke, 90.
343. **McFarlane, Duncan Herbert**
    1926   *The sociology of Rouville County, Province of Quebec*, M. A. Thesis, McGill University.

A BIBLIOGRAPHICAL INTRODUCTION...

344. **Pochopien, Kazimierz Marian**
    1952   *The District of Brome, a regional study*, M. A. Thesis, McGill University.
345. **Robitaille, André, and others**
    1955   *Sainte-Marie-de-Beauce, études d'urbanisme*, Presses Universitaires Laval, Québec, 24.
346. **Saint-Amant, Joseph-Charles**
    1932   *Un coin des Cantons de l'Est*, La Parole, Drummondville, 534.
347. **Sellar, R.**
    1888   *The history of the Country of Huntingdon*, Canadian Cleaner, Huntingdon, 584.

i) *The Montreal Region*

348. **Adair, E. R. and Wardleworth, E. S.**
    1933   The parish and church of l'Acadie, CHAR, 59-73.
349. **Allaire, J.-B.-A.**
    1905   *Histoire de la paroisse de Saint-Denis-sur-Richelieu*, Courrier de Saint-Hyacinthe, Saint-Hyacinthe, 539.
350. **Allard, Claude**
    1947   *Le Comté de Bonaventure*, Thesis, Laval University.
351. **Anonymous**
    1955   In the Laurentians, CGJ, 50, 62-69.
352. **Auclair, Elie-J.**
    1927   *Histoire de la paroisse de Saint-Joseph-de-Soulanges ou « Les Cèdres » (1702-1927)*, n. e., Montréal, 416.
353.   1934   *Saint-Jérôme de Terrebonne*, Labelle, Saint-Jérôme, 365.
354.   1935   *Histoire de Châteauguay, 1735-1935*, Beauchemin, Montréal, 243.
355. **Ballabon, M. B.**
    1952   *A Regional Study of the Richelieu Valley*, M. A. Thesis, McGill University.
356. **Brosseau, J.-D.**
    1913   *Saint-Georges-d'Henryville et la Seigneurie de Noyau*, Co. d'Imprimerie, Saint-Hyacinthe, 239.
357.   1937   *Saint-Jean-de-Québec*, Le Richelieu, Saint-Jean, 313.
358. **Brouillette, Benoît**
    1944   Varennes, AE, Montréal, 58.
359.   1944   L'industrie et le commerce à Varennes, AE, avril, 51-66.
360.   1944   Géographie, histoire et économie Agricole de Varennes, AE, mars, 460-90.
360-a.   1944   Le village de Varennes, AE, mai, 165-74.
361. **Buies, Arthur**
    1891   *Au Portique des Laurentides*, Darveau, Québec, 96.
362. **Choquette, C.-P,**
    1930   *Histoire de la ville de Saint-Hyacinthe*, Richer, Saint-Hyacinthe, 539.
363. **Cobban, A. A. and Lightgow, R. M.**
    1952   *A regional study of the Richelieu valley*, M. A. Thesis, McGill University.
364. **Courteau, Guy, et Lanoue, François**
    1949   *Une nouvelle Acadie, Saint-Jacques-de-l'Achigan*, Imp. Populaire, Montréal, 382.
365. **Dugas, G.**
    1900   *Histoire de la paroisse de Sainte-Anne-des-Plaines*, Granger, Montréal, 207.
366. **Dugas, A.-C.**
    1902   *Histoire de la Paroisse de Saint-Liguori, comté de Montcalm*, n. e., n. p., 221.
367. **Francœur, Jean**
    1954   *Saint-Hyacinthe, esquisse de géographie urbaine.* M. A. Thesis, University of Montreal.

A BIBLIOGRAPHICAL INTRODUCTION...

368. **Groulx, Lionel**
    1913 *Petite histoire de Salaberry-de-Valleyfield*, Beauchemin, Montréal, 31.
369. **Hamelin, Louis-Edmond**
    1948 *Aspect de géographie sociale de la cité de Joliette*, Thesis, Laval University.
370. **Jodoin, A. et Vincent, J.-L.**
    1889 *Histoire de Longueuil*, Gebhardt-Berthiaume, Montréal, 691.
371. **Lanctot, Gustave**
    1947 *Brève histoire de Saint-Jean-du-Richelieu*, Ducharme, Montréal, 24.
372. **Leduc, A.**
    1920 *Beauharnois, paroisse Saint-Clément, 1819-1919*, Co. d'Imprimerie, Ottawa, 320.
373. **Maheux, Louis-Philippe**
    1948 *Etude économique de Joliette*, Thesis, Ecole des Hautes Etudes Commerciales.
373-a. **Marchand, Laurent**
    1942 *Monographie économique du Comté de Beauharnois*, Thesis, Ecole des Hautes Etudes Commerciales.
374. **Marsolais, Jean-Marc**
    1948 *La Région de Joliette*, Thesis, Laval University.
375. **Montgrain, André**
    1944 *Monographie économique du Comté de Champlain*, Thesis, Ecole des Hautes Etudes Commerciales.
376. **Longstreth, T. Morris**
    1922 *The Laurentians, the hills and the habitant*, McClelland, Toronto, 456.
377. **Marie-Victorin, Fr.**
    1920 *Croquis Laurentiens*, Casterman, Paris, 249.
377-a. **Nault, Laurent**
    1950 *Monographie économique de Beauharnois*, Thesis, Ecole des Hautes Etudes Commerciales.
378. **Prud'homme, B.**
    1949 *Etude du peuplement du Comté de Vaudreuil*, Thesis, University of Montreal.
379. **Rondeau, Clovis**
    1953 *Saint-Félix-de-Valois*, Soc. des Missions Etrangères, Montréal, 466.
380. **Rozon, Paul**
    1946 *Monographie économique du Comté Laval-Deux-Montagnes*, Thesis, Ecole des Hautes Etudes Commerciales.
381. **Société Historique de Sainte-Thérèse-de-Blainville**
    1940 *Sainte-Thérèse-de-Blainville*, Etoile du Nord, Joliette, 340.

j) *Montreal City*

383. **Arelano, Ronald and others**
    1955 *Pontville, a socio-economic study of a French Canadian suburban community*, Thesis, McGill University.
384. **Ames, H. B.**
    1897 *The City below the Hill*, Montreal, 72.
385. **Angers, Pierre**
    1941 *Montreal, ville inconnue*, OT, nu. 269, Montréal, 16.
386. **Atherton, William Henry**
    1914 *Montréal, 1635-1914*, Clark, Montreal, 3 v.

A BIBLIOGRAPHICAL INTRODUCTION...

387. **Auclair, Elie**
     1924   *Saint-Jean-Baptiste-de-Montréal*, Québec, 130.
388.   1943   *Saint-Henri-des-Tanneries de Montréal*, TRSC, 37, 1-16.
389. **Beauregard, L.**
     1950   *Monographie géographique du boulevard Saint-Laurent et de la rue Saint-Denis de Montréal*, Thesis, University of Montreal.
390. **Bertrand, C.**
     1935-42   *Histoire de Montréal*, Beauchemin, Montréal, 2 v.
391. **Blanchard, Raoul**
     1947   *Montréal, esquisse de géographie urbaine*, Etudes Canadiennes, 2, 195.
393. **Bosworth, Newton**
     1839   *Hochelaga Depicta*, Greig, Montreal, 284.
394. **Brouillette, Benoît.**
     1943   *Le port et les transports à Montréal*, AE, jan., 193-260.
395.   1938   *Le développement industriel du port de Montréal*, AE, juin, 201-220.
396. **Bruchési, Jean**
     1942   *De Ville-Marie à Montréal*, L'Arbre, Montréal, 154.
397. **Brumath, A. Leblond de**
     1926   *Histoire populaire de Montréal*, Beauchemin, Montréal, 299.
398. **Campeau, Charles-Edouard**
     1944   *Les espaces libres à Montréal*, Relations, 4, 46, 258-61.
399. **Collaboration**
     1942   *Ville, O ma Ville*, Ecrivains Canadiens, Montréal, 405.
400. **Cooper, John Irwin**
     1942   *Montreal, the story of three hundred years*, n. e., Montréal, 133.
401. **Cousineau, A.**
     1944   *Urbanisation de Montréal*, Service d'Urbanisme, Montréal, 60.
402. **Dagenais, P. and others**
     1947   *Le Mont Royal*, RCG, 1, 4, 3-15.
403. **Dawson, Carl A.**
     1926   *The City as an organism with special reference to Montreal*, McGill University Publications, Montreal.
404. **Dupont Herbert, Roger**
     1940   *Le développement industriel de Montréal avant 1900*, Thesis, University of Montreal.
405. **Fisher, David**
     1940   *Montreal regional industrial pattern as compared with that of Toronto*, M. A. Thesis, McGill University.
406. **Frégault, Guy**
     1944   *Montréal, Capitale du Canada*, AH, février, 5-9.
407. **Gauthier, Paul**
     1949   *Le logement familial à prix réduit à Montréal*, Thesis, University of Montreal.
408. **Gazette**
     1907   *Montreal, the Metropolis of Canada*, Gazette, Montreal, 319.
409. **Guerin, Marc-Aimé**
     1952   *L'aménagement du sol dans la banlieue rurale de Montréal*, RCG, 4, 19-27.
410. **Heaton, Phyllis**
     1932   *Standard of living in Montreal*, M. A. Thesis, McGill University.
411. **Huguet-Latour, L.-A.**
     1863-82   *Annuaire de Ville-Marie*, Montréal, 476.

A BIBLIOGRAPHICAL INTRODUCTION...

412. **Huttemeyer, K.-G.-C.**
    1889 *Les intérêts commerciaux de Montréal et Québec et leurs manufactures*, Gazette, Montréal, 202.
413. **Lacoste, Sir Hormisdas**
    1901 *Les affaires municipales de Montréal, 1900-1*, n. e., Montréal, 100.
414. **Lamothe, J.-Cléophas**
    1903 *Histoire de la Corporation de la Cité de Montréal*, Montreal Printing, Montréal, 840.
415. **Laplante, Jean de**
    1952 *La Communauté montréalaise*, CESH, 1, 57-105.
416. **Lash, H. N.**
    1949 *Montreal rural-urban land use*, M. A. Thesis, McGill University.
417. **Leacock, Steven**
    1942 *Montreal, Seaport and City*, Doubleday, New York, 328.
418. **Massicotte, E.-Z.**
    1893 *La cité de Sainte-Cunégonde de Montréal*, Houlé, Montréal, 200.
419.   1933 *Memento de Montréal, 1636-1760*, TRSC, 27, 111-132.
420. **Massue, Huet**
    1940 *Financial and economic situation of Montreal compared with that of Toronto*, Shawinigan Water and Power, Montreal.
421. **Minville, Esdras and others**
    1943 *Montréal Economique*, Fides, Montréal, 430.
422. **Morin, Victor**
    1942 *Le Vieux Montréal*, Ed. des Dix, Montréal, 43.
423.   1949 *La légende dorée de Montréal*, Ed. des Dix, Montréal, 211.
424. **Nobbs, Percy E.**
    1944 *City-owned land and the housing problem in Montreal*, McGill Monographic Series, no 4, 196-203.
425. **Pick, Alfred John**
    1937 *The Municipal and Financial administration of Paris and Montreal*, M. A. Thesis, McGill University.
426. **Pye, J. L.**
    1939 *Point Saint Charles, an ecological study*, M. A. Thesis, McGill University.
427. **Richardson, Nigel A.**
    1954 *A study of the relationship between ecological and non-ecological factors in the development of natural areas of Montreal*, M. A. Thesis, McGill University.
428. **Roberts, Percy A.**
    1928 *Dufferin District, An area in transition*, M. A. Thesis, McGill University.
429. **Rocher, Guy**
    1952 *Industrialisation et culture urbaine*, CESH, 1, 165-170.
430. **Saint-Pierre, Arthur**
    1947 *Valeur de la propriété immobilière détenue par les Canadiens français dans la région métropolitaine de Montréal*, TRSC, 41, 89-99.
431. **Sandman, A.**
    1870 *Ville Marie, or sketches of Montreal*, Bishop, Montreal, 393.
432. **Tangue, Raymond**
    1928 *Géographie humaine de Montréal*, Lib. d'Action Française, Montréal, 325.
433.   1936 *Montréal*, Lévesque, Montréal, 188.
434.   1936 *Analyse du budget de la ville de Montréal*, AE, juin, 254-68.
435. **Tombs, L. C.**
    1926 *The port of Montreal*, Macmillan, Toronto, 177.
436. **Zakuta, Leo**
    1948 *The Natural Areas of the Montreal Metropolitan Community*, M. A. Thesis, McGill University.

31

A BIBLIOGRAPHICAL INTRODUCTION...

k) *The Ottawa-Abitibi-Temiscamingue Region*

437. **Benoist, Emile**
     1938 *L'Abitibi, pays de l'or*, Ed. du Zodiaque, Montréal, 194.
438. **Biron, Hervé**
     1948 *Nuages sur les brûlés, la colonisation au Témiscamingue*, Pilon, Montréal, 59.
439. **Brault, Lucien**
     1941 *Ottawa, de ses débuts à nos jours*, Ph. D. Thesis, University of Ottawa.
440.   1942 *Ottawa, capital of Canada*, Ed. de l'Université d'Ottawa, Ottawa, 310.
441.   1950 *Hull, 1800-1950*, Ed. de l'Université d'Ottawa, Ottawa, 262.
442. **Buies, Arthur**
     1889 *L'Outaouais Supérieur*, Darveau, Québec, 309.
443. **Chamberland, M.**
     1929 *Histoire de Montebello, 1815-1928*, Montréal, 410.
444.   1931 *Histoire de N. D.-des-Sept-Douleurs de Grenville*, Montréal, 310.
445. **Chenier, Henri**
     1937 *Notes historiques sur le Témiscamingue*, Ville-Marie, 137.
446. **Cloutier, Henri**
     1947 Le Royaume de Matagami, *Relations*, 75, 76-79.
447. **Collaboration**
     1938 *Le Nord de l'Outaouais*, Le Droit, Ottawa, 396.
448. **Dugré, Alexandre**
     1945 L'Abitibi veut mûrir, *Relations*, 56, 198-200.
449.   1949 Lenteur au Nord, *Relations*, 104, 219-221.
450.   1953 Le Témiscamingue et ses problèmes, *Relations*, 156, 324-6 ; 157, 6-9.
451. **Gosselin, A. and Boucher, G.-P.**
     1944 *Settlement problems in North Western Quebec and North Eastern Ontario*, Dept. of Agriculture, Ottawa, 9.
452. **Gourlay, J.-L.**
     1896 *History of the Ottawa Valley*, n. e., n. p., 288.
453. **Greber, Jacques**
     1950 L'Aménagement de la Capitale Nationale, RUO, 20, 3, 265-71.
454.   1950 *Projet d'aménagement de la Capitale Nationale*, Service d'Aménagement, Ottawa, 2 v.
455. **Laplante, Rodolphe**
     1945 Une région oubliée et ses problèmes (Pontiac), *Relations*, 50, 46-48.
456. **Légaré, Romain**
     1940 L'Abitibi, Région de Colonisation, *Culture*, 5, 2, 157-172.
457. **Mackay, J. R.**
     1949 *The regional geography of the lower Ottawa valley*, Ph. D. Thesis, University of Montreal.
458. **Ouellet, Gérard**
     1950 *Un royaume vous attend : l'Abitibi*, Ministère de la Colonisation, Québec, 84.
459. **Rossignol, Léo**
     1941 *Histoire documentée de Hull, 1792-1900*, Ph. D. Thesis, University of Ottawa.
460. **Trudelle, P.**
     1937 *L'Abitibi d'autrefois, d'hier et d'aujourd'hui*, Amos, 395.

3. Social Institutions

a) *Demography*

461. **Bouchette, Erol**
     1905 La population française du Canada, *Revue Canadienne*, 41, 368-83.
462. **Charles, Enid**
     1941 *The Changing Size of the Family in Canada*, Dominion Bureau of Statistics, Ottawa, 311.
463. **Cousineau, René**
     1947 Natalité et fécondité au Canada, AE, janvier, 732-44.
464. **Davidson, J.**
     1896 The growth of the French Canadian Race in North America, *The Annals*, 8, 213-35.
465. **Dumoreau, P.**
     1952 L'aspect et l'avenir démographique du Canada français, AE, 28, 5-26.
466. **Duncan, M.**
     1944 *The French Canadian population : its distribution and development*, M. A. Thesis, University of Aberdeen.
467. **Finestone, Harold**
     1944 *Trends in the population structure in the Sherbrooke sub-region*, M. A. Thesis, McGill University.
468. **Hall, Oswald**
     1937 *The size and composition of the Canadian family*, M. A. Thesis, McGill University.
469. **Henripin, Jacques**
     1953 Les mariages entre parents présentent-ils des risques ?, *Le Devoir*, 44, 19 déc., 4.
470.   1953 La mortalité des enfants de moins d'un an, chez nous, *Le Devoir*, 44, 28 nov., 4, 7.
471.   1954 *La population canadienne au début du XVIIIe siècle*, Presses Universitaires de France, Paris, 129.
472.   1955 Les divisions de recensement au Canada de 1871 à 1951, AE, 30, 4, 633-59 ; 31, 1, 102-27.
473. **Huot, L.**
     1936 Crise et problèmes de population dans le Québec, *Etudes Economiques*, 6, 179-223.
474. **Lalande, Gilles**
     1954 Un nouvel ouvrage sur la population du Canada, RCG, 8, 3-4, 94-98.
475. **Langlois, Georges**
     1934 *Histoire de la population canadienne-française*, Lévesque, Montréal, 309.
476. **Lemieux, A.-O.**
     1934 Factors in the growth of the rural population in Eastern Canada, *Proceedings of the Can. Pol. Assoc.*, 6, 196-219.
477. **Lewis, H. Harry**
     1940 *Population of the Quebec Province*, Economic Geography, Clark University.
478. **Maheu, Rodolphe**
     1933 Mouvements démographiques au Canada depuis le commencement du XXe siècle : immigration et émigration, *Etudes Economiques*, 5, 323-338.

479. **Parrot, Paul**
    1948   The division of demography, *Bulletin Sanitaire*, Ministry of Health, Quebec, 48, 3, 41-62.
480. **Poznanski, T.**
    1953   Quelques données numériques sur l'élément français au Canada, RUL, 7, 810-820.
481. **Prud'homme, L.-A.**
    1901   Vitalité de la race française au Canada, *Revue Canadienne*, 2, 18-29 ; 117-129.
482. **Sabagh, G.**
    1942   The fertility of the French Canadian women during the 17th century, AJS, 47, 680-89.
483. **Veyret, Paul**
    1953   *La population du Canada*, Presses Universitaires de France, Paris, 158.

b) *Kinship and the Family*

484. **Action Catholique, Hull**
    1943   *Semaine familiale mettant en honneur les familles nombreuses*, n. e., Hull, 74.
485. **Angers, F.-A.**
    1942   Standards nutritifs de la famille urbaine canadienne, AE, janvier, 267-75.
486. **Auteurs canadiens**
    1946   *Au Royaume du Foyer*, Congrégation de Notre-Dame, Montréal, 177.
487. **Anjou, Marie-Joseph d'**
    1953   L'autorité dans l'éducation familiale, CF, 10, 110-116.
488. **Beaudoin, Lucien**
    1949   *La dissolution du lien matrimonial en droit canonique et en droit civil canadien*, Ph. D. Thesis, University of Ottawa.
489. **Bernier, Gérard**
    1953   L'Institut Généalogique Drouin, Le Droit, 20 juin, 17-19.
490. **Boardman, F.-G.**
    1954   Ce que révèle le recensement à propos des familles, BESC, 6, 4, 4-6.
491. **Henri Bourassa**
    1925   Divorce et Mariage, Le Devoir, Montréal, 12.
492.   1930   Le Divorce, aspects constitutionnels et politiques, Le Devoir, Montréal, 21.
493. **Bouvier, Léon**
    1941   Le mariage mixte en Cour d'Appel, *Relations*, 10, 262-63.
494. **Breul, Frank Rennel**
    1951   *Family allowance in Canada*, M. A. Thesis, McGill University.
495. **Bruneau, Arthur-Aimé**
    1921   *Questions de Droit sur le mariage*, Ducharme, Montréal, 200.
496. **Brunelle, L.**
    1946   *Structure de la Famille Québecoise*, M. A. Thesis, Laval University.
497. **Brunet, Louis-Alexandre**
    1881   *La Famille et ses traditions*, Senécal, Montréal, 378.
498. **Bulletin Paroissial**
    1918   *Autour du Foyer canadien*, Messager, Montréal, 268.
499. **Cahiers d'Action catholique**
    1954   *Famille contemporaine et Problèmes étudiants*, Librairie Dominicaine, Montréal, 57.
500. **Côté, Marcel**
    1952   *Plan d'Etude sur la Famille*, ISP, no 459, Montréal, 32.
501. **Dépt. des Relations Industrielles**
    1951   *Sécurité de la Famille ouvrière*, Presses Universitaires Laval, Québec, 193.

A BIBLIOGRAPHICAL INTRODUCTION...

502. **Déry, Edouard**
    1953 *La Famille canadienne-française*, Imp. Saint-Joseph, Ottawa, 66.
503. **Dionne, N.-E.**
    1914 *Les Canadiens français, Origines des Familles*, Laflamme et Proulx, Québec, 611.
504. **Drouin, F.-M.**
    1936 *Autour de la famille*, Collège Dominicain, Ottawa, 30.
505. **Falardeau, Jean-Charles**
    1949 *Orientation nouvelle des familles canadiennes-françaises*, Conseil Canadien du Bien-Etre social, Ottawa.
506. **Filiatrault, Georgette**
    1946 *Guerre et désorganisation dans la famille*, Thesis, Laval University.
507. **Filion, Gérard**
    1940-41 La Famille paysanne canadienne-française, AN, 16, 4, 322-33 ; 17, 1, 46-62.
508. **Forest, M.-C.**
    1920 *Le Divorce*, Le Droit, Ottawa, 156.
509. **Gagnon (Famille)**
    1940 *Fête du troisième centenaire des Gagnon, 1640-1940*, n. e., n. p., 171.
509-a. **Garigue, Philip**
    1956 French Canadian kinship and urban life, *American Anthropologist*, 58, 3.
510. **Gérin, Léon**
    1932 Famille canadienne-française de Saint-Irénée, sa force, ses faiblesses, RTC, mars, 35-63.
511. 1934 Famille canadienne-française de Saint-Justin, RTC, juin, 18-31.
512. **Giroux, Paul-Emile**
    1955 *L'Enquête prénuptiale*, Fides, Montréal, 197.
513. **Godbout, Archange**
    1925 *Origine des Familles canadiennes-françaises*, Desclée, Lille, 225.
514. 1955 *Nos ancêtres au XVIIe siècle*, n. e., n. p., 96.
515. **Groulx, Lionel**
    1920 La vie familiale chez nos ancêtres, AF, 21-35.
516. **Lalande, Louis**
    1929 *Au Service de la Famille*, Messager, Montréal, 209.
517. **Lamontagne, M. et Falardeau, J.-C.**
    1947 The Life Cycle of French Canadian Urban Families, CJEPS, 13, 2, 233-47.
518. **Lebel, Léon**
    1951 Les allocations familiales au Canada, *Relations*, 122, 47-50 ; 124, 91-93 ; 126, 158-161.
519. **Lefevre, J.-J.**
    1945 Quand finira la légende, BRH, 156.
520. 1947 En marge de trois siècles d'histoire domestique, RUO, 33.
521. **Légaré, Thérèse**
    1947 *Conditions économiques et sociales des familles de Gaspé-Nord*, Thesis, Laval University.
522. **Lemieux, Gérard**
    1947 L'Institut d'études familiales, AN, déc., 273-80.
523. 1955 *Vu et vécu, La vie familiale des jeunes ruraux*, Ed. du Sol, Montréal, 38.
524. **Lemoine, A.**
    1950 *Questions de vie familiale*, n. e., Montréal, 90.
525. **Lery, Louis-C.**
    1955 *Le problème du Divorce*, Bellarmin, Montréal, 132.
526. **Lesage, G.**
    1953-54 Notre économie familiale, RUO, 1953, 23, 63-83 ; 23, 416-40 ; 24, 299-314.

A BIBLIOGRAPHICAL INTRODUCTION...

526-a. **Lévesque, Albert**
    1943   *Entrez donc*, Lévesque, Montréal, 165.
527. **McNaughton, M. A., and others**
    1950   *Farm family living in Nicolet County, Quebec, 1947-1948*, Dept. of Agriculture, Ottawa, 26.
528. **Mailloux, Alexis**
    1910   *Le Manuel des Parents chrétiens*, L'Action Sociale, Québec, 289.
529. **Michaud, Berthe**
    1950   *Un organisme d'éducation populaire : le service de préparation au mariage de Montréal*, Thesis, University of Montreal.
530. **Miner, Horace**
    1930   The French Canadian family Cycle, ASR, 3, 700-8.
531. **Morisset, T.**
    1945   *Condition de la famille ouvrière à Québec pendant la guerre*, Thesis, University of Montreal.
532. **Papillon, Marthe**
    1946   *Etude des familles de la ville de Québec*, Thesis, Laval University.
533. **Papkuskas, Ramuska-Antoine**
    1955   L'éducation familiale au tournant de l'histoire, RUO, 25, 103-8.
534. **Pascal, Mgr Albert**
    1916   *La famille et le mariage chrétien*, Langevin, Montréal, 251.
535. **Poulin, Gonzalve**
    1940   *Brève histoire de la famille canadienne*, Ed. La Famille, Montréal, 48.
536.   1940   La famille canadienne-française dans son évolution historique, AN, août, sept., oct.
537.   1940   Les responsabilités familiales de l'Etat, *Le Devoir*, 31, 14, 5.
538.   1941   La famille canadienne aux prises avec les difficultés économiques, *Culture*, sept., 273-88.
539.   1952   *Problèmes de la Famille canadienne-française*, Presses Universitaires Laval, Québec, 75.
540. **Rocher, Guy**
    1954   La famille dans la ville moderne, SS, 4, 80-84.
541.   1954   Le Père, *Food for Thought*, 14, 6, 6-10.
542. **Roy, Thérèse**
    1948   *Influence économique et sociale des allocations familiales*, Thesis, University of Montreal.
543. **Semaines Sociales du Canada**
    1923   *La Famille*, L'Action Française, Montréal, 360.
544.   1950   *Le Foyer, Base de la Société*, ISP, Montréal, 301.
545. **Société Généalogique canadienne-française**
    1944-55   *Mémoires*, 15 v.
546. **Tanguay, Cyprien**
    1871-90   *Dictionnaire Généalogique des Familles canadiennes-françaises de 1608- à 1890*, Sénécal, Québec, 7 v.
547.   1886   *A travers les Registres*, Lib. Saint-Joseph, Montréal, 235.
548. **Trottier, Louis**
    1938   Les Droits de succession de la Province de Québec, AE, juin, 445-61.
549. **Turcotte, Dominique-Augustin**
    1940   *Pour restaurer le Foyer*, Presse Dominicaine, Montréal, 167.
550. **Turgeon, Henri**
    1949   Le système successoral de la Province de Québec, n. e., Québec, 45.

c) *The Economic Organization*

I) *Economic History*

551. **Angers, F.-A.**
     1936 La route trans-canadienne et la Province de Québec, AE, fév., 365-68.
552. 1936 Les chemins de fer et la Province de Québec, AE, juin, 271-74.
553. 1939 La position économique des Canadiens français dans le Québec, AE, oct., 401-26.
554. 1941 La situation économique actuelle du Québec et les facteurs qui la conditionnent, *Culture*, 2, 3, 289-299.
555. 1941 Vue d'ensemble sur notre milieu économique, AE, 2, 1, 47-74.
556. 1945 Etude sur les revenus de la population de la Province de Québec, AE, avril, 32-89.
557. **Angers, F.-A. and Allen, Patrick**
     1953 Evolution de la structure des emplois au Canada, AE, avril-juin, 75-104 ; juil.-sept., 271-301 ; oct., 481-524.
558. **Archambault, Joseph-P.**
     1940 *Notre relèvement économique*, ESP, nu. 314, Montréal, 32.
559. **Asselin, Olivar**
     1927 Les Canadiens français et le développement économique du Canada, AF, 17, 5-6 ; 305-327.
560. **Ballabon, Maurice-Bernard**
     1955 *Area differentiation of the manufacturing belt in central Canada*, Ph. D. Thesis, McGill University.
561. **Barbeau, Victor**
     1936 *Mesure de notre taille*, Le Devoir, Montréal, 243.
562. 1937 *Pour nous grandir*, Le Devoir, Montréal, 242.
563. **Beaubien, L.-G.**
     1954 *Le placement au Canada*, Montréal, 83.
564. **Bédard, Charles-M.**
     1953 En marge du nouveau projet canadien de canalisation et d'aménagement hydro-électrique du réseau Grands Lacs-Saint-Laurent, AE, juillet-sept., 229-70.
565. **Benoist, Emile**
     1925 *Monographies économiques*, Le Devoir, Montréal, 274.
566. **Bergeron, Marius**
     1943 *Adaptation de nos institutions économiques à notre cas social*, Thesis, Laval University.
567. **Bouchette, Errol**
     1900 French Canada and Canada, *The Canadian Magazine*, 14, Feb., 313-20.
568. 1901 L'Evolution économique dans la Province de Québec, TRSC, 7, 117-147.
569. 1905 Etudes sociales et économiques sur le Canada, *Revue Canadienne*, 43 and 44, 125.
570. 1905 *Emparons-nous de l'industrie*, Revue Canadienne, Montréal, 195.
571. 1913 *L'Indépendance économique du Canada français*, Wilson, Montréal, 293.
572. **Buron, Edmond-J.-P.**
     1904 *Les richesses du Canada*, Librairie Orientale, Paris, 360.
573. **Campeau, Charles-Edouard**
     1955 Des insulaires ignorent l'histoire, *Relations*, 15, 187-8, 205-6.
574. **Camu, Pierre**
     1949 The traffic on the Upper Saint Lawrence River, RCG, 3, 3-42.
575. 1952 *L'axe économique du Saint-Laurent*, Ph. D. Thesis, University of Montreal.
576. 1952 Le projet de canalisation du Saint-Laurent, AE, avril, 27-56.

A BIBLIOGRAPHICAL INTRODUCTION...

577.   1953   Effets du projet de canalisation du Saint-Laurent sur le port de Montréal, AE, jan., 619-37.
578. **Chartier, Emile**
              1921   Le Canada français. La situation économique, politique et sociale, *Revue Canadienne*, 26, 175-185 ; 27, 272-285.
579. **Chevrier, Lionel**
              1955   *The Saint Lawrence seaway*, Printers to the Queen, Ottawa, 16.
580. **Côté, Pierre.**
              1943   *Les Canadiens français et le développement industriel du Québec*, Thesis, Ecole des Hautes Etudes Commerciales.
581. **Cousineau, Rosario**
              1945   Le rôle de l'Etat dans l'organisation de la vie économique, AE, 20, 2, 5, 398-430.
582.   1948   Employeurs religieux et employés laïques, AE, jan., 752-59.
583. **Craig, Isabel**
              1937   *Economic Conditions in Canada (1763-1783)*, M. A. Thesis, McGill University.
584. **Creighton, D. G.**
              1937   *The Commercial Empire of the Saint Lawrence*, Ryerson, Toronto, 441.
585. **Currie, A. W.**
              1951   *Canadian Economic Development*, Nelson, Toronto, 454.
586. **De Bray, A.-J.**
              n. d. *L'Essor industriel et commercial du peuple canadien*, Beauchemin, Montréal, 222.
587. **Deschamps, Jean**
              1955   Québec boude-t-il le progrès du Canada ?, AN, avril, 678-84.
588. **Durocher, René**
              1951   Pourquoi plus de faillites dans Québec que dans l'Ontario ?, AE, jan., 705-48.
589. **Ecoles des Hautes Etudes Commerciales**
              1931-37 *Etudes Economiques*, Beauchemin, Montréal, 7 v.
590. **Faucher, Albert**
              1946   Histoire économique et Unité canadienne, *Cahiers de la Faculté des Sciences Sociales*, Université Laval, 4, 5, 36.
591. **Faucher, A. et Lamontagne M.**
              1953   History of Industrial Development, in *Essays on Contemporary Quebec*, (ed. Falardeau, J. C.), Presses Universitaires Laval, Québec, 24-37.
592. **Fortier, de la Bruère**
              1938   L'Organisation du crédit foncier dans la Province de Québec, AE, jan., 201-23.
593. **Gagnon, Aurèle**
              1952   Etude des occupations de la population canadienne-française de la Province de Québec, CESH, 1, 135-164.
594. **Gibson, J. Douglas**
              1948   *Canada's Economy in a changing world*, Macmillan, Toronto, 380.
595. **Golberg, S. A.**
              1940   *The French Canadians and the Industrialization of Quebec*, M. A. Thesis, McGill University.
596. **Grenier, Jean**
              1954   Le Crédit Social, AN, juil., 567-82.
597. **Glazebrook, G. de T.**
              1938   *The history of transportation in Canada*, Yale University Press, New Haven, 475.
598. **Groulx, Lionel**
              1920   Le problème économique, AF, 4, 557-65 ; 6, 706-22.

599. **Guimont, Paul-Henri**
    1940   *La canalisation du Saint-Laurent*, ESP, nu. 313, Montréal, 32.
600. **Guy, Pierre Paul**
    1950   *La place de l'agriculture et de l'industrie dans l'économie de la Province de Québec*, Thesis, Ecole des Hautes Etudes Commerciales.
601. **Innis, H. A. and Lower, A. R. M.**
    1933   *Select Documents in Canadian Economic History, 1783-1885*, University of Toronto Press, Toronto, 846.
602. **Innis, M. Q.**
    1948   *An Economic History of Canada*, Ryerson, Toronto, 363.
603. **Innis, Harold, A.**
    1956   *The Fur Trade in Canada*, University of Toronto Press, Toronto, 475.
604. **Heaton, H. A.**
    1939   *A history of trade and commerce, with special reference to Canada*, Nelson, Toronto, 404.
605. **Lank, Herbert, H.**
    1945   Les carrières économiques et les Canadiens français, AE, mai, 101-108.
606. **Laplante, Rodolphe**
    1941   L'Avenir du magasin indépendant, *Relations*, 7, 177-179.
607. **Larivière, J.-A.**
    1932   L'Epargne et les Canadiens français, *Etudes Economiques*, 2, 7-69.
608. **Laurin, J.-E.**
    1942   *Histoire économique de Montréal et des Cités et Villes du Québec*, Ed. Laurin, Montréal, 287.
609. **Lefevre, James**
    1941   *Réalités et expériences canadiennes-françaises dans l'épargne-vie*, Thesis, Laval University.
610. **Leman, Beaudry**
    1929   Progrès économiques, facteur de survivance, RTC, 240-254.
611. **Ligue de l'achat chez-nous**
    1951   *Où acheter dans le Québec*, n. e., Montréal, 171.
612. **L'Heureux, Eugène**
    1930   *La participation des Canadiens français à la vie économique*, L'Action Catholique, Québec, 62.
613.   1933   La dictature économique dans le Québec, AN, 1, 2, 66-78.
614. **Martin, Jean-Marie**
    1947   Notre place dans l'économie canadienne, *Cahiers de l'Ecole des Sciences Sociales*, Québec, 4, 5, 32.
615. **Massue, Huet**
    1945   *Vingt-cinq années d'évolution économique au Canada et son effet sur la Province de Québec*, Chambre de Commerce, Montréal, 16.
616.   1953   Coup d'œil sur l'Economie canadienne, RTC, 39, 115-126.
617. **Mavor, James**
    1922   A chapter of Canadian economic history, 1791-1839, TRSC, 16, 19-33.
618. **McGee, J. C.**
    1948   L'indice du coup de la vie, *Relations*, 90, 178-181.
619. **Ménard, Gilles**
    1950   *La décentralisation de la population urbaine et de l'Industrie dans le Québec*, Thesis, Ecole des Hautes Etudes Commerciales.
620. **Minville, Esdras**
    1924   Le capital étranger, AF, 11, 6, 323-349.
621.   1924   Economie nationale, RTC, 9, 49-78.
622.   1928   L'Education économique, AF, 19, 5, 262-286.
623.   1935   *Histoire économique du Canada*, Beauchemin, Montréal, 126.
624.   1936   L'Economique et le National, AN, 7, 209-214.

A BIBLIOGRAPHICAL INTRODUCTION...

625.   1936   Le Budget canadien en 1935-36, AE, mai, 158-172.
626.   1936   Le Budget canadien en 1936-37, AE, mars, 464-78.
627.   1950   L'aspect économique du problème national canadien-français, AE, 26, 1, 48-77.
628.   1950   *L'aspect économique du problème national canadien-français*, ISP, no 436, Montréal, 32.
629.   1951   Les conditions de l'autonomie économique des Canadiens français, AN, mai, 260-84.
630. **Montpetit, Edouard**
        1935   *L'Avenir économique des Canadiens français*, n. e., Montréal, 5.
631.   1938   Les Canadiens français et l'économique, TRSC, 32, 55-80.
632.   1939   Pour une économie nationale, RTC, 25, 119-146.
633.   1942   *La conquête économique*, Valiquette, Montréal, 3 v.
634. **Montreal Daily Herald**
        1941   *French Canada's War Effort*, Daily Herald, 30 juin, 21.
635. **Morin, René**
        1944   Considérations sur la vie économique du Québec, AE, nov., 27-45.
636. **Nadeau, Jean-Marie**
        1942   La canalisation du Saint-Laurent, AE, avril, 31-56.
637. **Parenteau, Roland**
        1953   Finance provinciale, 1953, AE, 29, 343-351.
638.   1954   Salaires différentiels, AE, 30, 538-551.
639.   1955   Quelques raisons de la faiblesse économique de la nation canadienne-française, AN, 44, 316-331.
640. **Parizeau, Gérard**
        1937   Aperçu de la situation économique dans le Bas-Canada vers 1837, RTC, 23, 91, 272-284.
641. **Reid, S. W.**
        1947   The habitant's standard of living on the Seigneurie des Mille-Iles, CHR, sept., 266-278.
642. **Robitaille, Ernest**
        1941   La Beauharnois, entreprise excellente, *Relations*, 6, 143-6.
643. **Séguin, Maurice**
        1946   La conquête et la vie économique des Canadiens, AN, 308-326.
644. **Semaines sociales du Canada**
        1928   *Le problème économique*, Montréal, 320.
645. **Solowis, T.**
        1949   Développement des banques canadiennes-françaises, AE, avril, 3-10.
646. **Stead, Robert J. C.**
        1955   Taming the Saint Lawrence, CGJ, 51, 5, 176-189.
647. **Vézina, Roger**
        1954   La position des Canadiens français dans l'industrie et le commerce, *Culture*, 15, 3, 291-9.
648. **Wykes, Neville Georges**
        1941   *The highway transportation problem in Quebec*, M. A. Thesis, McGill University.

II) *Agriculture*

649. **Angers, F.-A.**
        1943   Quelques facteurs économiques et sociaux qui conditionnent la prospérité agricole, AE, jan., 261-315.
650.   1951   La sécurité sociale en agriculture, AN, sept., 6-21.
651. **Anonymous**
        1941   *La corporation des agronomes du Québec*, n. e., n. p., 163.

652. **Archambault, J.-P.**
　　1928　*L'Union Catholique des Cultivateurs de la Province de Québec*, Union Catholique des Cultivateurs, Montréal, 269.
653. **Assoc. Cath. de la Jeunesse C.-F.**
　　1918　*Le problème agricole au Canada français*, ACJC, Montréal, 292.
654. **Beaudin, Dominique**
　　1952　*L'U. C. C. d'aujourd'hui*, Ed. de l'U. C. C., Montréal, 160.
655. **Bergeron, Jean**
　　1943　*L'Agriculture et l'Eglise*, n. e., Québec, 210.
656. **Blais, Pierre-Paul**
　　1948　*Saint-Pierre-du-Sud. La mobilité des propriétés agricoles*, Thesis, Laval University.
657. **Blanchard, Raoul**
　　1949　Les excédents de population et l'agriculture dans la Province de Québec, AE, jan., 635-41.
658. **Bouchard, Georges**
　　1936　*La Renaissance Campagnarde*, Lévesque, Montréal, 200.
659. **Bouffard, Jean**
　　1921　*Traité du Domaine*, Le Soleil, Québec, 227.
660. **Burpee, Lawrence J.**
　　1940　A people that can stand alone, *Queen's Quarterly*, 47, 231-40.
661. **Canadian Historical Review**
　　1927　Some Canadian Villages, CHR, 8, 302-308.
662. **Charron, P.-E.**
　　1942　*Le Crédit Rural*, Thesis, Laval University.
663. **Corminbœuf, Fernand**
　　1943　*Essai Agrogéologique du Québec*, Institut Agricole d'Oka, Oka, 184.
664. 　　1944　Les sciences de la terre et l'agriculture dans la Province de Québec, AE, mai, 175-89.
665. 　　1944　Les ressources agraires dans la Province de Québec, AE, 1, 4, 353-371.
666. **Dagenais, Pierre**
　　1942　Monographie d'une exploitation agricole-type de plaine de Montréal, AE, mars, 461-77.
667. **De Calles, A. P.**
　　1920　The habitant, his origin and history, *Canada and its Provinces*, (ed. Shortt, A.), vol. 15, 17-117.
668. **Delorme, Joachim**
　　1938　L'Industrie du sucre d'érable dans la Province de Québec, AE, mars, 446-54.
669. **Filion, Gérard**
　　1942　Le Paysan et ses Institutions sociales, AE, oct., 79-82.
670. 　　1944　Nos ruraux s'organisent, *Relations*, 4, 37, 19-21.
671. **Gagné, Charles**
　　1924　Notre Problème agricole, AF, 11, 2, 91-102 ; 3, 156-170 ; 4, 221-237.
672. 　　1924　*Notre Problème agricole en 1924*, ESP, no 126-7, Montréal, 64.
673. **Gérin, Léon**
　　1923　*Le Problème du cultivateur canadien en 1923*, Soc. de l'industrie laitière, Québec, 20.
674. 　　1923　Notre Industrie Ovine, RTC, mars, 21-38.
675. 　　1948　*Le Type économique et social des Canadiens*, Fides, Montréal, 221.
676. **Godbout, Adélard**
　　1933　La Carrière agroéconomique, OT, nu. 174, Montréal, 16.
677. 　　1944　Agriculture in Quebec, past-present-future, CGJ, 28, 4, 157-181.

A BIBLIOGRAPHICAL INTRODUCTION...

678. **Groulx, Lionel**
    1933 Le problème de la terre. La survivance canadienne-française et la terre, *Semaines Sociales du Canada*, 227-47.
679.   1953 L'agriculteur canadien-français, *Le Devoir*, 5 sept., 4-5.
680. **Haythorne, G. V.**
    1938 *Agriculture and the farm worker in Eastern Canada*, Ph. D. Thesis, Harvard University.
681. **Haythorne, G. V. and Marsh, L. C.**
    1941 *Land and labour, a social survey of agriculture and farm labour market in central Canada*, Oxford University Press, Toronto, 431.
682. **Hudson, S. C. and others**
    1949 *Genres d'exploitation agricole au Canada*, Ministère de l'Agriculture, Ottawa, nu. 825.
683. **Hughes, Everett**
    1938 Industry and the rural system in Quebec, CJEPS, 4, 342-49.
684. **Jones, Robert Leslie**
    1946 Agriculture in Lower Canada, 1792-1815, CHR, 27, 1, 33-51.
685. **Laplante, Rodolphe**
    1946 Le Crédit agricole, *Relations*, 72, 373-376.
686.   1953 Quelques aspects du crédit agricole, *Relations*, 152, 218-221.
687.   1954 Réflexions sur les prêts agricoles, *Relations*, 161, 130-33.
688.   1953-54 L'électrification rurale dans le Québec, RTC, 39, 271-76.
689. **Leduc, Jean-Paul**
    1950 *Le Crédit agricole de la Province de Québec*, Thesis, Ecole des Hautes Etudes Commerciales.
690. **Lemelin, Charles**
    1952 *Agricultural development and industrialization of Quebec*, Ph. D. Thesis, Harvard, University.
691.   1953 Social impact of industrialization on agriculture in the Province of Quebec, *Culture*, 14, 34-46 ; 156-169.
692. **Lemieux, Omer Adrien**
    1940 *Development of agriculture in Canada during the sixteenth and seventeenth centuries*, Ph. D. Thesis, University of Ottawa.
693. **Lemonde, Jean-Luc**
    1950 *L'Electrification rurale de la Province de Québec*, Thesis, Ecole des Hautes Etudes Commerciales.
694. **Leslie-Jones, R.**
    1942 French Canadian Agriculture in the Saint Lawrence Valley, 1815-1850, *Agricultural History*, 16, 137-48.
695. **Lessard, Regis**
    1950 *La ferme familiale de Saint-Alexandre de Kamouraska*, Thesis, Laval University.
696. **Létourneau, Firmin**
    1949 *L'U. C. C.*, n. e., n. p., 248.
697.   1950 *Histoire de l'Agriculture (Canadienne-française)*, Imp. Populaire, Montréal, 324.
698. **Lettres Pastorales collectives**
    n. d. *Le Problème rural*, Action Catholique, Ottawa, 48.
699. **Minville, Esdras (éd.)**
    1943 *L'Agriculture*, Fides, Montréal, 555.
700. **Nagant, Henri**
    1915 Historical notes concerning agriculture, *Statistical Year Book*, Province of Québec, 413.
701. **Parenteau, Roland**
    1951 Nos fermiers, exploiteurs ou exploités, AE, avril, 144-52.

702. **Pasquier, Louis**
    1949 L'agriculture québecoise doit devenir intensive, *Relations*, 102, 153-155 ; 103, 178-181.
703. **Perron, Marc-A.**
    1955 *Un grand Educateur agricole, Edouard-A. Barnard, 1835-1898. Essai historique sur l'agriculture de 1700 à 1900*, n. e., n. p., 335.
704. **Rioux, Albert**
    1933 La Carrière agricole, OT, nu. 174, Montréal, 8.
705. 1942 L'Electrification rurale du Québec, Messager, Sherbrooke, 138.
706. **Riverin, Alphonse**
    1949 *L'Agriculture québecoise*, Thesis, Laval University.
707. **Séguin, Maurice**
    1948 *La nation canadienne et l'agriculture*, Ph. D. Thesis, University of Montreal.
708. **Semaines Sociales du Canada**
    1947 *La Vie Rurale*, ESP, Montréal, 289.
709. **Tellier, Maurice**
    1940 Etude sur la culture industrielle de tabacs à cigarettes dans le Québec, AE, nov., 25-48.
710. **Tremblay, Adélard**
    1950 *La ferme familiale du Comté de Kamouraska*, Thesis, Laval University.
711. **Van Bruyssel, Ferd.**
    1895 *Le Canada, agriculture, élevage*, Imp. du Roi, Bruxelles, 484.

III) *Forest and Fishing*

712. **Allaire, Jean**
    1940 Les ressources forestières de Québec, AE, mai, 150-57.
713. **Arsenault, Ernest**
    1945 Nos bûcherons, *Relations*, 53, 122-125.
714. **Asselin, Pierre**
    1934 L'Industrie de la pêche en Gaspésie et ses possibilités de développement, *Etudes Economiques*, 4, 105-131.
715. **Associa. des Ingénieurs Forestiers du Québec**
    1949 *Les Problèmes Forestiers du Québec*, Fides, Montréal, 112.
716. **Barbin, Gérard**
    1955 Québec, ses pêcheries, ses pêches, *Relations*, 177, 233-235.
717. **Bédard, Avila**
    1944 Forestry in Quebec, CGJ, 28, 6, 251-281.
718. **Bérubé, Louis**
    1941 *Coup d'œil sur les Pêcheries de Québec*, Ecole de Sainte-Anne-de-la-Pocatière, 215.
719. 1942 La guerre et les pêcheries du Québec, *Relations*, 19, 171-173.
720. **Chambers, E. T. D.**
    1912 *The Fisheries of the Province of Quebec, Historical Introduction*, Dept. of Mines and Fisheries, Quebec, 206.
721. **Dionne, Michel**
    1948 *Les Pêcheurs Unis du Québec*, Thesis, Ecole des Hautes Etudes Commerciales.
722. **Dugré, Alexandre**
    1949 Chantier. Nouvelle mode, *Relations*, 98, 52-54.
723. **Favreau, André**
    1944 La Forêt, Ressource capitale du Québec, *Technique*, 19, 9-10 ; 653-663 ; 726-731.
724. **Labrie, Napoléon-Alexandre**
    1948 L'Exploitation chrétienne de la Forêt, *Relations*, 90, 163-8.

A BIBLIOGRAPHICAL INTRODUCTION...

725. **Lamothe, G. E.**
    1949   The Forest of Quebec, *Culture*, 10, 230-249.
726. **Langlais, Hormisdas**
    1946   Considérations sur les pêcheries maritimes du Québec, AE, oct., 458-75.
727. **Lower, A. R. M.**
    1936   *Settlement and the forest in Eastern Canada*, Macmillan, Toronto, 424.
728.   1938   *The North American assault on the Canadian Forest : A History of the lumber trade between Canada and the United States*, Ryerson, Toronto, 377.
729. **Lussier, Omer**
    1952   Conservation des forêts du Québec, *Forêt et Conservation*, 18, 10, 8-12.
730. **Maher, Thomas**
    1952   *Pays de Cocagne ou terre de Caïn*, Presses Universitaires Laval, Québec, 252.
731. **Minville Esdras (éd.)**
    1944   *La Forêt*, Fides, Montréal, 414.
732.   1946   *La Pêche et la Chasse*, Fides, Montréal, 580.
733. **Préfontaine, Georges**
    1946   Le développement des connaissances scientifiques sur les pêcheries maritimes et intérieures de l'Est du Canada, AE, jan., 220-83.
734. **Risi, Joseph**
    1945   La petite industrie forestière, *Relations*, 60, 311-313.
735. **Tousignant, J. B.**
    1946   *Pêcheries maritimes du Québec*, Thesis, Laval University.

IV) *Mining and industries*

736. **ACJC**
    1922   *Le problème industriel au Canada français*, ACJC, Montréal, 308.
737. **Angers, F.-A.**
    1952   Progrès industriels de Québec, AE, 28, 329-241.
738.   1953   Le français dans l'industrie, AN, 4, 1, 70-77.
739. **Asselin, Olivar**
    1928   L'Industrie dans l'économie du Canada français, AF, 20, 3, 151-76.
740.   1938   L'Industrie dans l'économie du Canada français, ESP, Montréal, 32.
741. **Bouchette, Errol**
    1906   L'industrie nationale, *Journal de Françoise*, 5, 18 août, 149-51.
742.   1913   Les débuts d'une industrie et notre bourgeoisie, TRSC, 6, 143-57.
743. **Beauregard, Ludger**
    1953   Analyse sommaire des principales industries de Montréal, *Techniques*, 28, 7, 465-67.
744. **Brouillette, Benoît**
    1946   L'Aluminium au Saguenay, AE, oct., 417-46.
745. **Bussières, Yves**
    1952   *L'industrie du cuivre dans la Province de Québec*, Thesis, Laval University.
746. **Caron, Maximilien**
    1945   Le régime juridique des mines de la Province de Québec, AE, mai, 109-121.
747. **Côté, Fernand**
    1946   L'Industrie minière du Québec et le problème social, AE, mars, 409-27.
748. **Dagenais, Pierre**
    1940   L'Industrie de la construction maritime dans Québec, AE, juin, 220-38.
749. **Delorme, Gérard**
    1937   L'industrie du cuivre dans la Province de Québec, AE, oct., 450-60.
750. **Drolet, Jean-Paul**
    1954   Le domaine minier de la Province de Québec, *Culture*, 15, 4, 406-423.

A BIBLIOGRAPHICAL INTRODUCTION...

751. **Dufresne, A.-O.**
    1944 Quebec, a Mineral Store, CGJ, 29, 1, 12-26.
752. 1945 La production minière de la Province, AE, nov., 17-51.
753. 1948 Mining in Quebec, an historical sketch, *Canadian Mining Journal*, 69, 10, 110-115.
754. **Dutil, Lorenzo**
    1935 *Le régime de l'électricité dans la Province de Québec*, Editions Nouvelles, Montréal, 220.
755. **Filiatrault, Marcel**
    1945 *Etude préliminaire sur l'industrie de la pulpe et du papier dans la Province de Québec*, Thesis, Laval University.
756. **Frigon, Augustin**
    1933 Le Canadien français et l'industrie, RTC, 73, 1-11.
757. **Girard, Raymond**
    1949 *Les Industries canadiennes propres au Québec et leur physionomie particulière*, Thesis, Ecole des Hautes Etudes Commerciales.
758. **Guimont, Paul-Henri**
    1945 Le placement industriel au Canada français, AE, déc., 101-110.
759. **Gregg, Milton F.**
    1954 *Développement industriel et emploi dans le Québec*, RI, 9, 259-69.
760. **Lacroix, Gérard**
    1941 L'Industrie des eaux gazeuses dans la Province de Québec, AE, déc., 156-171.
761. **Lamontagne, Maurice**
    1948 Quebec, Rich resources for industries, *Public Affairs*, 4, 256-261.
762. **Laurent, Edouard**
    n. d. *Une enquête au pays de l'aluminium*, Cahiers de l'Ecole des Sciences Sociales, Québec, 45.
763. **Leroy, André**
    1906 *Les mines de Québec*, n. e., Québec, 147.
764. **Marquis, G.-E.**
    1925 Expansion industrielle dans le Québec, ESP, no 138, Montréal, 24.
765. **Marshall, H. and others**
    1936 *Canadian-American Industry. A Study in International Investment*, Yale University Press, New Haven, 360.
766. **Martin, Guy**
    1947 L'Industrie de la boulangerie dans la Province de Québec, AE, jan., 614-36.
767. **McGee, J.-C.**
    1950 L'importance relative des industries de la Province de Québec, AE, oct., 549-65.
768. **McGuire, B. J.**
    1951 Aluminium. The Story of fifty years of growth by the Canadian Industry, CGJ, 43, 4, 144-163.
769. **Melançon, Jacques**
    1949 L'Industrie canadienne-française et ses besoins de capitaux, AE, jan., 661-76.
770. **Mendels, Morton Meyer**
    1929 *The Asbestos industry in Canada*, M. A. Thesis, McGill University.
771. **Ministère de l'Industrie**
    1952 *La Province de Québec et ses Manufactures*, Ministère de l'Industrie, Québec, 6 v.
772. 1952 *Québec, puissance industrielle*, Ministère de l'Industrie, Québec, 135.
773. **Minville, Esdras**
    1947 Pour réformer le régime industriel, AN, nov., 164-71.
774. **Mhun, H.**
    1953 L'expansion minière du Québec-Sept-Iles transformé par le fer, *Carnets Viatoriens*, 18, 62-64.

775. **Morcel, Raymond**
 1951 L'influence de la politique tarifaire du Canada sur le développement de son industrie lainière, AE, oct., 512-47.
776. **Normandin, A.-B.**
 1945 L'Industrie Hydro-électrique du Québec et l'effort de guerre, *Relations*, 59, 298-301.
777. **Obalski, Joseph**
 1905 *Province de Québec, industries minérales*, Dussault et Proulx, Québec, 72.
778. **Pelletier, Georges**
 1921 Notre Industrie, AF, 322-356.
779. **Piché, Paul-Emile**
 1936 Où en est notre industrie du papier ?, AE, nov., 11-50.
780. **Retty, J. A.**
 1951 Iron Ore Galore, CGJ, 42, 1, 2-21.
781. **Saint-Pierre, Arthur**
 1922 *L'aspect social du problème industriel*, n. e., Montréal, 16.
782. **Statistical Year Book**
 1954 Mining, Province of Quebec, Quebec, 379-404.
783. **Thérien, Eugène**
 1939 Le bâtiment et la crise dans Québec et à Montréal, AE, avril, 43-60.

V) *Cooperative movement*

784. **Anonymous**
 1950 *Congrès international des Caisses Populaires Desjardins*, Fédération des Caisses Populaires, Lévis, 378.
785. 1942 Une Caisse d'épargne millionnaire, *Ensemble*, jan., 15-16.
786. **Allaire, Jean-Baptiste-Arthur**
 1916 *Nos premiers pas en coopérative agricole*, n. e., Saint-Hyacinthe, 58.
787. 1919 *Catéchisme des sociétés coopératives agricoles de Québec*, n. e., Saint-Hyacinthe, 72.
788. **Aubin, Florian**
 1949 *Une coopérative florissante, le comptoir agricole de Saint-Félix-de-Valois*, Comptoir Agricole, Saint-Félix-de-Valoix, 151.
789. **Barbeau, Victor**
 1938 La coopérative de consommation, AN, nov., 178-10.
790. 1940 Le coopératisme. Une solution au problème économique et social de notre province, AE, avril, 1-20.
791. 1944 Invitation à l'humain, Ed. de la Familiale, Montréal, 179.
792. **Bertrand, Jacques**
 1952 *Monographie de la société coopérative de Louiseville*, Thesis, Laval University.
793. **Bouvier, Emile**
 1941 En Gaspésie coopérative, *Relations*, 8, 218-219.
794. **Chiasson, Livian**
 1937 L'expérience d'Antigonish, OT, no 220, Montréal, 16.
795. **Conseil Supérieur de la Coopération**
 1939-55 *Annual Reports*.
796. 1944 L'inventaire du Mouvement coopératif, 259.
797. 1945 La Paix par la coopération, Québec, 316.
798. 1949 La législation coopérative, Québec, 220.
799. **Couture, A.-J.**
 1951 Qu'est-ce qu'une Caisse Desjardins ?, n. e., Manitoba, 100.
800. **Desjardins, Alphonse**
 1912 La Caisse Populaire, ESP, nu. 7-12, Montréal, 64.

A BIBLIOGRAPHICAL INTRODUCTION...

801. **Dubois, Emile**
     1949 *Les coopératives d'habitation de la Province de Québec*, Thesis, University of Montréal.
802. **Faucher, Albert**
     1944 *L'entreprise coopérative*, Cahiers de l'Ecole des Sciences Sociales, Québec, 3, 7, 30.
804. **Filion, Gérard**
     1937 La Coopération agricole dans Québec, AE, oct., 425-39.
805. **Girard, René**
     1949 Au service du petit peuple, *Relations*, 97, 18-22.
806. **Girardin, Emile**
     1949 Les Caisses d'Epargnes scolaires, *Relations*, 108, 331-332.
807. **Grondin, Philibert**
     1950 *Le Catéchisme des Caisses Populaires Desjardins*, Féd. des Caisses Populaires Desjardins, Montréal, 150.
808. **Guérin, Wilfrid**
     1921 *Les Caisses Populaires*, ESP, nu. 103, Montréal, 30.
809. **Le Franc, J.-P.**
     1910 *Catéchisme des Caisses Populaires*, Bon Livre, Québec, 82.
810. **Louard, Berthe**
     1953 L'habitation à prix modique à la portée de tous, *Relations*, 13, 221-223.
811. **Marquis, Paul**
     1942 *Les Caisses Populaires Desjardins*, Thesis, Laval University.
812. **Minville, Esdras**
     1943 *La Force conquérante de la Coopération*, Conseil Supérieur de la Coopération, 26.
813. **Paré, René**
     1953 Le Mouvement coopératif de la Province de Québec, *Ensemble*, 14, 8, 5-8.
814. 1954 Le mouvement coopératiste du Québec, *Relations*, 168, 343-46.
815. 1954 La Coopération et les Canadiens de langue française, *Ensemble*, 15, 7, 16-20.
816. **Pavan, Mgr P. et Bélanger, G.-M.**
     1952 *Syndicalisme et Coopération agricoles*, Presses Universitaires Laval, Québec, 77.
817. **Poirier, R.-F.**
     1942 La Coopération et les Caisses Populaires, *Forêt Québecoise*, 4, 9, 439-445.
818. **Poulin, Gonzalve**
     1940 Le mouvement coopératif au Canada, *Culture*, 5, 2, 137-156.
819. **Saint-Pierre, Arthur**
     1910 Les Caisses Populaires, *Messager Canadien*, mars, 123-128.
820. **Semaines Sociales du Canada**
     1937 *La Coopération*, ESP, Montréal, 336.
821. **Tessier, Albert**
     1950 *Le Miracle du Curé Chamberland*, Bien-Public, Trois-Rivières, 118.
822. **Thibault, Suzel**
     1946 *La ville de Rimouski et la coopération*, Thesis, Laval University.
823. **Toussaint, Jean**
     1948 *Les coopératives des pêcheurs de la Gaspésie*, Thesis, University of Montreal.
824. **Tremblay, Rosario**
     1950 *Les Caisses Populaires Desjardins, 1900-1950*, Féd. des Caisses Populaires Desjardins, 31.
825. **Vaillancourt, Cyrille**
     1950 *Alphonse Desjardins, pionnier de la coopération de crédit en Amérique*, Le Quotidien, Lévis, 232.

A BIBLIOGRAPHICAL INTRODUCTION...

VI) *Labour problems and trade unionism*

826. **Archambault, J.-P.**
     1919 *Les Syndicats catholiques*, Ed. de la Vie Nouvelle, Montréal, 82.
827. 1936 *Les Syndicats catholiques au Canada*, ESP, nu. 267, Montréal, 31.
828. 1950 *Un chef syndiqué, Gaudiose Hébert*, ISP, Montréal, 40.
829. **Battistella, Renzo**
     1954 *Le mouvement ouvrier*, ISP, nu. 470, Montréal, 32.
830. **Beaulieu, Marie-Louis**
     1955 *Les Conflits de Droit dans les rapports collectifs du Travail*, Presses Universitaires Laval, Québec, 540.
831. **Beausoleil, Gilles**
     1953 Considérations sur l'arbitrage 1952-56, RI, 9, 1, 29-49.
832. 1954 *Salaires du Québec et de l'Ontario*, C. T. C. C., Montréal, 52.
833. **Bercherman, Philip**
     1950 *Unions and wage rate in the newsprint in Quebec and Ontario, 1909-1948*, M. A. Thesis, McGill University.
834. **Bibeault, Réal**
     1954 *Le syndicat des débardeurs de Montréal*, Thesis, University of Montreal.
835. **Bolte, P. E. and others**
     1949 *Structural reforms in the Entreprise*, Dept. of Industrial Relations, Laval University, Quebec, 98.
836. **Bourassa, Henri**
     1919 *Syndicats nationaux ou internationaux*, Le Devoir, Montréal, 46.
837. 1931 *La loi des accidents du travail*, Le Devoir, Montréal, 22.
838. **Bouvier, Emile**
     1949 La profession en relations industrielles, AE, oct., 554-64.
839. 1950 Dix années d'assurance-chômage, *Relations*, 118, 300-3.
840. 1951 *Patrons et Ouvriers, Sect. des Relations Industrielles*, Université de Montréal, 209.
841. 1953 Le salaire annuel garanti, *Relations*, 148, 101-104.
842. 1954 *Le Droit au travail au Québec*, ISP, no 475, Montréal, 32.
843. **Bowker, E. Elwin**
     1933 *Unemployment among dock labourers in Montreal*, M. A. Thesis, McGill University.
844. **Cardin, Jean-Paul**
     1948 *L'influence du syndicalisme national catholique sur le droit syndical québécois*, Thesis, University of Montreal.
845. **Charpentier, Alfred**
     1920 *De l'internationalisme au nationalisme*, ESP, nu. 285, Montréal, 32.
846. 1944 *L'organisation du travail de demain*, CTCC, Montréal, 15.
847. 1945 *Syndicalisme ou politique*, CTCC, Montréal, 16.
848. 1946 *Ma Conversion au Syndicalisme catholique*, Fides, Montréal, 240.
849. 1946 *La CTCC, 20e anniversaire*, n. e., Québec, 17.
850. 1948 Situation actuelle de la collaboration patronale-ouvrière, *Culture*, 9, 241-6.
851. 1951 *Montée triomphante de la CTCC*, Thérien, Montréal, 126.
852. 1953 Problème de structure syndicale, *Culture*, 14, 56-9.
853. 1953 A propos de Cartels internationaux, *Culture*, 14, 423-7.
854. 1954 Répertoire des associations patronales, *Culture*, 15, 186-199.
855. 1954 Encore les associations patronales, *Culture*, 15, 312-8.
856. 1954 Groupes d'intérêts et corps intermédiaires, *Culture*, 15, 426-31.
857. 1955 Les conseils d'industrie, comment les constituer, *Culture*, 16, 307-15.
857a. 1956 L'Avenir du Syndicalisme au Canada, *Culture*, 17, 2, 180-90.
858. **Chartrand, Vitalien**
     1953 Prospective patronale du syndicalisme, RI, 9, 1, 52-58.

859. **Coats, R. H.**
    1914   Labour movement of Canada, *Canada and its Provinces*, (ed. Shortt and Doughty), vol. 9, 292.
860. **Collaboration**
    1954   *Les règlements des conflits de droit en relation du travail*, Presses Universitaires Laval, Québec, 137.
861. **Commission sacerdotale d'Etudes Sociales**
    1945-46   *L'organisation Professionnelle dans le Québec*, Bellarmin, Montréal, 36.
862.   1947   *La participation des travailleurs à la vie de l'entreprise*, Bellarmin, Montréal, 100.
863. **Congrès des Relations Industrielles**
    1946-54   *Annual reports*, Presses Universitaires Laval, Québec, 8 v.
864. **Corriveau, Laurent**
    1945   *Etude sur les relations industrielles du moulin Anglo-Canadien de pulpe et de papier*, Thesis, Laval University.
865. **Cousineau, Jacques**
    1941   La grève d'Arvida, *Relations*, 8, 212-213.
866. **C. T. C. C.**
    1950   *René Rocque, Prisonnier politique*, Imp. Judiciaire, Montréal, 48.
867. **Dagallier, M.**
    1947   Climat Chrétien à l'usine, Responsabilités patronales, *Relations*, 81, 284-6 ; 83, 329-31.
868. **Dallaire, Gérard**
    1952   *Relation des patrons et ouvriers de la forêt au Québec*, Thesis, University of Montreal.
869. **Dauseau, Fernand**
    1953   Le contrat collectif chez Dupuis Frères, *Relations*, 13, 302-3.
870. **D'Auteuil, Richard-Jean**
    1940   Le Syndicalisme catholique national au Canada, *Culture*, 3, 290-308.
871. **Davidson, Winnifred Hazel**
    1922   *Wages and Prices, particularly in the Province of Quebec, and with special reference to women workers*, Thesis, McGill University.
872. **De la Chevrotière, Jacques**
    1945   *Les comités mixtes de production*, Thesis, Laval University.
873. **Déom, André**
    1951   *La grève de Lachute*, Thesis, University of Montreal.
874. **Després, Jean-Pierre**
    1945   *Le marché du travail et les unions ouvrières*, Cahiers de l'Ecole des Sciences Sociales, Québec, 32.
875.   1947   *Le mouvement ouvrier canadien*, Fides, Montréal, 205.
876. **Dion, Gérard**
    1955   Les groupements syndicaux dans la Province de Québec, RI, 11, 1-24.
877. **Dion, Raymond**
    1943   *Action catholique et action syndicale*, Thesis, Laval University.
878. **Ecole Sociale Populaire**
    1921   *L'organisation ouvrière catholique au Canada*, ESP, nu. 105, Montréal, 39.
879.   1929   *Le Syndicalisme catholique canadien*, ESP, nu. 190, Montréal, 32.
880.   1937   *Le Syndicalisme national catholique*, ESP, nu. 285, Montréal, 31.
881.   1948   *Les positions des travailleurs catholiques canadiens*, ESP, nu. 414-5, Montréal, 64.
882. **Felteau, Cyrille**
    1941   *Chômage et assurance-chômage*, Thesis, Laval University.

A BIBLIOGRAPHICAL INTRODUCTION...

883. **Ferragne, Roger**
    1952 *Le Syndicalisme dans les hôpitaux catholiques de Montréal (1935-1951)*, Thesis, University of Montreal.
884. **Fortier, Emilien**
    1941 *L'assurance-chômage canadien*, Thesis, Laval University.
885. **Francq, G.**
    1948 *Code of Labour and Industrial Laws of the Province of Quebec and Federal Laws*, Mercantile Printing Co., Montreal, 488.
886. **Fraser, Blair**
    1950 Labor and the Church in Quebec, *Foreign Affairs*, 28, 247-55.
887. **Garneau, C. E.**
    1942 *Les conflits du travail*, Thesis, Laval University.
888. **Genest, Omer**
    1942 Nos ouvriers opprimés, *Relations*, 23, 291-3.
889. **Giroux, Georges-M.**
    1933 *Le privilège ouvrier. Etude sur l'article 2013 du code civil*, Lévesque, Montréal, 494.
900. **Giroux, Gilles**
    1954 *Le Syndicalisme dans l'industrie textile du Québec*, Thesis, University of Montreal.
901. **Gosselin, Louis-de-Gonzague**
    1953 Aperçu sur la conciliation, RI, 9, 1, 69-76.
902. **Greening, W. E.**
    1952 *Paper makers in Canada*, International Brotherhood of Paper Makers, Cornwall, 96.
903. **Guilbault, Jacques**
    1951 Les lois québecoises de conciliation et d'arbitrage, RB, 11, 221, 277, 329, 385.
904. **Institut Social Populaire**
    1953 Grève et Morale, ISP, nu. 464, Montréal, 16.
905. **Harvey, Pierre**
    1955 Les salaires dans la Province de Québec, AE, 31, 294-305.
906. **Jolicœur, Fernand**
    1953 Evolution de la mentalité ouvrière, *Le Devoir*, 12 sept., 13, 17.
907. **Lafortune, L.-A. et Tremblay, G.**
    1927 L'union ouvrière, ESP, nu. 165, Montréal, 32.
908. **Latham, Allan B.**
    1930 *The Catholic and National Unions of Canada*, Macmillan, Toronto, 120.
909. **Laures, Jean-Marie**
    1952 L'Eglise et le Syndicalisme, ISP, nu. 454, Montréal, 32.
910. **Ledit, Joseph-H.**
    1946 Les leçons d'une grève, *Relations*, 70, 312-4.
911. **Ledoux, Burton**
    1948 La Silicose, De Saint-Louis-d'Amherst à l'Ungava, *Relations*, 87, 65-87 ; 91, 1934.
912.   1949 Asbestos, East Broughton, Province of Quebec, Canada, n. e., n. p., 55.
913. **Héroux, Omer**
    1919 Le mouvement ouvrier catholique au Canada, OT, Montréal, 16.
914. **Logan, H. A.**
    1948 *Trade Unions in Canada*, Macmillan, Toronto, 412.
915. **Lorimier, François C. de**
    1952 *Les grèves de Sorel (1937)*, Thesis, Montreal University.
916. **Maltais, M.-F.**
    1925 *Les Syndicats catholiques canadiens. Etude socio-économique*, Catholic University of America Press, Washington, 146.

A BIBLIOGRAPHICAL INTRODUCTION...

917. **Marsh, Leonard C.**
     1940 *Canadians in and out of work,* McGill University, Montreal, 503.
918. **Melançon, Jacques**
     1946 Toronto vs. Montréal, *Relations,* 61, 7-10 ; 62, 42-45.
919. **Mercier-Gouin, Léon**
     1921 *Des Syndicats ouvriers au point de vue légal,* Beauchemin, Montréal, 84.
920. **Mindes, Evelyn**
     1947 *Confederation of Catholic Workers of Canada,* M. A. Thesis, McGill University.
921. **Minville, Esdras**
     1939 *Labour Legislation and Social Service in the Province of Quebec,* Printer to the King, Ottawa, 97.
922. 1944 Pour une documentation ouvrière, AE, jan., 264-85.
923. **Pelletier, Gérard**
     1954 Les bills 19 et 20, AN, 43, 351-362.
924. **Picard, Gérard**
     1947 L'avenir des syndicats, AN, déc., 243-55.
925. **Plante, Albert**
     1950 L'incident de Shawinigan, *Relations,* 137, 155-157.
926. 1955 Les grandes lignes d'un conflit industriel, *Relations,* 177, 227-230.
927. **Raynaud, André**
     1951 *La grève des instituteurs,* Thesis, University of Montreal.
928. **Regimbal, Albert**
     1954 Grève au pays de l'or, *Relations,* 158, 37-40.
929. **Rountree, George Meridith**
     1933 *The employment and unemployment Problems of the Railway Industry, with particular Reference to Montreal,* Thesis, McGill University.
930. **Roy André**
     1950 L'arbitrage de l'amiante, *Relations,* 111, 68-71.
931. 1950 Réflexions sur le chômage, *Relations,* 112, 96-98.
932. **Royal Commission**
     1889 *Report of the Royal Commission on the Relations of Capital and Labor in Canada. Evidence :* Quebec, Queen's Printer, Ottawa, 2 v.
933. **Saint-Pierre, Arthur**
     1911 L'organisation ouvrière dans la Province de Québec, ESP, nu. 2, 33.
934. 1914 Pour l'organisation ouvrière catholique, *Messager Canadien,* juin, 276-80.
935. 1914 La Fédération Américaine du Travail, ESP, nu. 30, Montréal, 32.
936. 1920 La question ouvrière au Canada, n. e., Montréal, 65.
937. n. d. L'accession des travailleurs à la propriété, L'Action Sociale, Québec, 30.
938. **Semaines Sociales du Canada**
     1921 Le Syndicalisme, L'Action Française, Montréal, 289.
939. 1922 Capital et Travail, L'Action Française, Montréal, 301.
940. **Shlakman, Vera**
     1931 *Unemployment in the Men's Clothing industry in Montreal,* M. A. Thesis, McGill University.
941. **Tétrault, C.-M.**
     1940 *La législation ouvrière de la Province de Québec,* M. A. Thesis, McGill University.
942. **Trudeau, P.-E. and others**
     1956 *La grève de l'amiante,* Les Ed. Cité Libre, Montréal, 430.
943. **Zrinyi, Joseph**
     1933 *Les conventions collectives et la Confédération des Travailleurs catholiques du Canada,* Thesis, University of Montreal.

A BIBLIOGRAPHICAL INTRODUCTION...

d) *The Political Organization*

I) *Political History*

944. **Action Française**
    1927 *Les Canadiens français et la Confédération canadienne*, Biblio. de l'Action Française, Montréal, 144.
945. **Anderson, Violet**
    1938 *Problems in Canadian Unity*, Nelson, Toronto, 153.
946. **Angers, F.-A.**
    1940 L'opinion d'un Anglo-canadien qui a lu le rapport Sirois, AE, déc., 170-78.
947. 1952 Comment la Centralisation progresse ?, AN, déc., 191-206.
948. 1952 Quand Ottawa s'en mêle, AN, avril, 214-47.
949. **Anonymous**
    1867 *La Confédération, couronnement de dix années de mauvaise administration*, Le Pays, Montréal, 48.
950. 1867 *Contre-poison. La Confédération, c'est le salut du Bas-Canada*, Senécal, Montréal, 72.
951. 1886 *Election de 1886. Situation politique et administrative de la Province de Québec*, Darveau, Québec, 417.
952. 1954 *Mémoire de la Corporation de l'Ecole Polytechnique de Montréal à la Commission d'enquête*, RTC, 4, 158, 19-45.
953. 1954 Mémoire à la Commission Tremblay, *Ensemble*, 15, 4, 22-31.
954. 1954 Mémoire présenté par la Société d'Etude rurale à la Commission Royale d'Enquête, VF, 8, 327-346 ; 388-406.
955. **Arès, Richard**
    1949 La Confédération, pacte ou loi, Action Nationale, Montréal, 76.
956. 1950 Défense et illustration du fédéralisme, AN, oct., 95-109.
957. 1950 Fédéralisme et organisation de la vie politique, AN, déc., 253-69.
958. **Armstrong, E. H.**
    1937 *The Quebec Crisis*, Columbia University Press, New York, 270.
959. **Arthur, Elizabeth**
    1949 *The French Canadians under British rule, 1760-1800*, Ph. D. Thesis, McGill University.
960. **Beaudry, David-Hercule**
    1861 *Le conseiller du peuple*, Senécal, Montréal, 218.
961. **Boissonnault, Charles-Marie**
    1936 *Histoire politique de la Province de Québec*, Ed. Frontenac, Québec, 373.
962. **Bonenfant, J.-C.**
    1948 La genèse de la loi de 1867, *Culture*, 9, 3-17.
963. 1952 Les Canadiens français et la naissance de la Confédération, CHAR, 39-45.
964. **Bourassa, Henri**
    1902 The French Canadians in the British Empire, *Monthly Review*, sept., 35.
965. 1902 *Grande-Bretagne et Canada*, Pionnier, Montréal, 42-80.
966. 1911 *La Convention Douanière entre le Canada et les Etats-Unis*, Le Devoir, Montréal, 38.
967. 1911 *The reciprocity agreement and its consequences*, Le Devoir, Montréal, 43.
968. 1911 *La Conférence Impériale et le rôle de M. Laurier*, Le Devoir, Montréal, 80.
969. 1912 *The spectre of annexation and the real danger of national desintegration*, Le Devoir, Montréal, 42.
970. 1915 *Que devons-nous à l'Angleterre ?*, n. e., Montréal, 420.
971. 1917 *La Conscription*, Le Devoir, Montréal, 46.
971-a. **Bruchési, Jean**
    1937 Les Etats-Unis et les rébellions de 1837-38 dans le Bas-Canada, RTC, 23, 89, 1-20.

972. 1945 *La situation politique et nationale il y a un siècle*, Imp. Populaire, Montréal, 22.
973. 1946 Sir Wilfrid Laurier et Mgr Bruchési, TRSC, 40, 3-22.
974. 1950 Service national et conscription, 1914-1917, TRSC, 44, 1-26.
975. 1951 *Le Canada français dans le monde*, Soc. Saint-Jean-Baptiste, Montréal, 30.
976. **Brunet, Ludovic E.**
     1908 *La Province du Canada. Histoire politique de 1840 à 1867*, Laflamme et Proulx, Québec, 305.
977. **Brunet, Michel**
     1953 Premières réactions des vaincus de 1760 devant leurs vainqueurs, RHAF, 6, 506-516.
978. 1954 La science politique au service de l'union canadienne, AN, déc., 272-92.
979. **Buies, Arthur**
     1876 *L'Ancien et le futur Québec*, Darveau, Québec, 43.
980. 1864 *Lettres sur le Canada*, Journal du Pays, Montréal, 26.
981. 1867 *Lettres sur le Canada*, Journal du Pays, Montréal, 52.
982. **Burt, Alfred Leroy**
     1933 *The Old Province of Quebec*, Ryerson, Toronto, 551.
983. **Canadian**
     1930 *A political and historical Account of Lower Canada*, London, 275.
984. **Caron, Ivanhoe**
     1929 Les Canadiens français et l'invasion Américaine de 1774-1715, TRSC, 23, 21-35.
985. **Caron, Maximilien**
     1938 La Province de Québec est-elle un état ?, AE, 1, 2, 121-132.
986. **Chambre de Commerce de la Province de Québec**
     1952 *Les relations fédérales-provinciales en matière d'impôts*, Chambre de Commerce, Montréal, 37.
987. **Chapais, Thomas**
     1919-34 *Cours d'histoire du Canada, de la conquête à la Confédération*, Garneau, Québec, 8 v.
988. **Choquette, P.-A.**
     1936 *Un demi-siècle de vie politique*, Beauchemin, Montréal, 350.
989. **Christie, Robert**
     1848-66 *A history of the late Province of Lower Canada*, Carry, Quebec, 6 v.
990. **Collaboration**
     1931 *Hommages à LaFontaine*, Comité du Monument LaFontaine, Montréal, 485.
991. **Coupland, Réginald**
     1925 *The Quebec Act, a study in Statesmanship*, Oxford University Press, Oxford, 224.
992. **Cousineau, Jacques**
     1944 Que sera notre révolution ?, *Relations*, 4, 42, 157-160.
993. **Dansereau, Arthur**
     1879 *The Quebec Political Crisis*, n. e., Quebec, 69.
994. **Dansereau, Fernand**
     1954 Pourquoi une marche sur Québec ?, AN, 43, 255-291.
995. **David, L. O.**
     1884 *Les Patriotes de 1837-38*, Senécal, Montréal, 300.
996. 1898 *L'Union des Deux-Canadas*, Senécal, Montréal, 332.
997. 1905 *Laurier et son temps*, Worcester, 159.
998. 1919 *Laurier, sa vie, ses œuvres*, L'Eclaireur, Beauceville, 266.
999. 1909 *Histoire du Canada depuis la Confédération*, Beauchemin, Montréal, 256.
1000. 1917 *Mélanges historiques et littéraires*, Beauchemin, Montréal, 338.

A BIBLIOGRAPHICAL INTRODUCTION...

1001. **Desjardins, L. G.**
 1918 *England, Canada and the Great War*, n. e., Quebec, 422.
1002. **Dexter, Grant**
 1945 *The conscription debate of 1917 and 1944, an analysis*, Winnipeg Free Press, Winnipeg, 10.
1003. **Dominion of Canada**
 1946 *Dominion-Provincial Conference (1945)*, Cloutier, Ottawa, 624.
1004. **Doughty, Arthur George**
 1915-35 *Documents relating to the constitutional history of Canada*, Printer to the King, Ottawa, 2 v.
1005. 1937 *The Elgin-Grey Papers, 1846-1852*, Printer to the King, 4 v.
1006. **Durham, (Earl)**
 1839 *Report on the Affairs of British North America*, House of Commons, London, 5 v.
1007. **Eggleston, Wilfrid**
 1946 *The Road to Nationhood*, Oxford University Press, Toronto, 337.
1008. **Fleming, John**
 1828 *Political Annals of Lower Canada*, Gazette, Montreal, 186.
1009. **Frégault, Guy**
 1943 Le Statut de Westminster demeure, *Le Quartier Latin*, 26, 10, 10 déc., 4.
1010. **Gaudron, Edmond**
 1940 Jusqu'où doit aller l'Union au Canada ?, *Culture*, 1, 129-36.
1011. **Gendron, Robert**
 1941 *Les Canadiens français et la Confédération*, M. A. Thesis, University of Ottawa.
1012. **Gérin-Lajoie, A.**
 1888 *Dix ans au Canada de 1840 à 1850*, Demers, Québec, 619.
1013. **Goforth, J. F.**
 1928 *The economic and ethnological basis of Canadian Confederation*, M. A. Thesis, McGill University.
1014. **Gosnell, R. E.**
 1918 *The story of Confederation with postscript on the Quebec situation*, n. e., n. p., 156.
1015. **Gouin, Lomer**
 1918 La Confédération canadienne, Le Soleil, Québec, 36.
1016. 1918 Quebec and the Confederation, Beauchemin, Montréal, 34.
1017. **Groulx, Lionel**
 1915-16 Nos luttes constitutionnelles, Le Devoir, Montréal, 102.
1018. 1918 La Confédération canadienne, Le Devoir, Montréal, 253.
1019. 1921 *Vers l'émancipation*, Action Française, Montréal, 308.
1020. 1920 *Lendemain de conquête*, Action Française, Montréal, 235.
1021. 1927 Les Canadiens français et l'établissement de la Confédération, AF, 17, 282-301.
1022. 1939 Une opinion anglo-canadienne, AN, 13, 466-76.
1023. 1949 *L'indépendance du Canada*, Action Nationale, Montréal, 175.
1024. **Hamel, Marcel-Pierre**
 1948 *Le Rapport de Durham*, Ed. du Québec, Montréal, 376.
1025. **Harvey, Jean-Charles**
 1938 *Can we achieve Canadian Unity*, Empire Club, 184.
1026. **Héroux, Maurice**
 1952 *L'Opinion canadienne devant la guerre de 1914*, Thesis, Montreal University.
1027. **Hudon, Théophile**
 1936 Est-ce la fin de la Confédération ?, Messager, Montréal, 188.
1028. **Mackay, Hector**
 1941 Le rapport Sirois, AE, jan., 201-227.

A BIBLIOGRAPHICAL INTRODUCTION...

1029. **Lamontagne, M.**
1954 *Le Fédéralisme canadien, Evolution et Problèmes*, Presses Universitaires Laval, Québec, 300.
1030. **Lanctot, Gustave**
1941 Le Québec et la révolution américaine, TRSC, 35, 91-112.
1031. **Landon, Fred**
1927 The American Civil War and Canadian Confederation, TRSC, 21, 2, 55-62.
1032. **Langelier, Charles**
1909-12 *Souvenirs Politiques*, Dussault et Proulx, Québec, 2 v.
1033. **Laurendeau, Arthur**
1930 Une heure avec l'abbé Groulx à propos de '37, AN, 7, 6, 325-49.
1034. **Laurendeau, André**
1941 La conscription et le prétendu droit de veto du Québec, AN, déc., 258-65.
1035. **Laurent, Edouard**
n. d. *Quelle est la nature de l'Acte de 1867 ?*, Ecole des Sciences Sociales, Québec, 36.
1036. **Legendre, Napoléon**
1878 *Notre Constitution et nos institutions*, Plinguet, Montréal, 42.
1037. **Léger, Jean-Marc**
1954 Mesure de notre influence réelle, AN, 44, 332-338.
1038. 1955 Des illusions qui peuvent être mortelles, AN, 45, 220-229.
1039. **Leman, Beaudry**
1941 Réflexions sur le Rapport Rowell-Sirois, AE, déc., 118-137.
1040. **Lemieux, Rodolphe**
1925 MacDonald et Laurier, TRSC, 19, 1, 1-14.
1041. 1927 Blake, Chapleau, Laurier, TRSC, 21, 1, 51-65.
1042. **Lower, A. R. M.**
1949 *From Colony to Nation*, Longmans, Toronto, 600.
1043. **Lucas, C. P.**
1912 *Lord Durham's Report on the Affairs of British North America*, Oxford University Press, Oxford, 3 v.
1044. **Maheux, Arthur**
1943 Durham et la nationalité canadienne-française, CHAR, 19-24.
1045. 1944 *Problems of Canadian Unity*, Quebec, 186.
1046. **Marie-Joseph, Fr.**
1953-54 Les Canadiens veulent conserver le régime seigneurial, RHAF, 7, 45-63 ; 224-240 ; 356-391 ; 490-504.
1047. **Martin, Chester**
1955 *Foundations of Canadian Nationhood*, University of Toronto Press, Toronto, 554.
1048. **McDougall, J. L.**
1927 Nationalism and Unity in Canada, *Dalhousie, Review*, 171-78.
1049. **McGee, J.-C.**
1948 *Histoire politique de Québec-Est*, Bélisle, Québec, 322.
1050. 1948 *Laurier, Lapointe, Saint-Laurent*, Bélisle, Québec, 332.
1051. **McLeish, John A. B.**
1940 *Quebec's role in the Confederation movement, 1863-1865*, M. A. Thesis, McGill University.
1052. **Michel, Jacques**
1938 *La participation des Canadiens français à la Grande Guerre*, ACF, Montréal, 138.
1053. **Mills, G. H. Stanley**
1947 *The annexation movement of 1849-50 as seen through Lower Canadian Press*, M. A. Thesis, McGill University.

A BIBLIOGRAPHICAL INTRODUCTION...

1054. **Moreau, Henri**
    1902   *Sir Wilfrid Laurier*, Plon, Paris, 299.
1055. **Neatby, Blair H.**
    1953   *Laurier and Quebec*, Ph. D. Thesis, University of Toronto.
1056. **Neatby, H. B. and Saywell, J. T.**
    1956   Chapleau and the Conservative Party in Quebec, CHR, 37, 1, 1-22.
1057. **Paré, Lorenzo**
    1951   *Les Canadiens français et l'organisation militaire*, OT, Montréal, 16.
1058. **Parenteau, Roland**
    1955   Autonomie et réalisme politique, AE, 31, 273-281.
1059. **Raymond, Maxime**
    1943   *Politique en ligne droite*, Ed. du Mont-Royal, Montréal, 239.
1060. **Reid, Escott**
    1933   The effect of the depression on Canadian politics, 1929-32, *American Political Science Review*, 27, 3, 455-465.
1061. **Rothney, Gordon, O.**
    1947   Quebec, Cradle of Democracy, *Culture*, 8, 405-417.
1062. **Roy, Joseph**
    1909   *Histoire du Canada 1841-1867*, Beauchemin, Montréal, 525.
1063. **Royal Commission**
    1937   *Report on the Royal Commission on the relationships between the Dominion and the Provinces*, Printer to the King, Ottawa, 3 v.
1064. **Rumilly, Robert**
    n. d.   *Pages d'histoire politique*, Ligue de l'autonomie des Provinces, n. e., n. p., 47.
1065.   1948   *L'autonomie provinciale*, Ed. de l'Arbre, Montréal, 302.
1066. **Saint-Pierre, Arthur**
    1909   *L'avenir du Canada français*, Ed. du Messager, Montréal, 20.
1067. **Saunders, Richard M.**
    1946   *French Canadian Outlook*, Ryerson, Toronto, 16.
1068. **Savard, Alfred**
    1918   *Quebec and Confederation*, n. e., Quebec, 136.
1069. **Skelton, O. D.**
    1922   *Life and letters of Sir Wilfrid Laurier*, Century Co., New York, 2 v.
1070. **Société Saint-Jean-Baptiste de Montréal**
    1954   *Canada français et Union canadienne*, Action Nationale, Montréal, 127.
1071. **State Trials**
    1839   *A general court-martial held at Montreal in 1838-39. A complete History of the late Rebellion in Lower Canada*, Armour and Ramsay, Montreal, 2 v.
1072. **Stevenson, John A.**
    1948   The problem of French Canada, *Quarterly Review*, 575, 113-125.
1073. **Tangue, Raymond**
    1940   Les fondements économiques de l'unité canadienne, AE, déc., 101-117.
1074. **Tremblay Commission**
    1956   Short version of the Report, *Montreal Star*, 7 april, 10-11, 48.
1075. **Trudeau, P.-E.**
    1954   De libro, tributo et quibusdam aliis, CL, 10, 1-16.
1076. **Trudel, Marcel**
    1949   *Louis XVI, le Congrès Américain et le Canada, 1774-89*, Ed. du Quartier Latin, Montréal, 259.
1077.   1952   *Le Régime militaire dans le Gouvernement de Trois-Rivières, 1760-1764*, Bien Public, Trois-Rivières, 236.
1078. **Vaillancourt, Emile**
    1942   *Canadian unity and Quebec*, n. e., Montreal, 16.

A BIBLIOGRAPHICAL INTRODUCTION...

1079. **Watson, Samuel James**
1874 *The constitutional history of Canada*, Adam, Toronto, 157.
1080. **Willinson, G. S.**
1903 *Sir Wilfrid Laurier and the Liberal Party*, Toronto, 2 v.
1081. **Wright, J.**
1849 *Debates of the House of Commons in the year 1774 of the bill for making more effectual provision for the government of the Province of Quebec*, Ridgeway, London, 303.

II) *Government*

1082. **Achintre, M.-A.**
1871 *Manuel électoral, portraits et dossiers parlementaires du Premier Parlement de Québec*, Duvernay, Montréal, 137-XXXIX.
1083. **Audet, François-J.**
1908 *Gouverneurs, Lieutenant-Gouverneurs et administrateurs de la Province de Québec, 1763-1908*, TRSC, 2, 85-124.
1084.   1943 *Les Députés de Montréal*, Ed. des Dix, Montréal, 455.
1085. **Audet, François-J. et Surveyer, E.-F.**
1946 *Les Députés au premier Parlement du Bas-Canada*, Ed. des Dix, Montréal, 316.
1086. **Auclair, Elie-J.**
1934 *Les paroisses et les municipalités dans la Province de Québec*, TRSC, 28, 1, 53-60.
1087. **Bernard, M. S.**
1901 *Manuel de Droit Constitutionnel et Administratif*, Montréal, 222.
1088. **Bonenfant, Jean-Charles**
1954 *Les Institutions politiques canadiennes*, Presses Universitaires Laval, Québec, 204.
1089. **Bourinot, Sir John George**
1902 *How Canada is Governed*, Copp, Clark, Toronto, 344.
1090. **Bouvier, Emile**
1954 *Pourquoi un impôt provincial sur le revenu ?*, *Relations*, 14, 63-65.
1091. **Brittain, Horace L.**
1951 *Local Government in Canada*, Ryerson, Toronto, 248.
1092. **British North America Act**
1943 *British North America Acts and Selected Documents, 1867-1943*, Printer to the King, Ottawa, 358.
1093. **Chausse, F.**
1948 *Le Civisme*, Ed. de l'U. C. C., p. 186.
1094. **Clokie, Hugh McDowall**
1945 *Canadian Government and Politics*, Longman, Toronto, 350.
1095. **Cole, Taylor**
1949 *The Canadian Bureaucracy. A study of Canadian Civil Servant*, Duke University Press, Durham, 279.
1096. **Côté, J.-O.**
1866 *Political appointments and elections in the Province of Canada, 1841-1865*, Desbarats, Ottawa, 129.
1097. **Crawford, Kenneth Grout**
1954 *Canadian Municipal Government*, University of Toronto Press, Toronto, 407.
1098. **Dagneau, Georges-Henri**
1947 *Les Canadiens français devant le fonctionnarisme fédéral*, FV, 8, 495-507.
1099. **Dawson, R. W.**
1929 *The Civil Service in Canada*, Oxford University Press, Oxford, 266.
1100. **Dawson, Robert MacGreggor**

A BIBLIOGRAPHICAL INTRODUCTION...

       1949 *Democratic Government in Canada*, University of Toronto Press, Toronto, 188.
1101.   1954 *The Government of Canada*, University of Toronto Press, Toronto, 622.
1102. **Denis, Gérard**
       1950 *Code Municipal de la Province de Québec*, Wilson and Lafleur, Montréal, 746.
1103. **Deschamps, C.-E.**
       1896 *Municipalités et Paroisses dans la Province de Québec*, Brousseau, Québec, 1295.
1104. **Desjardins, Joseph**
       1902 *Guide Parlementaire historique de la Province de Québec*, Québec, 396.
1105. **Gérin-Lajoie, A.**
       1851 *Catéchisme Politique*, Perrault, Montréal, 144.
1106. **Gérin-Lajoie, Paul**
       1950 *Constitutional Amendment in Canada*, University of Toronto Press, Toronto, 340.
1107.   1952 *Réflexions sur la Constitution canadienne*, ISP, no 455, Montréal, 26.
1108.   1953 *Origines de nos problèmes constitutionnels et fiscaux actuels*, *Relations*, 149, 118-120 ; 150, 149-152 ; 151, 183-185 ; 152, 208-211 ; 153, 231-234.
1109. **Kennedy, W. P. M.**
       1930 *Statutes, treaties and documents of the Canadian Constitution*, Oxford University Press, Oxford, 752.
1110.   1938 *The Constitution of Canada*, Oxford University Press, Oxford, 628.
1111. **Lamontagne, Maurice**
       1954 *Le rôle économique et social du Gouvernement*, RI, 9, 129-148.
1112. **Laplante, Pierre**
       1953 *L'assistance publique et les municipalités*, *Relations*, 13, 77-8.
1113. **MacKay, Robert A.**
       1926 *The unreformed Senate of Canada*, Oxford University Press, Oxford, 284.
1114. **Magnan, C.-J.**
       1896 *Manuel de Droit civique. Notre Constitution et nos Institutions*, Darveau, Québec, 239.
1115. **Magnan, Hormidas**
       1925 *Dictionnaire historique et géographique des paroisses, missions et municipalités de la Province de Québec*, Arthabaska, 739.
1116. **Montigny de, B. A. T.**
       1878 *Catéchisme politique*, Beauchemin et Valois, Montréal, 246.
1117. **Normandin, G. Pierre**
       1954 *The Canadian Parliamentary Guide*, Ottawa, 301.
1118. **Pouliot, Jean-François**
       1923 *Le nouveau Code municipal annoté*, Wilson et Lafleur, Montréal, 575.
1119. **Rumilly, Robert**
       1956 *Quinze années de réalisations*, n. e., Montréal, 237.
1120. **Smith, William**
       1928 *L'évolution du gouvernement au Canada*, n. e., Montréal, 274.
1121. **Tellier, Robert**
       1955 *Municipal Code of the Province of Quebec*, Wilson and Lafleur, Montréal, 627.
1122. **Trotter, Reginald George**
       1924 *Canadian Federation*, Dent, Toronto, 348.
1123. **Ward, Norman**
       1950 *The Canadian House of Commons*, University of Toronto Press, Toronto, 307.
1124. **Weir, Stanley Robert**
       1903 *The Municipal Code of the Province of Quebec*, Théorêt, Montréal, 453.

A BIBLIOGRAPHICAL INTRODUCTION...

III) *Political ideologies and political parties*

1125. **Anonymous**
      1864   Le Rougisme en Canada, Côté, Québec, 79.
1126.   1887   L'honorable J.-A. Chapleau. Biographie et discours, Senéchal, Montréal, 537.
1127.   1908   Elections provinciales de 1908. Deux régimes politiques comparés, n. e., Québec, 176.
1128.   1909   Sir Wilfrid Laurier. Discours, Beauchemin, Montréal, 472.
1129.   1912   Elections de 1912, the Gouin Government and its works, n. e., Montréal, 150.
1130.   1936   Report of the Committee on the Survey of Canadian political parties, Junior Board of Trade, Montreal, 53.
1131.   1938   Embryo Fascism in Quebec, Foreign Affairs, 454-466.
1132.   1944   Planning for freedom, 16 lectures on the CCF, CCF, Ottawa, 179.
1133. **Archambault, J.-L.**
      1887   Conservateurs et Libéraux, Montréal, 34.
1134. **Arthur, Elizabeth**
      1947   Adam Mabane and the French Party in Canada : 1760-1791, M. A. Thesis, McGill University.
1135. **Barthe, Ulric**
      1890   1871-1890, Wilfrid Laurier on the Platform, Ménard, Québec, 624.
1136. **Bourassa, Henri**
      1926   La politique et les partis. Comment voter ?, Imp. Populaire, Montréal, 42.
1137. **Brunet, Michel**
      1951   Les idées politiques de la Gazette Littéraire de Montréal, CHAR, 43-50.
1138. **Cadieux, Marcel et Tremblay, Paul**
      1943   Démocratie canadienne, RTC, 29, 113, 41-56.
1139. **Castor**
      1882   Le Pays, le Parti, le Grand'Homme, Martin, Montréal, 108.
1140. **Cervin, Vladimir**
      1955   Some correlates of voting behaviour in the 1952 Quebec Elections, CJPES, 21, 3, 370-373.
1141. **Cité Libre**
      1952   Special number on the provincial elections for the 16 July 1952, Cité Libre, 72.
1142. **Chaloult, René**
      1942   Pour notre libération, contre la lâcheté des vieux partis, Action Nationale, Montréal, 32.
1143. **Charpentier, Alfred**
      1955   Le mouvement politique ouvrier de Montréal, RI, Lo, 74-92.
1144. **Conservateur**
      1864   Le Rougisme en Canada, Côté, Québec, 79.
1145. **Cooper, George Irwin**
      1938   French Canadian Conservatism in principle and practice, Ph. D. Thesis, McGill University.
1146.   1942   The political ideas of Etienne Cartier, CHR, 23, 3, 286-294.
1147. **Cox, Robert W.**
      1948   The Quebec Provincial election of 1886, M. A. Thesis, McGill University.
1148. **Dansereau, Fernand**
      1953   La « gauche » au Canada, AN, 42, 92-102.
1149. **David, Athanase**
      1935   En marge de la Politique, Lévesque, Montréal.
1150. **Desrosiers, J.-B.**
      1938   Principe et description de l'organisation corporative, AN, 11, 2, 143-156.
1151. **Diamond, Rolland**
      1943   Les troisièmes partis et l'esprit de parti dans la Province de Québec, Thesis, Laval University.

59

1152. **Dufèvre, Bernard**
    1953 Une drôle d'élection en 1834, RUL, 7, 598-607.
1153. **Executive Committee of Liberal-Conservative Summer School**
    1933 *Canadian Problems*, Oxford University Press, Toronto, 320.
1154. **Gillis, Duncan Hugh**
    1951 *Democracy in the Canadas*, Oxford University Press, Toronto, 217.
1155. **Gosselin, Emile**
    1953 Rôle du Syndicalisme dans la vie politique, RI, 9, 1, 2-13.
1156. **Graham, W. R.**
    1955 Arthur Meighen and the conservative party in Quebec, the election of 1925, CHR, 36, 1, 17-35.
1157. **Gratton, Adrien**
    1937 Notion sur le Corporatisme, AE, 13, 1, 5-6, 318-326.
1158.   1937 Le Corporatisme et la Province de Québec, AE, 13, 5-6, 322-327.
1159. **Harvey, Pierre**
    1953 L'organisation corporative dans la Province de Québec, AE, oct., 411-33.
1160.   1954 Les corporations professionnelles dans la Province de Québec, AE, 30, 40-63.
1161. **Lamarche, M.-A.**
    1916 *Petit catéchisme politique*, n. e., Saint-Hyacinthe, 23.
1162. **Lareau, Edmond**
    1879 *Libéraux et Conservateurs*, Montréal, 44.
1163. **Laurendeau, André**
    1949 Notes sur la doctrine des partis politiques canadiens, *Chantiers*, 5, 6, 103-107.
1164. **Lévesque, G.-H.**
    1937 Représentation professionnelle dans la corporation, *Action Catholique*, Québec, 8 sept., 4.
1165. **Liberal Party**
    1908 *Le Gouvernement Laurier devant l'opinion publique. Campagne électorale 1908*, n. e., n. p., 19 pamphlets.
1166. **Lower, A. R. M.**
    1955 Political "partyism" in Canada, CHAR, 88-95.
1167. **Minville, Esdras**
    1936 *Comment établir l'organisation corporative au Canada ?*, ESP, nu. 272, Montréal, 32.
1168.   1943 Le Milieu politique, ESC, 22, 7, 525-532.
1169. **Morrison, N. M.**
    1940 *Industry and municipal politics in Quebec*, M. A. Thesis, McGill University.
1170. **Quinn, Herbert F.**
    1946 *The Quebec Provincial Election of 1914*, M. A. Thesis, McGill University
1171.   1949 The role of the Union Nationale in Quebec politics, 1935-48, CJPES, 15, 523-534.
1172.   1953 *The Nationalist movement in Quebec since 1930. The impact of industrialization on party politics*, Ph. D. Thesis, Columbia University.
1173.   1955 The Union Nationale Party, *Canadian Forum*, 35, 412, 29-30.
1174. **Quinn, H. F. and Coughlin, G. A.**
    1938 *The Bogey of Fascism in Quebec, and the Quebec "Padlock Law"*, OT, no 234, Montreal, 16.
1175. **Reid, Scott**
    1932 The rise of national Parties in Canada, *Proceedings Canadian Political Science Association*, 187-200.
1176. **Richer, Léopold**
    1935 *Nos chefs à Ottawa*, Lévesque, Montréal, 210.
1177.   1930 *Notre problème politique*, Ed. de l'ACF, Montréal, 210.
1178.   1940 *Silhouettes du monde politique*, Ed. du Zodiaque, Montréal, 264.

1179. **Royal, Joseph**
 1894 Le Socialisme aux Etats-Unis et au Canada, TRSC, XII, 1, 49-62.
1180. **Saint-Denis, Arthur**
 1939 Fascism in Quebec. A false alarm, RUO, 12.
1181. **Saint-Pierre, Arthur**
 1910 Le Socialisme à Montréal, *Messager Canadien du Sacré-Cœur*, mars, 109-11.
1182. 1914 L'utopie socialiste, ESP, nu. 30, Montréal, 32.
1183. 1917 Le parti ouvrier, *Le Semeur*, nov., 59-62.
1184. **Scott, F. R.**
 1939 *Canada Today*, Oxford University Press, Toronto, 184.
1185. **Surveyer, Edouard-Fabre**
 1927 Les élections de 1792, RTC, 13, 1-19.
1186. **Tassé, Joseph**
 1893 *Discours de Sir Georges Cartier*, Senécal, Montréal, 817.
1187. **Thatcher, Max B.**
 1951 *Political issues in Quebec. A study in Canadian federalism*, Ph. D. Thesis, North Western University.
1188. **Trudeau, Pierre-Elliott**
 1954 La démocratie est-elle viable au Canada français ?, AN, 44, 190-200.
1189. **Underhill, F. H.**
 1935 The development of national political parties in Canada, CHR, 4, 367-87.
1190. **Villeneuve, Card. J.-M.-R.**
 1945 Le corporatisme en regard de la liberté sociale, *Le Devoir*, 36, 220, 6-7.

IV) *Nationalism*

1191. **Action Française**
 1923 *Notre Avenir politique*, Biblio. de l'Action Française, Montréal, 269.
1192. **Action Nationale**
 1948 *Vers la République du Canada*, Ed. de l'Action Nationale, Montréal, 68.
1193. 1954 *Special number on Henri Bourassa*, AN, jan., 245.
1194. **Angers, François-Albert**
 1943 Vues canadiennes-françaises sur le problème canadien, *Culture*, 4, 482-494.
1195. 1955 L'autonomie est-elle une formule négative ?, AN, 44, 473-91.
1196. **Anonymous**
 1916 *Où allons-nous ? Le Nationalisme canadien*, Soc. d'édit. Patriotique, Montréal, 73.
1197. 1954 Conditions d'un Etat français dans la Confédération canadienne, AN, 43, 328-50.
1198. **Arès, R.**
 1943-47 *Notre Question nationale*, Ed. de l'Action Nationale, Montréal, 3 v.
1199. **Asselin, Olivar**
 1937 *Pensée française*, Ed. de l'ACF, Montréal, 214.
1200. 1923 *L'Oeuvre de l'Abbé Groulx*, Montréal, 123.
1201. 1909 *A Quebec view of Canadian Nationalism*, Guertin, Montreal, 61.
1202. **Bastien, Hermas**
 1923 *Energies rédemptrices*, Montréal, 160.
1203. 1925 *Conditions de notre destin national*, Lévesque, Montréal, 239.
1204. **Bonenfant, J.-C. et Falardeau, J.-C.**
 1946 Cultural and political implications of French Canadian nationalism, CHAR, 56-73.
1205. **Bouchard, T.-D.**
 1947 *Si nous voulons être de véritables patriotes*, n. e., Saint-Hyacinthe, 60.
1206. **Bouchette, Errol**
 1904 Vues patriotiques, *La Nouvelle France*, 3, oct., 449-63.

1207. **Baudoux, Maurice**
    1954 Le véritable patriotisme, VF, 449-435.
1208. **Bourassa, Henri**
    1902 Le patriotisme canadien-français, *La Revue Canadienne*, 1, 423-48.
1209.   1910 *Religion, langue, nationalité*, Le Devoir, Montréal, 30.
1210.   1914 *The duty of Canada at the present hour*, Montréal, 44.
1211.   1916 *Hier, aujourd'hui, demain, problèmes nationaux*, Le Devoir, Montréal, 178.
1212.   1923 *Patriotisme, nationalisme, impérialisme*, Le Devoir, Montréal, 63.
1213.   1927 *Examen de conscience national*, Le Devoir, Montréal, 16.
1214. **Brown, Clément**
    1948 *L'éveil de la nationalité canadienne-française*, Thesis, Laval University.
1215. **Brunet, Michel**
    1952 *Canadians et Canadiens*, Fides, Montréal, 173.
1216. **Caron, Maximilien**
    1938 La province de Québec est-elle un Etat ?, AE, mai, 121-32.
1217.   1940 Y a-t-il un provincialisme légitime ?, AE, mars, 401-15.
1218. **Cadieux, M. et Tremblay, P.**
    1939 Etienne Parent, un théoricien de notre nationalisme, AN, 13, 3, 203-19 ; 13, 4, 307-18.
1219. **Ciré-Côté, Eve**
    1924 *Papineau, son influence sur la pensée canadienne*, Mignault, Montréal, 247.
1220. **Chaloult, René**
    1942 *Pour une politique canadienne-française*, Ed. des Jeunes Patriotes, Montréal, 14.
1221. **Croteau, Lionel**
    1934 *Le milieu intellectuel de la rébellion de 1837*, M. A. Thesis, University of Ottawa.
1223. **D'Armours, J.-A.**
    1916 *Où allons-nous ?, le nationalisme canadien*, Soc. d'Editions Patriotiques, Montréal, 73.
1224. **David, L.-O.**
    1926 *La jeunesse et l'avenir*, Beauchemin, Montréal, 125.
1225. **Dexter, Robert C.**
    1923 French Canadian patriotism, AJS, 694-710.
1226. **Doughty, Arthur-J.**
    1926 Le drapeau de la Nouvelle-France, TRSC, XX, 43-46.
1227. **Dufèvre, Bernard**
    1955 Les ambitions d'un politicien, RUL, 10, 99-105.
1228. **Falardeau, Jean-Charles**
    1948 Canadian citizenship and national development, *Canada Looks Ahead*, Tower Books, Ottawa, 39-48.
1229. **Fauteux, Aegidius**
    1950 *Patriotes de 1837-1838*, Ed. des Dix, Montréal, 433.
1230. **Filion, Gérard**
    1955 Québec, province différente, AN, mai, 763-73.
1231. **Filteau, Gérard**
    1938-42 *Histoire des patriotes*, Ed. de l'ACF, Montréal, 3 v.
1232. **Frégault, Guy**
    1945 Louis Riel, Patriote canadien, AN, fév., 15-22.
1233. **Gérin, Léon**
    1924 Comment se maintiendra le groupe national canadien-français, *Revue de l'Amérique Latine*, 8.
1234.   1925 *Antoine Gérin-Lajoie, résurrection d'un patriote canadien*, Le Devoir, Montréal, 260.

A BIBLIOGRAPHICAL INTRODUCTION...

1235. **Gosselin, Paul-Emile**
　　　　1940　L'Education nationale, ESP, Montréal, 30.
1236. **Gouin, Léon-Mercier**
　　　　1941　L'idéal patriotique d'Honoré Mercier, RUO, 11, 2.
1237. **Gouin, Paul**
　　　　1938　Servir, la cause nationale, Les Ed. du Zodiaque, Montréal, 250.
1238. **Groulx, Lionel**
　　　　1928　Les périls actuels, AF, 19, 294-99.
1240.　　　1934　Le national et le religieux, AN, 3, 93-98.
1241.　　　1935　Nos positions, Action Catholique, Québec, 36.
1242.　　　1936　Dix ans d'action française, Lévesque, Montréal, 273.
1243.　　　1937　Une politique nationale, notre destin français, AN, 9, 130-42.
1244.　　　1937　Directions, Ed. du Zodiaque, Montréal, 271.
1245.　　　1941　Notre Mission française, Le Devoir, Montréal, 45.
1246. **Holmes, Charles-E.**
　　　　1944　Et le nôtre ? la question d'un drapeau national, Ducharme, Montréal, 42.
1247. **Lachance, Louis**
　　　　1936　Nationalisme et religion, Collège Dominicain, Ottawa, 195.
1248. **Lacroix, Benoit**
　　　　1954　« Je me souviens », donc je prévois, RD, 60, 1, 259-263.
1249. **Lalande, Hermas**
　　　　1919　Halte-là, Patriote, Progrès du Golfe, Rimouski, 219.
1250. **Laplante, Rodolphe**
　　　　1953　L'émiettement national se continuera-t-il encore longtemps ?, CV, 18, 203-208.
1251.　　　1953　Vue d'ensemble sur la vie de Bourassa, Chantiers, 9, 5, 41-53.
1252. **Laporte, Pierre**
　　　　1955　Château Maisonneuve, AN, mai, 754-62.
1253. **Laurendeau, Arthur**
　　　　1934　L'éducation nationale, AN, 3, 5, 260-280.
1254. **Laurendeau, André**
　　　　1935　Notre nationalisme, Tracts Jeune-Canada, Montréal, 52.
1255.　　　1941　Alerte aux Canadiens français, Ed. de l'Action Française, Montréal, 28.
1256.　　　1952　Y a-t-il une crise du nationalisme ?, AN, 40, 207-22 ; 41, 6-28.
1257.　　　1955　Québec devrait s'appeler la « Nouvelle-France », AN, 45, 220-229.
1258. **Le Devoir**
　　　　1952　Hommage à Bourassa, Le Devoir, Montréal, 216.
1259. **Ledit, Joseph-H.**
　　　　1944　L'Eglise et les nationalismes, CF, 31, 5, 321-36.
1260. **Leland, Morice**
　　　　1951　Quelques observations sur le nationalisme de M. Henri Bourassa, CHAR, 60-63.
1261. **Lemieux, Edmond**
　　　　1953　La force des idées nationalistes au Canada français, AN, juin, 466-70.
1262. **Lévesque, Albert**
　　　　1934　La Nation canadienne-française, son existence, ses droits, ses devoirs, Lévesque, Montréal, 161.
1263. **L'Heureux, Eugène**
　　　　1932　Une formule du patriotisme canadien-français, Action Sociale, Québec, 39.
1264.　　　1946　Opinions libres entre Canadiens de bonne volonté, n. e., Québec, 21.
1265.　　　1948　Ma Province et mon Pays, n. e., Québec, 251.
1266. **MacLennan, Hugh**
　　　　1949　The psychology of Canadian nationalism, Foreign Affairs, 27, 413-25.
1267. **Maheux, Arthur**
　　　　1941　Ton histoire est une épopée, Québec, 212.

1268. 1943 Durham et la nationalité canadienne-française, CHAR, 19-24.
1269. 1945 Le nationalisme canadien-français à l'aurore du XXe siècle, CHAR, 58-74.
1270. **Montpetit, Edouard**
   1937 *D'Azur à trois Lys d'or*, Ed. de l'A. C. F., Montréal, 148.
1271. **Morin, W.**
   1938 *Nos droits à l'indépendance politique*, Guillemat, Paris, 253.
1272. **O'Connell, M. P.**
   1953 *Henri Bourassa and Canadian nationalism*, Ph. D. Thesis, University of Toronto.
1273. 1953 The ideas of Henry Bourassa, CJEPS, 3, 361-76.
1274. **O'Leary, Dostaler**
   1937 *Le séparatisme, doctrine constructive*, Les Jeunesses Patriotes, Montréal, 218.
1275. **Pâquet, Mgr L.-A.**
   1925 *Le bréviaire du patriote canadien-français*, Biblio. de l'AF, Montréal, 59.
1276. **Paradis, Wilfrid-H.**
   1954 Le nationalisme canadien dans le domaine religieux, RHAF, 7, 465-82.
1277. **Pelletier, Charles**
   1955 Faut-il confier à Ottawa l'avenir de notre groupe ethnique ?, AN, 45, 22-35.
1278. **Perrault, Antonio**
   1924 Enquête sur le nationalisme, AF, 11, 2, 105-118.
1279. **Potvin, Pascal**
   1943 Papineau et l'orientation du nationalisme québecois, CHAR, 35-42.
1280. **Richer, Léopold**
   1938 *Notre problème politique*, Ed. de l'A. C. F., Montréal, 154.
1281. **Rothney, Gordon O.**
   1943 Nationalism in Quebec. Politics since Laurier, CHAR, 43-49.
1282. **Roy, Mgr Camille**
   1943 *Du fleuve aux océans*, Beauchemin, Montréal, 188.
1283. **Rumilly, Robert**
   1934 *Papineau*, Flammarion, Paris, 309.
1284. 1953 *Henri Bourassa*, Chantecler, Montréal, 791.
1285. **Scott, F. R.**
   1942 Political nationalism and confederation, CJEPS, 8, 3-30.
1286. **Séguin, Robert Lionel**
   1955 *Le mouvement insurrectionnel dans la presqu'île de Vaudreuil, 1837-1838*, Ducharme, Montréal, 132.
1287. **Tessier, Hector**
   1940 Le nationalisme canadien-français et la morale internationale, CV, juillet, 130-35.
1288. **Tremblay, Jean-Jacques**
   1940 *Patriotisme et nationalisme*, Publication de l'Université d'Ottawa, Ottawa, 233.
1289. **Turcotte, Edmond**
   1942 *Réflexions sur l'avenir des Canadiens français*, Valiquette, Montréal, 165.
1290. **Urbain, Yvon**
   1954 Les Canadiens français ne sont pas maîtres chez-eux, VF, 8, 532-641.

V) *The Saint Jean Baptiste Society*

1291. **Charette, P.-P.**
   1884 *Les noces d'Or de la Saint-Jean-Baptiste*, Le Monde, Montréal, 515.
1292. **Chouinard, Honoré-Julien-Jean-Baptiste**
   1881-03 *Annales de la Société Saint-Jean-Baptiste de Québec*, n. e., Québec, 4 v.

1292-a. **Fournier, Rodolphe**
    1948   *Le Manuel des Sociétés Saint-Jean-Baptiste*, Société Saint-Jean-Baptiste, n. p., 95.
1293. **Gagner, J.-Léopold**
    1952   *Duvernay et la Saint-Jean-Baptiste*, Chantecler, Montréal, 51.
1294. **Laplante, Rodolphe**
    1950   *Pourquoi une Fédération des Sociétés Saint-Jean-Baptiste ?*, OT, Montréal, 16.
1295. **Marson, Georges-Avila**
    1910   *Fêtes du 75e anniversaire de l'Association Saint-Jean-Baptiste de Montréal*, n. e., Montréal, 387.
1296. **Saintonge, F.**
    1945   *Témoin de la Lumière. Le culte de saint Jean-Baptiste*, Ed. Lumens, Montréal, 371.
1297. **Sulte, Benjamin**
    1916   La Saint-Jean-Baptiste, 1636-1836, TRSC, X, 1, 1-25.
1298.   1929   *La Saint-Jean-Baptiste, 1636-1852*, Mélanges Historiques, vol. 15, Montréal, 130.

VI) *Laws and the Legal System*

1299. **Anonymous**
    1954   Mémoire concernant l'administration de la justice dans la Province de Québec, RB, 14, 48-62.
1300. **Archambault, Joseph-P.**
    1955   *M. Antonio Perrault*, OT, no 413, Montréal, 12.
1301. **Beaudoin, Louis**
    1953   *Le Droit Civil de la Province de Québec*, Wilson and Lafleur, Montréal, 1366.
1302. **Beullac, Pierre**
    1938   La Profession d'avocat, RdD, 16, 10, 622-35.
1303. **Bouffard, J.**
    1915   Origine de la propriété privée dans la Province de Québec, *Annuaire statistique*, Québec, 253-65.
1304. **Buchanan, Arthur W. P.**
    1925   *The bench and bar of Lower Canada down to 1850*, Burton, Montréal, 219.
1305. **Bureau, J.-Aderville**
    1932   Le Privilège du For et nos tribunaux civils, CF, 19, 7, 550-62.
1306. **Caron, Edmond and others**
    1865   *Rapport des commissaires chargés de la codification des lois civiles du Bas-Canada*, Desbarats, Québec, 3 v.
1307. **Caron, Maximilien**
    1944   La lutte pour le droit français au Canada, *Culture*, 5, 422-36.
1308. **Chase-Casgrain, Th. Larue and others**
    1893-94   *First and Second reports of the Commission charged with the revision and amendment of the code of civil Procedure*, n. e., Quebec, 3 v.
1309. **Deguire, René**
    1953   *Code Civil de la Province de Québec*, Wilson et Lafleur, Montréal, 598.
1310. **De Lorimier**
    1871-90   *La Bibliothèque du Code Civil de la Province de Québec*, Senécal, Québec, 21 v.
1311. **Dorion, Noël**
    1954   Le rôle social de l'avocat, AN, 43, 7-8, 501-14.
1312. **Doutre, G. et Lareau, E.**
    1872   *Le Droit civil canadien*, Montréal, 2 v.

A BIBLIOGRAPHICAL INTRODUCTION...

1313. **Fabre-Surveyer, Edouard**
 1932 *La procédure sous le régime français*, Imprimeur du Roi, Ottawa, 16.
1314. **Gérin, Léon**
 1934 La transformation de la langue et des institutions juridiques, RTC, déc., 15.
1315. **Johnson, Walter S.**
 1953 Sources of the Quebec Law of Evidence in Civil and Commercial matters, *Canadian Bar Review*, 31, 1000-20.
1316. **Kennedy, Williams B. McClure**
 1931 Reports on the Laws of Quebec, 1767-70, *Canadian Archives*, no 12, 92.
1317. **Lareau, Edmond**
 1888 *Histoire du Droit canadien*, Périard, Montréal, 2 v.
1318. **Langelier, F.**
 1903-11 *Cours de Droit civil de la Province de Québec*, Wilson et Lafleur, Montréal, 6 v.
1319. **Lemieux, Rodolphe**
 1900 *Les origines du Droit franco-canadien*, Théorêt, Montréal, 482.
1320. **Massicotte, E.-Z.**
 1896 *Le Droit civil canadien, résumé en tableaux synoptiques*, n. e., Montréal, 128.
1321. **McCarthy, Justin**
 1809 *Dictionnaire de l'Ancien Droit du Canada*, Neilson, Québec, 247.
1322. **Mignault, P.-B.**
 1879 L'administration de la justice sous la domination française, *La Revue Canadienne*, 16, 105-119.
1323. 1895-1916 *Le Droit civil canadien*, Whiteford and Théorêt, Montréal, 9 v.
1324. 1927 L'indépendance des juges, TRSC, XXI, 1, 29-50.
1325. 1940 Le Code civil de la Province de Québec et son interprétation, *University of Toronto Law Journal*, 1, 104-36.
1326. **Minville, Esdras,**
 1943 Les traditions et les lois, ESC, 22, 3, 353-59.
1327. **Nantel, Maréchal**
 1938 Mœurs judiciaires — Le Barreau, RdD, 16, 7, 401-9.
1328. 1947 Nos institutions politiques et judiciaires, *Les Cahiers des Dix*, XI, 191-99.
1329. 1950 L'étude du Droit et du Barreau, RB, mars, 97-100.
1330. 1952 En marge d'un centenaire, *Les Cahiers des Dix*, 17, 233-44.
1331. **Neatty, Hilda, M.**
 1937 *The Administration of Justice under the Quebec Act*, University of Minnesota Press, Minneapolis, 383.
1332. **Pagnuelo, S.**
 1880 *Lettres sur la Réforme judiciaire*, Chapleau, Montréal, 241.
1333. **Perrault, Antonio**
 1919 *Pour la défense de nos lois françaises*, Biblio. de l'Action Française, Montréal, 35.
1334. 1923 L'Association du Barreau canadien, AF, 10, 3, 147-55.
1335. 1933 *Le Barreau*, OT, no 165, Montréal, 7.
1336. 1936 *Traité de Droit commercial*, Lévesque, Montréal, 3 v.
1337. 1953 La Cour Suprême du Canada, *Relations*, 145, 18-20.
1338. 1954 Les Etudes de Droit, RB, 14, 381-84.
1339. **Pigeon, Louis-Philippe**
 1945 *Nécessité d'une évolution du Droit civil*, Cahiers de l'Ecole des Sciences Sociales, Québec, 3, 9, 32.
1340. **Rinfret, Thibaudeau**
 1946 La Cour Suprême du Canada, RUO, 16, 3, 261-73.
1341. **Roy, Edmond-J.**
 1899-1902 *Histoire du Notariat au Canada*, Revue du Notariat, Lévis, 4 v.

1342. **Roy, Pierre-Georges**
    1933 *Les Juges de la Province de Québec,* Imprimeur du Roi, Québec, 585.
1343. **Sirois, Joseph**
    1933 *Le Notariat,* OT, Montréal, nu. 165, 16.
1345. **Surveyer, E.-F. et Beullac, P.**
    1954 Notre Code civil à l'Université de Bordeaux, RB, 14, 486-91.
1345. **Surveyer, E.-F. et Beulac, P.**
    1949 *Le Centenaire du Barreau de Montréal,* Ed. des Dix, Montréal, 232.
1346. **Sylvestre, Georges**
    1953 La profession du notaire dans la Province de Québec, NRC, 56, 195-208.
1347. **Testard de Montigny, B.-A.**
    1869 *Histoire du Droit canadien,* Senécal, Montréal, 984.
1348. **Walton, Frederick Parker**
    1907 *The scope and interpretation of the Civil Code of Lower Canada,* Wilson et Lafleur, Montréal, 159.
1349. **White, W. J.**
    1903 *Sources and development of the Law of the Province of Quebec,* Montreal, 57.

e) *The Religious Organization*

I) *History of the Catholic Church in Quebec*

1350. **Alexis, Fr. de Barbezieux**
    1897 *Histoire de la Province ecclésiastique d'Ottawa et de la colonisation dans la vallée de l'Ottawa,* n. e., Otawa, 2 v.
1351.   1914 *L'Eglise Catholique au Canada,* Action Sociale, Québec, 93.
1352. **Allaire, J.-B.-A.**
    1934 *Dictionnaire biographique du clergé canadien-français,* Imp. du Courrier de Saint-Hyacinthe, Saint-Hyacinthe, 4 v.
1353. **Anonymous**
    1900 *Le Diocèse de Montréal à la fin du XIXe siècle,* n. e., Montréal, 800.
1354. **Arès, Richard**
    1956 Note sur « la crise religieuse » au Canada français, *Relations,* 184, 88-91.
1355. **Archambault, Joseph-P.**
    1952 Les retraites fermées au Canada, *Relations,* 142, 273-75.
1356. **Auclair, Elie-Joseph-Arthur**
    1914-24 *Prêtres et religieux au Canada,* n. e., Montréal, 2 v.
1357.   1933 *Figures canadiennes,* Lévesque, Montréal, 199.
1358.   1940 Le rôle de l'Eglise dans les Cantons de l'Est, SCHEC, Rapport 1939-40, 89-97.
1359. **Beaubien, Irénée**
    1955 *L'unité chrétienne au Canada,* Bellarmin, Montréal, 79.
1360. **Bégin, Card. L.-N.**
    1915 Relations de l'Eglise et de l'Etat, TRSC, IX, 1, 165-72.
1361.   n. d. *Les conditions religieuses de la société canadienne,* OT, Montréal, 12.
1362. **Bellefeuille, L. de**
    1868 *Le Canada et les Zouaves Pontificaux,* Le Nouveau-Monde, Montréal, 206.
1363. **Bernier, Paul**
    1946 *La situation présente des catholiques au Canada,* ESP, no 384, Montréal, 32.
1364. **Biron, Hervé**
    1947 *Grandeurs et misères de l'Eglise trifluvienne (1615-1947),* Les Ed. Trifluviennes, Trois-Rivières, 242.
1365. **Bonnault, Claude de**
    1934 La vie religieuse dans les paroisses rurales canadiennes au XVIIIe siècle — Les curés, *Recherches Historiques,* nov., 645-75.

A BIBLIOGRAPHICAL INTRODUCTION...

1366. **Boubée, Joseph**
    1924 Le Canada et son clergé aux débuts du régime anglais (1760-1791), *Etudes*, 5 mars, 579-86.
1367. **Canada Ecclésiastique (Le)**
    1896 *Yearbook*, Beauchemin, Montréal, 50 v.
1368. **Canadian Catholic Historical Association**
    1933 *Yearly Report*.
1369. **Caron, Ivanhoé**
    1933 La nomination de Mgr Joseph-Octave Plessis, évêque de Québec au Conseil Législatif de Québec, TRSC, XXVII, 1, 1-22.
1370.   1934 Mgr Joseph-Octave Plessis, Archevêque de Québec et les premiers Evêques catholiques des Etats-Unis, TRSC, XXVIII, 1, 119-38.
1371.   1935 Les Evêques de Québec, leurs procureurs et leurs vicaires généraux, à Rome, à Paris et à Londres, 1734-1834, TRSC, XXIX, 1, 153-178.
1372.   1938 Mgr Joseph-Octave Plessis, curé de Notre-Dame-de-Québec, 1792-1805, TRSC, XXXII, 1, 21-40.
1373. **Carrière, Gaston**
    1954 L'Eglise canadienne vers 1841, RUO, 24, 66-89.
1374.   1954 Le Renouveau catholique en 1840, RUO, 24, 257-79.
1375. **Clark, S. D.**
    1944 Religious organization and the rise of the Canadian Nation, 1850-85, CHAR, 86-97.
1376. **Collaboration**
    1929 *Les Retraites fermées au Canada*, Imp. du Messager, Montréal, 214.
1377.   1928 *Pèlerinages canadiens*, Imp. du Messager, Montréal, 250.
1378. **Congrégation de Notre-Dame**
    1908 *Histoire de l'Eglise du Canada*, Montréal, 345.
1379. **Congrès Eucharistique**
    1911 *XXIe Congrès Eucharistique International, Montréal, 1910*, Beauchemin, Montréal, 1102.
1380. **Dandurand, Marcel**
    1955 Les premières difficultés entre Mgr Bourget et l'Institut Canadien de Montréal, 1844-1865, RUO, 25, 145-165.
1381. **David, L. O.**
    1896 *Le Clergé canadien, sa mission, son œuvre*, Montréal, 123.
1382. **D'Appolonia, Luigi**
    1949 Cinquante ans à la Délégation Apostolique, *Relations*, 99, 79-80 ; 100, 106-108.
1383. **Delorme, Arthur**
    1949 Il nous faut des prêtres, *Relations*, 100, 100-1.
1384. **Delorme, Napoléon**
    1943 Le recrutement sacerdotal dans les collèges classiques, ESC, 22, 8, 621-25.
1385. **Desrosiers, L.-A.**
    1950 *Le Clergé diocésain de Montréal en 1950*, Thérien, Montréal, 228.
1386. **Diocèse de Montréal**
    1953 *Le Synode de Montréal*, Archevêché de Montréal, Montréal, 311.
1387. **Dion, Gérard**
    1955 Les aumôniers dans les syndicats catholiques de Québec, *Ad Sursum Sacerdotum*, 6, 7-8, 124-38.
1388. **Dionne, N.-E.**
    1905 *Les Ecclésiastiques et les Royalistes français réfugiés au Canada*, Québec, 443.
1389. **Dominic de Saint Denis, Fr.**
    1956 *The Catholic Church in Canada*, Ed. Thiau, Montréal, 269.

1390. **D'Orléans, Jean**
    1949 *Notre-Dame-du-Cap,* Fides, Montréal, 227.
1391. **Drouin, Raoul**
    1946 *Mgr Georges Gauthier,* Fides, Montréal, 105.
1392. **Dugré, Adélard**
    1948 La religion des Canadiens français, *Relations,* 92, 226-9.
1393. **Duval, Roch**
    1949 *Une contribution de l'orientation professionnelle au recrutement sacerdotal,* M. A. Thesis, Laval University.
1394. **Falardeau, Jean-Charles**
    1951 Religious Sociology in Canada, *Lumen Vitæ,* VI, 1-2, 127-42.
1395.   1952 Rôle et importance de l'Eglise au Canada français, *Esprit,* août, 214-29.
1396. **Fortier, Antoine**
    1953 Vocations sacerdotales et familles canadiennes-françaises, *L'Action Catholique,* 9 avril, 4 ; 28 mai, 4.
1397.   1953 La famille canadienne-française à l'honneur, *La Semaine Religieuse de Montréal,* 112, 317-20.
1398.   1953 Paroisses et vocations religieuses, *L'Action Catholique,* 14 sept., 4.
1399. **Frenette, Eugène F.-X.**
    1947 *Notices biographiques et historiques sur le Diocèse de Chicoutimi,* n. e., Chicoutimi, 418.
1399-a. **Garigue, Philip**
    1956 Saint Joseph Oratory, NRC, 3, 5, 250-65.
1400. **Giroux, Henri**
    1869 *Histoire et statistiques des Institutions catholiques de Montréal,* La Minerve, Montréal, 80.
1401. **Giroux, Michel**
    1945 La situation juridique de l'Eglise catholique dans la Province de Québec, *Revue du Notariat,* oct.-nov.
1402. **Godbout, Archange**
    1941 La liste chronologique de l'Abbé Noiseux, *Culture,* II, 13-28. ;
1403. **Gosselin, Auguste**
    1900 Le clergé canadien et la déclaration de 1732, TRSC, VI, 1, 23-52.
1404.   1911-14 *L'Eglise du Canada depuis Mgr Laval jusqu'à la conquête,* Laflamme et Proulx, Québec, 3 v.
1405.   1916-17 *L'Eglise du Canada après la conquête,* Laflamme, Québec, 2 v.
1406. **Gosselin, D.**
    1887 *Histoire populaire de l'Eglise du Canada,* Langlois, Québec, 189.
1407. **Goyau, Georges**
    1934 *Une épopée mystique. Les origines religieuses du Canada,* Spes, Paris, 301.
1408. **Gravel, Albert**
    1952 *Aux sources de notre histoire religieuse dans les Cantons de l'Est,* Apostolat de la Presse, Sherbrooke, 140.
1409. **Groulx, Lionel**
    1936 Les patriotes de 1837 et le clergé, *Notre Maître, le passé,* Granger, Montréal, 89-109.
1410.   1942 La Situation religieuse au Canada français vers 1840, SCHER, Report 1941-42, 51-76.
1411. **Hamelin, L.-E. et Hamelin, C.-L.**
    1956 Industrialisation et structure de l'Eglise dans le Diocèse de Trois-Rivières. Dynamisme des milieux sociaux, CG, 7, 35-45.
1412.   1956 *Quelques matériaux de sociologie religieuse canadienne,* Ed. du Lévrier, Montréal, 156.

A BIBLIOGRAPHICAL INTRODUCTION...

1413. **Jouve, Odoric-M.**
   1917 *Le Troisième centenaire de l'établissement de la Foi au Canada*, Imp. Franciscaine Missionnaire, Québec, 498.
1414. **Laflèche, L. (abbé)**
   1866 *Quelques considérations sur les rapports de la société civile avec la religion et la famille*, Senécal, Montréal, 268.
1415. **Langevin, F.**
   1931 *Mgr Ignace Bourget*, Imp. du Messager, Montréal, 298.
1416. **Lanctot, Gustave**
   1942 *Situation politique de l'Eglise canadienne : servitude de l'Eglise sous le Régime français*, Ducharme, Montréal, 26.
1417.   1943 *Un abbé part en guerre contre un sulpicien*, Ducharme, Montréal, 32.
1418. **Lapointe, Alban**
   1943 Le manque de prêtres, ESC, 22, 3, 626-9.
1419. **Laurent, Laval**
   1945 *Québec et l'Eglise aux Etats-Unis sous Mgr Briand et Mgr Plessis*, Libr. Saint-François, Montréal, 245.
1420. **Lefevre, Eugène**
   1949 *Terres de Miracles, Sainte-Anne-de-Beaupré, 1927-1947*, Librairie Alphonsienne, Sainte-Anne-de-Beaupré, 210.
1421. **Legros, Hector et Paul-Emile Sr**
   1949 *Le Diocèse d'Ottawa, 1847-1949*, l'Archevêché, Ottawa, 905.
1422. **LeMoyne, Jean**
   1955 L'atmosphère religieuse au Canada français, CL, 12, 1-14.
1423. **Livernoche, Jean**
   1952 *Enquête sur la vie religieuse des élèves de 12e année au cours primaire supérieur*, Ed. Pédagogiques de l'Ecole Normale Secondaire, Montréal, 261.
1424. **Maurault, Olivier Mgr**
   1952 Tableau du Canada religieux de 1852, SCHEC, Rapport 1951-52, 19-28.
1425. **Pagnuelo, S.**
   1872 *Etudes historiques et légales sur la liberté religieuse au Canada*, Beauchemin et Valois, Montréal, 409.
1426. **Panneton, Georges et Magnan, Antonio**
   1953 *Le Diocèse de Trois-Rivières*, Bien-Public, Trois-Rivières, 377.
1427. **Panneton, Georges**
   1955 *Chronique mariale (Trois-Rivières, Cap-de-la-Madeleine)*, Bien-Public, Trois-Rivières, 116.
1428. **Paquet, Mgr L.-A.**
   1909 *Droit public de l'Eglise*, L'Evénement, Québec, 346.
1429.   1912 *Droit public de l'Eglise*, L'Evénement, Québec, 4 v.
1430. **Pépin, Paul**
   1952 *La formation apostolique de l'adolescent au niveau secondaire*, M. A. Thesis, University of Montreal.
1431. **Perrault, Antonio**
   1945 *Religion, Culture et Liberté au Canada*, ESP, Montréal, 80.
1432. **Perrault, Jacques**
   1945 La religion et notre société canadienne-française, *Culture*, VI, 294-306.
1433. **Perrier, Philippe**
   1935 Spiritualité du Clergé canadien, *Journées Thomistes*, I, 119-139.
1434. **Plessis, Mgr Joseph-Octave**
   1865 Voyage dans le Golfe Saint-Laurent et les provinces d'en-bas. Journal de la mission 1811 et 1812, *Le Foyer canadien*, 3, 73-281.
1435.   1903 *Journal des visites pastorales de 1815-1816*, Imp. Franciscaine Missionnaire, Québec, 75.

A BIBLIOGRAPHICAL INTRODUCTION...

1436. **Porter, Fernand**
    1949   L'Institution Catéchistique au Canada, Les Ed. Franciscaines, Montréal, 332.
1437. **Pouliot, Léon**
    1942   La réaction catholique de Montréal, 1840-1841, Imp. du Messager, Montréal, 119.
1438.   1955   Mgr Bourget et son temps, Beauchemin, Montréal, 203.
1439. **Prud'homme, L.-A.**
    1927   M. l'abbé Joseph-David Filion, TRSC, XXI, 1, 207-38.
1440. **Québec, Georges de**
    1944   L'Eglise catholique au Canada, L'Echo de Saint-François, Montréal, 82.
1441. **Rameau, de Saint-Pierre, E.**
    1866   Situation religieuse de l'Amérique anglaise, Douniol, Paris, 32.
1442. **Riddell, W. A.**
    1916   The rise of ecclesiastical control in Quebec, Columbia University Studies, vol. 74, no 1, 196.
1443. **Riddell, W. R.**
    1928   The status of Roman Catholicism in Canada, n. e., Toronto, 24.
1444. **Rumilly, Robert**
    1945   Mgr Laflèche et son temps, Simpson, Montréal, 491.
1445. **Ryan, Claude**
    1955   Les laïcs et la vie liturgique au Canada, Revue Eucharistique du Clergé, 58, 1, 47-58.
1446. **Savaete, Arthur**
    n. d.   Vers l'abîme. Histoire politico-religieuse du Canada de 1763 à nos jours, Librairie Générale catholique, Paris, 12 v.
1447. **Semaine Religieuse (La)**
    1936   Centenaire du Diocèse de Montréal, Thérien, Montréal, 205.
1448. **Simard, Georges**
    1933   La race et la langue française dans l'Eglise du Canada, RUO, 3, 2, 131-154.
1449. **Tanguay, Mgr**
    1868   Répertoire Général du Clergé canadien, Darveau, Québec, 321.
1450. **Têtu, Henri**
    1889   Les Evêques de Québec, Hardy, Québec, 692.
1451. **Têtu, Henri et Gagnon, C.-O.**
    1887-93   Mandements, lettres pastorales et circulaires des Evêques de Québec, Côté, Québec, 8 v.
1452. **Trudel, Marcel**
    1955   Inventaire de l'Eglise canadienne à la fin de 1764, RHAF, 9, 313-46.
1453.   1956   L'Eglise canadienne sous le régime militaire, Fides, Montréal, 2 v.
1454. **Trudelle, Joseph**
    1901-4   Les églises et chapelles de la ville et de la banlieue de Québec, 1608-1901, Le Soleil, Québec, 2 v.
1455. **Valois, Omer**
    1954   Diocèse de Joliette, 1904-1954, Revue Eucharistique du Clergé, 57, 51-56.
1456. **Vinette, Raymond**
    1949   Le recrutement sacerdotal, ESC, 26, 226.
1457. **Viger, J.**
    1850   Archéologie religieuse du Diocèse de Montréal, Gilson, Montréal, 114.

II) *Religious Orders*

1458. **A. M. B. G.**
    1926   Fêtes du 3e centenaire des Jésuites à Québec, n. e., Québec, 201.
1459. **A. M. D. G.**
    1863   Les Ursulines de Québec, Darveau, Québec, 4 v.

A BIBLIOGRAPHICAL INTRODUCTION...

1460. 1888 *Les Ursulines de Trois-Rivières*, Ayotte, Trois-Rivières, 560.
1461. **Anonymous**
 1915 *Vingt-cinq années de Vie franciscaine au Canada, 1890-1915*, Ed. Revue du Tiers-Ordre, Montréal, 335.
1462. 1939 *Frères-Prêcheurs en terre canadienne*, Ed. du Lévrier, Ottawa, 201.
1463. 1940 *Le Grand Séminaire de Montréal*, n. e., Montréal, 170.
1464. 1942 *La Compagnie de Jésus au Canada, 1842-1942*, Maison Provinciale, Montréal, 181.
1465. 1946 *La Congrégation de Jésus et de Marie (Eudistes) au Canada*, Besançon, 172.
1466. 1954 *Tiers-Ordre Dominicain, Canada, 1854-1954*, Couvent des Dominicains, Saint-Hyacinthe, 39.
1467. 1954 Moines et moniales de Citeaux au Canada, CV, 19, 211-26.
1468. 1955 *Les Récollets de Montréal*, Ed. Franciscaines, Montréal, 293.
1469. **Archambault, Joseph-Papin**
 1924 *Au service de l'Eglise*, Imp. du Messager, Montréal, 313.
1470. 1929 *Sur les pas de Marthe et de Marie*, Imp. du Messager, Montréal, 669.
1471. **Auclair, Elie-J.**
 1922 *Histoire des Sœurs de Sainte-Anne*, Imp. des Frères des Ecoles Chrétiennes, Montréal, 354.
1472. **Bastien, Hermas**
 1948 *L'Ordre Hospitalier de Saint-Jean-de-Dieu*, Ed. Lumen, Montréal, 211.
1473. **Conférence Religieuse canadienne**
 1954 *Actes du premier congrès religieux canadien*, Conférence Religieuse canadienne, Ottawa, 741.
1474. **Congrégation de Sainte-Croix**
 n. d. *Sainte-Croix au Canada, 1847-1947*, Fides, Montréal, 604.
1475. **Bernard, Antoine**
 1947-51 *Les Clercs de Saint-Viateur au Canada*, Les Clercs de Saint-Viateur, Montréal, 2 v.
1476. **Couet, Thomas-Cyrille**
 1925 *La Mère Marie-de-la-Charité et les Sœurs Dominicaines de Québec*, Action Sociale, Québec, 3 v.
1477. **Courteau, Guy**
 1948 *Sœurs du Bon-Conseil et Sisters of Service*, Relations, 93, 258-9.
1478. **Duchaussois, Pierre**
 1932 *Rose du Canada, Mère Marie-Rose, Fondatrice de la Congrégation des Sœurs des Saints-Noms-de-Jésus-et-de-Marie*, Spes, Paris, 352.
1479. **Duclos, Paul**
 1948 *Une Institution ecclésiastique : Les Clercs de Saint-Viateur*, M. A. Thesis, Laval University.
1480. **Ferland Angers, Albertine**
 1945 *Mère d'Youville*, Beauchemin, Montréal, 385.
1481. **Franciscains**
 1915 *Les Frères Mineurs, leur histoire, leur vie. Les Franscicains du Canada*, n. e., Montréal, 349.
1482. **Frères de l'Ecole Chrétienne**
 1921 *Les Frères de l'Ecole Chrétienne au Canada*, Montréal, 328.
1483. **Gauthier, Henri**
 1912 *La Compagnie de Saint-Sulpice au Canada*, Séminaire de Saint-Sulpice, Montréal, 145.
1484. **Jouve, Odoric-Marie**
 1905 *Les Frères-Mineurs à Québec, 1615-1905*, Couvent des Saints-Stigmates, Québec, 159.
1485. **Laroche-Héron, C. de**
 1855 *Les Servantes de Dieu en Canada*, Lovell, Montréal, 158.

A BIBLIOGRAPHICAL INTRODUCTION...

1486. **Montreuil, Anna-B.**
       1955 *Three came with gifts*, Ryerson, Toronto, 160.
1487. **Marie-Jean de Patmos, Sr.**
       1950 Les Sœurs de Sainte-Anne, un siècle d'histoire, 1850-1900, Les Sœurs de Sainte-Anne, Lachine, 640.
1488. **Marie-Michel-Archange, Sr.**
       1955 *Histoire de la Congrégation des Petites Franciscaines de Marie*, Baie Saint-Paul, 539.
1489. **Maurault, Mgr Olivier**
       1936 *Nos Messieurs*, Ed. du Zodiaque, Montréal, 323.
1490. **Morin, Hervé**
       1946 *Commentaire des règles de la Congrégation de Sainte-Croix*, Fides, Montréal, 423.
1491. **Nadeau, Eugène**
       1950 *Mère Léonie, Fondatrice des Petites Sœurs de la Sainte Famille*, Fides, Montréal, 169.
1492. **Paul-Emile, Sr**
       1945 *Mère Elizabeth-Bruyère et son œuvre*, Ed. de l'Université d'Ottawa, Ottawa, 405.
1493. **Saint-Pierre, Arthur**
       1932 Un fait social important ; services économiques rendus par nos Congrégations, *Messager Canadien du Sacré-Cœur*, juillet, 308-312.
1494. 1926 *L'Oratoire Saint-Joseph-de-Montréal*, Montréal, 144.
1495. n. d. *What are all these nuns good for ?* Biblio. Canadienne, Montréal, 14.
1496. **Sœurs de la Charité de Québec**
       1939 *Mère Mallet, 1805-1871*, Maison Mère des Sœurs de la Charité, Québec, 612.
1497. **Stuker, Eugène**
       1942 La Trappe de N.-D.-de-Mistassini, *Progrès du Saguenay*, 55, 46, 2 juillet, 1-7-8.
1498. **Viatte, Auguste**
       1952 *Histoire de la Congrégation de Jésus-Marie, 1810-1950*, Couvent de Jésus-Marie, Québec, 309.

III) *Missionary activities*

1499. **Anonymous**
       1930 *Le Semaine Missionnaire de Montréal*, Beauchemin, Montréal, 300.
1499a. 1955 *Esquimaux*, Union Missionnaire du Clergé, Québec, 118.
1500. **Bourassa, Henri**
       1919 *Le Canada apostolique*, Biblio. de l'Action Française, Montréal, 170.
1501. **Breton, Paul-Emile**
       1954 *Le Grand Chef des Prairies : Le Père Albert Lacombe, O. M. I., 1827-1916*, Ed. de l'Ermitage, Edmonton, 232.
1502. **Breynat, Gabriel Mgr**
       1948 *Cinquante ans au pays des neiges*, Fides, Montréal, 3 v.
1503. **Campbell, Thomas-Joseph**
       1908-19 *Pioneer priests of North America, 1642-1710*, Fordham University Press, New York, 3 v.
1504. **Carrière, Gaston**
       1955 L'honorable Compagnie de la Baie-d'Hudson et les missions des Oblats, 1844-1861, RUO, 25, 330-64.
1505. 1955 Cent ans d'apostolat au Labrador, RUO, 65, 693-699.
1506. **Campagne, Joseph-Etienne**
       1949 *Les Missions catholiques dans l'Ouest canadien*, Ed. de l'Université d'Ottawa, Ottawa, 208.

73

A BIBLIOGRAPHICAL INTRODUCTION...

1507. **Devine, E.-J.**
 1922 *Historic Caughnawaga*, Messenger Press, Montreal, 443.
1508. **Duchaussois, Pierre-Jean-Baptiste**
 1919 *The Grey Nuns in the Far North*, McClelland and Stewart, Toronto, 287.
1509. 1921 *Aux glaces polaires, Indiens et Esquimaux*, Oeuvre Apostolique de Marie-Immaculée, Lyons, 471.
1510. **Gasgrain, H.-R.**
 1895 *Mémoire sur les missions en Nouvelle-Ecosse (1760-1820)*, Darveau, Québec, 269.
1511. 1897 *Les Sulpiciens et les Prêtres des missions étrangères en Acadie*, Pruneau et Kirouac, Québec, 462.
1516. **Garnier, L.**
 1950 *Du traîneau à l'avion*, Bonne-Presse, Paris, 209.
1517. **Grouard, Mgr**
 n. d. *Souvenirs de mes soixante ans d'apostolat dans l'Athabaska-Mackenzie*, La Liberté, Winnipeg, 440.
1518. **Juneau, Roméo**
 1939 *Martyrs aux glaces polaires*, n. e., Montréal, 250.
1519. **Lacasse, Carmel**
 1951 *Terre d'attente*, Fides, Montréal, 226.
1520. **Lecompte, Edouard**
 1925 *Les missions modernes de la Compagnie de Jésus au Canada, 1842-1924*, Imp. du Messager, Montréal, 2 v.
1521. **Lesage, Germain**
 1946 *Capitale d'une solitude*, Ed. des Etudes Oblates, Otawa, 185.
1522. **Nadeau, Eugène**
 1939 *Un homme sortit pour semer*, Beauchemin, Montréal, 207.
1523. 1954 *Sapier, prêtre de misère (1856-1946)*, n. e., Montréal, 366.
1524. 1954 *A l'origine des missions de la Baie-James*, RUO, 24, 53-65.
1525. **Oblate Commission**
 1953 *Atlas des missions indiennes et esquimaudes confiées aux Oblats de Marie-Immaculée du Canada*, Oblate Commission, University, Ottawa, 48.
1526. **Paul-Emile, Sr**
 1952 *La Baie James, ou Amiskawaki, la terre des castors*, Ed. de l'Université d'Ottawa, Ottawa, 402.
1527. **Quatrième Semaine d'Etudes Missionnaires**
 1951 *Le Laïcat et les Missions*, Ed. de l'Université d'Ottawa, Ottawa, 276.
1528. **Rousseau, Pierre**
 1930 *Saint-Sulpice et les Missions catholiques*, Garaud, Montréal, 188.
1529. **Roy, Elia**
 1950 *Efforts missionnaires du Canada en 1948*, La Vie des Communautés Religieuses, 8, 152-6.
1530. **Saindon, Emile**
 1928 *En missionnant. Essai sur les missions*, Le Droit, Ottawa, 79.
1531. **Secrétariat du Comité Missionnaire**
 1948 *Ville-Marie missionnaire*, n. e., n. p., 616.
1532. **Thériault, Yvon**
 1952 *L'apostolat missionnaire en Mauricie*, Bien-Public, Trois-Rivières, 144.
1533. **Trudel, P.-E.**
 1936 *Les missions canadiennes*, n. e., Trois-Rivières, 366.

IV) *Social Catholicism*

1554. **A. C. J. C.**
 1915 *Le devoir social au Canada*, Bureau de l'ACJC, Montréal, 307.

A BIBLIOGRAPHICAL INTRODUCTION...

1555. **Aganier, Hozael**
    1954   La J. E. C. canadienne, *Cahiers d'Action catholique*, 167, 310.
1556. **Aird, Roger**
    1952   *Rapport entre l'A. C. et l'organisation professionnelle ouvrière et patronale d'inspiration chrétienne*, Thesis, Laval University.
1557. **Anonymous**
    1953-4 Positions de la J.E.C. secondaire, CAC, 59-58 ; 167, 28-40.
1558. **Archambault, J.-P.**
    1917   *La question sociale et nos devoirs de catholiques*, ESP, Montréal, 112.
    1918   *Le clergé et l'Action sociale*, ESP, Montréal, 103.
1560.   1930   *Esquisses sociales*, Librairie d'Action canadienne-française, Montréal, 331.
1561.   1932   *La restauration de l'ordre social d'après les encycliques « Rerum Novarum » et « Quadragesimo Anno »*, ESP, Montréal, 106.
1562.   1937   *L'Action catholique au Canada*, ESP, no 287, Montréal, 37.
1563.   1938   *L'Action catholique d'après les textes pontificaux*, ESP, Montréal, 156.
1564.   1939   *Les Voyageurs catholiques*, ESP, Montréal, 80.
1565.   1945   *La moralité publique*, ESP, no 383, Montréal, 32.
1566.   1950   *Figures catholiques*, ISP, Montréal, 193.
1567. **Asselin, Joseph-François-Olivar**
    1915   *Les Evêques et la propagande de l'Action catholique*, n. e., Montréal, 60.
1568. **Aumôniers de la L. O. C. et de la J. E. C.**
    1952   *L'Action catholique ouvrière*, Montréal, 50.
1569. **Baudoux, Maurice**
    1953   Collaboration des éducateurs à l'Action catholique, CAC, 155, 20-29.
1570. **Cadieux, Fernand**
    1952   La J. E. C. des collèges secondaires, CAC, 147, 69-74.
1571. **Chagnon, Louis**
    1937   *Directions sociales catholiques*, L'Action Paroissiale, Montréal, 214.
1572. **Courchesne, Georges**
    1925   *L'Association catholique de la Jeunesse canadienne-française*, OT, no 77, Montréal, 16.
1574. **Civardi, Mgr L.**
    1936   *Manuel d'Action catholique*, Ed. Jocistes, Montréal, 383.
1575. **Charbonneau, Mgr Joseph**
    1947   *Lettre pastorale : L'Action catholique*, Fides, Montréal, 63.
1576. **Chicoine, Fidèle**
    1948   *Précis de doctrine rurale à l'usage des Canadiens français*, Ed. Franciscaines, Montréal, 255.
1577. **Cholette, G.**
    1944   *Le Comité d'Action catholique de Saint-Charles-de-Limoilou*, Thesis, Laval University.
1578. **Collaboration**
    1947   *Six ans après... réalisations de l'Action catholique du Diocèse de Montréal*, Ed. Unitas, Montréal, 207.
1579. **Courchesne, Mgr**
    1946   *Notre Jeunesse*, ESP, no 387-8, Montréal, 64.
1580. **Ecole Sociale Populaire**
    1933   *Pour la Restauration sociale au Canada*, ESP, no 232-3, Montréal, 64.
1581.   1936   *Les vingt-cinq ans de l'Ecole Sociale Populaire, 1911-1936*, ESP, no 269-70, Montréal, 61.
1582.   1945   *Le 25e anniversaire des Semaines Sociales du Canada*, ESP, no 38, Montréal, 32.
1583. **Filion, Jean**
    1938   *Jeunesse et Politique*, ESP, Montréal, 32.

A BIBLIOGRAPHICAL INTRODUCTION...

1584. **Gaudreau, Sr Agnès-de-Rome**
1946 *The social thought of French Canada as reflected in the Semaines Sociales du Canada*, Catholic University of America, Washington, 266.
1585. 1946 *La pensée sociale du Canada français, telle que reflétée dans les Semaines Sociales*, ESP, no 391, Montréal, 30.
1585a **Gaudrault, P.-M.**
1946 *Neutralité, non-confessionnalité et l'Ecole Sociale Populaire*, Ed. du Lévrier, Montréal, 63.
1586. **Gauthier, Laurenzo**
1942 *Pour un Ordre social chrétien*, ESP, Montréal, 200.
1587. **Gratton, Adrien**
1937 *L'orientation de la Province de Québec vers le corporatisme social*, AE, août, 318-347.
1588. **Groulx, Lionel**
1938 *Une croisade d'adolescents*, Granger, Montréal, 253.
1589. **J. O. C.**
1942 *Rapports des journées d'études sacerdotales de la J. O. C.*, Fides, Montréal, 382.
1590. **Journées Thomistes (II)**
1937 *Témoignages de la Jeunesse canadienne-française*, Ed. du Lévrier, Ottawa, 87.
1591. **Lalande, Germain-L.**
1950 *Conversion au réel, un essai sur l'Action catholique*, Fides, Montréal, 315.
1592. **Lettre Pastorale collective**
1941 *La restauration de l'Ordre social*, Action-Catholique, Québec, 36.
1593. 1950 *Le problème ouvrier en regard de la doctrine sociale de l'Eglise*, Documents Sociaux, Québec, 86.
1594. **L. O. C. et L. O. C. F.**
1947 *La L.O.C. canadienne, mystique et technique*, Fides, Montréal, 286.
1595. 1947 *Espoir des Familles ouvrières*, n. e., Montréal, 60.
1596. **Nadeau, Eugène**
1952 *Un Louis d'or, le Chevalier Louis Emond, 1876-1949*, Ed. Oblates, Montréal, 198.
1597. **Ouellet, Fernand**
1955 *Etienne Parent et le mouvement du catholicisme social 1848*, Bull. des Recherches historiques, 61, 3, 99-119.
1598. **Paquet, Mgr Louis-Adolphe**
1922 *Thèmes Sociaux*, Imp. Franciscaines Missionnaires, Québec, 333.
1599. **Saint-Pierre, Arthur**
1911 *Vers l'Action*, Ed. du Messager, Montréal, 108.
1600. 1931 *Législation sociale et l'encyclique « Rerum Novarum »*, La Santé, Montréal, 8.
1601. **Semaines Sociales du Canada**
1920-55 *Yearly Report*.
1602. 1920 *Rerum Novarum*, Bibliothèque de l'Action Nationale, Montréal, 201.

V) *Parish Organization*

1603. **Alexis, Père de Barbezieux**
1902 *Une Paroisse canadienne*, La Nouvelle-France, 1, 2, 66-85.
1604. **Archevêché de Montréal**
1953 *Feuillet de l'administration temporelle des paroisses*, Archevêché de Montréal, Montréal, 46.
1605. **Beaumont, G.**
1947 *Les centres paroissiaux à Québec*, Thesis, Laval University.

1606. **Boissinot, Y.**
    1952   La Salle paroissiale de Limoilou, Thesis, Laval University.
1607. **Brisson, L.**
    1947   La paroisse Saint-Sauveur au service du peuple, Thesis, Laval University.
1608. **Denis, Gérard**
    1953   Codes des Fabriques, Wilson et Lafleur, Montréal, 320.
1609. **Desmarchais, Philémon**
    1938   La Paroisse, facteur d'économie, RTC, 24, 95, 300-327.
1610. **Dugré, A.**
    1929   La Paroisse au Canada français, ESP, no 183-4, Montréal, 64.
1611. **Falardeau, Jean-Charles**
    1949   The parish as an institutional type, CJEPS, 15, 353-69.
1612.   n. d.   Paroisses de France et de Nouvelle-France, Cahiers de l'Ecole des Sciences Sociales, Québec, 38.
1613.   1951   Parish Research in Canada, The Sociology of the Parish, ed. Nuesse, C. J. and Harte, T. J., The Bruce Publishing Co., Milwaukee, 254-71.
1614. **Filion, Gérard**
    1953   La paroisse rurale, Le Devoir, 44, 26 sept., 4, 10.
1615. **Gariépy, Wilfrid**
    1953   La paroisse urbaine, ISP, Montréal, 30.
1616. **Gérin, Léon**
    1894   Le rang et la paroisse, Science Sociale, Paris, 16.
1617. **Guimont, Cléophas-Regis-Roméo**
    1921   Le Droit paroissial, Action Française, Montréal, 260.
1618. **Lemelin, Roméo**
    1954   Les registres paroissiaux, n. e., Québec, 209.
1619. **Mignault, Pierre-Basile**
    1893   Le Droit paroissial, Beauchemin, Montréal, 690.
1620. **Poulin, Gonzalve**
    1936-7   L'Evolution historico-juridique de l'institution paroissiale au Canada français, Nos Cahiers, 2 v.
1621. **Pouliot, Jean-François**
    1919   Le Droit paroissial de la Province de Québec, Imp. le Saint-Laurent, Fraserville, 636.
1622.   1936   Traité de Droit fabricien et paroissial, Wilson et Lafleur, Montréal, 1010.
1623. **Roy, Mgr M.**
    1950   Paroisse et Démocratie au Canada français, OT, Montréal, 16.
1624. **Semaines Sociales du Canada**
    1953   La Paroisse, cellule sociale, ISP, Montréal, 204.

VI) *Non-Catholic Religious organizations in Quebec*

1625. **Audet, F.-J.**
    1900   Le clergé protestant du Bas-Canada, 1760-1800, TRSC, VI, 1, 133-42.
1626. **Amaron, C.-E.**
    1885   The evangelization of the French Canadians, Lovell, 90.
1627. **Baird, C.-H.**
    1885   History of the Huguenot immigration in America, Dodd, Mead and Co., New York, 2 v.
1628. **Bergeron, René**
    1947   Les « Témoins » d'une sottise, OT, no 332, Montréal, 16.
1629. **Brosseau, Jean-Dominique**
    1954   Notre apostolat auprès des protestants, Relations, 14, 19-21.
1630. **Cammi, E.**
    n. d.   Les protestants aujourd'hui en France et au Canada, Hébert, Montréal, 48.

A BIBLIOGRAPHICAL INTRODUCTION...

1631. **Clark, S.-D.**
1948 *Church and Sect in Canada*, University of Toronto Press, Toronto, 458.
1632. **Duclos, R. P.**
1913 *Histoire du Protestantisme français au Canada et aux Etats-Unis*, Librairie Evangéline, Montréal, 2 v.
1633. **Forest, C.**
1935 *La question juive au Canada*, La Presse Dominicaine, Montréal, 52.
1634. **Garland, S. G.**
1929 *The Church in a changing City*, Thesis, McGill University.
1635. **Jasmin, Damien**
1947 *Les Témoins de Jéhovah*, Ed. Lumens, Montréal, 209.
1636. **Hampden**
1871 *The political state and conditions of Her Majesty's Protestant subjects in the Province of Québec*, Canadian News, Toronto, 74.
1637. **Ledit, Joseph-H.**
1945 Dans la jungle protestante, *Relations*, 50, 44-46.
1638. 1947 Les Témoins de Jéhovah, *Relations*, 74, 43-46.
1639. **Maheux, Arthur**
1940 Le problème protestant, SCHEC, Rapport 1939-40, 43-50.
1640. **Rinfret, Thibaudeau**
1953 *La Cour Suprême et les Témoins de Jéhovah*, ISP, no 468, Montréal, 32.
1641. **Rosser, F. T. and Wilson, Stuart**
1956 *The Baptists in Upper and Lower Canada before 1820*, University of Toronto Press, Toronto, 240.
1642. **Therrien, Eugène-A.**
1954 *Baptist work in French Canada*, Grande Ligue Mission, Montreal, 67.
1643. **White, Thomas**
1876 *The Protestant Minority in Quebec and its political Relations with the Roman Catholic Majority*, Dawson, Montreal, 419.

VII) *Anti-clericalism*

1644. **A Catholic**
1905 *The Ultramondane policy in Quebec and its results*, n. e., n. p., 32.
1645. **Archambault, J.-P.**
1935 *La menace communiste au Canada*, ESP, no 254-5, Montréal, 64.
1646. **Arès, Richard**
1952 Le problème de l'anticléricalisme au Canada français, *Relations*, 143, 282-5.
1647. 1952 Anticléricalisme, cléricalisme et sens de l'Eglise, *Relations*, 144, 310-14.
1648. **Bernard, Henri**
1904 *La Ligue de l'Enseignement. Histoire d'une conspiration maçonnique à Montréal*, n. e., Montréal, 150.
1649. **Buies, Arthur**
1884 *La lanterne*, n. e., Montréal, 336.
1650. **Chiniquy, Charles**
1946 *Mes Combats*, L'Aurore, Montréal, 691.
1651. **De Lery, Louis-C.**
1954 *La Franc-Maçonnerie*, Bellarmin, Montréal, 48.
1652. **Dessaulles, L.-A.**
1873 *La grande guerre ecclésiastique*, Doutre, Montréal, 130.
1653. **Dougall, John**
1875 *History of the Guibord Case*, n. e., Montreal, 150.
1654. **Ferland, Joseph**
1924 Le Laïcisme, AF, 12, 6, 322-30.

1655. **Favre, Mgr Charles-Edouard**
    1894 *La Grande Cause ecclésiastique*, Lovell, Montréal, 350.
1656. **Germain, Noël**
    1942 *La Franc-maçonnerie du Québec est-elle protestante ?*, Messager, Montréal, 56.
1657. **Gauthier, Mgr Georges**
    1938 *Lettre sur le communisme*, OT, no 226, Montréal, 16.
1658. **Hudon, Théophile**
    1938 *L'Institut canadien de Montréal et l'affaire Guibord*, Beauchemin, Montréal, 170.
1659. **Huot, Antonio**
    1906 *Le fléau maçonnique*, Dussault et Proulx, Montréal, 178.
1660. **Lacasse, Z.**
    1892 *Une nouvelle Mine, le prêtre et ses détracteurs*, Librairie Saint-Joseph, Montréal, 276.
1661. **Laurent, Edouard**
    1939 *Une enquête sur le communisme à Québec*, ESP, no 303, Montréal, 32.
1662. **Lenoir, Maurice**
    1940 *Clericalism in Quebec*, *New Republic*, CIII, 12, 379-81, 13, 408-10.
1663. **Lindsey, C.**
    1877 *Rome in Canada*, Lovell, Toronto, 308.
1664. **Marie-Médéric, Fr.**
    1939 *Un siècle de voltarianisme au Canada français*, Ph. D. Thesis, University of Ottawa.
1665. **Robertson, John Ross**
    1900 *The history of Freemasonary in Canada, 1749-1858*, Morong, Toronto, 2 v.
1666. **Sait, Edouard McChesnay**
    1911 *Clerical control in Quebec*, The Sentinel, Toronto, 158.
1667. **Théodore-Vibert, Paul**
    1908 *La Nouvelle-France catholique*, Schleicher, Paris, 496.
1668. **Trudeau, P.-E. and Rolland, Roger**
    1953 Matériaux pour servir à une enquête sur le cléricalisme, *Cité Libre*, 7, 29-43.
1669. **Trudel, M.**
    1945 *L'influence de Voltaire au Canada*, Fides, Montréal, 2 v.
1670.   1955 *Chiniquy*, Bien-Public, Trois-Rivières, 339.

4. FRENCH-SPEAKING GROUPS OUTSIDE THE PROVINCE OF QUEBEC

a) *Acadiens*

1671. **Anonymous**
    1955   Communautés religieuses en Acadie, *Evangéline*, 12, 141, 25 août, 25.
1672. **Arsenault, Bona**
    1955   *L'Acadie des ancêtres*, Conseil de la Vie française en Amérique, Québec, 400.
1673. **Aucuin, Louis**
    1955   Le rôle de l'Eglise dans le « miracle » acadien, *La Presse*, 71, 24 juin, 47, 52.
1673-a. **Beaudry, René**
    1955   Aux sources de l'histoire de l'Acadie et des Provinces Maritimes, CHAR, 62-68.
1674. **Bernard, Antoine**
    1935   *Histoire de la survivance acadienne, 1755-1935*, Clercs de Saint-Viateur, Montréal, 465.
1675.   1936   *Le drame acadien depuis 1604*, Clercs de Saint-Viateur, Montréal, 459.
1676.   1949   *La renaissance acadienne au XXe siècle*, La Survivance-française, Québec, 189.
1677. **Blanchard, J.-H.**
    1927   *Histoire des Acadiens de l'Ile du Prince-Edouard*, Imp. de l'Evangile, Moncton, 120.
1678. **Breault, Arthur**
    1933   *Education française en Acadie*, Thesis, University of Ottawa.
1679. **Campbell, G. G.**
    1948   *The History of Nova Scotia*, Ryerson, Toronto, 288.
1680. **Casgrain, H.-R.**
    1887   Les Acadiens après leur dispersion, 1755-75, TRSC, V, 1, 15-92.
1681. **Cormier, Clément**
    1951   En route pour l'Acadie, *Relations*, 127, 178-80.
1682.   1955   La mission et le message des écrivains de l'Acadie, *La Presse*, 71, 210, 24 juin, 37.
1683. **Cyriaque, Daigle-L.**
    1948   *Histoire de Saint-Louis de Kent. Cent cinquante ans de vie paroissiale française en Acadie*, L'Imp. Acadienne, Moncton, 246.
1684. **Dubois, Emile**
    1920   *Chez nos frères les Acadiens*, L'Action Française, Montréal, 173.
1685. **Dugré, Alexandre**
    1954   Acadie, 1755-1955, *Relations*, 168, 334-7.
1686. **Frégault, Guy**
    1954   La déportation des Acadiens, RHAF, 8, 3, 321-339.
1687. **Ganong, W. F.**
    1945   *Saint Croix Island*, New Brunswick Museum, Saint John, 125.
1688. **Gaudet, Laura C.**
    1945   *Songs of Acadia*, Broadcast Music Inc., New York, 32.
1689. **Gidéon, Augustus**
    1955   L'Agriculture, facteur de survivance, *L'Evangéline*, 12, 14, 15 août, 85.
1690. **Gosselin, Gilberte**
    1955   La liaison française en Acadie, VF, 10, 11-23.

A BIBLIOGRAPHICAL INTRODUCTION...

1691. **Groulx, Lionel**
  1917 *L'Histoire acadienne*, Soc. Saint-Jean-Baptiste, Montréal, 32.
1692. **Lauvrière, E.**
  1924 *La tragédie d'un peuple*, Goulet, Paris, 2 v.
1693. **Le Blanc, D. J.**
  1937 *The true story of the Acadians*, Tribune Publishing Co., Lafayette, 256.
1694. **Leblanc, Emery**
  1955 L'Acadie appelée à jouer un rôle accru en politique, *La Presse*, 71, 210, 24 juin, 34, 38.
1695. **Leblanc, Henri-P.**
  1955 La société l'Assomption, *La Presse*, 71, 210, 24 juin, 38.
1696. **Legère, Martin, J.**
  1955 Le mouvement coopératif, *L'Evangéline*, 12, 141, 15 août, 78.
1697. **Le Gresley, Omer**
  1926 *L'Enseignement du français en Acadie, 1604-1926*, Enault, Paris, 256.
1698. **Michaud, Marguerite-Marie**
  1949 *La reconstruction française au Nouveau-Brunswick, Bouchote, paroisse-type*, Ph. D. Thesis, University of Montreal.
1699.   1955 Le rôle de l'Acadienne, *La Presse*, 71, 210, 24 juin, 39.
1700.   1955 *La reconstruction française au Nouveau-Brunswick, Bouchote, paroisse-type*, Presses Universitaires, Frederiction, 221.
1701. **Plante, Albert**
  1955 Les fêtes du deuxième centenaire de la déportation des Acadiens, *Relations*, 15, 178, 270-71.
1702. **Poirier, Pascal**
  1908 Des Acadiens déportés à Boston en 1755, TRSC, IV, 1, 125-80.
1703.   1927 Comment une langue évolue, TRSC, XXI, 1, 239-45.
1704. **Rameau de Saint-Pierre, E.**
  1889 *Une colonie féodale en Amérique : L'Acadie (1604-1881)*, Plon, Paris, 2 v.
1705. **Richard, Edouard**
  1916-18 *Acadie, reconstruction d'un chapitre perdu de l'histoire d'Amérique*, Laflamme, Québec, 2 v.
1706. **Robichaud, Mgr**
  1943 *Le Français en Acadie*, OT, no 282, Montréal, 15.
1707. **Robichaud, Norbert**
  1954 Radio-Canada en Acadie, VF, 8, 456-63.
1708. **Rumilly, Robert**
  1955 *Histoire des Acadiens*, Fides, Montréal, 2 v.
1709. **Sloat, Prudence**
  1946 *La Survivance française au Nouveau-Brunswick*, M. A. Thesis, McGill University.
1710. **Taillon, Léopold**
  1952 *Au service de la culture française en Acadie, 1938-1952*, Fides, Montréal, 159.
1711.   1955 Progrès réalisés par l'Ecole acadienne, *La Presse*, 71, 210, 24 juin, 35.

b) *Other groups in Canada*

1712. **Anonymous**
  1949 *Folklore franco-ontarien*, Soc. Historique du Nouvel-Ontario, Sudbury, 48.
1713. **Association canadienne-française d'éducation d'Ottawa**
  1912 *The bilingual schools of Ontario*, Ottawa Printing Co., Ottawa, 55.
1714.   1912 *Bilingualism in Ontario*, n. e., Ottawa, 27.
1715. **Baudoux, Maurice**
  1941 La vie rurale et la famille. Conditions de survivance dans l'Ouest, *La Survivance*, 14, 3.

81

A BIBLIOGRAPHICAL INTRODUCTION...

1716. **Bélanger, Roger**
   1949 Région agricole de Nipissing-Sudbury, *Relations*, 106, 263-6 ; 107, 306-7.
1717. **Belcourt, N.-A.**
   1923 The French Canadians outside Quebec, *The Annals*, CVII, 13-24.
1718. **Béliveau, Mgr**
   1927 Le Canadien français et le rôle de l'Eglise dans l'Ouest, AF, 83-84.
1719. **Benoît, J.-P.-A.**
   1904 *Vie de Mgr Taché*, Beauchemin, Montréal, 2 v.
1720. **Bernard, Antoine**
   1949 *Nos pionniers de l'Ouest*, La Survivance-française, Québec, 141.
1721. **Bernier, Alfred**
   1953 La Vie française au Manitoba, *Relations*, 151, 192-194.
1722. **Biays, Pierre**
   1952 *Un village terreneuvien, Capt Saint-Georges*, Presses Universitaires Laval, Québec, 30.
1723. **Blais, Moïse**
   1902 *Le Manitoba ; renseignements et conseils aux Canadiens français*, n. e., n. p., 74.
1724. **Bouchette, Errol**
   1912 L'Ontario français économique, *Revue Franco Américaine*, IX, 389-409.
1725. **Bourassa, Henri**
   1905 *Les Ecoles du Nord-Ouest*, Nationaliste, Montréal, 31.
1726.   1912 *Pour la Justice, historique de la législation scolaire du Nord-Ouest*, Le Devoir, Montréal, 44.
1727. **Carrière, L.**
   1952 *Le vocabulaire français des écoliers franco-ontariens*, Ph. D. Thesis, University of Montreal.
1728. **Charles, Enid and Anthony, Sylvia**
   1943 The community and family in Prince Edward Island, *Rural Sociology*, 8, 37-57.
1729. **Clague, Robert-Ernest**
   1939 *The political Aspect of the Manitoba school Question, 1890-96*, M. A. Thesis, University of Manitoba.
1730. **Chauvin, F.-X.**
   1946 Les Canadiens français d'Essex et de Kent, *Relations*, 72, 365-9.
1731. **Comeau, Joseph-Edouard**
   1949 *L'Enseignement du français dans les écoles publiques de la Nouvelle-Ecosse depuis 1900*, Thesis, University of Montreal.
1732. **Daignault, P.-M.**
   1905 *Les Français de la Nouvelle-Ecosse*, Lib. Centrale, Besançon, 278.
1733. **Dawson, C. A.**
   1934 *The settlement of the Peace River Country*, Macmillan, Toronto, 284.
1734.   1936 *Group settlement. Ethnic communities in Western Canada*, MacClelland and Stuart, Toronto, 395.
1735. **Dorion, Léo-Martin**
   1946 *La langue française en Nouvelle-Ecosse*, Thesis, University of Montreal.
1736. **Dugas, G.**
   1906 *Histoire de l'Ouest canadien de 1822 à 1869*, Beauchemin, Montréal, 154.
1737. **Edwards, C.-E.**
   1946 *La survivance de la culture française en Nouvelle-Ecosse*, M. A. Thesis, McGill University.
1738. **Ewart, John S.**
   1894 *The Manitoba school Question*, Copp, Clarke Co., Toronto, 401.
1739. **Felteau, Cyrille**
   1953 Les minorités françaises de l'Ouest canadien, *Culture*, 14, 434-39.

A BIBLIOGRAPHICAL INTRODUCTION...

1740. **Frémont, D.**
 1935 *Mgr Provencher et son temps*, Ed. la Liberté, Winnipeg, 292.
1741. 1947 Les Français dans l'Ouest canadien, TRSC, XLI, 1, 15-26.
1742. 1954 Les établissements français à l'ouest du Lac Supérieur, TRSC, XLVIII, 1, 7-12.
1743. 1954 Les Français dans l'Alberta, *Amérique Française*, 12, 1, 29-39.
1744. **Giroday, Boyer de la**
 1949 L'expansion française en Colombie Britannique, *Relations*, 102, 164-5.
1745. **Godbout, Arthur**
 1953 Les écoles franco-ontariennes d'avant 1800, CHAR, 25-35.
1746. **Goldren, Harvey**
 1924 *The French settlement in the Red River Valley*, M. A. Thesis, McGill University.
1747. **Groulx, Lionel**
 1928 Lettre du Manitoba, AF, 20, 35-48.
1748. 1935 *L'enseignement français au Canada*, Vol. 2, Granger, Montréal, 271.
1749. **Jean-Augustin, Sr Marie**
 1950 *Douze années d'immigration française au Manitoba, 1870-1882*, Thesis, University of Ottawa.
1750. **Jolys, J.-M.**
 1914 *La paroisse de Saint-Pierre-Jolys au Manitoba*, n. e., n. d., 236.
1751. **Hurtubise, Raoul**
 1939 *Les Canadiens français et le Nouvel-Ontario*, OT, no 244, Montréal, 16.
1752. **Lachance, Gérard**
 1955 Pour abattre le « rideau de pierre », AN, 44, 754-62.
1753. **Lanctot, Gustave**
 1954 Aperçu des premiers peuplements de l'Ouest, TRSC, XLVIII, 13-18.
1754. **Martineau, Gloriana G.**
 1947 *La Survivance française dans Prescott et Russell*, M. A. Thesis, McGill University.
1755. **Mombourquette, Francis Alexander**
 1948 *Administration of bilingual schools with special reference to the Province of Nova Scotia*, M. A. Thesis, University of Toronto.
1756. **Morice, A.-G.**
 1914 *L'histoire abrégée de l'Ouest canadien*, n. e., Saint-Boniface, 162.
1757. 1921 *Histoire de l'Eglise catholique dans l'Ouest canadien*, Granger, Montréal, 4 v. (also in english).
1758. **Morton, A. S.**
 1939 *A history of the Canadian West to 1870-71*, Nelson, New York, 987.
1759. **Morton, W. L.**
 1951 The Manitoba school and Canadian nationalism, CHAR, 51-59.
1760. **Perret, R.**
 1913 *La géographie de Terre-Neuve*, Guilmoto, Paris, 372.
1761. **Plante, Albert**
 1952 *Les écoles séparées d'Ontario*, Bellarmin, Montréal, 104.
1762. **Plante, Albert et Hurtubise, J.-Raoul**
 1954 *Les Ecoles bilingues d'Ontario*, Société Historique du Nouvel-Ontario, Sudbury, 48.
1763. **Prud'homme, L.-A.**
 1923 Le premier parlement du Manitoba, 1870-1874, TRSC, XVII, 1, 165-82.
1764. 1933 L'élément français au Nord-Ouest et son action bienfaisante, TRSC, XXVII, 1, 185-192.
1765. **Oliver, Edmund H.**
 1926 The settlement of Saskatchewan to 1914, TRSC, XX, 1, 63-88.

1766. **Ready, William**
       1948 *Political factors affecting the Manitoba school question, 1896-1916*, M. A. Thesis, University of Manitoba.
1767. **Regimbal, Albert**
       1945 Le français en Ontario-Sud, *Relations*, 58, 258-60.
1768. **Stanley, G. F. G.**
       1936 *The birth of Western Canada*, Longmans, Toronto, 475.
1769.   1954 French settlement west of Lake Superior, TRSC, XLVIII, 2, 107-115.
1770. **Tassé, J.**
       1878 *Les Canadiens de l'Ouest*, Co. d'Imp. Canadienne, Montréal, 2 v.
1771. **Tessier-Lavigne, Yves**
       1925 *Le bilinguisme dans l'Ouest canadien*, Arbour et Dupont, Montréal, 32.
1772. **Tremaudan, Auguste-Henri de**
       1918 *Le Sang français*, Libre-Parole, Winnipeg, 240.
1773. **Tremblay, Rodolphe**
       1951 *Timmins, métropole de l'or*, Collège du Sacré-Cœur, Sudbury, 48.
1774. **Vincent, Gaston**
       1954 Perspective d'Amour, VF, 8, 476-96.
1775. **Walter, Bernal-Ernest**
       1941 *A study of the reading, writing, oral and aural skills of French students in Alberta*, Thesis, University of Alberta.
1776. **Woods, David Scott**
       1926 *The two races in Manitoba*, M. A. Thesis, University of Manitoba.

c) *Metis*

1777. **Dugas, Georges**
       1905 *Histoire véridique des faits qui ont préparé le mouvement des métis à la Rivière Rouge en 1869*, Beauchemin, Montréal, 228.
1778. **Giraud, Marcel**
       1945 *Le Métis canadien*, Institut d'Ethnographie, Paris, 1296.
1779. **Frémont, Donatien**
       1948 Les métis de l'Ouest canadien, TRSC, XLIII, 1, 53-77.
1780.   1952 Henri Jackson et l'insurrection du Nord-Ouest, TRSC, XLVI, 19-49.
1781.   1953 *Les secrétaires de Riel*, Chantecler, Montréal, 205.
1782. **Groulx, Lionel**
       1944 *Louis Riel et les événements de la Rivière-Rouge en 1869-70*, Action Nationale, Montréal, 23.
1783. **Le Chevalier, Jules**
       1939-40 Les Oblats de Marie-Immaculée de la colonie de Saint-Laurent dans l'insurrection métisse de 1885, RUO, 1939, oct., 449-69 ; 1940, avril, 215-36 ; juillet, 354-80.
1784. **Morice, A.-G.**
       1908 *Dictionnaire historique des Canadiens et des Métis français de l'Ouest*, Garneau, Québec, 322.
1785.   1935 *A critical history of the Red River Insurrection*, Canadian Publishers, Winnipeg, 375.
1786. **Morton, Arthur S.**
       1939 The New Nation : the Métis, TRSC, XXXIII, 2, 137-46.
1787. **Prud'homme, L.-A.**
       1934 François Beaubien, patriarche des Métis français, TRSC, XXVIII, 1, 45-62.
1788. **Symington, D. F.**
       1953 Métis Rehabilitation, CGJ, 46, 4, 128-39.

A BIBLIOGRAPHICAL INTRODUCTION...

1789. **Tremaudan, A. H. de**
    1935 Histoire de la Nation métisse dans l'Ouest canadien, Lévesque, Montréal, 450.
1790. **Valentine, V. F.**
    1954 Some problems of the Métis of Northern Saskatchewan, CJPES, 20, 89-92.
1791. **Valentine, V. F. and Young, R. C.**
    1954 The situation of the Métis of Northern Saskatchewan in relation to his physical and social environment, CG, 4, 49-56.

d) *French Speaking groups in the United States*

1792. **Association Canado-américaine**
    1936 Les Franco Américains peints par eux-mêmes, Lévesque, Montréal, 284.
1793. **Barbe-Marbois, M.**
    1829 Histoire de la Louisiane, Didot, Paris, 476.
1794. **Baxter, J. P.**
    1894 The pioneers of New France in New England, Munsell, Albany, 450.
1795. **Bélisle, A.**
    1911 Histoire de la Presse franco-américaine, Opinion Public, Worcester, 434.
1796. **Benoit, J.**
    1935 L'âme franco-américaine, Lévesque, Montréal, 245.
1797. **Bernard, Antoine**
    1953 Histoire de la Louisiane, de ses origines à nos jours, Presses Universitaires Laval, Québec, 446.
1798. **Bourassa, Henri**
    1929 L'affaire de Providence et la crise religieuse en Nouvelle-Angleterre, Le Devoir, Montréal, 22.
1799. **Daigneault, E.-J.**
    1936 Le vrai mouvement Sentinelliste en Nouvelle-Angleterre, 1923-1929, et l'affaire du Rhodes Island, Ed. du Zodiaque, Montréal, 246.
1800. **Ditchy, Jay Karl**
    1932 Les Acadiens louisianais et leur parler, John Hopkins Press, Baltimore, 272.
1801. **Comité de la Survivance en Amérique**
    1937-56 Vie franco-américaine (Yearly report).
1802.   1950 La vie française en Amérique en 1950, La Survivance Française, Québec, 112.
1803.   1950 Centenaire franco-américain, 1849-1949, n. e., Québec, 643.
1804. **Dubé, Claudia, M.**
    1935 La Survivance française dans la Nouvelle-Angleterre, Thesis, McGill University.
1805. **Ducharme, J.**
    1943 The shadows of the trees, Harper, New York, 258.
1806. **Fabre-Surveyer, Edouard**
    1945 From Montreal to Michigan and Indiana, TRSC, XXXIX, 45-84.
1807. **Forget, Ulysse**
    1946 Les franco-américains et le "Melting Pot" et onomastique franco-américaine, n. e., n. p., 52.
1808. **Foley, Allen R.**
    1940 From French Canadian to Franco-American, Ph. D. Thesis, Harvard University.
1809. **Goulet, A.**
    1934 Une Nouvelle-France en Nouvelle-Angleterre, Duchemin, Paris, 158.
1810. **Hamon, E.**
    1891 Les Canadiens français de la Nouvelle-Angleterre, Hardy, Québec, 483.

A BIBLIOGRAPHICAL INTRODUCTION...

1811. **Hubert-Robert, Régine**
 1941 *L'histoire merveilleuse de la Louisiane française*, Ed. de la Maison Française, New York, 364.
1812. **Jalbert, Eugène-L.**
 1941 Ecoles franco-américaines du Rhodes Island, *Relations*, 12, 311-13.
1813. **Jehin de Prume, J.**
 n. d. *Les Canadiens français à New York*, Pigeon, Montréal, 70.
1814. **Lachapelle, J.-B.**
 1937 L'esprit français en Louisiane, *Le Devoir*, 28, 148, 9.
1815. **Laflamme, J.-L.-K.**
 1901-2 Les Canadiens aux Etats-Unis, *La Revue Canadienne*, 1901, 1, 485-95 ; 2, 72, 153, 232, 311, 385, 471 ; 1902, 1, 57, 129, 209 ; 2, 137, 400.
1816. **Lauvrière, Emile**
 1940 *Histoire de la Louisiane française, 1673-1939*, Louisiana State University Press, 445.
1817. **Léger, Card. Emile**
 1954 Le fait français en Amérique, *Documentation Catholique*, 36, 51, 1180, 1070-76.
1818. **Locke, William N.**
 1946 The French Colony at Brunswick, Maine, AdF, 1, 97-111.
1819. **Magnan, D.-M.-A.**
 1913 *Histoire de la Race française aux Etats-Unis*, Amat, Paris, 396.
1820. **Marie-Carmel, Sr**
 1945 *La littérature française de la Nouvelle-Angleterre*, Ph. D. Thesis, Laval University.
1821. **Morin, Victor**
 1930 Une société secrète de patriotes canadiens aux Etats-Unis, TRSC, XXIV, 1, 45-58.
1822. **Mulvey, M. D.**
 1936 *French Canadian missionaries in the present United States, 1604-1791*, Catholic University of America Press, Washington, 158.
1823. **Parenton, V. J.**
 1948 *The rural French-speaking People of Quebec and south Louisiana, a comparison*, Ph. D. Thesis, Harvard University.
1824. **Pellerin, Eveline**
 1937 *La langue française en Louisiane*, M. A. Thesis, McGill University.
1825. **Plante, Albert**
 1954 Problème franco-américain, *Relations*, 168, 331-4.
1826. **Pousland, Edouard**
 1933 *Etude sémantique de l'anglicisme dans le parler franco-américain de Salem*, Droz, Paris, 309.
1827. **Prior, G. T.**
 1932 *The French Canadians in New England*, M. A. Thesis, Brown University.
1828. **Read, William Alexander**
 1931 *Louisiana-French*, Louisiana State University Press, Bâton-Rouge, 253.
1829. **Revue trimestrielle canadienne**
 1921 *L'Evolution de la Race française en Amérique*, Beauchemin, Montréal, 277.
1830. **Rimbert, Sylvie**
 1954 L'Immigration franco-canadienne au Massachusetts, RCG, 8, 3-4, 75-85.
1831. **Robert, Adolphe**
 1946 *Mémorial des actes de l'Association canado-américaine*, L'Avenir national, Manchester, 483.
1832. **Robert, Adolphe**
 1952 *Inventaire franco-américain, 1952*, n. e., n. p., 24.

A BIBLIOGRAPHICAL INTRODUCTION...

1833. **Saint-Pierre, Arthur**
    1942   Quelques aspects de la démographie franco-américaine, *L'Action Universitaire*, 9, 3, 7-10.
1834. **Saint-Pierre, T.**
    1895   *Histoire des Canadiens de Michigan et du Comté d'Essex*, Imp. de la Gazette, Montréal, 348.
1835. **Sansouci, Lucien et Thérèse**
    1946   *Guide officiel franco-américain*, R. I., Woonsocket, 1278.
1836. **Thierrault, Mary Carmel**
    1946   *La littérature française de Nouvelle-Angleterre*, Fides, Montréal, 325.
1837. **Truesdell, Léon, E.**
    1943   *The Canadian born in the United States*, Yale University Press, New Haven, 260.
1838. **Twaithes, R. G.**
    1908   *Wisconsin, the americanization of a French settlement*, Houghton Miffin and Co., New York, 466.
1839. **Verrette, Adrien**
    1949   *Le Comité de la survivance française en Amérique*, OT, Montréal, 16.
1840. **Wilson, B.**
    1921   *L'Evolution de la race française en Amérique*, Beauchemin, Montréal, 277.
1841. **Wright, C. D.**
    1882   *The Canadian French in New England*, Rand, Avery and Co., Boston, 92.

5. Social Changes and Social Problems

a) *Migration to the United States*

1842. **Anonymous**
    1849 *Rapport du Comité spécial de l'Assemblée Législative de l'émigration du Bas-Canada vers les Etats-Unis*, Perrault, Montréal, 96.
1843. **Bilodeau, Georges-Marie**
    1926 *Pour rester au pays, étude sur l'émigration des Canadiens français aux Etats-Unis*, L'Action Sociale, Québec, 165.
1844. **Brink, Reginald M.**
    1925 *A study of the population movements between the United States and Canada*, M. A. Thesis, University of British Columbia.
1845. **Durand, Louis-D.**
    1924 L'émigration aux Etats-Unis, AF, 3, 130-40 ; 4, 194-211.
1846. **Dugré, Alexandre**
    1946 Désertions ou Victoires, *Relations*, 67, 196-8.
1847. **Hamilton, Andrew W.**
    1930 *Migration of population between Canada and the United States*, M. A. Thesis, McGill University.
1848. **Robitaille, Adrien**
    1947 L'émigration canadienne aux Etats-Unis, *Relations*, 75, 86-7.
1849. **Schwab, Jean G.**
    1936 *Migration between Canada and the United States*, M. A. Thesis, McGill University.
1850. **Tessier-Lavigne, Yves**
    1924 Perte du capital humain, AF, 11, 2, 66-76.
1851. **Rimbert, Sylvie**
    1954 L'immigration franco-canadienne au Massachusetts, RCG, 8, 3-4, 75-85.
1852. **Williard, Eugene Wallace**
    1924 *The migration of people from Canada to the United States*, M. A. Thesis, McGill University.

b) *Rural-Urban Migration and Urbanization*

1853. **Blais, Roger**
    1954 L'exode rural, CV, XIX, 5-15.
1854. **Blanchet, Jean**
    1947 L'exode rural et l'état de crise, AN, oct., 93-111.
1855. **Bouvier, Emile**
    1945 Déplacement de notre population, *Relations*, 5, 49, 10-12.
1856. **Ferencz, Agnes**
    1945 *The impact of urbanization on French Canadian medical attitudes*, M. A. Thesis, McGill University.
1857. **Goldberg, Simon**
    1940 *The French Canadians and the industrialization of Quebec*, M. A. Thesis, McGill University.
1858. **Hamelin, L.-E.**
    1955 Emigration rurale à l'échelon paroissial, CG, 5, 53-61.

1859. **Lapointe, J.-Alphonse**
    1951 Y a-t-il encore un exode rural ?, AN, sept., 22-31.
1860. **Lieff, Pearl J.**
    1940 *The urbanization of the French Canadian parish*, M. A. Thesis, McGill University.
1861. **Matteau, Arthur**
    1948 *L'émigration des jeunes à Saint-Sylvère, 1925-1945*, Thesis, University of Montreal.
1862. **Semaines Sociales du Canada**
    1929 *La Cité*, ESP, Montréal, 320.
1863. **Tessier-Lavigne, Yves**
    1924 L'Emigration vers les villes, AF, 11, 2, 66-86.

c) *Social Stratification*

1864. **Allen, Patrick**
    1951 Tendances occupationnelles dans les provinces canadiennes, 1901-1941, AE, jan., 749-78.
1865. **Baby, L.-F.-G.**
    1899 *L'exode des classes dirigeantes lors de la cession du Canada*, Montréal, 45.
1866. **Beique, F. L. Mme**
    1939 *Quatre-vingts ans de souvenirs*, Valiquette, Montréal, 290.
1867. **Biographical Society of Canada**
    1923-4 *Prominent people of the Province of Quebec*, Montréal, 3 v.
1868. **Boisseau, Fernand**
    1947 Les classes moyennes dans un monde troublé, *Relations*, 81, 260-62.
1869. **Bouchette, Errol**
    1912 Les débuts d'une industrie et notre classe bourgeoise, TRSC, VI, 1, 143-57.
1870. **Brazeau, J.**
    1951 *The French Canadian doctor in Montreal*, M. A. Thesis, McGill University.
1871. **Brunet, Michel**
    1955 La conquête anglaise et la déchéance de la bourgeoisie canadienne, *Amérique Française*, XIII, 2, 19-84.
1872. **Campeau, Charles-Edouard**
    1943 Nos classes moyennes à Montréal, *Relations*, 27, 67-69.
1873. **Couillard-Després, A.**
    1916 *La noblesse de France et du Canada*, Coll. Laurentienne, Montréal, 73.
1874. **Daniel, F.**
    1867 *Histoire des grandes familles françaises du Canada*, Senécal, Montréal, 2 v.
1875. **Falardeau, Jean-Charles**
    1942 La place des professions libérales dans le Québec, *Revue Dominicaine*, XLVIII, 274-81.
1876.   1945 Stratifications sociales de notre milieu, TRSC, 39, 1, 65-72.
1877.   1945 Stratifications sociales, *Revue Dominicaine*, mars, 272-79.
1878.   1951 Réflexions sur nos classes sociales, *Nouvelle Revue Canadienne*, 3, 1-9.
1879. **Fauteux, Aegidius**
    1940 *Les Chevaliers de Saint-Louis au Canada*, Ed. des Dix, Montréal, 252.
1880. **Fortin, J.-A.**
    1948 *Biographies canadiennes-françaises*, Publications Provinciales, Montréal, 544.
1881. **Groulx, Lionel**
    1931 *La déchéance incessante de notre classe moyenne*, Imp. Populaire, Montréal, 16.
1882. **J. I. C.**
    1939 *L'avenir de notre bourgeoisie*, Valiquette, Montréal, 138.

A BIBLIOGRAPHICAL INTRODUCTION...

1883. **Larkin, William**
1950   Tendances occupationnelles au Canada, 1891-1941, AE, oct., 448-509.
1884. **Lecompte, Edouard**
1923   *Sir Joseph Dubuc, 1840-1914*, Imp. du Messager, Montréal, 270.
1885. **Les journalistes associés**
1950   *Les biographies françaises*, n. e., Montréal, 913.
1886. **Minville, Esdras**
1939   La bourgeoisie et l'économique, AE, mars, 401-25.
1887. **Morin, Victor**
1941   *Seigneurs et Censitaires, Castes disparues*, Ed. des Dix, Montréal, 94.
1888. **Munro, W. M.**
1920   *The seigneurs of old Canada*, Glasgow, Brook and Co., Toronto, 155.
1889. **Ouellier, Fernand**
1955   Toussaint Pothier et le problème des classes sociales, *Bull. des Recherches Historiques*, 61, 4, 147-161.
1890. **Ouimet, Raphaël**
1921-48   *Biographies canadiennes*, Montréal, 15 v.
1891. **Plante, Albert**
1955   Le fonctionnaire, un personnage, *Relations*, 15, 284-86.
1892. **Roy, Pierre-Georges**
1933   *Fils de Québec*, n. e., Québec, 4 v.
1893. **Rumilly, Robert**
1934   *Chefs de file*, Ed. du Zodiaque, Montréal, 263.
1894. **Ryan, Claude**
1950   *Les classes moyennes au Canada français*, Action Nationale, Montréal, 61.
1895. **Soc. Nouvelle de Publicité**
1953   *Vedettes, le fait français au Canada*, Soc. Nouvelle de Publicité, Montréal, 714.
1896. **Sulte, Benjamin**
1914   La noblesse au Canada avant 1914, TRSC, VIII, 1, 103-36.

d) *The Status of Women*

1897. **Aikman, Mary E.**
1937   *The Nature of women's Employment with special Reference to Montreal*, M. A. Thesis, McGill University.
1898. **Anjou, Marie-Joseph d'**
1954   Préambule à une éducation féminine, *Collège et Famille*, 11, 201-11.
1899. **Béchard-Deslandes, Monique**
1953   Activités, tâches et professions féminines, CeF, 10, 193-201.
1900. **Bergeron, Rita**
1955   Expériences d'une ouvrière du vêtement, *Relations*, 15, 257-9.
1901. **Boucher, Monique**
1946   *Le travail féminin dans la Province de Québec*, Thesis, Laval University.
1902. **Bouvier, Emile et Angers, L.-A.**
1942   *Le travail féminin à l'usine et l'effort de guerre*, Le Devoir, Montréal, 53.
1903. **Bourassa, Henri**
1925   *Femmes-Hommes ou Hommes et Femmes*, Le Devoir, Montréal, 80.
1904. **Chartier, Roger**
1952   *Problèmes du travail féminin*, Centre de Culture Populaire de Laval, Québec, 64.
1905.   1953   La rémunération du travail féminin, RI, 8, 309-27.
1906. **Cleverdon, Catherine L.**
1950   *The woman suffrage movement in Canada*, University of Toronto Press, Toronto, 324.

A BIBLIOGRAPHICAL INTRODUCTION...

1907. **Deylau, Jean**
    1907 Le vrai féminisme, *Revue Canadienne*, 52, 561.
1908. **Daveluy, Marie-Claude**
    1934 L'Education nationale et le couvent, AN, 4, 2.
1909. **Dorion, C.-E. and others**
    1930 *Commission des Droits civils de la femme*, n. e., Québec, 3 v.
1910. **Duguay, Martine-Hébert**
    1936 La femme et l'étude du Droit, *L'Action Universitaire*, jan., 9.
1911. **Ecole Sociale Populaire**
    1942 *Le travail féminin et la guerre*, ESP, no 342, Montréal, 32.
1912. **Fadette**
    1938 L'influence des femmes dans le monde, *Le Devoir*, 29, 18, 24 jan.
1913. **Fouché-Delbosc, I.**
    1940 Women of New France, CHR, XXI, 2, 132-49.
1914. **Frégault, Guy**
    1943 Les mères de la Nouvelle-France, *Programme de la Société Saint-Jean-Baptiste de Montréal*, 24 juin 1943, 21-25.
1915. **Gérin-Lajoie, Sr**
    1932 *Le retour de la mère au foyer*, ESP, Montréal, 30.
1916. **Laplante, Germaine**
    1936 La femme ordinaire et la politique, CF, jan.
1917. **Leblanc, Eveline**
    1948 *La femme au foyer*, Cahiers de l'Ecole des Sciences Sociales, Québec, 5, 9, 28.
1918. **Ligue des droits de la femme**
    1946 Le Code civil et la femme mariée dans la Province de Québec, *Le Devoir*, 28-29 jan. 1948.
1919. **Marie-du-Rédempteur, Sr**
    1927 *Femme canadienne-française*, Thesis, University of Ottawa.
1920.   1935 *La femme canadienne-française*, OT, no 121, Montréal, 16.
1921. **Métivier, Jeanne**
    1935 La femme dans le journalisme, *L'Action Universitaire*, mai, 9.
1922. **Loranger, Louis-J.**
    1899 *De l'incapacité légale de la femme mariée*, Senécal, Montréal, 138.
1923. **Paquet, Mgr**
    1928 L'influence maternelle, CF, mars, 451-521.
1924. **Perrault, Antonio**
    1952 Condition juridique de la femme mariée, *Relations*, 135, 58-61.
1925.   1955 La femme mariée, RB, 15, 37-39.
1926. **Poulin, Gonzalve**
    1944 Orientation nouvelle de la femme canadienne, *Culture*, V, 403-14.
1927. **Price, Enid Margaret**
    1919 *The changes in the industrial occupation of women in the environment of Montreal during the period of the war 1914-18*, Canadian Reconstruction Association, Montreal, 86.
1928. **Riddel, William Renwick**
    1928 Women Franchise in Quebec, a Century ago, TRSC, XXII, 2, 85-100.
1929. **Saint-Pierre, Arthur**
    1917 Le travail des femmes au Canada, *La Bonne Parole*, juin, 8-12.
1930. **Tessier, Albert**
    1946 *Canadiennes*, Fides, Montréal, 160.
1931. **Trudel, Gérard**
    1948 Capacité de la femme mariée, *The Canadian Bar Review*, 26, 1, 147-57.

e) *Relationship with other Ethnic Groups*
I) *French-English Relationships*

1932. **Acal, Alice**
   1949 *A Study of mutual Attitudes of English (speaking) Canadian and French (speaking) Canadian children*, M. A. Thesis, University of Toronto.
1933. **Bailey, A. G.**
   1947 On the nature of the distinction between the French and English in Canada, CHAR, 63-72.
1934. **Ballantyne, Murray**
   1942 Les milieux anglophones du Canada, *Relations*, 20, 199-202.
1935. **Banks, Margaret Amelia**
   1950 *Toronto opinion of French Canada during the Laurier Regime, 1896-1911*, M. A. Thesis, University of Toronto.
1936. **Bell, Aubrey F.**
   1945 Deux conceptions de la vie, *Relations*, 51, 74-6.
1937. **Bourassa, Henri**
   1914 *French and English, frictions and misunderstandings*, Le Devoir, Montréal, 23.
1938. **Cadieux, Marcel et Tremblay, Paul**
   1941 Le dualisme canadien, RTC, XXVII, 63-75.
1939. **Canadian Institute of International Affairs**
   1938 *Relations between English and French Canadians*, Canadian papers, series, 14-19.
1940. **Chapais, Thomas**
   1916 La Province de Québec et la minorité anglaise, *La Nouvelle France*, 4, 145-64.
1941. **Charpentier, Fulgence**
   1924 L'Anglomanie, AF, 12, 4, 194-209.
1942. **Clark, James B. M.**
   1927 French and English in the Province of Quebec, *Nineteenth Century*, 327-336.
1943. **Davidson, Mary**
   1933 *The social Adjustment of British immigrant Families in Verdun and Pointe-Saint-Charles*, M. A. Thesis, McGill University.
1944. **Gordon, R. S.**
   1944 Equality for French Canadians is essential for Canadian Unity, *Today*, 1, 6-7, 28-30.
1945. **Groulx, Lionel**
   1943 *Pourquoi sommes-nous divisés ?*, Ed. de l'Action Nationale, Montréal, 42. (also in english)
1946. **Falardeau, Jean-Charles**
   1949 Mariage de raison, *Food for Thought*, X, 34-37.
1947. **Gervais, Raphaël**
   1906 A propos d'un livre perfide, André Siegfried « Le Canada, les deux races », *La Nouvelle France*, 340-53 ; 436-47 ; 485-99.
1948. **Holmes, C. E. A.**
   1919 *Meeting the French Canadians Half-Way*, Canadian Advertising Agency, Montreal, 24.
1949. **Howes, Helen C.**
   1942 *Inside Quebec*, Fellowship for Christian Order, Toronto.
1950. **Hughes, Everett C.**
   1933 The French-English margin in Canada, AJS, 39, 1, 1-11.
1951. 1938 Position and status in a Quebec industrial town, ASR, III, 5, 709-17.
1952. 1943 *French Canada in Transition*, University of Chicago Press, Chicago, 227.
1953. 1948 The study of Ethnic relations, *Dalhousie Review*, XXVII, 477-82.

A BIBLIOGRAPHICAL INTRODUCTION...

1954. **Hughes, E. C. and McDonald, M. L.**
 1941 French and English in the economic structure of Montreal, CJEPS, VII, 493-505.
1955. **Hunter, Jean I.**
 1939 *The French invasion of the Eastern Townships*, M. A. Thesis, McGill University.
1956. **Jamieson, S.**
 1935 *French and English in the institutional structure in the Province of Quebec*, M. A. Thesis, McGill University.
1957. **Lanctot, Gustave**
 1949 Influences réciproques des deux cultures, TRSC, XLIII, 1, 59-67.
1958. **Laurendeau, André**
 n. d. *Nos écoles enseignent-elles la haine des Anglais ?*, Action Nationale, Montréal, 22.
1959. **Lavère, Georges-J.**
 1954 Chronique, *Culture*, 15, 1, 83-92.
1960. **Lorrain, Léon**
 1952 L'incompatibilité de génie du français et de l'anglais, TRSC, XLVI, 1, 60-69.
1961. **Lortie, Monique**
 1952 Les relations biculturelles au Canada, CESH, 1, 11-52.
1962. **Lower, A. R. M.**
 1943 Two ways of life. The primary antithesis of Canadian History, CHAR, 5-17.
1963. **Lucas, Rex**
 1950 *Occupational Orientation of High School entrants in a biethnic Railroad town*, M. A. Thesis, McGill University.
1964. **Maheux, Arthur**
 1943 *Pourquoi sommes-nous divisés ?*, Radio-Canada, Montréal, 213.
1965. 1944 *What keeps us apart*, n. e., Quebec, 176.
1966. 1944 *Problems of Canadian unity*, n. e., Quebec, 186.
1967. 1954 Avons-nous changé ?, *Queen's Quarterly*, 60, 532-37.
1968. **Moore, William Henry**
 1918 *The Clash*, Dent, Toronto, 333.
1969. **Morley, Percival F.**
 1919 *Bridging the Chasm*, Dent, Toronto, 182.
1970. **Percival, W. P.**
 1954 The Province of Quebec, Where French and English meet, *English speaking World*, 36, 3, 21-23.
1971. **Pierce, Lorne**
 1929 *Towards the "Bonne Entente"* Ryerson, Toronto, 43.
1972. **Prat, Henri**
 1930 La pensée franco-britannique, RTC, 50-62.
1973. **Racine, Loris**
 1955 La situation des Canadiens français à l'O.N.F., AN, 44, 411-19.
1974. **Rennie, Douglas L. C.**
 1953 *The ethnic division of labour in Montreal*, M. A. Thesis, McGill University.
1975. **Reynolds, Lloyds G.**
 1933 *The occupational adjustment of the British immigrant in Montreal*, M. A. Thesis, McGill University.
1976. **Ross, Eileen D.**
 1941 *The French and English social Elites in Montreal*, M. A. Thesis, University of Chicago.
1977. 1942 The cultural effects of population changes in the Eastern Townships, CJPES, IX, 447-60.

A BIBLIOGRAPHICAL INTRODUCTION...

1978. 1950 *Ethnic Relations and social Structures, a Story of the invasion of French speaking Canadians into an English Canadian district*, Ph. D. Thesis, University of Chicago.
1979. 1953 Ethnic group contacts and status dilemma, *Phylon*, 15, 3, 267-75.
1980. 1954 French and English Canadians contacts and institutional changes, CJEPS, 20, 3, 281-95.
1981. **Rousse, J.-B.**
       1945 Unity in Diversity, *Educational Review*, LIX, 12-15.
1982. **Roy, Ferdinand**
       1917 *L'appel aux armes et la réponse canadienne-française, étude sur le conflit des races*, Garneau, Quebec, 45.
1983. **Roy, W. J.**
       1935 *The French-English division of labour in the Province of Quebec*, M. A. Thesis, McGill University.
1984. **Sanders, Wilfrid**
       1943 *Jack and Jacques*, Ryerson, Toronto, 46.
1985. **Sellar, Robert**
       1910 *The tragedy of Quebec*, Ontario Press, Toronto, 258.
1986. **Siegfried, André**
       1906 *Le Canada : les deux races, problèmes politiques contemporains*, Paris, 415.
1987. 1907 *The race question in Canada*, Appleton, New York, 343.
1987-a. **Steward, J. and Blackburn, J.**
       1956 Tensions between English-speaking and French-speaking Canadians, CESH, 3, 145-68.

II) *Relationship with other Ethnic Groups*

1988. **Anonymous**
       1951 *Rapport des travaux de la conférence nationale sur le problème des immigrants*, Action Catholique, Montréal, 75.
1989. **Angers, François-Albert**
       1954 Le Canada français et l'immigration, AN, 43, 423-440.
1990. **Audet, Lucille**
       1950 *Chinatown*, Ed. Mission Chinoise, Montréal, 63.
1991. **Beaudin, Dominique**
       1953 La vérité est amplement suffisante, 41, 509-18.
1992. **Benoist, Emile**
       1940 Un aperçu de nos colonies étrangères, *Le Devoir*, 31, 46, 24 fév., 45-47.
1993. **Boyes, F. C. and others**
       1948 *Living together in Canada, Problems in democratic Citizenship*, Dent, Toronto, 201.
1994. **Bruchési, Mgr Paul**
       1915 Le problème des races au Canada, TRSC, IX, 1, 5-12.
1995. **Casgrain, Philippe**
       1937 L'immigration au Canada, CF, 25, 2, 131-37.
1996. **Cormier, D.**
       1951 *Psychologie de groupe de la population de Montréal, touchant le problème de l'immigration*, Thesis, University of Montreal.
1997. **Couture, Clovis**
       1956 L'intégration des immigrants au Canada français, BESC, 8, 1, 14-16.
1998. **D'Appolonia, Luigi**
       1950 Tels sont les Italo canadiens, *Relations*, 110, 36-40.
1999. 1955 *Tolérance raciale et religieuse*, ISP, no 479, Montréal, 32.

2000. **Dubreuil, Guy**
    1951 *Psychologie de groupe de la population de Montréal touchant le problème de l'immigration*, Thesis, University of Montreal.
2001.   1953 L'immigration et les groupes canadiens, CESH, 2, 95-148.
2002. **Ehman, Daniel**
    1949 Les Catholiques allemands du Canada, Relations, 100, 91-93.
2003. **Falardeau, Jean-Charles**
    1953 Problèmes et méthodes d'enquêtes sur les immigrants et les nationaux canadiens, SS, 3, 213-231.
2004. **Forest, Ceslas**
    1935 *La question juive au Canada*, Presse Dominicaine, Montréal, 52.
2004a. **Fugère, Jean-Paul**
    1945 Le fait néo-canadien dans la vie montréalaise et dans la vie canadienne, AN, XXV, 4, 354-68 ; 5, 445-58.
2005. **Gauthier, René**
    1951 *Les Néo-canadiens*, OT, no 377, Montréal, 15.
2006. **Godbout, Benoît**
    1938 A-t-on raison d'être antisémite ?, Jeunesse, 4, 3, 3-4.
2007. **Grandbois, J.-M.**
    1953 *Etude sur la réceptivité des étudiants canadiens-français à l'égard des étudiants émigrés*, M. A. Thesis, University of Montreal.
2008. **Guérin, Wilfrid**
    1931 A propos de la question scolaire juive, Le Devoir, 13 et 18 mars 1931.
2009. **Jones, Frank E.**
    1950 *Work organization in the structural steel industry*, M. A. Thesis, McGill University.
2010. **Kisilewski, V. J.**
    1948 L'immigration allemande au Canada, Relations, 96, 353-55.
2011. **Klock, Pierre**
    1953 Dangers de l'immigration au Canada, Relations, 156, 316-8.
2012. **Krakowski, François**
    1955 Embauchage des émigrants dans les villes, BESC, 7, 1, 7-11.
2012-a. **Kulbis, Stanislas**
    1950 Les Lithuaniens au Canada, Relations, 116, 228-30.
2013. **Laporte, Pierre**
    1954 Panorama de l'immigration, la leçon et les faits, AN, 43, 395-408.
2014. **Laundry, Lydia**
    1953 *Recherches sur la réceptivité d'un groupe d'étudiantes canadiennes-françaises envers les émigrés*, Thesis, University of Montreal.
2015. **Léger, Jean-Marc**
    1954 Le devoir du Québec envers l'immigrant, AN, 43, 410-22.
2016.   1954 Notre devoir envers l'immigrant, AN, 43, 277-84.
2017.   1956 *Le Canada français face à l'immigration*, ISP, no 482, Montréal, 32.
2018. **Lemieux, Edmond**
    1953 La force des idées nationalistes au Canada français, AN, 41, 466-70.
2019. **Mailhiot, Bernard**
    1956 La psychologie des relations inter-ethniques à Montréal, CESH, 3, 7-24.
2020. **Malone, Anne G.**
    1952 *The group Opinions and Attitudes of the Quebec population concerning Immigration*, Thesis, University of Montreal.
2021. **Sack, Benjamin**
    1945 *History of the Jews in Canada*, Canadian Jewish Congress, Montreal, 285.
2022. **Séguin, Alexandre**
    1953 L'immigration vue par un immigrant, AN, 42, 144-52.

A BIBLIOGRAPHICAL INTRODUCTION...

2023. **Semaines Sociales du Canada**
    1954   *Etablissement rural et immigration*, ISP, Montréal, 260.
2024. **Vanier, Anatole**
    1933   Les Juifs au Canada, AF, 2, 1, 5-24.

f) *Social Problems*

2025. **Archambault. J.-P.**
    1947   *Le logement populaire, problème capital*, ESP, no 397, Montréal, 32.
2026. **Beaupré, Henri**
    1953-4   La délinquance juvénile à Québec, *Culture*, 14, 385-405 ; 15, 46-57 ; 150-163.
2027. **Blais, Hervé**
    1942   *Les tendances eugénistes au Canada*, L'Institut Familial, Montréal, 199.
2028. **Bourassa, Henri**
    1921   *Une mauvaise loi, l'assistance publique*, Le Devoir, Montréal, 40.
2029. **Caron, François**
    1954   Enquête sur la moralité à Montréal, *La Presse*, 8 oct. 1954.
2030. **Comité d'Enquête sur l'hygiène à Montréal**
    1928   *Enquête sur les activités en hygiène publique*, Metropolitan Life Insurance Co., Montréal, 156.
2031. **Commission Royale**
    1909-10   *Rapport de la Commission Royale de la Tuberculose*, Province de Québec, 157.
2032. **Charbonneau, Mgr Joseph**
    1948   *Le problème de l'habitation*, ESP, no 410, 32.
2033. **Daveluy, Marie-Claire**
    1933   *L'Orphelinat Catholique de Montréal*, Lévesque, Montréal, 344.
2034. **David, Anathase**
    1934   *Deux questions sociales*, n. e., Québec, 20.
2035. **Deschamps, Paul**
    1947   L'habitation à Montréal, AE, 23, 3, 446-72.
2036. **Deschamps, Jean**
    1949   La politique du logement à Québec, AN, mars, 149-56.
2037. **Dufault, Paul**
    1943   Mortalité et tuberculose dans le Québec, *Relations*, 3, 31, 176-79.
2038. **Fortin, Berthe**
    1946   *Le problème du logement à Montréal*, Thesis, University of Montreal.
2039. **Frères de la Charité**
    1948   *La délinquance vue par le Mont Saint-Antoine*, Granger, Montréal, 176.
2040. **Gingras, Paul-Emile**
    1954   Une politique de sobriété, *Relations*, 14, 103-5.
2041. **Groulx, Adélard**
    1943   *La mortalité maternelle et la mortalité infantile à Montréal*, Union médicale du Canada, Montréal, 4.
2042.   1945   Certains problèmes de santé publique et leur solution, Camsi Journal, 4, 1.
2043.   1948   *Le service de Santé de la Ville de Montréal*, n. e., Montréal, 36.
2044. **Laliberté, Jacques**
    1948   Problème de l'inadaptation de l'enfance à Québec, Cahiers de l'Ecole des Sciences Sociales, Québec, 5, 7, 25.
2045. **Laplante, Rodolphe**
    1949   Le logement dans le Québec, AN, juin, 462-69.
2046. **Lecavalier, Marc**
    1955   La délinquance juvénile à Montréal, *Relations*, 178, 262-5.

2047. **Lefèvre, Fernand**
       1954 La vie à la prison de Montréal au XIXe siècle, RHAF, 7, 524-37.
2048. **Lemieux, Gérard**
       1946 Jeunesse du Québec, J.E.C., Montréal, 48.
2049. 1952 Vers une sécurité plus démocratique, AE, avril, 90-104.
2049-a. **Mailloux, Noël**
       1956 Le problème de la délinquance au Canada, CESH, 3, 193-206.
2050. **Massicotte, Valière**
       1944 La délinquance juvénile et la guerre, OT, no 298, Montréal, 16.
2051. **Mathieu, Lucille**
       1952 *Conditions de vie de la femme âgée indigente*, Thesis, University of Montreal.
2052. **Minville, Esdras**
       1938 Quelques aspects du problème social dans la Province de Québec, AE, octobre, 401-24.
2053. 1940 Notre problème social, AE, juin, 201-29.
2054. **Nadeau, Jean-Marie**
       1951 L'état actuel de la question sociale au Canada français, AN, mars, 174-88.
2055. **Oban, Maurice**
       1953 *Le rôle de l'Eglise dans les problèmes sociaux*, ISP, no 458, Montréal, 32.
2056. **Parisien, Roch**
       1952 *Les vieillards de Montréal vivant sous l'assistance publique*, Thesis, University of Montreal.
2057. **Patenaude, J.-Z.-Léon**
       1953 Le comité de moralité publique, *Relations*, 29, 246-8.
2058. **Plante, Pacifique**
       1950 *Montréal sous le Régime de la Pègre*, Ed. de l'Action Nationale, Montréal, 96.
2059. **Richard, d'A. et Poulin, Gonzalve**
       1944 Le problème du logement, *Ensemble*, 5, 6, 4-5 and 34.
2060. **Saint-Pierre, Arthur**
       1915 Un problème ardu : l'habitation ouvrière saine et à bon marché, *Le Petit Canadien*, sept., 137-40.
2061. 1925 *Le problème social*, Ed. de la Bibliothèque Canadienne, Montréal, 203.
2062. 1931 Le problème de la misère, *La Santé*, jan., 12, 17.
2063. 1947 La protection de l'enfance dans la Province de Québec, RTC, 130, 1-19.
2064. 1950 *Le problème actuel du logement*, ISP, no 438, Montréal, 32.
2065. 1955 La sécurité sociale, AE, juillet, 195-217.

g) *Social Work and Social Legislation*

2066. **Anonymous**
       1934 *Histoire de l'Hôtel-Dieu de Saint-Vallier-de-Chicoutimi*, Imp. du Progrès du Saguenay, Chicoutimi, 421.
2067. 1949 Le service social et le problème du logement, *Relations*, 98, 48-50.
2068. **Angers, F.-A.-A.**
       1941 Secours direct, AE, jan., 274-79.
2069. 1944 Un nouveau pas dans la législation sociale, AE, fév., 368-78.
2070. 1944 Assurance-santé et sécurité sociale, AE, avril, 67-83.
2071. 1945 Les allocations familiales fédérales de 1944, AE, juin, 228-62.
2072. **Barré-Dufresne, Monique**
       1948 *Recherches sur la nature et les conditions d'exercice du service social dans la Province de Québec*, Thesis, University of Montreal.

A BIBLIOGRAPHICAL INTRODUCTION...

2073. **Beaudry, Joseph**
    1944   *Civisme et sociologie appliqués par questions et réponses*, Fides, Montréal, 122.
2074. **Beaupré, Louis**
    1953   La famille, notre centre d'intérêt, BESC, 5, 2, 1-6 ; 3, 3-6.
2075. **Bilodeau, Joseph**
    1956   Assistance publique au Québec, BESC, 8, 1, 3-13.
2076. **Boucher, J.-Emile**
    1948   Les Clubs Richelieu, *Relations*, 96, 366-7.
2077. **Bourgeois, Charles-E.**
    1946   *L'enfance abandonnée dans la Province de Québec*, Thesis, University of Ottawa.
2078.   1946   *L'enfance sans soutien*, Le Centre familial, Montréal, 256.
2079.   1952   *Le service social diocésain*, n. e., Trois-Rivières, 29.
2080. **Bouvier, Emile**
    1940   *Le Samaritanisme moderne au service social*, ESP, no 317, Montréal, 21.
2081. **Bowers, Swithun**
    1955   Pourquoi faut-il des œuvres catholiques en service social ?, BESC, 7, 2, 4-11.
2082. **Cadieux, Joseph-Michel**
    1937   Les sourds-muets, *Messager du Sacré-Cœur*, août, 407-15.
2083. **Cantin, Léo-G.**
    1955   La Fédération des Oeuvres du Diocèse de Québec, SS, 5, 105-7.
2084. **Charland, Raymond**
    1941   Les œuvres de bienfaisance neutres, *Revue Dominicaine*, 47, 313-16.
2085. **Cloutier, Jeanne**
    1955   La préparation des praticiens. Formation dans les œuvres. Une expérience du service social aux familles de Montréal, SS, 5, 25-34.
2086. **Conseil des Œuvres**
    1953   *Répertoire des Oeuvres sociales de Montréal*, Commission Diocésaine des Oeuvres de Charité et de Service social, Montréal, 312.
2087. **Davis, R.-E.-G.**
    1956   L'œuvre inachevée du Bien-Etre social au Canada, *Revue Dominicaine*, LXII, 1, 14-25.
2088. **Denault, Hayda**
    1945   *Les services sociaux à Québec*, Thesis, University of Montreal.
2089.   1952   Service social familial et institutions, SS, 2, 162-70.
2090.   1954   Avant le conseil central des œuvres, SS, 5, 67-78.
2091.   1955   Problèmes pratiques des écoles de service social, SS, 5, 35-42.
2091-a. **Desmarais, Lucien**
    1942   *Le Service social*, OT, no 281, Montréal, 8.
2092. **Dion, Gérard**
    1943   *L'œuvre des terrains de jeu de Québec*, Ed. du Cap Diamant, Québec, 122.
2093. **Gérin-Lajoie, Marie**
    1944   La protection des jeunes filles à Montréal, *Relations*, 4, 46, 268-9.
2094. **Germain, V.**
    1943   Relations du service d'adoption avec la fille-mère qui abandonne son enfant, *Semaine Religieuse de Québec*, 65, 779-582 ; 595-7.
2095. **Gingras, Gustave**
    1953   Allons-nous instituer la réhabilitation ?, SS, 3, 8-12.
2096. **Guillemette, A.-M.**
    1955   La formation professionnelle universitaire en service social, SS, 5, 4-7.
2097. **Julien, J.-A.**
    1936   *La Société Saint-Vincent-de-Paul à Montréal*, OT, 158, Montréal, 16.
2098. **Lebel, Léon**
    1927   *Les allocations familiales*, ESP, no 159-60, Montréal, 64.

2099. **Leclerc, Pierre**
  1953   Rôle et importance de la récréation dans le cadre familial et paroissial, SS, 3, 77-82.
2100.   1954   Rôle préventif du travailleur social dans la communauté paroissiale, SS, 4, 77-79.
2101. **Lemieux, Gérard**
  1953   Une association des familles, Le Devoir, 44, 7 février, 4.
2102. **Levesque, Georges-Henri**
  1944   Service social et charité, Cahiers de l'Ecole des Sciences Sociales, Québec, 3, 2, 20.
2103. **Lussier, Gabriel-M.**
  1942   Pour une enfance déshéritée, Revue Dominicaine, 48, 2, 65-75.
2104. **Maria-Laetitia, Sr**
  1952   Un service social à l'enfance, SS, 2, 177-9.
2105. **Marie-du-Précieux-Sang, Sr**
  1952   Services sociaux professionnels de nos institutions, SS, 2, 171-6.
2106. **Meek, Suzanne**
  1949   Deux facteurs sociaux de délinquance juvénile, Thesis, University of Montreal.
2107. **Miville-Déchêne, Elzéar**
  n. d.   Le secrétariat des familles, OT, no 82, Montréal, 16.
2108. **Minville, Esdras**
  1944   Schéma d'une politique de sécurité économique et sociale pour la Province de Québec, EA, déc., 123-86.
2109. **Painchaud, Maurice**
  1953   Qu'est-ce que le service familial de Québec ?, SS, 3, 83-9.
2110. **Paré, Simone**
  1949   La méthode du service social des groupes, Cahiers de l'Ecole des Sciences Sociales, Québec, 5, 10, 37.
2111.   1954   Revue rétrospective sur l'Ecole de Service Social de l'Université Laval, 1943-54, SS, 4, 85-92.
2112.   1955   La méthode de service social de groupes, Revue Dominicaine, 61, 2, 27-34, 40.
2113.   1956   Groupes et Service social, Presses Universitaires Laval, Québec, 280.
2114. **Patenaude, J.-Z.-Léon**
  1956   Le rôle de l'Eglise catholique dans la lutte antialcoolique au Canada, Chronique Sociale de France, 64, 1, 107-110.
2115. **Plante, Albert**
  1944   Une réussite aux Trois-Rivières, Relations, 4, 48, 314-7.
2116. **Poulin, Gonzalve**
  1947   Le service social dans la cité, Cahiers de l'Ecole des Sciences Sociales, Québec, 4, 10, 22.
2117.   1952   Institutions de charité et services sociaux dans la Province de Québec, SS, 2, 146-54.
2118.   1954   Evolution historique des services d'assistance de la Province de Québec, SS, 4, 112-26.
2119.   1955   L'Ecole du service social et le Conseil des Oeuvres de Québec, SS, 5, 79-87.
2120.   1955   Le contrôle du crime chez nous, SS, 5, 118-23.
2121.   1956   La carrière du travailleur social, Revue Dominicaine, LXII, 1, 95-103.
2122. **Roch, Hervé**
  1951   L'adoption dans la Province de Québec, Wilson et Lafleur, Montréal, 205.
2123. **Saint-Pierre, Arthur**
  1914   Questions et Oeuvres sociales chez nous, ESP, Montréal, 264.
2124.   1932   L'Oeuvre des Congrégations religieuses de Charité dans la Province de Québec, Bibliothèque Canadienne, Montréal, 245.

A BIBLIOGRAPHICAL INTRODUCTION...

2125.   1926   Oeuvres charitables ou Oeuvres sociales, *La Veilleuse*, fév., 77-84.
2126.   1931   Un ministère du service social, *La Santé*, déc., 3.
2127.   1932   L'Assistance conditionnelle dans la Province de Québec, *La Santé*, fév., 20.
2128.   1945   *Témoignages sur nos orphelinats*, Fides, Montréal, 153.
2129. **Pelletier, Gérard**
             n. d.   *Histoire des enfants tristes*, Action Nationale, Montréal, 95.
2130. **Robitaille, Robert**
             1942   Montréal, Grand centre médical, *Quartier Latin*, 24, 25, 24 avril, 5.
2131. **Rumilly, Robert**
             1946   *La plus riche aumône. Histoire de la Société de Saint-Vincent-de-Paul au Canada*, Ed. de l'Arbre, Montréal, 235.
2132. **Semaines Sociales du Canada**
             1951   *Le rôle social de la charité*, ISP, Montréal, 210.
2133. **Villeneuve, Rudolph**
             1955   *Catholic Social Work*, Grand Séminaire de Montréal, University of Montreal, 146.
2134. **Vinay, M.-P.**
             1949   *Le Service social*, Laplante et Langevin, Montréal, 278.

6. Cultural Characteristics

a) Folklore and Traditions

2135. **Alloway, Mary Wilson**
 1889 *Famous Firesides of French Canada,* Lovell, Montreal, 217.
2136. **Archives du Folklore**
 1947 Hommage à Marius Barbeau, *Archives du Folklore,* Québec, 2, 7-96.
2137. **Barbeau, Marius**
 1916 Le folklore canadien-français, TRSC, II, 1, 3-12.
2138. 1916 Contes populaires canadiens, 1re série, JAF, XXIX, 1-154.
2139. 1917 Contes populaires canadiens, 2e série, JAF, XXX, 1-161.
2140. 1919 Contes populaires canadiens, 3e série, JAF, 32, 90-168.
2141. 1934 *Cornelius Krieghoff,* Macmillan, Toronto, 152.
2142. 1934 *Au Cœur de Québec,* Ed. du Zodiaque, Montréal, 200.
2143. 1935 *Folk Songs of old Quebec,* National Museum, Ottawa, 72.
2144. 1936 *The Kingdom of the Saguenay,* Macmillan, Toronto, 167.
2145. 1936 *Quebec where ancient France lingers,* Garneau, Québec, 173.
2146. 1937 *Romancero du Canada,* Macmillan, Toronto, 254.
2147. 1938 Nos traditions, RTC, 24, 290-99.
2148. 1941 *Henri Julien,* Ryerson, Toronto, 44.
2148a. 1945 *Ceinture Fléchée,* Paysana, Montréal, 110.
2149. 1946 *Alouette,* Ed. Lumen, Montréal, 210.
2150. 1947 *L'arbre de rêve,* Ed. Lumen, Montréal, 188.
2151. 1949 Maple Sugar, CGJ, 38.
2152. 1952 *Les contes du grand-père Sept-heures,* Chantecler, Montréal, 65.
2153. 1954 How the folk songs of French Canada were discovered, CHJ, 49, 2, 58-69.
2154. **Barbeau, Marius and Sapir, E.**
 1925 *Folk Songs of French Canada,* Yale University Press, New Haven, 216.
2155. **Bernard, Antoine**
 1924 Le folklore gaspésien, AF, 12, 6, 346-67.
2156. **Beaugrand, Honoré**
 1904 *New studies in Canadian Folklore,* Renouf, Montréal, 130.
2157. **Biron, Fernand**
 1948 Le chant et la musique dans la vie quotidienne populaire, Cahiers de l'Ecole des Sciences Sociales, Québec, 5, 8, 38.
2158. **Bouchard, Georges**
 1926 Les petites industries féminines à la campagne, TRSC, XX, 1, 121-37.
2159. 1927 *Les petites industries féminines à la campagne,* ESP, no 164, Montréal, 32.
2160. 1931 *Vieilles choses, vieilles gens,* Lib. d'ACF, Montréal, 181.
2161. 1944 Habitant ou Paysan ?, TRSC, XXXVIII, 1, 27-35.
2162. **Boucher, Thomas**
 1952 *Mauricie d'autrefois,* Bien-Public, Trois-Rivières, 206.
2163. **Burque, François-Xavier**
 1921 *Chansonnier canadien-français,* Imp. Nationale, Québec, 283.
2164. **Carrière, Joseph-M.**
 1946 The present state of French folklore studies in North America, *Southern Folklore Quarterly,* 10, 4, 219-226.
2165. **Croff, E. Mme**
 1931 *Nos ancêtres à l'œuvre à la Rivière-Ouelle,* Lévesque, Montréal, 212.

2166. **Daviault, Pierre**
 1940 Contes populaires canadiens, 7e série, JAF, LIII, 89-190.
2167. 1948 Le nom de lieux au Canada, TRSC, XLII, 1, 43-52.
2168. **Deffontaines, Pierre**
 1955 Hiver et genres de vie au Canada français, RCG, IX, 2-3, 73-92.
2169. **De Lorimier, Louis-Raoul**
 1920 *Au cœur de l'histoire*, Le Devoir, Montréal, 316.
2170. **Gagnon, Ernest**
 1905 *Choses d'autrefois*, Dussault et Proulx, Québec, 320.
2171. **Gagnon, Marcel**
 1865 *Chansons populaires du Canada*, Bureau du Foyer canadien, Québec, 375.
2172. **Gaspé, Philippe-Aubert de**
 1863 *Les anciens Canadiens*, Foyer Canadien, Québec, 369.
2173. **Gérin-Lajoie, Antoine**
 1949 *Jean Rivard* (8th edition), Beauchemin, Montréal, 294.
2174. **Gilles, R. F.**
 1918 *Les choses qui s'en vont*, La Tempérance, Montréal, 186.
2175. **Groulx, Lionel**
 1920 *Chez nos ancêtres*, Biblio. de l'Action Française, Montréal, 102.
2176. **Lacourcière, L. et Savard, F.-A.**
 1946 Folklore et Histoire, AdF, 1, 14-24.
2177. **Lacourcière, Luc**
 1946 Les études de folklore français au Canada, *Culture*, 6, 3-9.
2178. 1946 La langue et le folklore, AdF, Québec, 14.
2179. **Lalande, Louis**
 1919 *Silhouettes paroissiales*, Imp. du Mesager, Montréal, 299.
2180. **Lanctot, Gustave**
 1926 Contes populaires canadiens, JAF, XXXIX, 371-449.
2181. 1931 Contes populaires canadiens, JAF, XLIV, 225-294.
2182. **Lanctot, Gustave et Lambert, Adélard**
 1923 Contes populaires canadiens, JAF, XXXVI, 205-272.
2183. **Laramée, Jean et Gingras, Jean-Paul**
 1936 *Chansons du vieux Québec*, Beauchemin, Montréal, 260.
2184. **Lemieux, Germaine**
 1954 Folklore et folkloristes, *Relations*, 166, 280-1.
2185. **Marie-Ursule, Sr**
 1951 *La civilisation traditionnelle des Lavalois*, Presses Universitaires Laval, Québec, 395.
2186. **Massicotte, E.-Z.**
 1913 *Mœurs, coutumes et industries canadiennes-françaises*, Beauchemin, Montréal, 140.
2187. 1925 Une noce populaire il y a cinquante ans, TRSC, XVII, 1, 25-31.
2188. 1927 Auberges et cabarets d'autrefois, TRSC, XXI, 1, 97-112.
2189. 1928 Hostelleries, clubs et cafés à Montréal, 1760-1850, TRSC, XXII, 1, 37-62.
2190. **Morin, Victor**
 1927 La chanson canadienne, TRSC, XXI, 1, 161-205.
2191. 1937 Superstition et croyances populaires, TRSC, XXXI, 1, 51-60.
2192. **Morisset, Alfred**
 1929 Le langage populaire en médecine, CF, 16, 7, 441-553.
2193. **Rioux, Marcel**
 1944 Le blason populaire canadien, CF, XXXII, 259-65.
2194. **Rivard, Adjutor**
 1914 *Chez nous*, L'Action Sociale, Québec, 143.
2195. 1918 *Chez nos gens*, L'Action Sociale, Québec, 135.

2196. **Roy, Mgr Camille**
  1924 *Propos rustiques*, Beauchemin, Montréal, 119.
2197.   1928 *Etudes et Croquis*, Carrier, Montréal, 145.
2198. **Roy, Carmen**
  1952 *Contes populaires Gaspésiens*, Fides, Montréal, 160.
2199. **Roy, Pierre-Georges**
  1939 Nos coutumes et traditions françaises, *Les Cahiers des Dix*, 4, 59-118.
2200. **Saunders, R.-M.**
  1940 Coureurs de Bois, la définition, CHR, XXI, 2, 123-31.
2201. **Société Historique de Montréal**
  1919 *Veillées du bon vieux temps*, Ducharme, Montréal, 103.
2202. **Taché, J.-C.**
  1924 *Trois légendes de mon pays*, Beauchemin, Montréal, 123.

b) *Linguistics and Language problems*

2203. **Angers, François-Albert**
  1941 L'art de déplacer les questions, AN, XVII, 1, 3-24.
2204. **Arès, R.**
  1954 *Positions du français au Canada*, ISP, no 474, Montréal, 64.
2205. **Barbeau, Victor**
  1939 *Le ramage de mon pays*, Valiquette, Montréal, 222.
2206. **Béliveau, Arthur**
  1953 La langue française, VF, 8, 212-228.
2207. **Blanchard, Etienne**
  1949 *Dictionnaire du bon langage*, Frères des Ecoles Chrétiennes, Montréal, 281.
2208.   1925 *En garde*, Beauchemin, Montréal, 122.
2209.   1919 *Le bon parler en affaires*, n. e., Montréal, 95.
2210. **Bourassa, Henri**
  1913 *La langue française et l'avenir de notre race*, L'Action Sociale, Québec, 22.
2211.   1915 *La langue française au Canada*, Le Devoir, Montréal, 52.
2212.   1918 *La langue, gardienne de la foi*, Le Devoir, Montréal, 84.
2213. **Bruneau, Charles**
  1940 *Grammaire et Linguistique*, Valiquette, Montréal, 54.
2214. **Buies, Arthur**
  1888 *Anglicismes et canadianismes*, Darveau, Québec, 106.
2215. **Charbonneau, Hector**
  1945 Les archaïsmes du parler madelinois, TRSC, XXXIX, 1, 19-38.
2216. **Charbonneau, René**
  1955 *La polatisation de t/d en canadien-français*, University of Montreal, Faculty of Letters, 145.
2217. **Chartier, Emile**
  1921 Le Canada français : la langue, *Revue Canadienne*, 26, 574-85 ; 649-661.
2218.   1932 Le patois canadien-français, RUO, II, 2, 129-44.
2219.   1945 Notre dette lexicologique envers Montaigne, TRSC, XXXIX, 1, 45-65.
2220. **Clapin, Sylva**
  1894 *Dictionnaire canadien-français*, Beauchemin, Montréal, 388.
2221.   1918 *Ne pas dire, mais dire*, Beauchemin, Montréal, 182
2222. **Congrès de la Langue Française au Canada**
  1913 *1er Congrès*, Action Sociale, Québec, 2 v.
2223.   1938 *2e Congrès*, Le Soleil, Québec, 3 v.
2224.   1953 *3e Congrès*, Ferland, Québec, 2 v.
2225. **Daviault, Pierre**
  1933 *Question de langage*, Lévesque, Montréal, 183.
2226.   1936 *L'expression juste en traduction*, Lévesque, Montréal, 247.

2227. 1944 Traducteurs et traduction au Canada, TRSC, XXXVIII, 1, 67-87.
2228. 1951 Langage et culture, NRC, 1, 1, 3-14.
2229. 1952 L'élément canadien-français de l'anglais d'Amérique, TRSC, XLXI, 1, 5-18.
2230. **Décelles, (fils)**
1929 *Notre beau parler de France*, Le Progrès, Hull, 104.
2231. **Denis, Roland**
1949 *Les vingt siècles du français*, Fides, Montréal, 437.
2232. **Descelles, Alfred**
1927 *La beauté du verbe*, Beauchemin, Montréal, 58.
2233. **Désy, Jean**
1953 Le français dans la vie canadienne, RUL, 8, 20-31.
2234. **Dionne, N.-E.**
1909 *Le parler populaire des Canadiens français*, Laflamme et Proulx, Montréal, 671.
2235. **Donnay, Joseph**
1942 *La grande source de nos anglicismes*, Société du Parler Français, Québec, 34.
2236. **Dulong, Gaston**
1952 La langue franco-canadienne, PO, 6, 2, 148-55.
2237. **Geddes, James**
1902 *Canadian French*, Junge and Sons, Erlangen, 66.
2238. 1806 *Bibliographie du parler français au Canada*, Société du Parler français au Canada, Québec, 99.
2239. **Gendron, Jean-Denis**
1953 La Société du Parler français, son activité durant l'année 1952-1953, RUL, 8, 189-92.
2240. **Geofirion, Louis-Philippe**
1925-27 *Zig-Zags autour de nos parlers*, n. e., Québec, 3 v.
2241. 1928 Le parler des habitants de Québec, TRSC, XXII, 1, 63-80.
2242. **Gosselin, P.-E.**
1936 La langue gardienne de la foi, CF, 24, 4, 301-9.
2243. **Guérin, Marc-Aimé**
1955 Quelques aspects géographiques du terme canadien-français, RCG, IX, 1, 32-41.
2244. **Guérin, Wilfrid**
1916 Le patois canadien-français, RC, 16, 115-34.
2245. **Groulx, Lionel**
1934 Langage et survivance, AN, 4, 1, 46-63.
2246. **Holmes, Charles-E.**
1941 *L'antibritannisme et l'unilinguisme*, Valiquette, Montréal, 29.
2247. **Homier, Pierre**
1913 *La langue française au Canada*, n. e., Montréal, 93.
2248. **Lande, Harold Bernard**
1930 *Economic Factor affecting the trend of Language in the Province of Quebec*, M. A. Thesis, McGill University.
2249. **LaRue, Gabriel**
1938 Notre français, CF, 25, 9, 965-92.
2250. 1938 *Pour que vive notre français*, ESP, no 293, Montréal, 32.
2251. **Laurence, Jean-Marie**
1947 *Notre français sur le vif*, Centre de Psychologie et de Pédagogie, Montréal, 301.
2252. 1955 Premiers principes d'une théorie de l'anglicisme, TRSC, 49, 17-19.
2253. **Legendre, Napoléon**
1899 *La langue française au Canada*, Darveau, Québec, 177.
2254. **Léger, Jean-Marc**
1955 La langue française menacée au Québec, AN, 45, 43-58.

2255. **Ligue des Droits du français**
   1916-37   *Almanach de la Langue française*, Montréal, 21 v.
2256. **Lorrain, L.**
   1952   Le français dans les affaires, AN, 40, 3, 183-190.
2257. **Martin, Ernest**
   1934   *Le français du Canada est-il un patois ?*, L'Action Catholique, Québec, 143.
2258. **Montigny, Louvigny de**
   1916   *La langue française au Canada*, Ottawa, 187.
2259.   1948   *Ecrasons le Perroquet*, Fides, Montréal, 107.
2260. **Montpetit, Edouard**
   1924   *Le parler français au Canada*, Le Devoir, Montréal, 19.
2261. **Nantel, Maréchal**
   1941   Autour d'une décision judiciaire sur la langue française au Canada, *Les Cahiers des Dix*, 6, 145-65.
2262. **Racine, Paul**
   1941   *Henri Bourassa à Notre-Dame*, Frangipani, Montréal, 52.
2263. **Richard, Louis-Arthur**
   1919   La langue que nous parlons, RTC, 4, 411-422.
2264. **Richer, A.-M.**
   1952   Parler canadien ou parler français, RUL, 7, 84-91.
2265. **Rivard, Adjutor**
   1914   *Etudes sur les parlers de France au Canada*, Garneau, Québec, 280.
2266. **Roy, P.-G.**
   1906   *Les noms géographiques de la Province de Québec*, Le Soleil, Québec, 514.
2267. **Saint-Jean, Albert**
   1944   Le langage technique, *Technique*, 19, 8, 565-68.
2268. **Saint-Pierre, Arthur**
   1916   Le français à l'Hôtel de ville, *Le Petit Canadien*, juin, 94-96.
2269. **Société du Parler français au Canada**
   1903   *L'origine et le parler des Canadiens français*, Université Laval, Québec, 30.
2270.   1930   *Glossaire du Parler français au Canada*, L'Action Sociale, Québec, 709.
2271.   1955   *Etudes sur le Parler français au Canada*, Presses Universitaires Laval, Québec, 220.
2272. **Sulte, Benjamin**
   1886   L'enseignement du français, RC, 22, 758-68 ; 23, 27-31.
2273.   1898   *La langue française au Canada*, Roy, Lévis, 107.
2274. **Surveyer-Fabre, Edouard**
   1903   Une vieille question, RC, I, 91-96.
2275. **Tardivel, J.-P.**
   1880   *L'anglicisme, voilà l'ennemi*, Imp. du Canadien, Québec, 28.
2276.   1901   *La langue française au Canada*, La Canadienne, Montréal, 69.
2277. **Tassé, Joseph**
   1888   *The French Question*, Imp. Générale, Montréal, 87.
2278. **Tougas, Gérard**
   1954   La langue française au Canada, illusions et réalités, *French Review*, 28, 2, 160-65.

c) *Bilingualism*

2279. **Allen Patrick**
   1955   Peut-on se documenter en français à Ottawa ?, AN, fév., 547-58.
2280. **Bastien, Hermas**
   1925   Le bilinguisme dans les Provinces Maritimes, AF, 13, 250-68.
2281.   1938   *Le bilinguisme au Canada*, Ed. de l'A.C.F., Montréal, 202.

2282. **Bruchési, Emile**
      1925   Le bilinguisme dans le Québec, AF, 14, 1, 4-19.
2283. **Désy, Jean**
      1953   Bilingues ? Pourquoi ?, *L'Action Universitaire*, 4, 3-17.
2284.   1955   Le Monde bilingue, TRSC, 49, 1-15.
2285. **Doucet, R. P.**
      1896   Dual language in Canada, Globe Press, Saint John, 15.
2286. **Downie, Donald**
      1916   *Notre droit d'aînesse ou la question bilingue*, La Publicité, Québec, 30.
2287. **Dugré, Alexandre**
      1946   Bilinguisme pour les autres, *Relations*, 63, 84-6.
2288. **Gauthier, Charles**
      1925   Le bilinguisme dans les services fédéraux, AF, 13, 3, 130-48.
2289. **Gérard, Fernand**
      1955   Le bilinguisme, AN, 44, 798-811.
2290. **Gervais, Emile**
      1944   Un écran de fumée, *Relations*, 4, 46, 262-4 ; 52, 87-90 ; 56, 201-2.
2291. **Groulx, Lionel**
      1925   Le bilinguisme avant 1867, AF, 13, 4-23.
2292. **Laurendeau, André**
      1940   La mort par le bilinguisme, AN, 16, 4, 314-17.
2293. **Lanctot, Gustave**
      1952   De l'influence sociale du bilinguisme, TRSC, XLIV, 1, 49-60.
2294. **Mackey, William**
      1953   Bilinguism and linguistic structure, *Culture*, 14, 141-49.
2295. **Perrault, Antonio**
      1925   Le bilinguisme fédéral, aspect juridique, AF, 13, 2, 66-94.
2296. **Tessier-Lavigne, Yves**
      1925   Le bilinguisme dans l'Ouest canadien, AF, 13, 5, 266-81 ; 13, 6, 330-42.
2297. **Rothney, Gordon**
      1946   Bilingual Canada and the World, *Culture*, VII, 129-40.
2298. **Vanier, Anatole**
      1925   Le bilinguisme et l'unité nationale, AF, 14, 3, 130-41.

d) *Journalism, Radio, Television and Public Spectacles*

2299. **Anonymous**
      1954   Ici, Radio-Canada, *Actualités*, 7, 4, 32.
2300. **Bélanger, Ferdinand**
      1924   La mauvaise presse, AF, 12, 1, 5-18.
2301. **Bernard, Harry**
      1924   Théâtre et Cinéma, AF, 12, 2, 69-80.
2302. **Bertrand, Théophile**
      1954   Les lectures populaires, *Lectures*, 10, 389-94.
2303. **Bisson, Margaret Mary**
      1931   *Le théâtre français à Montréal, 1878-1931*, M. A. Thesis, McGill University.
2304. **Boucher, Pierre**
      1953   Nos publics de théâtre, RUL, 8, 351-57.
2305. **Bourassa, Henri**
      1915   *Le Devoir, son origine, son passé, son avenir*, Le Devoir, Montréal, 53.
2306.   1921   *La presse catholique et nationale*, Le Devoir, Montréal, 80.
2307.   1921   *Le Devoir, ses promesses d'avenir, ses conditions de survie*, Le Devoir, Montréal, 46.
2308. **Bruchési, Jean**
      1951   Ancienne et nouvelle Revue canadienne, TRSC, XLV, 1, 1-8.

A BIBLIOGRAPHICAL INTRODUCTION...

2309. **Buies, Arthur**
    1875   *A French Canadian Press and the Improvements of Quebec*, Davreau, Québec, 21.
2310. **CBC**
    1943   Radio-Canada, Réseau français, 1936-1941, n. e., n. p., 76.
2311. **Conroy, Patricia**
    1936   A History of the Theatre in Montreal prior to the Confederation, M. A. Thesis, McGill University.
2312. **Dagneau, Georges-Henri**
    1945   L'attitude de la presse canadienne-française à l'égard de la religion, *Culture*, 6, 307-18.
2313.   1946   Remarques sur les conditions du journalisme canadien-français, *Culture*, 7, 454-59.
2314.   1947   Remarques sur l'influence des quotidiens de langue française au Canada, *Culture*, VIII, 3, 243-53.
2315. **Fournier, Jules**
    1922   *Mon encrier*, n. e., Montréal, 2 v.
2316. **Gervais, Emile**
    1954   Pour que notre T.V. trouve sa voie, *Relations*, 163, 186-8.
2317. **Gingras, Paul-Emile**
    1947   Radio Saint-Boniface, *Relations*, 73, 24-6.
2318. **Jouvert, Louis**
    1944   Sous l'anesthésique des brasseurs et distillateurs, AN, 23, 1, 64-77.
2319. **Marie-Germain, Fr.**
    1941   *Un siècle de journalisme canadien*, Thesis, University of Ottawa.
2320. **Gagnon, Henri**
    1934   *Les journées de Presse française à Québec*, n. e., n. p., 215.
2321. **Gérin, Elzéar**
    1864   *La Gazette de Québec*, Duquet, Québec, 65.
2322. **Gervais, Emile**
    1954   Télévision 1953, *Relations*, 14, 48-50 ; 84-85 ; 133-4.
2323. **Gingras, Paul-Emile**
    1954   La presse ordurière nous pourrit, AN, 44, 124-30.
2324. **Girard, Roméo**
    1948   *Qui nous mène ?*, Les Ed. Ouvrières, Montréal, 156.
2325. **Gosselin, Auguste**
    1898   Un épisode de l'histoire du théâtre au Canada, TRSC, IV, 1, 53-72.
2326. **Houlé, Léopold**
    1941   Notre théâtre et la critique, TRSC, XXXV, 1, 77-90.
2327.   1942   Retour des classiques, TRSC, XXXVI, 1, 59-69.
2328.   1944   Sermo vulgaris, sermo urbanis, TRSC, XXXVIII, 1, 143-9.
2329.   1945   *L'histoire du théâtre du Canada*, Fides, Montréal, 172.
2330. **Johnstone, Ken**
    1956   Who'll Le Devoir battle next ?, *MacLean's*, 69, 8, 36-7, 94-8.
2331. **Laurendeau, André**
    1941   Sur trois écrivains de la radio, *Revue Dominicaine*, 47, 255-60.
2332. **Laurent, Edmond**
    1945   Réflexions sur le théâtre, *Culture*, 6, 39-54.
2333. **Lavergne, Edouard**
    1924   *Sur les remparts*, Action Sociale, Québec, 319.
2334. **Legendre, Paul**
    1951   *La radio, puissance sociale*, Institut Littéraire du Québec, Québec, 238.
2335. **L'Heureux, Eugène**
    1942   *Le journalisme*, OT, Montréal, 16.

A BIBLIOGRAPHICAL INTRODUCTION...

2336. **L'Œuvre des Tracts**
   1946 *Omer Héroux, 1896-1946, 50 ans de journalisme catholique*, OT, Montréal, 16.
2337. **Nicol, John and others**
   1954 *La tribune radiophonique rurale au Canada*, UNESCO, Paris, 261.
2338. **O'Neil, Louis**
   1955 Pourquoi le clergé soutient-il Le Devoir ?, *Ad Usum Sacerdotum*, 1, 5, 76-80.
2339. **Orlier, Blaise**
   1941 *Louis Francœur, journaliste*, Le Droit, Ottawa, 32.
2340. **Peck, Robert-Alfred**
   1942 *Les grands quotidiens du Québec*, M. A. Thesis, McGill University.
2341. **Péloquin, Bonaventure**
   1953 *La presse catholique et le journalisme catholique*, Séminaire des Saints-Hôtes, La Prairie, 53.
2342. **Points de Vue**
   1956 La Télévision (special number), 1, 7, 42.
2342a. 1956 La Radio (special number), 1, 8, 45.
2343. **Rivard, Adjutor**
   1923 De la liberté de la Presse, TRSC, XVII, 1, 33-104.
2344. 1923 *De la liberté de la Presse*, Garneau, Québec, 125.
2345. **Robert, Guy**
   1956 Trois romans canadiens télévisés, *Revue Dominicaine*, LXII, 1, 82-88.
2346. **Ross, Mgr François-Xavier**
   1913 *Louis Veuillot et la Presse catholique*, n. e., Québec, 51.
2347. **Roy, Elias**
   1924 *La Presse catholique*, OT, Montréal, 16.
2348. **Russell, Jack David**
   1903 Acadian magazines, TRSC, 2, 9, 2, 173-203.
2349. **Saint-Georges, Jean**
   1954 Le réseau français de Radio-Canada, AN, 43, 363-71.
2350. **Société canadienne d'éducation des adultes**
   1951-6 *Emissions éducatives*, S.C.E.A., Montréal, 5 v.
2351. **Tétu, Horace**
   1881 *Journaux et revues de Montréal*, n. e., Québec, 51.
2352. 1889 *Historique des journaux de Québec*, n. e., Québec, 107.
2353. **Thiero, Adrien**
   1954 *Jules Fournier, journaliste de combat*, Fides, Montréal, 224.
2354. **White, Thomas**
   1883 *Newspapers, their development in the Province of Quebec*, n. e., Montréal, 15.

e) *Literature*

2355. **Barbeau, Victor**
   1944 *La Société des écrivains canadiens*, Ed. de la Soc. des Ecrivains canadiens, Montréal, 117.
2356. **Bashert, Gérard**
   1955 Le sentiment religieux dans le roman canadien-français, RUL, 9, 868-86 ; 10, 41-61.
2357. **Bastien, Hermas**
   1933 *Témoignages, études et profils littéraires*, Lévesque, Montréal, 213.
2358. **Bélanger, Jeannine**
   1939 *Poésie au Canada sous le régime français*, Ph. D. Thesis, University of Ottawa.

A BIBLIOGRAPHICAL INTRODUCTION...

2359. **Bender, P.**
1881 *Literary Sheaves*, Dawson, Montreal, 215.
2360. **Bernard, Harry**
1929 *Essais critiques*, Ed. de l'A.C.F., Montréal, 196.
2361. **Bisson, Laurence**
1932 *Le romantisme littéraire au Canada français*, Droz, Paris, 285.
2362. **Blain, Jean**
1955 A quand la république des lettres ?, AN, 44, 418-26.
2363. 1956 Notre littérature, AN, 45, 418-26 ; 548-52.
2364. **Bouchard, Paul**
1936 Régionalisme littéraire, AN, 7, 5, 293-305.
2365. **Bronner, Frédéric**
1944 *L'influence du romantisme dans le Canada français de 1855 à 1914*, Ph. D. Thesis, University of Ottawa.
2366. **Brouillard, Carmel**
1935 *Sous le signe des Muses*, Granger, Montréal, 241.
2367. **Bruchési, Jean**
1941 *Rappels*, Valiquette, Montréal, 231.
2368. 1947 *Evocations*, Ed. Lumen, Montréal, 213.
2369. **Brunet, Berthelot**
1946 *Histoire de la littérature canadienne-française*, Ed. de l'Arbre, Montréal, 186.
2370. **Charbonneau, Jean**
1935 *L'Ecole Littéraire de Montréal*, Lévesque, Montréal, 320.
2371. **Chartier, Mgr Joseph-Etienne-Emile**
1921-2 Le Canada français, *Revue Canadienne*, 26, 735-46 ; 27, 25-39 ; 100-13 ; 177-92.
2372. 1928 L'école régionaliste dans le Canada français, TRSC, 22, 1, 7-22.
2373. 1941 *La vie de l'esprit, 1760-1925*, Valiquette, Montréal, 355.
2374. **Choquette, Adrienne**
1939 *Confidences d'écrivains canadiens-français*, Bien-Public, Trois-Rivières, 236.
2375. **Crouzet, Paul**
1946 *Poésie au Canada*, Didier, Paris, 372.
2376. **Dandurand, Albert**
1935 *Littérature canadienne-française — la prose*, Le Devoir, Montréal, 208.
2377. 1939 *Nos Orateurs*, Ed. de l'A.C.F., Montréal, 232.
2378. **Dantin, Louis**
1928 *Poètes de l'Amérique française*, Carrier, Montréal, 250.
2379. **Daveau, Louis-Michel**
1873 *Nos hommes de lettres*, Stevenson, Montréal, 280.
2380. **Desmarchais, Rex**
1954 L'écrivain au Canada français, *L'Action Universitaire*, 20, 3, 23-35.
2381. **Doutremont, Henri**
1925 Quelques marques distinctives de la littérature canadienne, CF, 13, 4, 260-66.
2382. **Dugas, Marcel**
1929 *Littérature canadienne*, Didot, Paris, 202.
2383. **Félix, Walter**
1940 French Canadian letters, *Letters in Canada*, ed. Woodhouse, A.S.P., University of Toronto Quarterly, 9, 308-19.
2384. **Fortier, Lévis**
1954 *Le message poétique de Saint-Denys-Garneau*, Ed. de l'Université d'Ottawa, Ottawa, 230.
2385. **Fraser, Ian Forbes**
1939 *The spirit of French Canada*, Ryerson, Toronto, 219.

109

A BIBLIOGRAPHICAL INTRODUCTION...

2386. **Freeman, Audrey**
 1946 *Portrait de la femme canadienne-française d'après la littérature du pays, 1850-1945*, M. A. Thesis, McGill University.
2387. **Gauthier, Joseph-Delphis**
 1948 *Le Canada français et le roman américain*, Tolra, Paris, 356.
2388. **Greig, Janet-T.**
 1926 *Le canadianisme de la littérature canadienne-française de l'école de 1860*, M. A. Thesis, University of British Columbia.
2389. **Grignon, Claude-Henri**
 1933 *Ombres et Clameurs*, Lévesque, Montréal, 204.
2390. **Halden, Charles ad der**
 1904 *Etudes de la littérature canadienne-française*, Paris, 352.
2391. 1907 Nouvelles études de la littérature canadienne-française, Rudeval, Paris, 377.
2392. **Harvey, Jean-Charles**
 1926 *Pages critiques sur quelques aspects de la littérature canadienne-française*, Le Soleil, Québec, 187.
2393. **Haynes, David M.**
 1945 *The historical novel and French Canada*, Ph. D. Thesis, University of Ottawa.
2394. **Howe, Ruth**
 1939 *Evolution du roman au Canada français*, D.LL. Thesis, University of Montreal.
2395. **Huston, J.**
 1893 *Le Répertoire national ou Recueil de Littérature canadienne*, Valois, Montréal, 4 v.
2396. **Jobin, Antoine-Joseph**
 1941 *Visages littéraires du Canada français*, Ed. du Zodiaque, Montréal, 270.
2397. **Jones, Frederick-Mason**
 1931 *Le roman canadien-français*, Imp. de la Charité, Montpellier, 202.
2398. **Lacroix, Benoît-M.**
 1954 *Vie des lettres et histoire canadienne*, Ed. du Lévrier, Montréal, 76.
2399. **Lapointe, Jeanne**
 1954 Quelques aspects positifs de notre littérature, CL, 10, 17-36.
2400. **Légaré, Romain**
 1945 Le roman canadien-français d'aujourd'hui, *Culture*, 6, 55-75.
2401. 1947 Le renouveau du conte au Canada français, Culture, 8, 51-66.
2402. **Lamarche, Marcolin-Antonio**
 1930 *Ebauches critiques*, Ménard, Montréal, 169.
2403. **Lareau, Edmond**
 1874 *Histoire de la littérature canadienne*, Lovell, Montréal, 496.
2404. **Léger, Jules**
 1938 *Le Canada français et son expression littéraire*, Nizet et Bastard, Paris, 211.
2405. **Mahon, Rose-Kathryn**
 1950 *Les mœurs et les coutumes rurales au Canada français dans le roman canadien-français depuis les origines jusqu'à 1900*, M. A. Thesis, McGill University.
2406. **Marie-Victorin, Fr.**
 1928 *A travers la littérature canadienne-française*, Frères des Ecoles Chrétiennes, Montréal, 265.
2407. **Marion, Séraphin**
 1931 *En feuilletant nos écrivains*, Ed. de l'A.C.F., Montréal, 216.
2408. 1950 Lamartine et le Canada français, RUO, 20, 1, 23-46.
2409. 1939-54 *Les lettres canadiennes-françaises d'autrefois*, Ed. de l'Université d'Ottawa, 8 v.

A BIBLIOGRAPHICAL INTRODUCTION...

2410. **Mary-Ignatia, Sr**
    1946 *Les Canadiens français d'après les romans canadiens-français de 1840 à 1900*, Ph. D. Thesis, Laval University.
2411. **Maurel, Charles**
    1946 *Nos héros de romans*, n. e., Québec, 34.
2412. **McNamara, Mary-Frances C.**
    1940 *L'histoire dans la poésie canadienne-française, 1860-1900*, M. A. Thesis, McGill University.
2413. **Michel, Eleanor**
    1943 *Les Canadiens français d'après le roman contemporain*, Ph. D. Thesis, Laval University.
2414. **Montigny, Louvigny de**
    1937 *La Revanche de Maria Chapdelaine*, Ed. de l'A.C.F., Montréal, 210.
2415. **O'Leary, D.**
    1954 *Le roman canadien-français*, Cercle du Livre de France, Ottawa, 195.
2416. **Patterson, Marion Isabel Arnott**
    1948 *Nationalism as expressed in French Canadian poetry of the Quebec school*, M. A. Thesis, University of Toronto.
2417. **Pelletier, Albert**
    1933 *Egrappages*, Lévesque, Montréal, 234.
2418. **Perrault, Antonio**
    1944 A propos de roman social, Jean Rivard et le fils de l'esprit, TRSC, XXXVIII, 1, 151-69.
2419. **Radicot, Paul-Emile**
    1954 Nos romans de 1953, *Relations*, 162, 155-7.
2420.   1955 Nos romans de 1954, *Relations*, 175, 214-16.
2421. **Roy, Mgr Camille**
    1909 *Nos origines littéraires*, L'Action Sociale, Québec, 354.
2422.   1914 *Nouveaux essais sur la littérature canadienne*, L'Action Sociale, Québec, 390.
2423.   1915 Notre Patriotisme littéraire en 1860, CF, 14, 2, 51-58.
2424.   1923 *Erables en fleurs*, n. e., Québec, 234.
2425.   1925 *Essais sur la littérature canadienne*, Beauchemin, Montréal, 201.
2426.   1930 *Histoire de la littérature canadienne*, Action Sociale, Québec, 310.
2427.   1931 *Regards sur les lettres*, L'Action Sociale, Québec, 240.
2428.   1934 *Poètes de chez nous*, Beauchemin, Montréal, 132.
2429.   1935 *Romanciers de chez nous*, Beauchemin, Montréal, 196.
2430. **Saint-Pierre, Arthur**
    1950 La littérature sociale canadienne-française avant la Confédération, TRSC, XLIV, 1, 67-94.
2431. **Sœurs de Sainte-Anne**
    1928 *Précis d'histoire littéraire*, Sœurs de Sainte-Anne, Lachine, 336.
2432.   1944 *Histoire des littératures françaises et canadiennes*, Sœurs de Sainte-Anne, Lachine, 566.
2433. **Sylvestre, Guy**
    1941 *Situation de la poésie canadienne*, Le Droit, Ottawa, 30.
2434.   1951 Où en est notre littérature ?, RUO, 21, 4, 427-48.
2435.   1951 Naissance de nos lettres, TRSC, XLV, 1, 71-78.
2436.   1952 Le rapport Massey et l'écrivain, TRSC, XLVI, 1, 81-88.
2437.   1952 L'année littéraire 1951-52, RUO, 22, 446-66.
2438.   1952 *The recent Development of the French Canadian novel*, University of Toronto Press, Toronto, 12.
2439.   1953 Introduction à l'histoire de la littérature canadienne, RUO, 23, 84-109 ; 187-215.
2440. **Tanguay, Jean-Charles**
    1954 Notre littérature, AN, 44, 153-58.

A BIBLIOGRAPHICAL INTRODUCTION...

2441. **Taylor, Margaret Ellen Bresce**
1942 *Le roman historique canadien-français, des origines jusqu'à 1914*, M. A. Thesis, McGill University.
2442. **Turnbull, Jane Mason**
1938 *Essential traits of French Canadian poetry*, Macmillan, Toronto, 288.
2443. **Watts, Aileen, M.**
1950 *Le héros contre le milieu dans le roman canadien-français de 1938 à 1950*, M. A. Thesis, McGill University.
2444. **Wearing, Parker Lovell**
1949 *Studies in Canadian Nature Poetry*, M. A. Thesis, McGill University.

f) *Arts and Music*

2445. **Adair, E. R.**
1939 French Canadian Art, CHAR, 9-102.
2446.   1944 Philip Liebert, sculptor, *Culture*, 5, 169-73.
2447. **Anonymous**
1946 *The arts of French Canada*, National Gallery of Canada, Ottawa, 52.
2448. **Barbeau, Marius**
1939 Deux cents ans d'Orfèvrerie chez nous, TRSC, 33 1, 1-10.
2449.   1941 Backgrounds in Canadian Art, TRSC, 35, 2, 29-40.
2450.   1942 *Maîtres artisans chez nous*, Ed. du Zodiaque, Montréal, 220.
2451.   1943 *Côté, the wood carver*, Ryerson, Toronto, 43.
2452.   1943 Louis Jobin, statuaire, TRSC, 37, 1, 33-48.
2453.   1944 *Saintes artisanes, Les Brodeuses*, Fides, Montréal, 117.
2454.   1945 La Confrérie de Sainte-Anne, TRSC, 39, 1, 1-18.
2455.   1946 *The Arts of French Canada*, Arts Quarterly, 18.
2456.   1946 *Painters of Quebec*, Ryerson, Toronto, 50.
2457. **Barkham, Brian**
1955 *The development of land Settlement and rural Architecture in the Province of Quebec*, Thesis, McGill University.
2458. **Bellerive, Georges**
1925-6 *Artistes-peintres canadiens-français*, Garneau, Québec, 2 v.
2459. **Bland, John**
1948 Domestic architecture in Montreal, *Culture*, 9, 399-407.
2460. **Bruchési, Jean**
1943 A la recherche de nos œuvres d'art, TRSC, 37, 1, 25-35.
2461. **Buchanan, D. W. (ed)**
1945 *Canadian Painters*, Oxford University Press, Toronto, 117.
2462. **Canadian Art**
1948 *Special Quebec Issue*, Canadian Art, 5, 3, 95-162.
2463. **Chauvin, Jean**
1928 *Ateliers*, Ed. du Mercure, Montréal, 268.
2464. **Colgate, William**
1943 *Canadian Art*, Ryerson, Toronto, 278.
2465. **Culture**
1941 Special number on Art, *Culture*, 3, 145-219.
2466. **Déziel, Julien**
1955 Deux petites églises, *Arts et Pensée*, 19, 6-13.
2467. **Dunn, Joséphine Hambleton**
1952 The wood Carver of Saint Jean Port Joly, CGJ, 45, 6, 234-41.
2468. **Gagnon, Maurice**
1945 *Sur l'état actuel de la peinture canadienne*, Pascal, Montréal, 158.
2469. **Gauvreau, Jean-Marie**
1940 *Artisans du Québec*, Bien-Public, Trois-Rivières, 224.

A BIBLIOGRAPHICAL INTRODUCTION...

2470. 1944 Evolution et tradition des meubles canadiens, TRSC, 38, 1, 121-28.
2471. 1946 Pour un renouveau de l'art sacré au Canada, TRSC, XL, 1, 23-35.
2472. 1949 L'artisanat du Québec, TRSC, XLIII, 1, 23-38.
2473. **Gauvreau, Jean-Marie et Riou, Paul**
1954 Le rôle économique, social et culturel de l'artisanat, AE, 29, 624-50.
2474. **Gouin, Paul**
1956 Nos monuments historiques, *Vie des Arts*, 1, 9-13.
2474a. **Gowans, Alan**
1949 Quebec's great baroque Churches, *Culture*, 8, 6-12.
2475. 1949 From baroque to neo-baroque in the Church Architecture of Quebec, *Culture*, 10, 140-50.
2475a. 1956 *Church Architecture in New France*, University of Toronto Press, Toronto, 162.
2476. **Greening, W. E.**
1955 The new Spirit of religious Architecture in French Canada, CGJ, 50, 3, 104-111.
2477. **Hébert, Maurice**
1944 L'habitation canadienne-française, TRSC, 38, 1, 129-41.
2478. **Houlé, Léopold**
1946 Nos compositeurs de musique, TRSC, PL, 1, 51-59.
2479. **Lapierre, Eugène**
1937 *Calixa Lavallée, musicien national du Canada*, Ed. de l'A.C.F., Montréal, 214.
2490. 1948 Le mouvement musical dans le Québec et son orientation, *Culture*, 9, 361-70.
2491. **Lemieux, E. and others**
1952 L'art religieux contemporain au Canada, n. e., Québec, 68.
2492. **Macmillan, Ernest**
1955 *Music in Canada*, University of Toronto Press, Toronto, 232.
2493. **McInnis, Graham**
1939 *A short History of Canadian art*, Macmillan, Toronto, 125.
2494. **Massicotte, E.-Z.**
1924 La ceinture fléchée, chef-d'œuvre de l'industrie domestique au Canada, TRSC, 28, 1, 1-14.
2495. **Maurault, Mgr Olivier**
1929 *L'Art au Canada*, Ed. de l'A.C.F., Montréal, 310.
2496. **Morin, Léo-Pol**
1930 *Papiers à musique*, Lib. d'Action Canadienne, Montréal, 228.
2497. 1945 *Musique*, Beauchemin, Montréal, 484.
2498. **Morisset, Gérard**
1936-7 *Peintres et tableaux*, Ed. du Chevalet, Québec, 2 v.
2499. 1941 *Coup d'œil sur les arts en Nouvelle-France*, Charrier et Dugal, Québec, 170.
2500. 1948 Les arts au Canada sous le régime français, CHAR, 23-27.
2501. 1949 *L'architecture en Nouvelle-France*, Charrier et Dugal, Québec, 150.
2502. 1951 Old Churches of Quebec, CGJ, 43, 3, 100-115.
2503. **Pelletier, J.-R.**
1932 *L'évolution de la musique religieuse au Canada français*, Thesis, Laval University.
2504. **Riou, Paul et Gauvreau, Jean-Marie**
1947 Les formes de l'activité artisanale, TRSC, XLI, 1, 69-88.
2505. **Riou, Paul**
1953 Le rôle économique, social et culturel de l'artisanat, TRSC, 47, 1, 33-55.
2506. **Roy, Pierre-Georges**
1923 *Les monuments commémoratifs de la Province de Québec*, Imp. du Roi, Québec, 2 v.

A BIBLIOGRAPHICAL INTRODUCTION...

2507. 1925 *Les vieilles églises de la Province de Québec, 1647-1800*, Commission des Monuments Historiques de la Province de Québec, Imp. du Roi, Québec, 323.
2508. 1927 *Vieux manoirs, vieilles maisons*, Imp. du Roi, Québec, 376.
2509. **Sœurs de Sainte-Anne**
 1935 *Dictionnaire bibliographique des musiciens canadiens*, Sœurs de Sainte-Anne, Lachine, 299.
2510. **Traquair, Ramsay**
 1925 *The old Architecture of the Province of Quebec*, McGill University Publications, series 13, 1, 7.
2511. 1926 *The Cottages of Quebec*, McGill University Publications, Montreal, 14.
2512. 1940 *The old Silver of Quebec*, Macmillan, Toronto, 169.
2513. 1947 *The old Architecture of Quebec*, Macmillan, Toronto, 324.
2514. **Vaillancourt, Emile**
 1920 *Une maîtrise d'art en Canada, 1800-1823*, Ducharme, Montréal, 115.
2515. **Venne, Emile**
 1951 Des livres sur l'architecture du Québec, *Culture*, 12, 143-51 ; 262-71.

g) *Cultural Values*

2516. **Adam, Marcel**
 1955 Des malades qui s'ignorent, AN, 45, 155-58.
2517. **Angers, Charles (Jean de Sol)**
 1912 *Le docteur Hubert Larue et l'idée canadienne-française*, Le Soleil, Québec, 232.
2518. **Angers, François-A.**
 1943 Vues canadiennes-françaises sur le problème canadien, *Culture*, 4, 482-94.
2519. 1946 Suite au culte de notre incompétence, AN, février, 120-6.
2520. 1946 Et nos responsabilités, qu'en faisons-nous ?, AN, avril, 301-12.
2521. **Anonymous**
 1955 " To be or not to be ", RUL, 9, 836-42.
2522. **Arès, Richard**
 1952 Sommes-nous des Canadiens français ?, AN, jan., 30-36.
2523. **Ballantyne, Murray**
 1954 Les Canadiens français n'ont pas confiance en nous, VF, 542-48.
2524. **Barbeau, Marius**
 1935 Survival of French Canada, *Canadian Forum*, 15, 290, 313-4.
2525. 1936 Changing Quebec, *University of Toronto Quarterly*, 5, 318-33.
2526. 1941 Notre tradition, que devient-elle ?, *Culture*, 2, 3-12.
2527. 1949 La survivance française en Amérique, AdF, 4, 65-75.
2528. **Bastien, Hermas**
 1923 *Les énergies rédemptrices*, Biblio. de l'Action Française, Montréal, 160.
2529. **Baudoux, Maurice**
 1952 Notre peuple a grandi dans sa lutte ; c'est ce qui fait sa force, VF, 7, 202-19.
2530. **Belzile, Thuribe**
 1935 *Nos déficiences, conséquences, remèdes*, Le Devoir, Montréal, 37.
2531. **Benoît, Auguste**
 1942 Le façonnement canadien de notre génie français, CV, 7, 2, 97-110.
2532. **Bernier, Robert**
 1947 Problèmes d'adaptation au Canada français, *Relations*, 72, 356-7 ; 73, 5-9 ; 74, 41-3 ; 75, 68-70.
2533. **Bourassa, Henri**
 1932 *Honnêtes ou Canailles ?*, Le Devoir, Montréal, 23.
2534. 1943 *Que seront nos enfants ?*, Le Devoir, Montréal, 39.

A BIBLIOGRAPHICAL INTRODUCTION...

2535. **Brouille, Léo**
    1940   La destinée catholique de la nation canadienne-française, *L'Action Catholique*, 4, 1, 6.
2536. **Brunet, Michel**
    1955   Les crises de conscience et la prise de conscience du Canada français, AN, 44, 591-603.
2537. **Chalifour, Rosaire**
    1955   Québec à la conquête de son avenir, AN, 44, 773-84.
2538. **Chartier, Emile**
    1921   La Race canadienne-française, RTC, 7, 113-36.
2539. **Closse, Lambert**
    1936   *La réponse de la race*, n. e., Montréal, 546.
2540. **Couture, C.-F.**
    1947   L'avenir de l'élément français au pays, AN, nov., 211-23.
2541. **Dalbis, L.-J.**
    1925   *Le bouclier canadien*, Déom, Montréal, 246.
2542. **Dandurand, Joséphine**
    1901   *Nos travers*, Beauchemin, Montréal, 232.
2543. **Daviault, Pierre**
    1954   Français, Américains ou Canadiens, NRC, 3, 1-7, 64-74.
2544. **David, Athanase**
    1933   *Vers notre avenir*, RUO, 3, 1, 7-19.
2545. **De-la-Tour-Fondue, G.**
    1952   *Interviews canadiennes*, Chantecler, Montréal, 261.
2546. **Désilets, Alphonse**
    1926   *Pour la terre et le foyer*, Désilets, Québec, 215.
2547. **Desjardins, Edouard**
    1933   *Initiation au devoir*, Déom, Montréal, 283.
2548. **Désy, Jean**
    1954   *Les sentiers de la culture*, Fides, Montréal, 224.
2549. **Dumas, Paul**
    1934   *Nos raisons d'être fiers*, Le Devoir, Montréal, 30.
2550. **Filion, Gérard**
    1953   A new society grows in French Canada, *Saturday Night*, May 9, 7-9.
2551. **Fortin, Fernand-M.**
    1955   Le Canadien français, une jeunesse de vieille race, n. e., Mexico, 12.
2552. **Frégault, Guy**
    1937   Révolution et liberté, AN, avril, 232-39.
2553.   1937   Voix de jeunesse : où est la révolution ?, AN, mars, 81-90.
2554.   1955   Québec est-elle une enclave culturelle dans le Canada anglais, AN, 45, 253-56.
2555. **Gagnier, Leglius A.**
    1926   *Droits et devoirs de la médecine et des médecins canadiens-français*, Le Devoir, Montréal, 122.
2556. **Garrigou-Lagrange, Réginald**
    1939   Le meilleur des traditions canadiennes, *Revue Dominicaine*, 45, 172-82.
2557. **Gérin, Léon**
    1901   Notre mouvement intellectuel, TRSC, VII, 1, 145-72.
2558. **Greening, W. R.**
    1951   French Canadian Culture comes of Age, *Forthnightly*, 1010, 118-23.
2559. **Groulx, Lionel**
    1906   L'éducation de la volonté en vue du devoir social, *La Revue Canadienne*, 2, 58-79.
2560.   1916   *Les Rapailles*, Le Devoir, Montréal, 160.
2561.   1930   *Quelques causes de nos insuffisances*, n. e., n. p., 15.

A BIBLIOGRAPHICAL INTRODUCTION...

2562. 1939 Les bases de notre survivance, *Le Devoir*, 30, 146, 1.
2563. 1941 *Paroles à des étudiants*, Ed. de l'Action Nationale, Montréal, 80.
2564. 1953 *Pour bâtir*, L'Action Nationale, Montréal, 217.
2566. 1953 Survivre ou vivre ?, VF, 8, 146-53.
2567. 1954 La mission de la jeunesse canadienne-française, VF, 8, 347-59.
2568. 1955 *L'appel de la race* (introduction by Bruno Lafleur, 93), Fides, Montréal, 252.
2569. **H. E. C.**
    1920 *Ce que dit la Jeunesse*, La société des conférences, Montréal, 170.
2570. **Hertel, François**
    1936 *Leurs inquiétudes*, Lévesque, Montréal, 244.
2571. 1945 *Nous ferons l'avenir*, Fides, Montréal, 135.
2572. 1954 Les évolutions de la mentalité au Canada français, CL, 10, 140-52.
2573. **Humphrey, John and others**
    1943 Inside Quebec, *Relations*, 25, 16-9.
2574. **Hurteau, Philippe**
    1944 La subconscience d'infériorité, *L'Action Universitaire*, XI, 1, 21-24.
2575. **Joly, Richard**
    1954 Quelles traditions défendons-nous ?, CF, 11, 91-102.
2576. **Journées catholiques des Intellectuels canadiens**
    1950 *La personne humaine et le travail intellectuel*, CCIC, Montréal, 94.
2576a. 1951 *Les laïcs dans l'Eglise*, Fides, Montréal, 156.
2577. **Kistler, Ruth B.**
    1947 *Religion, Education and Language as factors in French Canadian cultural Survival*, New York University, Ph. D. Thesis.
2578. **Labelle, Antoine**
    1883 *La mission de la race canadienne-française au Canada*, Senécal, Montréal, 15.
2579. **L'Action Nationale**
    1941 D'une culture canadienne-française, AN, 27, 1-7 ; 28, 1-3 ; 27, 2, 125-46 ; 3, 207-221 ; 4, 310-21 ; 5, 297-405 ; 6, 538-45.
2580. **Laplante, R.**
    1945 Les traits francos-canadiens, AN, 25, 247-66.
2581. **Laplante, Germaine**
    1955 L'éducation nationale au foyer, VF, 10, 36-49.
2582. **Ledoux, Burton**
    1941 French Canada, a modern feudal State, *Virginia Quarterly Review*, XVII, 206-22.
2583. 1942 Le Canada français à la croisée des chemins, *Relations*, 22, 255-8.
2584. **Lemont, A.**
    1919 *Notre jeunesse et l'ère nouvelle*, n. e., Montréal, 126.
2585. **Lussier, Gabriel-Marie**
    1941 Culture canadienne-française, *Regards*, 2, 97-107.
2586. **Lussier, Doris**
    1954 Images d'une révolution, *Revue Dominicaine*, LX, 1, 5-15.
2587. **Maheux, Arthur**
    1949 A dilemma for our Culture, CHAR, 1-6.
2588. **Marchand, Clément**
    1936 La culture chez nous, *Les Idées*, 3, 6, 337-52.
2589. **Massey, Vincent**
    1948 *On being Canadian*, Dent, Toronto, 198.
2590. **Minville, Esdras**
    1933 *Le capitalisme et ses abus*, ESP, Montréal, 26.
2591. 1934 Le choc en retour de l'anglomanie, AN, 3, 195-220.
2592. 1944 Les Canadiens français ont-ils le sens des affaires ?, AE, 432-449.
2593. 1946 *Le Citoyen canadien-français*, Fides, Montréal, 2 v.
2594. 1949 *L'Homme d'affaires*, Fides, Montréal, 184.

A BIBLIOGRAPHICAL INTRODUCTION...

2595. 1953 Une question d'hommes, AN, 42, 112-24.
2596. **Montpetit, Edouard**
       1935 Climat de culture, RTC, 21, 156-173.
2597. 1942 Notes sur la double culture, TRSC, 36, 1, 77-81.
2598. 1946 *Propos sur la Montagne*, Ed. de l'Arbre, Montréal, 178.
2599. **Morin, Wilfrid**
       1938 *L'Avenir au Canada*, Sorlot, Paris, 250.
2600. 1943 *Nos Droits minoritaires*, Fides, Montréal, 431.
2601. **O'Leary, Dostaler**
       1935 *L'"inferiority Complex"*, Le Devoir, Montréal, 27.
2602. **Pelletier, Gérard**
       1952 Crise d'autorité ou crise de liberté ?, CL, 5, 1-10.
2603. **Perrault, Jacques**
       1945 La religion et notre société canadienne-française, *Culture*, 6, 294-306.
2604. **Perrier, Philippe**
       1927 Les Canadiens français et la vie morale et sociale au Canada, AF, 27, 5-6, 344-356.
2605. **Pruche, Benoît**
       1951 Vocation du Canada français, *Revue Dominicaine*, 57, 140-51.
2606. **Radio-Canada**
       1939 *Quelques problèmes d'actualité dans le Québec*, Beauchemin, Montréal, 196.
2607. **Rainville, Joseph**
       1933 La race canadienne-française dans vingt-cinq ans, RUO, III, 277-99.
2608. **Rioux, Albert**
       1950 Notre civilisation rurale est-elle en péril ?, *Culture*, 12, 248-65.
2609. 1955 Pour une révolution rurale, *Culture*, 14, 4, 424-36.
2610. **Rioux, Marcel**
       1955 Idéologie et crise de conscience au Canada français, CL, 14, 1-29.
2610a. 1956 Remarques sur les valeurs et les attitudes des adolescents d'une communauté agricole du Québec, CESH, 3, 133-44.
2611. **Roy, Mgr Camille**
       1929 Provincialisme intellectuel au Canada, CF, 17, 3, 148-67.
2612. 1941 *Pour former des hommes nouveaux*, Valiquette, Montréal, 206.
2613. **Rothney, Gordon O.**
       1947 *Quebec, cradle of democracy*, Culture, VIII, 4, 405-17.
2614. **Ryan, Claude**
       1950 Entre la sortie de l'école et le mariage, *Relations*, 109, 18-21.
2615. **Savard, Félix-A.**
       1955 Le Canadien français, *Notre-Temps*, X, 15, 26 février, 6.
2616. **Simard, Georges**
       1938 *Etudes canadiennes*, Beauchemin, Montréal, 224.
2617. **Stanley, Carleton W.**
       1929 Changing Quebec, *Dalhousie Review*, 20-27.
2618. **Symposium**
       1941 *French Canadian Background*, Ryerson, Toronto, 101.
2619. **Tremblay, Laurent**
       1941 La confiance en nous-mêmes, RUO, XI, 20-41.
2620. **Tremblay, Jean-Paul**
       1949 Culture et loisirs au Canada français, RUO, 19, 3, 360-78.
2621. **Trotter, R. G.**
       1950 Has Canada a National culture ?, *Queen's Quarterly*, XLIV, 215-227.
2622. **Turcotte, Edmond**
       1942 *Réflexions sur l'avenir des Canadiens français*, Valiquette, Montréal, 166.
2623. **Vadboncœur, P. and others**
       1952 Pour une dynamique de notre culture, CL, 5, 11-30.

2624. **Vandry, Ferdinand**
   1951 French culture and Canadian civilization, *Dalhousie Review*, XXXI, 73-81.
2625. **Vattier, Georges**
   1928 *Essai sur la mentalité canadienne-française*, Champion, Paris, 377.
2626. **Zay, Nicholas**
   1952 Problèmes du Canada français, *Le Devoir*, 43, 15 novembre, 4, 10.

h) *The influence of the United States*

2627. **Angers, François-A.**
   1940 L'américanisation du Saint-Laurent, AE, fév., 359-64.
2628. **Benoît, F.-E.-C.**
   1942 *L'influence américaine dans la littérature de nos premiers journaux canadiens-français*, Ph. D. Thesis, University of Ottawa.
2629. **Brebner, John Bartlet**
   1945 *North Atlantic Triangle, the interplay of Canada, the United States and Great Britain*, Yale University Press, New Haven, 385.
2630. **Buxton, Georges**
   1929 *L'influence de la révolution américaine sur le développement constitutionnel du Canada, 1774-1791*, Boccard, Paris, 128.
2631. **France-Amérique**
   1939 Le problème de la survivance française au Canada et les influences américaines, *France-Amérique*, août, 221-29.
2632. **Goldenberg, H. Carl**
   1936 The Americanization of Canada, *Forthnightly*, 824, 688-95.
2633. **Hansen, M. L. and Brebner, J. B.**
   1940 *The mingling of the Canadian and American peoples*, Yale University Press, New Haven, 2 v.
2634. **Lanctot, Gustave**
   1937 Influences américaines dans le Québec, TRSC, XXXI, 1, 119-125.
2635.   1941 *Les Canadiens français et leurs voisins du Sud*, Valiquette, Montréal, 322.
2636. **Leman, Beaudry**
   1928 Les Canadiens français et le milieu américain, RTC, 263-276.
2637. **Minville, Esdras**
   1923 Les Américains et nous, AF, 10, 2, 97-105.
2638. **Munro, W. B.**
   1929 *American influences on Canadian Government*, Macmillan, Toronto, 153.
2639. **Revue Dominicaine**
   1937 *Notre américanisation*, Ed. du Lévrier, Montréal, 272.
2640. **Robillard, Jean-Paul**
   1955 Les Etats-Unis nous envahissent, AN, 44, 632-640.
2641. **Wade, Mason**
   1944 Some aspects of the relations of French Canada with the United States, CHAR, 16-39.
2642. **Ware, N. J. and others**
   1937 *Labor in Canadian-American Relations*, University of Chicago Press, Chicago, 427.

i) *The influence of France*

2643. **Auclair, Elie-J.**
   1902 L'idée française et catholique chez les Canadiens, *La Revue Canadienne*, 1, 86-94 ; 166-75.
2644. **Barthe, Joseph-Guillaume**
   1885 *Le Canada reconquis par le France*, Ledoyen, Paris, 416.

A BIBLIOGRAPHICAL INTRODUCTION...

2645. **Beauveau-Craon, Prince de**
    1914 *La survivance française au Canada*, Paul, Paris, 233.
2645-a. **Bronner, Frederick-J.-L.**
    1936 *La survivance française*, M. A. Thesis, McGill University.
2646. **Cahiers français d'Information**
    1951 *Les relations historiques, économiques et culturelles, France-Canada*, Gouvernement Français, Paris, 36.
2647. **Charbonneau, Jean**
    1916-20 *Des influences françaises au Canada*, Beauchemin, Montréal, 3 v.
2648. **Charbonneau, R.**
    1947 *La France et nous*, Ed. de l'Arbre, Montréal, 77.
2649. **Chartier, Emile**
    1920 *La vitalité française au Canada*, Revue Canadienne, 25, 589-605.
2650. **Comité « France-Amérique »**
    1910 *France et Canada, l'avenir des relations franco-canadiennes*, n. e., Paris, 56.
2651. **Fabre-Surveyer, E.**
    1953 *Les Canadiens à Paris à la fin du siècle dernier*, Amérique Française, 11, 5, 41-47.
2652.   1953 *Les Canadiennes à Paris à la fin du siècle dernier*, Amérique Française, 11, 6, 38-43.
2653. **Faucher-de-Saint-Maurice, Edouard**
    1890 *La question du jour, resterons-nous français ?*, Québec, 136.
2653-a. **Fecteau, Edward**
    1945 *French contribution to America*, French-American Historical Society, Soucy Press, 339.
2654. **Gerbie, Frederic**
    1885 *Le Canada et l'émigration française*, Challamel, Paris, 448.
2655. **Gouin, Paul**
    1951 *Pour une technique de refrancisation*, Technique, 26, 6, 376-385.
2656. **Hébert, Joseph**
    1937 *La survivance du parler français et de l'esprit français*, RUO, 7, 4, 417-23.
2657. **Jones, H. M.**
    1928 *America and French Culture, 1750-1848*, University of North Carolina Press, 615.
2658. **Legendre, Paul**
    1952 *Les étudiants canadiens à Paris*, PO, 6, 4, 6069 ; 7, 1, 41-49.
2659. **Montpetit, Edouard**
    1914 *Les survivances françaises au Canada*, Plon, Paris, 91.
2670.   1920 *Au service de la tradition française*, Action Française, Montréal, 249.
2671. **Rivard, Antoine**
    1942 *Nous maintiendrons*, OT, no 273, Montréal, 16.
2672. **Roy, Mgr Camille**
    1937 *Pour conserver notre héritage français*, Beauchemin, Montréal, 185.
2673. **Tremblay, Maurice**
    1911 *Le Canada et la France, 1886-1911*, Chambre de Commerce, Montréal, 356.

7. The Educational System

a) *History of Education*

2674. **Action Nationale**
1935 *L'Education nationale*, Lévesque, Montréal, 209.
2675. **Allen, Howard C.**
1937 *The organization and administration of the educational Systems of the Canadian Provinces of Quebec and Ontario*, Thesis, Syracuse University.
2676. **Archambault, Joseph-Papin**
1948 *Vers la compétence*, OT, Montréal, 15.
2677. **Association canadienne des éducateurs de langue française**
1952 *L'enseignement du français au Canada*, Centre de psychologie et de pédagogie, Montréal, 311.
2678. **Audet, Louis-Philippe**
1941 *Le Frère Marie-Victorin*, Ed. de l'Erable, Québec, 283.
2679. 1947 *Le centenaire du système scolaire de la Province de Québec*, Cahiers de l'Ecole des Sciences Sociales, Québec, 4, 8, 43.
2680. 1950-55 *Le Système Scolaire de la Province de Québec*, Les Ed. de l'Erable, Québec, 5 v.
2681. 1954-5 Les écoles indépendantes dans le Bas-Canada, 1800-1825, *Culture*, XV, 3, 266-80 ; 4, 279-391 ; XVI, 1, 3,-50.
2682. **Beaudoin, Paul-Emile**
1949 Finances et Education, *Relations*, 106, 260-3.
2683. **Boucher-de-la-Bruère, Pierre**
1918 *Le Conseil de l'Institution et le Comité catholique*, Le Devoir, Montréal, 272.
2684. **Bouchette, Errol**
1905 L'Education nationale, *Revue Canadienne*, 41, 612-22.
2685. **Bruchési, Jean**
1942 Premiers livres scolaires canadiens, TRSC, 36, 1, 26-33.
2686. n. d. *Le Chemin des Ecoliers*, Valiquette, Montréal, 151.
2687. **Bureau, Robert**
1952 *Les bibliothèques scolaires masculines de langue française de la Ville de Québec*, Thesis, Laval University.
2688. **Cité Libre**
1954 Chez les instituteurs, *Cité Libre*, 9, 1-26.
2689. **Chapais, Thomas**
1928 La guerre des éteignoirs, TRSC, XXII, 1, 1-6.
2690. **Chartier, Emile Mgr**
1921 L'enseignement libre et chrétien, RC, 26, 7-18 ; 33-44.
2691. **Chauvreau, Pierre-Joseph-Olivier**
1876 *Instruction publique au Canada*, Côté, Québec, 367.
2692. **Cloutier, J.-E.**
1937 Nos écoles du soir, RD, mars, 134-47.
2693. **Collaboration**
1953 *Perspectives*, Sainte-Marie, Montréal, 140.
2694. **Comité catholique de l'Instruction**
1932 *Règlements du Comité catholique du Conseil de l'Instruction de la Province de Québec*, Québec, 318.

2695. **Cousineau, Jacques**
　　　　1941　Le problème des doubleurs, *Relations*, 9, 233-37.
2696. 　　　1942　Fréquentation scolaire au degré moyen de l'enseignement, *Relations*, 15, 64-9.
2697. **D'Anjou, Marie-Joseph**
　　　　1952　Visiteurs d'écoles à Montréal, *Relations*, 141, 229-32.
2698. **De Cazes, Paul**
　　　　1900　L'Instruction publique dans la Province de Québec, TRSC, VI, 1, 53-72.
2699. 　　　1905　*L'Instruction publique dans la Province de Québec*, Dussault et Proulx, Québec, 67.
2700. 　　　1912　*Code scolaire de la Province de Québec et Règlements du Comité catholique*, Le Soleil, Québec, 310 et 102.
2701. **De Lery, Louis-C.**
　　　　1941　L'Instruction obligatoire dans le passé, *Relations*, 11, 283-5.
2702. **Desrosiers, Adélard**
　　　　1909　*Les Ecoles Normales Primaires de la Province de Québec*, Arbour et Dupont, Montréal, 290.
2703. 　　　1940　Montréal, Centre d'Education, *Le Devoir*, 31, 46, 29.
2704. **Dugré, Alexandre**
　　　　1944　Bibliothèques et Forums, *Messager Canadien du Sacré-Cœur*, 53, 12, 609-17.
2705. **Dupuy, Pierre**
　　　　1925　L'Enseignement au Canada français, RTC, 11, 253-65.
2706. **Farley, P.-E.**
　　　　1933-5　*Orientation professionnelle*, Clercs de Saint-Viateur, Joliette, 2 v.
2707. **Fauteux, Aegidius**
　　　　1916　*Les Bibliothèques canadiennes*, Arbour et Dupont, Montréal, 45.
2708. **Fédération des Commissions scolaires catholiques**
　　　　1954　*Questions scolaires*, Mémoire présenté à la Commission Royale, Fédération des Commissions scolaires catholiques, 262.
2709. **Filteau, Gérard**
　　　　1950　*Les constances historiques de notre système scolaire*, Montréal, 59.
2710. 　　　1952　L'Education en Mauricie, 1852-53, SCHEC, 74-84.
2711. 　　　1952-3　Un siècle au service de l'Education, *Relations*, 144, 317-20 ; 146, 39-41.
2712. **Frégault, Guy**
　　　　1944　L'Education dans la vie nationale, Société Saint-Jean-Baptiste, *Programme du 24 juin 1944*, 69-74.
2713. **Gagnon, Onésine**
　　　　1952　*Cultural developments in the Province of Quebec*, University of Toronto Press, Toronto, 21.
2714. **Gallacher, J. C.**
　　　　1942　*A study of French influence on Canadian education with special Reference to Quebec*, M. A. Thesis, McGill University.
2716. **Gendron, Gérard**
　　　　1946　*La contribution financière du clergé et des communautés religieuses à l'enseignement dans la Province de Québec*, Thesis, Ecole des Hautes Etudes Commerciales.
2717. 　　　1947　La contribution financière du clergé à l'enseignement dans la Province de Québec, AE, juillet, 266-84.
2718. **Gervais, Albert**
　　　　1953　La corporation des instituteurs, *Relations*, 150, 152-5.
2719. 　　　1954　Pour une promotion de l'instituteur, *Relations*, 161, 127-30.
2720. 　　　1955　La tragédie scolaire de l'heure, *Relations*, 179, 289-91.
2721. **Gingras, Paul-Emile**
　　　　1955　L'Education : désarroi, AN, 44, 824-30.
2722. 　　　1955　L'Education, *Relations*, 45, 36-42 ; 106-111 ; 245-52.

2723. **Gosselin, Mgr Amédée**
   1911 *L'Instruction au Canada sous le régime français*, Laflamme et Proulx, Québec, 501.
2724. **Groulx, Lionel**
   1916 *La liberté scolaire*, Le Devoir, Montréal, 23.
2725. 1932 *Le français au Canada*, Delagrave, Paris, 236.
2726. 1934-5 *L'Enseignement français au Canada*, Granger, Montréal, 2 v.
2727. **Huberdeault, Jean**
   1947 *Problème de l'éducation en regard de la famille et de l'école*, Thesis, University of Montreal.
2728. **Laframboise, J.-C.**
   1951 L'Orientation de l'enseignement de l'administration publique au Canada, RUO, 21, 1, 17-26.
2729. **Lalande, P.-H.**
   1919 *L'Instruction obligatoire*, Imp. du Messager, Montréal, 148.
2730. **Lavergne, Armand-Renaud**
   1907 *Les écoles du Nord-Ouest*, Imp. du Nationaliste, Montréal, 63.
2731. **Lebel, Maurice**
   1945 Le rôle de l'enseignement dans la vie de nos institutions, *Culture*, 6, 4, 401-412.
2732. 1955 The teaching of French and English in the French Schools of Quebec, *Culture*, 16, 4, 381-92.
2733. **Lefèvre, Paul**
   1955 L'éducation populaire au Canada français, CL, 13, 21-33.
2734. **Legendre, Napoléon**
   1890 *Nos écoles*, Darveau, Québec, 95.
2735. **Lortie, Léon**
   1943 Problèmes de l'enseignement québecois, *Culture*, 4, 524-31.
2736. **Lowry, Curtis Henry**
   1944 *Early Jesuit education*, M. A. Thesis, Bishop's University.
2737. **Magnan, Charles-Joseph**
   1905 L'Instruction publique, RC, 41, 193-207.
2738. 1919 *A propos de l'éducation obligatoire*, L'Action Sociale, Québec, 120.
2739. 1922 *Eclairons la route*, Garneau, Québec, 246.
2740. 1932 *L'Instruction publique dans la Province de Québec*, n. e., Québec, 125.
2741. **Maheux, Arthur**
   1941 *Propos sur l'éducation*, L'Action Catholique, Québec, 260.
2742. **Mathieu, Mgr O.-E.**
   1916 *Education in the Province of Quebec*, Regina, 28.
2743. **Maurault, Mgr Olivier**
   1941 *Propos et portraits*, Valiquette, Montréal, n. p.
2744. **Morin, Victor**
   1953 Le Musée de Montréal, TRSC, XLVII, 1, 57-64.
2745. **Parenteau, Roland**
   1953 Le fonctionnement des fonds d'éducation, *Relations*, 153, 231-4.
2746. **Parmelee, G.-W.**
   1914 *Education in the Province of Quebec*, Dépt. de l'Instruction Publique, Québec, 156.
2747. 1931 *The Education Act of the Province of Quebec*, Dept. of Education, Québec, 286.
2748. **Paul, Victor**
   1941 *Nos institutions scolaires et l'impôt scolaire dans la Province de Québec*, Thesis, Ecole des Hautes Etudes Commerciales.
2749. **Plante, Albert**
   1953 Désirs des Commissions scolaires, *Relations*, 147, 59-62.

2750. 1953 Une thèse étonnante, *Relations*, 153, 238-41.
2751. 1953 Education et octroi statutaires, *Relations*, 1954, 260-63.
2752. 1954 Les Commissions scolaires à Chicoutimi, *Relations*, 167, 305-9.
2753. **Porter, Fernand**
　　　　1952 L'éducation en Mauricie, 1634-1852, SCHEC, 65-73.
2754. 1954 *Perspectives pédagogiques au Canada français*, Les Ed. Franciscaines, Montréal, 47.
2755. **Poulin, Gonzalve**
　　　　1939 *Le peuple est-il éducable ?*, Ed. de l'A.C.F., Montréal, 149.
2756. 1943 *Education populaire et loisirs d'après-guerre*, Cahiers de l'Ecole des Sciences Sociales, Québec, 32.
2757. **Province de Québec**
　　　　1950 *Code scolaire de la Province de Québec*, Gouvernement de la Province de Québec, Québec, 679.
2758. **Richer, Léopold**
　　　　1934 L'éducation nationale populaire, AN, 4, 4, 219-37.
2759. **Roy, Mgr Camille**
　　　　1935 *Nos problèmes d'enseignement*, Lévesque, Montréal, 221.
2760. **Roy, Egide-M.**
　　　　1924 *La formation du régime scolaire canadien-français*, Laflamme, Québec, 259.
2761. **Roy, Pierre-Georges**
　　　　1946 Les premiers manuels scolaires canadiens, BRH, 52, 231-303.
7262. **Royal Commission on the Advancement of Arts, Letters and Sciences**
　　　　1949-51 *Studies and Report*, Printers to the King, Ottawa, 2 v.
2763. **Saint-Pierre, Arthur**
　　　　1912 *L'Instruction obligatoire dans la Province de Québec*, ESP, no 13, Montréal, 23.
2764. **Simard, Georges**
　　　　1945 *Pour l'éducation dans un Canada souverain*, Ed. de l'Université d'Ottawa, Ottawa, 246.
2765. **Sissons, Charles Bruce**
　　　　1917 *Bi-lingual schools in Canada*, Dent, Toronto, 242.
2766. **Société canadienne d'enseignement post-scolaire**
　　　　1949 *Répertoire national de l'Education Populaire au Canada français*, Société Canadienne d'Enseignement post-scolaire, Québec, 332.
2767. **Tangue, Raymond**
　　　　1941 Réforme de l'enseignement et pain quotidien, AE, mai, 155-64.
2768. **Vincent, Joseph-Ulric**
　　　　1915 *La Question scolaire*, Ottawa Printing Co., Ottawa, 123.
2769. **Vinette, R.**
　　　　1953 The Catholic Normal Schools of Quebec, *Canadian Education*, 8, 35-39.
2770. **Wade, Mason**
　　　　1954 The Contribution of Abbé John Holmes to Education in the Province of Quebec, *Culture*, 15, 1, 2-16.
2771. **Weir, George M.**
　　　　1934 *The separate school Question in Canada*, Ryerson, Toronto, 298.

b) *Elementary Education*

2772. **Angers, François-Albert**
　　　　1945 *Le salaire de l'instituteur et de l'institutrice dans la Province de Québec*, Fédération des Instituteurs et Institutrices, Montréal, 47.
2773. **Audet, Louis-Philippe**
　　　　1948 *Où mène le cours primaire de la Province de Québec*, Ecole de Pédagogie et d'Orientation de l'Université Laval, Québec, 50.

2774. 1949 *La paroisse et l'éducation*, Ecole de Pédagogie et d'Orientation de l'Université Laval, Québec, 36.
2775. **Bellefeuille, Gustave**
1946 *Nos écoles laïques, 1846-1946*, Commission des Ecoles catholiques de Montréal, Montréal, 345.
2776. **Bruchési, Jean**
1939 Regards sur l'Ecole, AN, 13, 2, 92-105.
2777. **Casgrain, Thérèse-F.**
1944 La grande pitié de nos institutrices rurales, *Relations*, 5, 41, 130-1.
2778. **Comité catholique du Conseil de l'Instruction publique**
1953 *Programme d'études des Ecoles Primaires Elémentaires*, Comité Catholique, Montréal, 614.
2779. **Desjardins, Georges**
1950 *Les écoles du Québec*, Bellarmin, Montréal, 128.
2780. **Guénette, René**
1935 Une méthode d'éducation nationale à l'école primaire, AN, VI, 1, 7-31.
2781. **Maurault, Mgr Olivier**
1939 L'histoire de l'enseignement primaire à Montréal, de la fondation à nos jours, TRSC, XXXIII, 1, 1-18.
2782. **Pagé, Joseph**
1941 *Réformes de l'enseignement primaire*, Alliance catholique des Professeurs de Montréal, Montréal, 61.
2783. **Poulin, Leroy**
1934 *L'enseignement primaire rural dans la Province de Québec*, Thesis, Ecole Supérieure d'Agriculture de Sainte-Anne.
2784. **Saint-Pierre, Arthur**
1912 Nos enfants vont à l'école, *Messager Canadien du Sacré-Cœur*, déc., 5-49.

c) *Collège Classique and Secondary Education*

2785. **Angers, Pierre**
1954 Collège libre ou école publique ?, *Relations*, 14, 158-61.
2786. 1955 L'autonomie des Collèges classiques, *Relations*, 178, 259-61.
2787. **Anonymous**
1954 *Mémoire du Collège Jean-de-Brébeuf à la Commission Royale*, Collège Jean-de-Brébeuf, Montréal, 192.
2788. **Aumont, Gérard**
1950 La géographie dans l'enseignement secondaire au Canada français, RCG, IV, 1-2, 8-22.
2789. **Chartier, Emile**
1934 *The English and French systems of Secondary education in Quebec*, Montreal, 19.
2790. **Choquette, Philippe-B.**
1911-2 *Histoire du Séminaire de Saint-Hyacinthe*, Imp. des Sourds-Muets, Montréal, 2 v.
2791. **Congrès de l'Enseignement secondaire**
1948 *La Formation religieuse*, Comité Permanent de l'Enseignement Secondaire, Montréal, 438.
2792. **Desjardins, Paul**
1940 *Le Collège Sainte-Marie de Montréal*, Collège Sainte-Marie, Montréal, 318.
2793. **Douville, Joseph-Antoine-Irenée**
1903 *Histoire du Collège-Séminaire de Nicolet, 1803-1903*, Beauchemin, Montréal, 2 v.

2794. **Dugas, A.-C.**
    1914   Gerbes de souvenirs... du Collège de Joliette, Arbour et Dupont, Montréal, 2 v.
2795. **Fédération des Collèges classiques**
    1954   L'Organisation et les besoins de l'Enseignement classique dans le Québec, Fides, Montréal, 325.
2796. **Forget, Athanase**
    1932   Histoire du Collège de l'Assomption, 1893-1933, Imp. Populaire, Montréal, 809.
2797. **Gingras, Paul-Emile**
    1955   Le mémoire des Collèges classiques, AN, 44, 706-14.
2798. **Groulx, Lionel**
    1948   Professionnels et Culture classique, Le Devoir, 39, 112, 15 mars, 1, 8.
2799. **Joly, Richard**
    1952   Vers la réforme du baccalauréat, Presses Universitaires Laval, Québec, 32.
2800.   1953   Chronique collégiale 1951-2, ES, 32, 147-57.
2801.   1954   Les carrières des bacheliers, ES, 34, 57-63.
2802.   1954   Chronique collégiale, 1952-3, ES, 33, 201-16.
2803.   1955   Chronique collégiale, 1953-4, ES, 34, 245-63.
2804. **Laliberté, Joseph**
    1953   L'élite et la pédagogie du cours classique, CV, 18, 219-227.
2805. **Lamarche, Gustave**
    1951   Le Collège sur la Colline, petite histoire du Collège Bourget de Rigaud, Ed. de L'Echo de Bourget, Rigaud, 197.
2806. **Lauzon, Marcel**
    1949   Enquête sur les besoins d'Orientation scolaire au début du cours classique, Dépt. de Pédagogie et d'Orientation de l'Université Laval, Québec, 95.
2806a. **Lebon, Wilfrid**
    1948-9 Histoire du Collège de Sainte-Anne-de-la-Pocatière, Charrier et Dugal, Québec, 2 v.
2807. **Marie-du-Bon-Secours, Sr**
    1954   Valeur formatrice du cours classique pour les jeunes filles, CF, 11, 6-14.
2808. **Paquin, Denis**
    1955   Enquête sur les bibliothèques des Collèges classiques, ES, 34, 4, 155-68.
2809. **Pellard, Léo**
    1941   Défense et illustration de nos Collèges classiques, Les Carnets Viatoriens, Joliette, 16.
2810. **Picard, Robert**
    1954   Que représente notre baccalauréat ès Arts ?, Relations, 165, 254-8.
2811. **Plante, Gérard**
    1952   Pour un enseignement secondaire bien « coordonné », Relations, 137, 115-8.
2812. **Porter, Fernand**
    1949   Chronique collégiale, ES, 29, 224-32.
2813.   1950   Vocations choisies par les finissants des Collèges classiques et Séminaires affiliés aux Universités Laval et de Montréal, 1925-1950, Vie des Communautés Religieuses, 18, 5, 151.
2814. **Robert, Damien**
    1937   La formation scolaire dans nos Collèges classiques, ESP, no 282, Montréal, 32.
2815.   1939   Questions actuelles dans l'enseignement secondaire, ES, mars, 518-24.
2816. **Rioux, Marcel**
    1953   Remarques sur l'éducation secondaire, CL, 8, 34-42.
2817. **Roy, Mgr Camille**
    1935   Nos disciplines classiques, RTC, 21, 138-53.
2818. **Senécal, Wilfrid**
    1935   L'enseignement de la philosophie dans nos Collèges classiques, Journées Thomistes, I, 95-103.

2819. **Simard, Georges**
       1923   *Traditions et évolutions dans l'enseignement classique*, Ed. de l'Université d'Ottawa, Ottawa, 36.
2820. **Tremblay, Arthur**
       1954   La culture de nos bacheliers, ES, 33, 197-200.
2821.   1954   *Les Collèges et les Ecoles publiques : Conflit ou Coordination*, Presses Universitaires Laval, Québec, 140.

d) *Technical Education*

2822. **Anonymous**
       1955   L'Ecole des textiles de la Province de Québec, *Technique*, 30, 7, 8-12.
2823. **Buteau, J.-A.**
       1919   *Notre enseignement technique industriel*, Le Soleil, Québec, 124.
2824. **Ethier, Wilfrid**
       1953   L'Institut canadien d'Orientation professionnelle, *Vie des Communautés Religieuses*, 11, 139-43.
2825. **Gauvreau, Jean-Marie**
       1931   *L'Enseignement de l'ébénisterie à l'Ecole Technique de Montréal*, Imp. de l'Ecole Technique, Montréal, 12.
2826.   1943   *L'Ecole du Meuble*, Revue Technique, Montréal, 12.
2827. **Gibeau, Philippe**
       1949   Pour qui les écoles techniques ?, *Relations*, 100, 94-5.
2828. **Jean, François-Xavier**
       1947   Un siècle d'évolution agronomique, *Relations*, 78, 171-4.
2830. **Massue, Huet**
       1952   Contribution de Polytechnique au génie canadien, RTC, janvier.
2831. **Minville, Esdras**
       1940   L'Ecole des Hautes Etudes Commerciales, *Culture*, 458-69.
2832. **Montpetit, Edouard**
       1917   *L'Enseignement professionnel et la constitution d'une élite*, Revue Trimestrielle canadienne, Montréal, 19.
2833. **Rousseau, Gabriel**
       1939   Le développement des Ecoles d'Arts et Métiers, *Technique*, 14, 2, 85-9, 129.
2834. **Tessier, Albert**
       1943   *L'Enseignement ménager dans la Province de Québec*, n. e., Québec, 141.
2835. **Turcotte, Marguerite**
       1954   L'Orientation dans la mode canadienne-française, *Relations*, 14, 166, 275-7.
2836. **Vandandaigne, Anna**
       1945   L'Orientation professionnelle au service du foyer par l'enseignement ménager, PO, 5, 3, 161-90.

e) *University Education*

2837. **Angers, F.-A.**
       1952   Le Fédéral et les Universités, AN, jan., 7-29.
2838. **Auclair, Elie-J.**
       1938   L'Ecole Victoria de Montréal, TRSC, XXXII, 1, 1-20.
2839. **Audet, Francis-J.**
       1936   Simon Sanguinet et le projet d'Université de 1790, TRSC, XXX, 1, 53-70.
2840. **Barbeau, Antonio**
       1942   *Evolution de la médecine canadienne-française*, n. e., Montréal, 7.
2841. **Bastien, Hermas**
       1936   *L'Enseignement de la philosophie*, Lévesque, Montréal, 220.

2842. **Beaugrand-Champagne, Aristide**
       1933   *L'Architecture*, OT, Montréal, 16.
2842-a. **Benoît, Auguste**
       1954   La tragédie de l'Université, CV, 19, 81-93.
2843. **Blair, Hervé**
       1941   L'Enseignement de la théologie au Canada, *Culture*, 3, 206-20.
2844. **Bovey, Wilfrid**
       1933   Le rôle des Universités canadiennes-françaises en Amérique du Nord, RTC, 19, 341-52.
2845. **Bruchési, Jean**
       1949   Aspect intellectuel et universitaire du Canada d'après-guerre. *Culture*, X, 3, 215-30.
2846. 1953   *L'Université*, Presses Universitaires Laval, Québec, 117.
2847. **Carrière, Gaston**
       1951   Le Cardinal Villeneuve et les Universités canadiennes, *Culture*, 12, 31-42.
2848. **Collaboration**
       1944   L'Université et le Monde de demain, AU, XI, 2, 68.
2849. **Dansereau, Pierre**
       1944   Science in French Canada, *Scientific Monthly*, 59, 348, 188-94 ; 349, 261-72.
2850. **Falardeau, Jean-Charles**
       1956   Manquons-nous d'Universités ?, *Le Devoir*, 47, 86, 87, 88, 11, 12, 13 mars, 4.
2851. **Forest, Ceslas-M.**
       1951   Vingt-cinq ans de philosophie à l'Université de Montréal, *Actualités Philosophiques*, Centre de Psychologie et Pédagogie, Montréal, 9-30.
2852. **Institut Social Populaire**
       1953   Problèmes d'étudiants à l'Université, ISP, no 465, Montréal, 32.
2853. **L'Action Universitaire**
       1945   *Université de Montréal*, AS, 132.
2854. **Lévesque, Georges-Henri**
       1948   Les Universités et l'Union nationale, RD, LIV, 2, 76-81.
2855. **Lortie, Léon**
       1950   Canadian Universities and a Canadian Culture, AU, avril, 46-57.
2856. 1952   The B. A. degree in our French-speaking Universities, *Culture*, XIII, 21-32.
2857. **Maheux, Arthur**
       1952   L'Université Laval et la Culture française au Canada, *Culture*, 13, 2, 117-26.
2858. **Maurault, Mgr Olivier**
       1938   L'Enseignement supérieur au Canada, RTC, 24, 95, 22-38.
2859. 1952   L'Université de Montréal, *Les Cahiers des Dix*, 17, 11-49.
2860. **Minville, Esdras**
       1935   A l'Université, AN, jan., 5, 5-25.
2861. **Montpetit, Edouard**
       1940   L'Enseignement supérieur est-il américanisé ?, RTC, 26, 13, 229-73.
2862. **O'Bready, Maurice**
       1954   L'Université de Sherbrooke, ES, 34, 53-6.
2863. **Mercier, André**
       1948   *Education physique dans les Universités canadiennes-françaises*, M. A. Thesis, Montreal University.
2864. **Parent, Mgr A.-M.**
       1946   Le rôle des Universités canadiennes-françaises, AN, 28, 1, 22-32.
2865. **Prévost, H.**
       1952   L'Université Laval et la vie nationale, AN, juin, 353-60.
2866. **Stucker, E.**
       1942   La superbe Université de Montréal, *Technique*, 17, 9, 553-60.

8. SPECIAL PROBLEMS IN THE STUDY OF FRENCH CANADA

a) *Historical Interpretation and "Historicism"*

2867. **Adair, E. R.**
    1942   The Canadian contribution to Historical science, *Culture*, 4, 63-83.
2868. **Anonymous**
    1944   *Un manuel d'histoire unique*, Imp. Populaire, Montréal, 11.
2869. **Arès, Richard**
    1936   Histoire nationale et Education, AN, 7, 5, 306-20 ; 8, 1, 41-55.
2870.   1950   Sur une prédiction d'Arnold Toynbee, *Relations*, 112, 93-5.
2871. **Arles, Henri d'**
    1921   *Nos historiens*, L'Action Française, Montréal, 243.
2872. **Benoît, Auguste**
    1952   Deux « Histoire du Canada », Groulx, Rumilly, CV, 17, 2, 113-25.
2873. **Bouchard, T.-D.**
    1944   *The Teaching of Canadian History*, Yamaska Printing Co., St-Hyacinthe, 24.
2874. **Bruchési, Jean**
    1946   History and National life, *Culture*, 7, 177-93.
2875.   1953   *L'enseignement de l'histoire du Canada*, Canadian Historical Association, 13.
2876. **Brunet, Michel**
    1954   *Canadiens et Canadians*, Fides, Montréal, 173.
2877. **Careless, J. M. S.**
    1950   History and Canadian Unity, *Culture*, 12, 118-24.
2878. **Culture**
    1944   Special number on the teaching of History, june, 56.
2879. **Dufebvre, Bernard**
    1954   M. Séguin et « sa » vérité historique, RUL, 9, 312-19.
2880. **Erskine, John Stewart**
    1942   *Les Historiens canadiens-français*, M. A. Thesis, McGill University.
2881. **Frégault, Guy**
    1940   L'Art de l'Historien, *Le Quartier Latin*, 22, 19, 8 mars, 4.
2882.   1941   Notre Culture française, AN, oct., 144-47.
2883.   1942   Culture historique, *Amérique Française*, déc., 13-15.
2884.   1943   Francis Parkman, *Amérique Française*, fév., 27-31.
2885.   1944   Michel Bidaud, historien loyaliste, AU, XI, 4, 1-7.
2886.   1944   Le mythe de M. le Chanoine Groulx, AN, déc., 163-93.
2887.   1945   Actualité de Garneau, AU, XI, 7, 8-15.
2888.   1945   L'Enseignement de l'histoire, AU, XI, 9, 18-21.
2889.   1941-5   L'Enseignement de l'histoire au Canada, *L'Ecole Canadienne*, nov. 1941, 117-20 ; fév. 1945, 294-98 ; avril 1945, 398-403.
2890. **Gérin, Léon**
    1915   L'intérêt sociologique de notre histoire au lendemain de la conquête, RTC, mai, 3-14.
2891. **Godbout, Archange**
    1942   Sociétés historiques de langue française, *Culture*, 3, 67-89.
2892.   1943   Les préoccupations en histoire et les thèses de M. l'abbé Maheux, *Culture*, 4, 28-43.
2893.   1944   Enquête sur l'enseignement de l'histoire au Canada, *Culture*, 5, 156-68.

A BIBLIOGRAPHICAL INTRODUCTION...

2894. **Groulx, Lionel**
    1920 Veillons sur notre histoire, AF, nov., 5, 5-20.
2895. 1937 L'histoire, gardienne de traditions vivantes, *Directives*, Ed. du Zodiaque, Montréal, 205-43.
2896. 1950 Aux tournants de l'histoire, *Relations*, 113, 61-3.
2897. 1951 Vue d'ensemble sur l'histoire du Canada français, AN, oct., 89-97.
2898. 1952 Quel sort attend les Canadiens français ?, *Relations*, 144, 328-30.
2899. 1952 Henri Bourassa et la chaire d'histoire du Canada à l'Université de Montréal, RHAF, 6, 430-39.
2900. **Lacroix, Benoît-M.**
    1949 Avons-nous des historiens ?, RD, 55, 86-96.
2901. 1955 Culture française et Histoire canadienne, RD, oct., 143-53.
2902. **Lanctot, Gustave**
    1946 *Garneau, historien national*, Fides, Montréal, 207.
2903. 1946 Evolution de notre historiographie, AU, 13, 1, 3-6.
2904. **Ledoux, Burton**
    1942 Psychologie historique du Canada français, *Relations*, 15, 61-4 ; 17, 115-8 ; 22, 255-8.
2905. **Lefèvre, Jean-Jacques (ed)**
    1945 *Centenaire de l'histoire du Canada de François-Xavier Garneau*, Société Historique de Montréal, Montréal, 460.
2906. **Lefranc, A.**
    1890 Nos quatre historiens modernes, Bidaud, Garneau, Ferland et Faillon, RC, 3, 19-31.
2907. **Léger, Jean-Marc**
    1948 Robert Rumilly, *Notre-Temps*, 3, 15, 24 jan., 1, 4.
2908. **Lemoine, J.-M.**
    1882-3 Nos quatre historiens modernes, Bidaud, Garneau, Ferland, Faillon, TRSC, 1, 1, 1-12.
2909. **Maurault, Mgr Olivier**
    1929 *Marges d'histoire*, Lib. d'A.C.F., Montréal, 308.
2910. **O'Reilly, John B.**
    1955 Mason Wade, Historian, *Canadian Messenger of the Sacred-Heart*, 65, 580-90 ; 647-56 ; 703-9.
2911. **Pierce, D. J.**
    1937 *The historiography of French Canada*, Ph. D. Thesis, University of Toronto.
2912. **Roy, Mgr Camille**
    1935 *Historiens de chez nous*, Beauchemin, Montréal, 190.
2913. **Sage, Walter N.**
    1945 Where stands Canadian History, CHAR, 5-14.
2914. **Saunders, R. M.**
    1943 History and French Canadian survival, CHAR, 25-34.
2915. **Yon, Armond**
    1940 L'abbé Verreau, historien canadien, 1828-1901, TRSC, XXXIV, 1, 119-137.
2916. 1946 *L'abbé H.-A. Verreau*, Fides, Montréal, 208.

b) *Theories and Methods in Social Research*

2917. **Blanchard, Raoul**
    1938 Enquête historique locale, ES, 17, 5, 334-40.
2918. **Brouillette, Benoît**
    1944 Comment faire une monographie géographique ?, Cahiers de la Faculté de Sciences Sociales de l'Université Laval, 32.

2919. **Brunet, Michel**
　　　1955　Nécessité et importance des recherches en Sciences sociales, RCG, 9, 2-3, 115-18.
2920. **Caron, Ivanhoé**
　　　1926　Les monographies, leur rôle, leur caractère, *Semaine d'histoire du Canada*, 1ère session, Société d'histoire de Montréal, Montréal, 252-72.
2921. **Clément, Marcel**
　　　1949　*Sciences sociales et Catholicisme*, ESP, no 423, Montréal, 32.
2922. **Conway, Pierre H.**
　　　1942　*Life and French Canada*, Cahiers de l'Ecole des Sciences Sociales, Québec, 51.
2923. **Equipes de Recherches sociales**
　　　1949　*Recherches*, Université de Montréal, Montréal, 53.
2924. **Falardeau, Jean-Charles**
　　　1944　*Analyse sociale des Communautés rurales*, Cahiers de la Faculté des Sciences Sociales, Québec, 31.
2925.　　1949　Analyse des Communautés rurales, RUL, IV, 3, 210-17.
2926.　　1944　Problems and first experiments of Social research in Quebec, CJEPS, X, 3, 365-71.
2927. **Garigue, Philip**
　　　1956　Mythes et réalités dans l'étude du Canada français, CESH, 3, 123-32.
2928. **Gérin, Léon**
　　　1905　La vulgarisation de la science sociale chez les Canadiens français, TRSC, XI, 1, 67-88.
2929.　　1909　La Science sociale, TRSC, 3, III, 1, 129-66.
2930.　　1914　La Sociologie, le mot et la chose, TRSC, VIII, 1, 321-56.
2931.　　1925　La Science sociale en histoire, RTC, déc., 352-81.
2932.　　1937　L'Observation monographique de milieu social, RTC, 17, 378-89.
2933. **Groulx, Lionel**
　　　1945　L'œuvre d'Esdras Minville, AN, 34, 6-14.
2934.　　1953　Pour inaugurer la chaire de Civilisation canadienne-française, AN, fév., 122-44.
2935. **Hamelin, L.-E.**
　　　1954　L'Enseignement de la géographie et l'éducation nationale, VF, 8, 497-504.
2936.　　1955　Quelques aspects méthodologiques de l'enseignement de la géographie dans le Québec, *Culture*, XVI, 1, 66-89.
2937.　　1956　Un centre de recherches d'expression française dans l'Ungava, AN, 45, 7, 596-611.
2938. **Hughes, Everett-C.**
　　　1943　*Programmes de recherches sociales pour le Québec*, Cahiers de la Faculté des Sciences Sociales, Université Laval, Québec, 2, 4, 41.
2939.　　n. d.　*The natural history of a Research project*, (MS), Redpath Library, McGill University, 20.
2940. **Lévesque, Georges-Henri**
　　　1942　*Catholique, es-tu social ?*, Cahiers de l'Ecole des Sciences Sociales, Québec, 1, 4, 38.
2941.　　1948　L'Enseignement de la doctrine sociale de l'Eglise à la Faculté des Sciences Sociales de Laval, *Ad Sum Sacerdotum*, 4, 2, 21-34.
2942.　　1952　Humanisme et Sciences sociales, RD, LVIII, 2, nov., 212-23.
2943. **Mailhiot, Bernard**
　　　1952　Orientations présentes de nos recherches en Psychologie sociale, CESH, 1, 117-34.
2944. **Mailloux, Noël**
　　　1944　Nouveaux horizons de la psychologie contemporaine, *Culture*, 5, 3, 249-57.
2945.　　1953　Le dixième anniversaire de l'Institut de Psychologie de l'Université de Montréal, CESH, 2, 7-12.

2946. **Minville, Esdras**
    1944 *Invitation à l'étude*, Fides, Montréal, 169.
2947. **Poulin, Gonzalve**
    1941 L'Enseignement des Sciences dans les Universités canadiennes, *Culture*, 3, 338-49.
2948. **Radelet, Louis-A.**
    1953 The University of Montreal workshop on community Relations, CESH, 2, 169-79.
2949. **Saint-Pierre, Arthur**
    1954 Léon Gérin, un disciple canadien de Frédéric Le Play, TRSC, XLVIII, 1, 91-103.

9. BIBLIOGRAPHIES

2950. **Bergerin, André**
 1954 Les œuvres de Bourassa, AN, 43, 199-244.
2951. **Brown, Charles Raynor**
 1927 Bibliography of Quebec or Lower Canada Laws, 1764-1841, *Law Library Journal*, 19, 4, 22.
2952. **Bond, Donald F. and others**
 1945 Anglo-French and Franco-American studies, a current bibliography, *Romantic Review*, oct., 161-90.
2953. **Brault, Lucien**
 1940 *Francis J. Audet, bio-bibliography*, n. e., Ottawa, 96.
2954. 1954 Bibliographie d'Ottawa, RUO, 24, 345-75.
2955. **Brouillette, Benoît**
 1950 Un pionnier de la géographie au Canada, Emile Miller, RCG, IV, 1-2, 94-96.
2956. **Bonenfant, Jean-Charles**
 1948 French Canadian books and reviews published in Canada during the last ten years, *Statistical Year-Book*, Province of Quebec, 221-32.
2957. **Cardin, Clarisse**
 1947 *Bio-bibliographie de Marius Barbeau*, Fides, Montréal, 96.
2958. **Chabot, J.**
 1948 *Bio-bibliographie d'écrivains canadiens-français*, Ecole des Bibliothécaires, Montréal, 12.
2959. **David, A.**
 1927 *The books of French Canada*, Montréal, 47.
2960. **Dionne, N.-E.**
 1905-9 *Inventaire chronologique des livres, brochures, journaux et revues*, n. e., Québec, 4 v.
2961. **Drolet, Antonio**
 1955 *Bibliographie du Roman canadien-français, 1900-1950*, Presses Universitaires Laval, Québec, 126.
2962. **Gagnon, Philéas**
 1895-1913 *Essai de Bibliographie canadienne*, Québec et Montréal, 2 v.
2963. **Geddes, James et Rivard, Adjutor**
 1906 *Bibliographie du parler français au Canada*, Marcotte, Québec, 99.
2964. **Lanctot, Gustave**
 1951 *L'Oeuvre de la France en Amérique du Nord*, Fides, Montréal, 185.
2965. **Lapierre, Richard**
 1955 Bibliographie sommaire de Benoît Brouillette, RCG, IX, 1, 4-7.
2966. **Laurent, Edouard**
 1941 *Essai bibliographique autour de « Rerum Novarum »*, Les Ed. de Culture, Québec, 86.
2967. **Lortie, Lucien**
 1942 *Bibliographie analytique de l'œuvre de l'abbé Arthur Maheux*, n. e., Québec, 159.
2968. **Ludovic, Fr.**
 1941 *Bio-bibliographie de Mgr Camille Roy*, n. e., Québec, 181.
2969. **Malchelosse, Gérard**
 1916 *Benjamin Sulte et son œuvre, essai de bibliographie*, Pays Laurentien, Montréal, 78.

A BIBLIOGRAPHICAL INTRODUCTION...

2970.   1954 La bibliothèque acadienne, *Les Cahiers des Dix*, 19, 263-86.
2971. **Marin, A.**
           1946 *Bibliographie de l'Honorable Pierre-Basile Mignault*, Fides, Montréal, 135.
2972. **Morgan, Henry James**
           1867 *Bibliotheca Canadensis*, Desbarats, Ottawa, 411.
2973. **Nadeau, Gabriel**
           1952 Notes pour servir à une bibliographie franco-américaine, *Bull. de la Société Historique franco-américaine*, 64-74.
2974. **Ratté, Alice et Gagnon, Gilberte**
           1952 *Bibliographie analytique de la littérature pédagogique canadienne-française*, ACELF, 108.
2975. **Roy, Antoine**
           1938 Bibliographie de monographies et histoires de paroisse, *Rapport de l'Archiviste de la Province de Québec*, 1937-8, Québec, 252-83.
2976.   1941 Bibliographie de généalogies et histoires de familles, *Rapport de l'Archiviste de la Province de Québec*, 1940-1, 95-332.
2977. **Société des Ecrivains canadiens**
           1937-56 *Biographical Bulletin*, Société des Ecrivains canadiens, 19 v.
2978.   1955 *Répertoire bio-bibliographique 1944-1954*, Ed. de la Société des Ecrivains canadiens, Montréal, 256.
2979. **Staton, Frances**
           1924 *The rebellion of 1837-38, a bibliography*, Toronto Public Library, Toronto, 81.
2980. **Staton, F. M. and Tremaine, Marie**
           1934 *A bibliography of Canadiana*, Public Library of Toronto, Toronto, 828.
2981. **Tod, D. D. and Cordingley, A.**
           1950 *A check-list of Canadian Imprints, 1900-1925*, Printer to the King, Ottawa, 370.
2982. **Tremaine, Marie**
           1952 *A bibliography of Canadian Imprints, 1751-1800*, University of Toronto Press, Toronto, 706.
2983. **Trotter, R. C.**
           1934 *Canadian history, a syllabus and guide to reading*, Macmillan, Toronto, 193.
2984. **Woodley, Elsie Caroline**
           1932 *The history of education in the Province of Quebec, a bibliographical guide*, M. A. Thesis, McGill University.

Confederation

Canadian Historical Readings
A selection of articles from the *Canadian Historical Review*
and other volumes

1 *Approaches to Canadian History*
2 *Upper Canadian Politics in the 1850's*
3 *Confederation*
4 *Politics of Discontent*

Edited by Ramsay Cook / Craig Brown / Carl Berger

Confederation

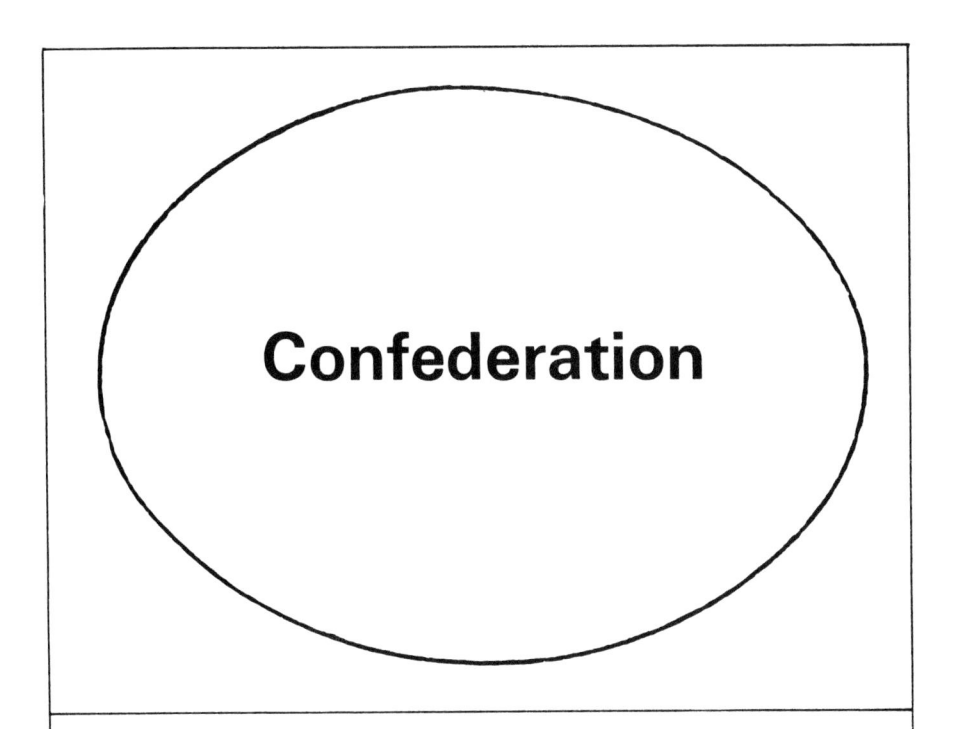

Essays by D. G. Creighton / C. P. Stacey / P. B. Waite
Walter Ullmann / A. G. Bailey / G. F. G. Stanley

Introduction by Ramsay Cook

University of Toronto Press

Copyright, Canada, 1967, by
University of Toronto Press
Toronto Buffalo London
Printed in Canada
Reprinted 1974, 1978
ISBN 0-8020-1456-9
CN ISSN 0068-8886
LC 23-16213

Contents

Introduction/RAMSAY COOK	vii
Economic Nationalism and Confederation/D. G. CREIGHTON	1
Britain's Withdrawal from North America, 1864–1871/C. P. STACEY	9
Edward Cardwell and Confederation/P. B. WAITE	23
The Quebec Bishops and Confederation/WALTER ULLMANN	48
The Basis and Persistence of Opposition to Confederation in New Brunswick/ALFRED G. BAILEY	70
Act or Pact? Another Look at Confederation/G. F. G. STANLEY	94

Contents

Introduction/RAMSAY COOK	vii
Economic Nationalism and Confederation/D. G. CREIGHTON	1
Britain's Withdrawal from North America, 1864–1871/C. P. STACEY	9
Edward Cardwell and Confederation/P. B. WAITE	23
The Quebec Bishops and Confederation/WALTER ULLMANN	48
The Basis and Persistence of Opposition to Confederation in New Brunswick/ALFRED G. BAILEY	70
Act or Pact? Another Look at Confederation/G. F. G. STANLEY	94

Introduction

RAMSAY COOK

CONFEDERATION, unlike the American Civil War which it paralleled in time, has not been the subject of acrimonious disputes among academic historians. Nor has it given rise to a massive and enduring tradition of patriotic hero worship. There have, nevertheless, been divergent interpretations of Confederation, both between English-speaking and French-speaking writers and within each of the two groups. Naturally, these changing perspectives have reflected the periods in which they were developed and the dominant interests of their authors. Though seldom rendered in epic proportions, Confederation has appeared as a major critical event in our national past in the writing of every Canadian historian, French or English. But in the century since 1867 there have been several subtle shifts in the interpretation of the events which culminated in the establishment of the "new nationality."

For not a few Canadians in the late nineteenth century, Confederation was looked upon as a prelude to a larger federation—that of the British empire—not the first giant step in the establishment of an independent Canada. Thinking of themselves as British in traditions and in "race," they viewed Australia, New Zealand, Canada, and Britain as different sections of the same nation. Convinced that this single nation already existed, united by ties of history, tradition, and "race," they suggested that this unity be formalized either by a written federal constitution or, less rigidly, by systematic continuous consultation and collaboration.

For writers like Principal G. M. Grant of Queen's University, and George Parkin, a Canadian who acted as secretary of the Rhodes Trust, the significance of Canadian Confederation was that it marked an advance toward the ultimate goal of imperial federation and offered an example of the organization that could be applied to the constituent parts of the empire. The views and hopes of these writers appear to contrast sharply with those of the gloomy custodian of the Grange in Toronto, Goldwin Smith. Smith, once enthusiastic about the prospects of Canadian nationalism, had concluded by the 1880's that Confederation was an entirely unnatural constitutional order. Since, in his view, the geographic determinants of North America ran north and south, and since Canadians and Americans had so much in common, the future promised political union for all the English-speaking people of North America. Smith also saw this union as a means of dealing with the "French" problem (by assimilation). These views he cogently presented in his widely read *Canada and the Canadian Question*, published in 1891, and also in a flood of journalistic outpourings.

The difference between Smith, the continentalist, and imperial federationists like G. M. Grant is obvious. But their similarities are almost as important. Both saw Confederation as a temporary way station for a country whose ultimate destiny was to form part of a larger English-speaking federation. But the dream was never achieved, either in its continentalist or its imperial federationist form. The Canadian people and their politicians showed little interest in these long-range plans, concerning themselves with more prosaic questions of trade, tariff, and immigration, and ignoring, for the most part, the demands of the outside world except when a crisis such as the Boer War was pressed upon their attention. And the division which that event produced in the country convinced many that concentration on domestic questions was far safer than speculation about the destiny of Canada and the empire.

The failure of the imperial federation ideal, a failure which was abundantly clear by the end of the Great War, and the gradual ascendancy of the view that Canada should attain full autonomy within the Empire-Commonwealth was accompanied by a revised view of the significance of Confederation. Where the imperial federationists had seen in it an anticipation of something broader and more elevating, the exponents of the later school were convinced that all Canadian history pointed toward self-sufficient, autonomous nationhood. In this scheme the achievement of 1867 had to be placed in an entirely different framework. The major theme of the new version was the gradual broadening of Canadian self-government from precedent to precedent. The major signposts were the 1837 rebellions and the consequent granting of responsible government, the passing of the British North America Act, and the gradual breakdown of British control over Canadian economic, military, and foreign affairs, all culminating in the Balfour Declaration and the Statute of Westminster. This view was sustained by the conviction that all human history is the story of increasing liberty, that the irresistible force of progress made the process inevitable, and that the nation state was a natural and desirable goal. This school of Canadian history was best represented by the writings of O. D. Skelton, Laurier's biographer and, significantly, Under-Secretary of State for External Affairs during the interwar years, of J. W. Dafoe, editor of the influential *Free Press* in Winnipeg, of F. H. Underhill, teacher and essayist, and of A. R. M. Lower, whose *Colony to Nation* (Toronto, 1946) effectively summed up the liberal-nationalist version of the Canadian past.

But even during the liberal-nationalist ascendancy another group of scholars was beginning to work out a new view of Canadian history which had a profound impact upon the interpretation of Confederation. Partly in reaction to the heavy political emphasis of his predecessors and contemporaries, and deeply influenced by studies in geography and economic history, Harold Adams Innis offered a novel and challenging version of the Canadian experience. Innis turned his mind to the staple trades, beginning with fur, that had played such a crucial role in the establishment and development of the country. His examination of this feature of Canadian history convinced him that, contrary to the dominant autonomist view, dependence upon Europe had been both necessary and beneficial. Where the politically oriented, liberal-nationalist historians had viewed Canadian dependence upon Britain as limiting and colonial, Innis argued that the strength of Canada, its economic and political survival, had been built upon this very relationship. Implicit in this argument was the view that the emphasis which the autonomists gave to the North American character of Canada was exaggerated. In fact, Canada had always maintained a close tie with Europe, and this was a natural outgrowth of Canadian geographical and trading patterns. Here Innis was challenging the still widely accepted view of Goldwin Smith that the natural geographic lines of North America ran north and south; the history of the staple trades, based on the St. Lawrence waterway system, showed plainly that the natural axis of the continent was, in fact, east-west. Confederation, then, was merely a constitutional structure built on a natural geopolitical base. In the conclusion to his *Fur Trade in Canada* (Toronto, 1930, revised 1956), Innis summarized his thesis in a famous sentence: "The present Dominion," he declared, "emerged not in spite of geography, but because of it."

Innis wrote no major study of Confederation himself. That task fell to his colleague, D. G. Creighton. Like Innis, and several other historians of the depression years, Creighton began with an interest in economic history. His first book, *The Commercial Empire of the St. Lawrence* (Toronto, 1937), brilliantly expanded and illustrated the

Laurentian thesis. Then, working with the Rowell-Sirois Commission, Creighton wrote *British North America at Confederation*, which placed a heavy emphasis on the economic motives and goals of the founders of the new union. In his great biography of Macdonald (Toronto, 1952, 1955) and in *The Road to Confederation* (Toronto, 1964) the story of Confederation was again told, this time with great sensitivity to personalities and with a keen sense of the drama of political history. But underlying all of these works was the theme of the triumph of Canadian nationality over the attractions of continentalism. As Creighton wrote in 1956, "the idea of the St. Lawrence as the inspiration and basis of a transcontinental, east-west system, both commercial and political in character, is still central in my interpretation of Canadian history."

The Laurentian theme remains the dominant one in English-Canadian studies of Confederation. Though giving more emphasis to Toronto as a metropolitan centre than previous writers, the underlying thesis of J. M. S. Careless's *Brown of The Globe* places it well within the orbit of the Innis-Creighton approach. The same may be said of W. L. Morton's writings on Confederation. This scholar is especially interesting in that while he continues to emphasize the role of the West in Confederation, his earlier protests against the imperialist implications of the Laurentian thesis have now been replaced by an acceptance of the doctrine.

No French-Canadian historian has written a full-scale, documented study of Confederation that can be compared with those published by English-speaking scholars. That in itself is a significant fact. Confederation has never held, for French Canadians, the same all-important place in the nation's history as it has for English Canadians. Indeed, some French-Canadian nationalist writers have viewed Confederation not as a triumph, but rather as a tragedy for their people. In this, they have echoed the views of some of the leading French-Canadian politicians at the time of Confederation. In the late nineteenth century, writers like L.-O. David and Ludovic Brunet expressed the same judgments on Confederation as those delivered by A.-A. Dorion in the Confederation Debates: Confederation, because of its centralized character, was a serious threat to the survival of French Canada. In so far as these writers approved Confederation at all, it was because it represented a step toward Canadian independence from Great Britain, a view which stands in marked contrast to that held by English-Canadian writers of the same period.

French-Canadian writers from Confederation onward judged Confederation from the standpoint of its effect upon the French culture in Canada. Abbé Lionel Groulx, writing at the end of the Great War, presented a divided view. On the one hand, Confederation had certainly been useful in preventing absorption of the country into the United States, and it had also helped to advance Canada on the road to freedom from Britain. On the other hand, it had failed to provide adequate guarantees for the French-speaking minorities living outside Quebec. By the beginning of the 1920's Groulx was convinced that Confederation was in an advanced stage of disintegration and that an independent Quebec would eventually emerge. Thomas Chapais, writing in the same years as Groulx, took a different view. He noted that the primary fact about Confederation was the federal system which it had established. Federalism had been adopted because it was necessary to accommodate the needs and aspirations of the French-speaking minority. It gave them their own province where they were a majority and could thus protect their way of life from any threats from the English-speaking majority. It was true, he admitted, that the French-speaking minorities outside Quebec had fared badly, but that was not the fault of Confederation—it would have happened under any system, given the intolerance of the English-speaking majority.

Thus French-Canadian writers have always emphasized two facets of Confederation: federalism and the status of the French culture in Canada. With respect to federalism, French Canadians were relatively quick to adopt, though they did not invent, the interpretation of Confederation as a compact among the provinces. This theory sought to provide historical support for the doctrine of provincial rights by insisting that Confederation, since it was the result of an agreement among the provinces, left the provinces primacy over the central government. This view appealed to French Canadians who feared that their rights might be tampered with by a highly centralized federal government in which English Canadians held the majority. French-Canadian writers also developed a second version of the compact theory which contended that Confederation was a compact or *entente* between French and English Canadians, thus guaranteeing equal rights to both groups. This view became especially widespread among French Canadians during the years when minority school rights were being challenged outside Quebec.

It is not surprising during the contemporary revival of nationalism in Quebec that Confederation should again come under historical review. While there is still no full-scale study of the subject by a French-Canadian scholar, some new tendencies can be discerned. Perhaps the most obvious is that many French-Canadian scholars have now accepted the English-Canadian contention that Confederation was, in origin, a highly centralized federation and that the concept of a provincial compact is baseless. Jean-Charles Bonenfant has been the main exponent of this view. Others have gone even further insisting that the concept of a cultural compact is also a "myth" that should be exploded. The writings of Professor Michel Brunet of the Université de Montréal provide the basis for this view. It is interesting to observe that these new views have come as part of Quebec's demand for radical alterations in the Canadian constitution. Where the old cultural compact theory was devised to defend the minority groups outside of Quebec, the rejection of that theory has been accompanied by the insistence that the minorities are no longer of any significance. For Quebeckers, the new theory runs, what is important is Quebec, not French Canada.

The essays included in this volume do not, of course, attempt to illustrate all of the interpretations of Confederation. They do, however, provide detailed studies against which the major interpretations may be measured. The subject can be examined in greater detail in a wide variety of historical works. Those of Donald Creighton, already mentioned, are essential reading. *The Life and Times of Confederation, 1864–1867* (Toronto, 1962) by Peter Waite, *The Critical Years: The Union of British North America, 1857–1873* (Toronto, 1965), by W. L. Morton, and J. M. S. Careless's *Brown of* The Globe, II, *Statesman of Confederation, 1860–1880* (Toronto, 1963) are also studies of first importance. An older, but still useful, book is W. M. Whitelaw, *The Maritimes and Canada before Confederation* (Toronto, 1934, reprinted 1966).

French-Canadian views of Confederation may be gleaned from Abbé Lionel Groulx' *La Confédération canadienne, ses origines* (Montreal, 1918) and Volume VIII of Thomas Chapais' *Cours d'histoire du Canada* (Quebec, 1934). Jean-Charles Bonenfant's important article, "L'Esprit de 1867," appeared in *La Revue d'histoire de l'Amérique française*, XVII (juin 1963). Two studies which present the various views of the compact theory are Volume I of *The Report of the Royal Commission of Inquiry on Constitutional Problems* (Quebec, 1956) and Père Richard Arès' *Dossier sur le pacte fédératif de 1867* (Montreal, 1967). Some further discussion of this question may be found in Ramsay Cook, *Canada and the French-Canadian Question* (Toronto, 1966).

To place Confederation in its international setting the following works may be examined: C. P. Stacey, *Canada and the British Army, 1846–1871* (Toronto, 1936, revised 1963); R. W. Winks, *Canada and the United States: The Civil War Years* (Baltimore, 1960); and W. L. Morton, "British North America and a Continent in Dissolution, 1861–1871," *History*, XLVII (June, 1962).

Finally the following pamphlets issued by the Canadian Historical

Association deserve specific mention: W. L. Morton, *The West and Confederation, 1857–1871*; P. B. Waite, *The Charlottetown Conference*; J. Murray Beck, *Joseph Howe, Anti-Confederate*; Paul G. Cornell, *The Great Coalition*; W. M. Whitelaw, *The Quebec Conference*; and Jean-Charles Bonenfant, *The French Canadians and the Birth of Confederation*.

Confederation

Economic Nationalism and Confederation

D. G. CREIGHTON

I

IT should be emphasized at once that in this paper I make no attempt to supply what might be called an "economic interpretation" of Confederation. The effort to explain one group of phenomena supposedly "political" in character by reference to another group of phenomena supposedly "economic" in character seems to me as mechanical and unreal as the historical dichotomy upon which it is based. I am interested, not in seeking such simple causal connections, but in exploring some small part of the enormously complicated relationships of industrialism and nationality in the nineteenth century. In the British Empire, Germany, and the United States, the rise of the new industry and the new transport was accompanied by a strong tendency towards territorial expansion and by an equally marked impulse towards political union and centralization. It seems to me that the foundation and early growth of the Dominion of Canada afford a small but fairly typical example of this complex politic-economic process. Within the short space of less than fifteen years, the British North American provinces reached four major decisions: they decided upon political union, westward expansion, transcontinental railways, and a protective tariff. The coincidence of these decisions was surely not accidental: they were all products of a vast complex system of related forces which were continually acting and reacting upon each other. It is this process of interaction that I propose to explore—in a very general fashion—this afternoon. And I shall focus attention upon only one of these four decisions—the determination to establish a protective tariff—in an endeavour to trace its origins and estimate its significance in the general historical process.

In the middle 1840's, the point at which this analysis must begin, the great triumphs of industrialism and nationality were still in the future. Except in England, the broad general interests of agriculture and commerce still dominated affairs. The economic order was characterized by wooden shipping, wind- and water-power, ocean and river transport. The relatively tranquil world of politics was made up of little states, small provinces, unconsolidated federations and sprawling, decentralized empires. The provinces of British North America had grown up in this world and they were fairly happily adjusted to it. Their economies were based upon the St. Lawrence River and the Atlantic Ocean; agriculture, lumbering, and fishing were their staple industries; and they had put their money into canals to improve the inland waterways and into wooden ships to peddle their goods around the world. It was their settled habit to think in terms of remote markets, of commercial systems which extended far beyond their narrow boundaries and vastly transcended their parochial interests. They were members—and fairly satisfied members—of the low-tariff British mercantile system; and the idea of reciprocity, of interchange of privileges, of economic and political give-and-take, was familiar and acceptable to them. Their trade relations with each other were almost negligible; they had no political link beside their common allegiance to Great Britain; and nobody had yet conceived the idea of a transcontinental British North American

Reprinted from Canadian Historical Association, *Report*, 1942 union. There was little interest in the remote West, little conception of the future of railways, and little appreciation of the vast potentialities of the tariff.

This innocent and idyllic world of our great grandfathers must have appeared to possess a most comforting substantiality. But in actual fact it was already ominously threatened with approaching dissolution. The first major shock which fell upon it came, appropriately enough, from the original industrialist country, Great Britain. In Great Britain, as in Germany, the United States, and British North America, the problem of commercial policy in general and of the tariff in particular was of essential importance in this period of rapid economic and political change. There were few measures which summed up the interests and expressed the philosophy of the new industrialism and the new nationality more completely and effectively than the repeal of the Corn Laws. To John Bright and the other reforming manufacturers, who somehow contrived to suggest that they ran their mills as unimportant side-shows to the main business of professional moralizing, the principle of free trade was a timeless truth of universal validity. It was not only economic orthodoxy: it was certainly Christian morality: there were even inspired moments when it seemed to take on the awful grandeur of divine revelation. In the light of these heavenly intimations it was easy for the free traders to convince themselves—and very nearly to convince posterity—that they acted in a spirit of cosmic altruism. Obsessed with the elevation of humanity in general, they drove straight towards the goal of national self-interest. In the main, the Anti-Corn Law League was an association of British manufacturers who preferred, with natural Christian humility, to conceal their real identity; and the repeal of the Corn Laws was just as strictly and exclusively a policy of economic nationalism as the tallest tariff on earth. In the interest of industrial specialization at home, and world trade abroad, the free traders had sacrificed both the agriculture of Great Britain and the commerce of British North America. "Blessed are the free in trade," ran the new British industrial beatitude, "for they shall inherit the earth." This terrestrial paradise of world commerce glimmered radiantly in the distance; but to win it, to make oneself worthy of it, it was first necessary to cast off the fleshly trammels of the old British Empire. For Great Britain the new nationality was at first inevitably written as "Little Englandism." It meant the withdrawal of colonial preferences, the recall of colonial troops, the abandonment of colonial obligations. Just as Prussia was forced to break up the ramshackle Germanic Confederation before she could achieve the consolidated German Empire, so Great Britain had to shake herself free from the Old Colonial System before she could begin to realize the world empire of free trade.

This sudden assertion of British national independence was the first formidable impact of the new order on British North America. It was followed almost immediately by another shock, the direct introduction of the new technology. The repeal of the Corn Laws compelled the provinces to grope their way towards a new commercial policy: the construction of the first railways equipped them with the rudiments of the new industrial system. In Great Britain, the first rapid growth of machine manufacture had preceded the construction of railways; but in North America—and for obvious reasons—this order was almost exactly reversed. In the new continent the railway was the first great embodiment of the age of iron and steam; and the construction of the Grand Trunk and the other railways of the 1850's formed the first stage of the slow industrialization of British North America. From that time onward, the development of the provinces was guided by the compulsion of two forces, one external and one native to the provinces themselves. The external pressure was to come from those two great industrialized nationalities, Great Britain and the United States: the internal pressure was to originate in the movement towards industrialism and nationality within British North America. Each of these influences was driving the provinces towards a new policy, political and commercial. And in time it was to be discovered that the goal of both was one and the same.

II

There was, however, nothing very novel in the first British North American reaction to the new world order. The original responses ran along safely traditional lines. Flung rudely out of the shelter of the Old Colonial System, the provinces could not believe themselves capable of enduring what the British industrial monopolists could complacently refer to as the "bracing atmosphere" of free trade; and except for a moment, during the deep depression of 1849, there was not much serious discussion of a protective tariff. In fact, the provinces had not the slightest intention of taking any action which, in the elephantine language of modern diplomacy, could be described as unilateral. Through long membership in the British Empire, they were accustomed to the idea of an interchange of privileges, of a rough balance of benefits and concessions. And when Great Britain had summarily and forcibly ejected them from their first commercial association, they turned naturally to that other imperialist power, the United States. In 1854, they concluded with the American Republic a treaty of Reciprocity, which established a series of reciprocal preferences and concessions, more systematic certainly than anything the provinces had known before, but roughly on the same lines as the old imperial system.

Within the comforting protection of these new fiscal arrangements, the provinces intended to carry on pretty much as they had done before. They were still largely absorbed in commerce, not manufacturing. They still thought, not in terms of a British North American economy, but in terms of great international commercial systems based on the ocean and the continental rivers. Even though they now began to use the new technology of steam and iron, they used it instinctively to buttress and strengthen commercial empires which had been built up long before in the pre-industrial age. It was significant that the Intercolonial, the one serious railway project which was intended to link the Maritimes with the Province of Canada, was taken up by governments rather than by private capitalists; and it was significant also that all the governments concerned, at one time or another, extricated themselves from agreements for its construction with the most surprising agility. The Grand Trunk, which was by far the biggest British American railway enterprise of the period, was obviously planned to strengthen the old international trading system of the St. Lawrence. It was intended, like the St. Lawrence canals before it, to capture the trade of the American Middle West.

All this implied—or seemed to imply—merely a slight modification of the old objectives and methods. The revised arrangement looked durable: but there were elements of disturbance within it. And of these variables perhaps the most important was the ominously uncertain condition of the United States. The Reciprocity Treaty—and it is essential to remember this—was negotiated *before* the triumph of industrialism and coercive centralized nationality in the United States. It was a typical product of the period when the agrarianism and commercialism of the South still struggled against the encroaching industrialism of the North. The South had taught the continent its ideas of equalitarian democracy, preached the principle of local autonomy for the benefit of little states and provinces, struggled to defend a rough balance of agricultural, commercial, and industrial interests within the republic. The Reciprocity Treaty was in part injurious to southern interests; but the South supported it precisely because it believed that the arrangement would satisfy the British provinces and prevent or delay their annexation to the United States. The passage of the Reciprocity Treaty was, in fact, one of the last efforts of the South to preserve the economic and political balance of power on the continent, to save North America from what Parrington has called "an unquestioning and uncritical consolidation." It was one of the South's last successes. For the Treaty was accepted in the year that witnessed the enactment of the Kansas-Nebraska Bill, which in effect destroyed the Missouri Compromise. From that moment the struggle between North and South for the control of the western domain approached its final paroxysm. And the new Republican party, which represented big business, coercive centralization, and truculent imperialism, adopted a protectionist creed which was to make such arrangements as the Reciprocity Treaty an idle dream for the next half-century.

But the approaching crisis, which was to transform the United States into an industrial and centralized nation, had not yet actually arrived. In the meantime, while North and South were slowly marshalling their forces for the conflict, the first results of railway building began to show themselves in British North America. One at least of these consequences might have been anticipated with tolerable certainty. From the earliest times, the governments of North America including those of the northern British provinces, had been compelled to make one peculiar and significant modification in the doctrine of the *laissez-faire*, non-interventionist state. They had been compelled to accept the idea that the state in North America must clear and prepare the way for the beneficent operations of the capitalist. In the past this had meant the lavish construction of roads and canals; and now it came to imply substantial contributions to railways. In the Maritimes, partly through choice and partly through necessity, the state itself frankly undertook the construction and management of its new transport system. In the Province of Canada, where the Northern, the Great Western, and the Grand Trunk Railway Companies were supposedly independent commercial concerns, the state subsidized, rehabilitated, and revived these enterprises with a frequency which almost earned it the title of ownership. All this involved what to British North America was a new and alarming drain upon the treasury; and when the capital imports incidental to railway building had ceased, and the depression of 1857 had descended, the customs revenue dwindled alarmingly. The province, as its financier Galt explained, had cheapened the cost of British manufactures in Canada, and enhanced the value of Canadian products in England, by its expenditures on canals and railways. The traffic therefore could very well bear an increased toll. The government needed the money. And, to make a long story short, it proposed to raise the tariff. Thus the Cayley-Galt tariff of 1858-9 was one of the first results of the railway construction programme. But there was, in addition, another important consequence which perhaps had not been anticipated by even the most hard-headed of the farmers and merchants who had wanted the railways in the first place. The railway boom provided the basis for the new industrialism in British North America. It brought, in volume and numbers such as had never been seen before, the new industrial materials, the new industrial techniques, the new industrial labourers. There was a widening of the economic horizon, a quickening of the tempo of economic life; and the little provincial foundries and manufacturies profited from the better markets of the period, and also from the high prices which were partly a result of the Crimean War and partly of the railway boom itself. The little colonial establishments profited; but not, unhappily, as much as they could have wished. Even while the boom was at its height, they were astonished and outraged to discover how much of the profits of Canadian railway construction were going into the pockets of American manufacturers. "The very spades and shovels, axes and hammers used by the workmen and labourers were of American make," wrote one contemporary with indignation. As Galt had intimated, the Canadian canals and the American and Canadian railways were already removing the natural shelter of the northern manufacturers. Their situation had been annoying enough during the boom; it was far worse when the depression of 1857 brought a collapse of prices. They suffered; but this time they suffered in highly important company, for their distress coincided with the financial embarrassment of the government. They desired a higher tariff for protection: the government desired it for increased revenue. And the result of this happy union of sentiments was the Cayley-Galt customs duties of 1858-9. Thus, on the eve of the American Civil War, an important qualification had already been introduced into the traditional commercial policy of British North America. The provinces stood committed to a system of low tariffs and reciprocal preferences. But Canada had abruptly increased her duties with protectionist approval though ostensibly for revenue purposes. This discrepancy was immediately detected in the United States. And disagreements might have followed this discovery, if all such problems had not been momentarily engulfed in the torrent of hatred unloosed by the American Civil War.

III

For the next fifteen years, the American Civil War and its consequences constituted perhaps the dominant factor in British North American affairs. Nothing is more obvious now than that the new order of nationality and industrialism meant war; and nothing is more ironical than the conviction of its apologists that it meant peace. John Bright stood for pacification with the same moral earnestness that he opposed factory acts and denounced colonies. To these middle-class reformers war was unthinkable precisely because they had just succeeded in raising politics to such a high moral plane. As Mr. Gladstone said reverently of John Bright, he had "elevated political life to a higher elevation and to a loftier standard." The Manchester School introduced moral earnestness into English politics: the American Slavery Abolitionists introduced moral indignation into North American affairs. Surely this ought to have improved human conduct; but the strange fact was that human conduct remained obstinately unregenerate. Far from becoming better, it seemed to be getting steadily worse. The aristocratic intriguers who met at the Congress of Vienna had given Great Britain nearly forty years of peace. But the ushering in of the Manchester men's millennium was followed almost immediately by the Crimean War; and the great humanitarian crusade of the Abolitionists ended in a bloody civil conflict. From 1854 to 1878, the bulk of the period covered by this paper, there were few years indeed which did not see armed struggle among the great powers of Europe and America.

In many ways, which cannot be examined here, the American Civil War was destined to effect the development of British America. Its influence, for example, on the formation of commercial policy was decisive in the end. So far as the Province of Canada was concerned, it helped from the start to promote the industrial growth which had begun during the previous decade. "I trust," said James Watson, President of the Manufacturers' Association of Ontario at a special meeting held in 1875, "I trust that it will be borne in mind that the rapid development of manufacturing [in this country] during the past few years is almost entirely due to the peculiar position of the United States from the commencement of the late civil war." Inevitably the war and the economic dislocation resulting from it focused the manufacturing industry of the United States upon the home market and limited its export trade. In all probability there were a good many Canadian manufacturers like Edward Gurney of the Gurney Stove Company who declared in 1876 that his business had quadrupled since 1861 and that, in effect, it was the war-time rise in values in the United States which had sufficed to give him the home market.

Thus one result of the war was to increase the number of people in the Province of Canada who were likely in future to want a protective tariff. Its far more important consequence, however, was to complete the supremacy of those interests in the United States which would never again submit to such a measure as the Reciprocity Treaty. The war was a struggle between an awakening industrial society and a planter community, a struggle for nationality against local independence. And its result, as Parrington has said, was to throw "the coercive powers of a centralizing state into the hands of the new industrialism." The men who stood for transcontinental railways, large-scale manufacture, and western exploitation were to determine, in large measure, the pattern of future American development. They represented unification and expansion within the country and imperialism without. The purchase of Alaska, the freely expressed desire for the annexation of British North America, are evidences of this renewed impulse towards territorial aggrandizement. The establishment of a passport system for the first time against the northern provinces, the threat to repeal the Rush-Bagot Treaty limiting naval armaments on the Great Lakes, the proposal to stop the bonding privileges for trade through United States territory— all illustrate a new truculence of tone.

Again, as in the case of England, commercial policy summed up and expressed the character of the new America which arose from the wreckage of the Civil War. Before the conflict began, the new Republican party had declared in favour of a protective tariff. The financial necessities of the war brought an enormous increase in the customs duties: and the need for war-time goods and services gave an immense impetus to manufacturing. When the war was over, the tariff was unquestioningly continued as one of the sacred institutions of the unified continental state. In home affairs, it expressed the victory of the industrial North over the agrarian South: in external relations, it signified the triumph of national exclusiveness over international co-operation. In such circumstances as these the Reciprocity Treaty had inevitably to disappear. In the winter of 1866, when the British Americans journeyed down to Washington, in the vain hope of negotiating a new agreement, Mr. Morrill, the principal author of the new American tariff, had only a very singular proposal to make to them. He proposed that, in return for the inshore fisheries and the navigation of the St. Lawrence and its canals, the United States would consider reciprocal free trade in five articles of great commercial importance. These articles were: unfinished millstones and grindstones, gypsum, firewood, and rags.

The tremendous alteration in the whole position of British North America had now been brought to an end. The change had begun with the downfall of the Old Colonial System of Great Britain: it had been completed by the wreck of the old federal system of the United States. The insignificant northern provinces were now flanked by two reorganized consolidated nationalities, heavily industrialized, each of which had adopted a realistic political and commercial policy in its own exclusive interest. In the complete absence, in the apparent impossibility of those reciprocal preferences which had supported the St. Lawrence route in the past, what hope was there for an international commercial system based upon it? Even under the favourable circumstances of the past, the St. Lawrence had never really won the trade of the American Middle West; and there was all the more reason now why it could never do so. This collapse of the old hopes in the wreckage of the old world of trade and politics brought the provinces to the threshold of economic and political nationalism. In the light of the successful examples around them, they saw now how they could use the new concepts of union and expansion as the United States had adapted them for the North American continent. They decided upon a strongly centralized federal union: they determined upon transcontinental railways and the opening of the West. All this was pretty strictly in accordance with the programme which had been developed in the United States during and after the Civil War. But there was one significant difference. There was no lofty protective tariff. In Canada, the decisive change in commercial policy had yet to come.

The fact was that for a decade longer the new federation still clung obstinately to the old economic notions which had been the stand-by of the provinces. The interests of the state, and the interests of the principal groups composing it, seemed still to be satisfied with a moderate commercial policy. In the Maritimes, the financial pressure of railway and railway commitments might have forced up the customs duties; and actually, just before Confederation, the tariff in New Brunswick was probably the highest in British North America. But, on the other hand, the revenue position in the Province of Canada was easier; and in 1866, as a pre-Confederation concession to opinion in the Maritimes, it lowered the level of the old Cayley-Galt duties. The manufacturers of Canada strongly protested this reduction; but in general the agricultural, commercial, and railway interests were stronger; and both in Canada and the Maritimes they still wanted what Galt called "modified free trade." They put their hopes in the free-trade area of four million people which Confederation would create. They expected that they could make arrangements for preferential exchange of goods with the West Indies and South America. And, of course, they obstinately continued to believe that in the end they would yet get a new Reciprocity Treaty with the United States.

Yet twelve years after Confederation the National Policy was an established fact. The twin pressures, internal and external, continued to act in unison: and together they were driving the new Dominion towards the complete American variant of economic nationalism. Gradually the hope of a Reciprocity Treaty with the United States was crushed out of existence by repeated disappointments. Macdonald failed to obtain a new arrangement at the time of the Washington Treaty: George Brown was unsuccessful in the negotiations of 1874. While the prospect of these international agreements faded, the idea of national exclusiveness had already begun to grow. The phrase "a national policy for Canada" appears as early as 1869. By the next year it has become definitely associated with the tariff. In the election of 1872 Macdonald made an open appeal to manufacturers and workingmen with a proposal to support domestic industry with a protective tariff. In the Maritimes, and in old commercial towns like Montreal, the trading interests were strongly entrenched and resisted stoutly; but Hamilton, Toronto, and the other industrial centres of the future were already converted or half-converted to the new views. All this had occurred while prosperity still ruled and while American manufactures had yet to enter the Canadian market in volume. After 1873 the drift towards protection became accelerated and irresistible. The situation was in many respects analogous to that which had existed in the Province of Canada in 1857-9 when the first Canadian protective tariff had come into being. Again depression had exposed the weaknesses of Canadian industry: again the mass-production American manufacturers had invaded the northern market: and again the Canadian government was badly in need of funds. There was one major difference, however—a difference which aggravated rather than alleviated the problem in the 1870's. In 1857-9, British North America had enjoyed a reciprocal commercial agreement with the United States. Now there was no Reciprocity Treaty and no prospect of one. The forces of industrialism and nationality, internal and external to British North America, had finished their work. And the Dominion of Canada completed its programme of national unification with the National Policy of Protection.

Britain's Withdrawal from North America[1]
1864-1871

C. P. STACEY

ONE of the most familiar vices of historians is their inveterate tendency to compart history. We partition it off chronologically, chopping it into neat periods. Thus the student who is being taught about the fifteenth century is only too likely to get the impression that at some date during that century a new heaven and a new earth suddenly came into being. The date varies according to the particular course to which the student is being subjected at the moment: it may be 1453, or 1485, or 1492, or 1494. That sort of thing is probably in some degree inevitable. More serious is our tendency to compart by topics. A person who writes a textbook—or even a book—on a period of modern British history is almost certain to divide it into topical chapters or groups of chapters. Thus a long chapter on "Domestic Problems" is usually followed by a rather shorter one on "The Ebb and Flow of Foreign Policy." Next comes a still shorter chapter entitled "Colonial Policies and Problems." Finally, the book almost invariably ends with a chapter called "Intellectual Currents."

The weakness of this kind of approach is most evident in cooperative works where the chapters are written by different hands, but even where the book is the work of one author there is a tendency for the division between the chapters to become absolute. The reader forgets that the men sitting around the table in Downing Street and controlling events (or trying to) were dealing simultaneously with all departments of policy, domestic, colonial and foreign; to say nothing of the fact that they were doubtless swayed by intellectual currents.

The same tendency to compart appears in more specialized fields, and here I come to my theme. Students of British foreign policy in the mid-Victorian era are familiar with the difficulties which resulted from Bismarck's wars; they are also acquainted

[1]This paper was read before Section II of the Royal Society of Canada at the June meeting of 1955. In a book called *Canada and the British Army, 1846–1871*, published in 1936, the present writer ventured the remark, with respect to the Danish War, "The fashion in which, at this period, the uncertainty of the situation in America hampered Britain's action in Europe, and *vice versa*, has been too little studied" (p. 154, n. 5). In this paper he attempts to expand that suggestion.

Reprinted from *Canadian Historical Review*, XXXVI (3), September, 1955

with the fact that the same period witnessed a prolonged and severe crisis in Anglo-American relations (though it must be said that scholars in the United Kingdom have usually been less interested in this than in the continental developments). It is rather extraordinary, however, that so few students on either side of the Atlantic should have noted the extent to which these two aspects of British policy were practically interconnected. The same statesmen who dealt with Prince Bismarck and Napoleon III had to deal with President Lincoln and President Grant; and it was this fact that was basically responsible for the ineffectiveness of British policy in both hemispheres. Historians have rightly recognized that it was military weakness that paralysed the action of the United Kingdom in Europe;[2] they have failed to point out that that weakness was the more serious in that British statesmen had to face the fact that if compelled to fight in Europe they would quite probably find themselves fighting the United States in North America at the same time. The British Army in the years dealt with in this paper was an inadequate instrument to deal with either of these emergencies singly; it was monstrously inadequate to deal with a war on two fronts, one on each side of the Atlantic. British policy has rarely if ever been faced with a more unpleasant dilemma. It was painfully evident to contemporaries, and it is really surprising how completely it has escaped the authors of such valuable and scholarly works as the *Cambridge History of British Foreign Policy*. Comparing that history published soon after the First World War with earlier British writings in the same field, one applauds the increased (though still inadequate) attention given to relations with the United States; but one remains impressed by the failure to observe the effects in Whitehall of the interaction of events in America and events in Europe.[3]

Such interaction was not, of course, entirely a new thing in the 1860's. It had appeared half a century before, during the Congress of Vienna, when British statesmen confronting Prussia and Russia found it embarrassing that their best troops should be fighting in America, and hastened to make peace with the United States so Britain's hands might be freed for more important matters.[4] In

---

[2]See, e.g., Arthur Hassall, *The History of British Foreign Policy, from the Earliest Times to 1912* (Edinburgh and London, 1912), 281.

[3]A. J. P. Taylor shows some awareness of the matter in *The Struggle for Mastery in Europe, 1848–1918* (Oxford, 1954); see pages 129 and 199. But he does not mention the *Alabama* question, indicate how serious was the problem confronting Gladstone's ministry in 1868–71, or describe the means adopted to deal with it.

[4]A. T. Mahan, *Sea Power in its Relations to the War of 1812* (2 vols., London, 1905), II, 423–34.

those days the United States was weak. Britain had in fact fought the French and the Americans simultaneously for three years without incurring fatal results. But half a century worked great changes. It is true that as late as 1861, when the *Trent* affair brought war between Britain and the United States very close, some Englishmen were still able to view the prospect with comparative equanimity. Lord Palmerston's Secretary of State for War, in the midst of hurrying off reinforcements to Canada, observed "We shall soon *iron the smile* out of their face."[5] The United States had just been disrupted by civil war; the breathless withdrawal of the Northern army from the field of Bull Run was fresh in the public mind; and for the moment Europe was comparatively quiet.

During the next three years the whole scene was transformed. The Southern Confederacy's early hopes of victory and independence were not realized. The Northern States became the greatest military power on earth, and their hostility to Britain was as evident as their strength. At the same time new and terrible forces were on the march in Europe. Bismarck had become Minister-President of Prussia in 1862 and had set about strengthening the army, in defiance of Parliament, and preparing for those trials of strength with Austria and France that were necessary preliminaries to unifying Germany under Prussian leadership. Britain's first real embarrassment came early in 1864, when Prussia and Austria attacked Denmark over Schleswig-Holstein. Palmerston had made the mistake of saying loudly that aggressors would find that "it will not be Denmark alone with whom they will have to contend." But the German monarchies were quite unmoved by such threats.[6]

At the same time the British Government discovered that nearly 15,000 of its regular troops were in British North America and that this would add greatly to the difficulty of collecting any kind of expeditionary force for Denmark. Orders were accordingly issued to reduce the force in Canada. What alarmed Canadians most was a proposal that the troops remaining in their country should be concentrated entirely at Quebec and Montreal, leaving

[5] Lewis to Twisleton, Dec. 5, 1861: Sir G. F. Lewis, ed., *Letters of the Right Hon. Sir George Cornewall Lewis* (London, 1870), 406.

[6] *Cambridge History of British Foreign Policy*, II, chap. XIII. Schleswig-Holstein ("Handbooks prepared under the Direction of the Historical Section of the Foreign Office," no. 35, London, 1920), 75 ff. Palmerston and Russell, in spite of the country's weakness, showed a tendency to persist in a warlike policy, but were restrained by their colleagues and by the Queen. It was at this time that the Queen described her two senior ministers as "those two dreadful old men" (to King Leopold, Feb. 25, 1864, G. E. Buckle, ed., *The Letters of Queen Victoria, Second Series*, I, 168).

Upper Canada without a British soldier.[7] This clearly reflected the British Government's new and solid respect for American military power; and in the course of the next few months editorials in The Times and debates in Parliament testified to the extent to which the scorn and bluster with which so many Englishmen had regarded the Northern forces and the Northern cause had now changed to apprehension and dismay.[8] The British governing class never appeared to worse advantage than in its attitude to the Civil War in the United States; and there is a certain poetic justice in the fact that that war did so much to advance the cause of political democracy in Britain and the transfer of power to other hands.

The Cabinet's position with respect to North America at this period was extremely difficult. No administration headed by Palmerston was likely to adopt a policy of scuttle, even when so many voices were raised in favour of it. The Government in fact steered a middle course. It refused to have anything to do with the ideas of Little Englanders like Robert Lowe, who urged that every Imperial soldier should be withdrawn from Canada at once; and on the other hand it argued that Canada's defence must rest "mainly and principally upon Canada herself."[9] The determination to maintain the Imperial military connection with Canada was strikingly symbolized by the decision taken at the beginning of 1865 to set about strengthening the fortress of Quebec at British expense. It was significant, however, that this decision was fiercely contested at the Cabinet table by the Chancellor of the Exchequer, W. E. Gladstone.[10]

The other aspect of the Government's policy was expressed mainly by the Colonial Secretary, Edward Cardwell. It appears very strikingly in the ministry's attitude towards the Canadian political developments of 1864. Back in 1858 the Colonial Office had been more hostile than friendly when dispatches arrived from Canada suggesting the possible desirability of a federal union of British North America.[11] Things were different now. When the Quebec Conference's resolutions reached London Cardwell was almost comically eager to embrace the scheme. On November 26, 1864, he wrote the Lieutenant-Governor of New Brunswick that the resolutions had been circulated to the Cabinet only the night

[7]*Canada and the British Army*, 154–60.
[8]*Ibid.*, 171–3.
[9]*Ibid.*, 173. The words quoted are Cardwell's. See Palmerston's report to the Queen, March 13, 1865, *Letters of Queen Victoria*, Second Series, I, 262–3.
[10]*Canada and the British Army*, 171–2.
[11]D. G. G. Kerr, *Sir Edmund Head: A Scholarly Governor* (Toronto, 1954), 194–200.

before, and it "would, of course, be premature for me to anticipate their decision." Then he proceeded:

> ... But I think I may safely assure you that they are one and all most anxious to promote the end in view, that they will allow no obstacles to prevent it, if those obstacles can be surmounted: and that if there are provisions which they do not entirely approve, they will be very slow to consider those provisions as rising to the magnitude of insurmountable obstacles.
>
> I fully expect that I shall soon have to instruct you in their name to promote the scheme of the Delegates to the utmost of your power.[12]

This forecast proved accurate. One week later Cardwell wrote officially, warmly approving the Quebec scheme.[13]

From this moment the Imperial Government steadily supported the federation plan. And there is little doubt that the chief reason for this was the scheme's obvious military importance. In the spring of 1865 a Canadian delegation went to London to discuss the defence of the country with the British Government. One result was a formal exchange of assurances of the two governments' determination to devote all their resources, if need be, to maintain the connection between Britain and Canada. Another was the mobilization of the fullest degree of Imperial influence to ensure the victory of the confederate cause in the Maritime Provinces. In a dispatch sent to the Maritime governors in June, 1865, Cardwell instructed them to inform their legislatures that it was "the strong and deliberate opinion of Her Majesty's Government" that it was desirable that all the British North American colonies should "unite in one Government." The paramount argument employed was that of defence. Cardwell wrote:

Looking to the determination which this country has ever exhibited to regard the defence of the Colonies as a matter of Imperial concern, the Colonies must recognize a right and even acknowledge an obligation incumbent upon the Home Government to urge with earnestness and just authority the measures which they consider to be most expedient on the part of the Colonies with a view to their own defence. Nor can it be doubtful that the Provinces of British North America are incapable, when separated and divided from each other, of making those just and sufficient preparations for national defence, which would be easily undertaken by a Province uniting in itself all the population and all the resources of the whole.[14]

---

[12]Public Record Office, London, 30/48, Cardwell Papers, Box 6/39 (Microfilms in Public Archives of Canada), Cardwell to Gordon, Nov. 26, 1864. The recent acquisition of these microfilms is due to the laudable initiative of the Dominion Archivist, Dr. W. Kaye Lamb.
[13]Cardwell to Monck, Dec. 3, 1864, P.A.C., G 21, vol. 26.
[14]*Papers relating to the Conferences which have taken place between Her Majesty's Government and a Deputation from the Executive Council of Canada* . . . (Quebec, 1865), Cardwell to Lieut.-Governor of New Brunswick, June 24, 1865.

In October, 1865, Palmerston died. Lord Russell carried on the government until the following summer, when a Conservative ministry headed by Lord Derby came into office. During these months the British ministers watched with alarm as Bismarck manipulated the Schleswig-Holstein question to produce the war he wanted with Austria. But they had learned their humiliating lesson, and there was no more loose talk of intervention. Russell's Foreign Secretary, Lord Clarendon, wrote to the Queen: "We have spoken in defence of right; we cannot actively interfere with those who are quarrelling over the spoils; and in the present state of Ireland, and the menacing aspect of our relations with the United States, the military and pecuniary resources of England must be husbanded with the utmost care."[15] Three days after the formation of Derby's Government the Prussian Army humbled Austria at Sadowa, displaying in the process an efficiency which Englishmen found both unfamiliar and alarming. As a result, Army reform suddenly became an important political issue.

The Government could draw some comfort, it is true, from the fact that in America the Civil War had ended, the Union Army had been largely disbanded, and the wanton attack on Canada which had been feared when fighting ended in the South had not eventuated. But on the other hand the Fenians were enjoying their heyday; they mounted a large-scale operation in 1866. The Canadian Government begged for help from England, and England sent a very considerable regular reinforcement. It was the last time such a thing was to happen. The action taken was not popular with Derby's chief lieutenant, Disraeli; it was at this moment that he wrote to the Prime Minister, "what is the use of these colonial deadweights which *we do not govern?*"[16]

In 1867 the Dominion of Canada duly came into being. The London *Times*' comment on the event was severely practical: "We look to Confederation as the means of relieving this country from much expense and much embarrassment. . . . We appreciate the goodwill of the Canadians and their desire to maintain their relations with the British Crown. But a people of four millions ought to be able to keep up their own defences."[17] Nevertheless, in the first instance Confederation brought no relief to Britain's strained "military and pecuniary resources." In all the circumstances of the time, it is perhaps not surprising that some Englishmen found

[15]March 31, 1866, *Letters of Queen Victoria, Second Series*, I, 314-15.
[16]*Canada and the British Army*, 191-4.
[17]March 1, 1867.

themselves regretting that the British Empire had a North American frontier. Early in 1867 Derby's son and Foreign Secretary, Lord Stanley, wrote to the British Minister in Washington, who had suggested the possibility of giving British North America representation in the House of Commons at Westminster, that he had once held the idea himself: "But I have never found it take in this Country. Many people would dislike the long boundary line with the United States (they look now to an early separation of Canada). . . ."[18] A few weeks later Stanley, fresh from putting a stop to the dangerous idea of calling the new political entity the Kingdom of Canada, wrote to Sir Frederick Bruce again: "There is no idea of a new monarchy, and that may as well be explained. The Colonies will remain Colonies, only confederated for the sake of convenience. If they choose to separate, we on this side shall not object: it is they who protest against the idea. In England separation would be generally popular."[19]

Late in 1868, a general election put the Conservatives out and brought in a Liberal ministry, headed by Gladstone, with a large majority behind it. The Continental situation remained uncertain. The Army remained unreformed; a proper Reserve could not be organized without an increased supply of recruits, and recruiting would not improve as long as British soldiers spent most of their lives abroad. For some twenty years successive British governments had been striving to reduce the colonial garrisons; but not much had been accomplished. Above all, the *Alabama* question remained unsettled, the Fenians were still active, and therefore Anglo-American relations were in a constant state of crisis.

Almost the first act of the new ministry was an attempt at settlement with the United States. Following a line already charted by the Conservatives, they signed the Johnson-Clarendon Convention in January, 1869. It was a disastrous failure. The Convention was thrown out by the United States Senate by a vote of 54 to 1 after a speech by Charles Sumner which seemed to estimate the amount of the *Alabama* claims at half the total cost of the Civil War. When this news reached London, Lord Clarendon wrote grimly, "I believe that Grant and Sumner mean war; or rather that amount of insult and humiliation that must lead to it."[20]

[18]P.A.C., Transcripts of Derby Papers from Knowsley Hall, Stanley to Bruce, Jan. 25, 1867.   [19]*Ibid.*, March 23, 1867.
[20]Allan Nevins, *Hamilton Fish: The Inner History of the Grant Administration* (New York, 1936), 147–52. Sir Herbert Maxwell, *The Life and Letters of George William Frederick, Fourth Earl of Clarendon* (2 vols., London, 1913), II, 358, Clarendon to Lady Salisbury, May 9, 1869.

For the Gladstone Cabinet's appreciation of the situation that now confronted it there is considerable evidence. The essence of it was the fact that as long as things in North America did not improve British policy in Europe would be hamstrung. In the spring of 1869 the Foreign Secretary was writing to the Queen of the dangers latent in the treaties concerning Belgium and Portugal to which Britain was a party. "It seems to be the duty of your Majesty's Government to bear in mind how widely different are the circumstances of this country now to when those Treaties were concluded, and that, if their execution were to lead us into war in Europe, we should find ourselves immediately called upon to defend Canada from American invasion and our commerce from American privateers."[21] This was before the news of Sumner's speech arrived. When it came, Clarendon wrote to the Queen again: "It is the unfriendly state of our relations with America that to a great extent paralyses our action in Europe. There is not the smallest doubt that if we were engaged in a Continental quarrel we should immediately find ourselves at war with the United States."[22] These views were not confined to Clarendon. His successor at the Foreign Office, Lord Granville, wrote to John Bright when Bright resigned from the government:

... Your guidance would have been invaluable as regards the United States.

I can conceive no greater object than to put our relations on a satisfactory footing with them. Our present position cripples us in every way. Not only would it do so if we wished for war, but it impedes our pacific efforts, making people attribute to fear that which is prompted by a sense of duty.[23]

The First Lord of the Admiralty had already suggested to Granville, when there seemed to be danger of a war with Russia over the Black Sea, that it was "very important" to get the differences with the United States out of the way: "Otherwise there can be little doubt that, however unprepared they may be just now, sooner or later we shall have them on our hands."[24]

What remedy could the Government provide? One obvious procedure was to liquidate the quarrel with the States at any cost which the British taxpayer could be made to swallow. In point of fact this was ultimately done, and historians would be well advised not to forget the European situation in interpreting British

[21] April 16, 1869, *Letters of Queen Victoria, Second Series*, I, 589–91.
[22] May 1, 1869, *ibid.*, 594–5.
[23] Nov. 21, 1870, Lord Edmond Fitzmaurice, *The Life of Granville George Leveson Gower, Second Earl Granville* . . . (2 vols., London, 1906), II, 28–9.
[24] Spencer Childers, *The Life and Correspondence of the Right Hon. Hugh C. E. Childers, 1827–1896* (2 vols., London, 1901), I, 173–4, Childers to Granville, Nov. 19, 1870.

BRITAIN'S WITHDRAWAL FROM NORTH AMERICA 17

policy in connection with the Treaty of Washington and the Geneva Arbitration. But in 1869 the Americans had struck aside the hand that Britain offered, and it would be two years before real negotiation would again be practicable.

There was however another possibility. That was to get out of North America. At the beginning of 1869 Great Britain was still deeply involved in this continent, and the symbol of this investment was the 12,000 British regular troops stationed in Canada and Newfoundland.[25] There is ample evidence that many influential Englishmen considered these troops "hostages . . . for British good behaviour"[26] and an incitement to the Americans to make war. It was obvious that merely to get them home would be an advantage to the security of the United Kingdom; it would be doubly so if their removal from Canada made conflict with the United States less likely. And the fact that, with the mother country's encouragement, a new political unit capable of assuming national responsibilities had now been created in British North America, gave such a policy more than a colour of justification.

There is no doubt that some members of Gladstone's Government would have welcomed a complete severance of the ties with Canada. However, they found themselves faced with an obstacle— that rather inconvenient Canadian loyalty which Lord Stanley had noted. In a crisis, this loyalty would probably have found considerable support in the British House of Commons. But the separatists were influential, and the high point of their activity was reached in the gloomy days after the rejection of the Johnson-Clarendon Convention. For many years British public men had been in the habit of referring to the relation between Britain and the colonies in terms which suggested that it was a temporary arrangement. Now this idea appeared in an official Colonial Office dispatch. On June 16, 1869, Lord Granville wrote confidentially to the Governor General of Canada, saying that the Imperial Government had no desire to maintain the connection "a single year" after it became "injurious or distasteful" to Canada, and concluding with an order: "You will . . . be good enough to bring to my notice any line of policy or any measures which without implying on the part of Her Majesty's Government any wish to change abruptly our relations, would gradually prepare both Countries for a friendly relaxation of them."[27]

[25]Parliamentary Papers, House of Commons, United Kingdom, 1870, no. 254, vol. XLII (12,014 all ranks on March 31, 1869).
[26]*The Times*, March 29, 1867.
[27]*Canada and the British Army*, 216.

On their own side Granville and his colleagues were slackening off the painter. Cardwell, now Secretary of State for War, was actively setting about the reform of the Army; and he had explained to Gladstone on undertaking the task, "The with-drawal of Troops from distant Stations is at the bottom of the whole question of Army Reform...."[28] In the spring of 1869 Canada was told that her garrison, apart from the troops at Halifax, was to be reduced to about 4,000 men, and it was indicated that even this force was not to remain long.[29]

At this moment the British Cabinet was faced with a fundamental decision, summed up by Granville in a private letter to Cardwell thus: ". . . the practical question is whether Quebec is to be considered an Imperial or a Colonial Fortress."[30] Although the British Government had been striving for years to reduce its force in Canada, it had never before been seriously suggested that Imperial troops would cease to garrison Quebec. In 1863 the Defence Committee had reported on the strategic importance of the fortress in these terms: "Since Quebec is the place through which all succours from Great Britain to Canada must pass, it is obviously necessary that this fortress should be maintained in the most efficient and secure condition. If it fell into the hands of an enemy, the military communication between the province and the mother country would be cut off. The Committee are therefore of opinion that Quebec should be kept up as a first class fortress. . . . "[31] This was the thinking that led Palmerston and his Cabinet to override their colleague Gladstone and undertake improvements in the fortress in 1865. By 1869 a great new fortified bridgehead had appeared on the south shore of the St. Lawrence opposite Quebec; but now Gladstone was Prime Minister and a different spirit ruled in Whitehall. It is evident that in April, 1869, Granville and Cardwell brought the question of the status of Quebec before the Cabinet.[32] I have been unable to find any definite record of the discussion or the decision; but it seems likely that the Cabinet decided at this time that Quebec was no longer to be an Imperial fortress, though it would appear that no final moment for withdrawal was fixed.

The Government's determination not to be turned from its course was demonstrated after the news of Sumner's speech arrived.

[28]Jan. 9, 1869, Cardwell Papers, Box 2/6.
[29]*Canada and the British Army*, 214.
[30]April 14, 1869, Cardwell Papers, Box 5/28.
[31]Report of Jan. 8, 1863, *ibid.*, Box 6/40 (confidential print).
[32]Correspondence in *ibid.*, Box 5/28.

Although, as we have seen, members of the Cabinet felt that it might be a sign of coming war, it caused no change in the plans for withdrawing troops from Canada. In the Cardwell papers there is what is evidently a note passed by Cardwell to Gladstone in the House of Commons in connection with a question on this point. It remarks that he proposes to reply simply that the orders were being executed, and it was not intended to countermand them. Gladstone's minute on the paper reads, "By all means."[33] However, events in North America did complicate the later stages of the withdrawal. There was a Fenian raid in the spring of 1870, and at the same time the need arose for sending an expedition to Red River. The Imperial Government consented to allow its troops to take part in the Red River operation; but it did so only on very strict conditions, and particularly emphasized that the regulars should be absolutely certain of getting back to the East before the winter. It is worth recalling that the London *Times*, in commenting on the Imperial share in the Red River expedition, remarked, "The British Parliament is now called upon to intervene for the last time in the affairs of the American Continent."[34]

These events in Canada were overshadowed by contemporary happenings in Europe. In July, 1870, war broke out between France and Prussia. In London there was great anxiety over an apparent threat to Belgium, and at the very outset of the struggle Gladstone asked Cardwell "to study the means of sending 20,000 men to Antwerp with as much promptitude as at the Trent affair we sent 10,000 to Canada."[35] The withdrawals from the colonies had allowed the Government to cut the cost of the British Army and reduce its over-all size while at the same time increasing the force in the United Kingdom. This happy situation now ended; 20,000 additional men were hastily voted for the Army, and the estimates leaped up in proportion.[36] In the minds of Englishmen the mistrust of France, which was so marked at the beginning of the war, changed, as the war progressed, to fear of Prussia. Lord Kimberley, the new Colonial Secretary, wrote to one of his colleagues in September, 1870, "We are only at the end of the first act of the tragedy, & we shall be fortunate if the next acts are not more gloomy & horrible still."[37] With the safety of Britain herself

[33]March 13, 1869, Cardwell Papers, Box 2/6. Cf. *Canada and the British Army*, 213.   [34]*Canada and the British Army*, 243.
[35]Morley, *Life of Gladstone*, II, 339.
[36]*Canada and the British Army*, 247–8. See Cardwell's speech in the House of Commons in introducing the Army Estimates, Feb. 16, 1871.
[37]Kimberley to Cardwell, Sept. 7, 1870, Cardwell Papers, Box 5/31.

apparently in question, the urge to liquidate the country's responsibilities in North America was even stronger than before.

The day before the Battle of Sedan, Cardwell asked Kimberley whether the time had come to offer officially the transfer to Canada of the Citadel of Quebec. Although the Dominion had already been given an indication that the Imperial force would be withdrawn in 1871, Kimberley preferred not to pursue the question at that moment and it was shelved for a few months.[38] But it came up again in December, 1870, by which time the British force in central Canada was down to a small remnant. Kimberley inclined to the view that it would do no harm to leave this force at Quebec, for the moment, as a concession to Canadian feeling; but Cardwell remarked, "A single Regiment & two Batteries at Quebec may be considered by the Cabinet a very awkward committal for the British Flag in case of rupture with the U. States."[39] It was agreed that the matter should go to the Cabinet for decision. Kimberley laid it before the Prime Minister in a letter and said he would "bring the matter forward at the next Cabinet."[40] No doubt he did, and it is evident that the decision was in favour of withdrawal. The Canadian Government tried hard to get the men in Whitehall to change their minds, but it was no use. In the autumn of 1871 the last British troops left Quebec, and thereafter the only British garrison in Canada was that of Halifax.[41] By this time the Treaty of Washington had made provision for settlement of the various issues between Britain and the United States. There was another period of serious anxiety early in 1872, and then the award of the Geneva Tribunal finally laid the *Alabama* claims to rest.

The departure of the 60th Rifles from the Citadel of Quebec on November 11, 1871, was a landmark in the foreign as well as the colonial policy of Britain. Eight years before, the highest military authorities in the Empire had declared that it was essential to maintain Quebec as an Imperial fortress. Six years before, the British Government had decided to renovate the defences at great expense. Now about a quarter of a million British pounds had been spent, the new forts were still not quite complete, and yet the Imperial troops departed. This somewhat peculiar train of events reflects the course of British policy in this troubled era.

[38]Cardwell to Kimberley, Aug. 31, 1870, Kimberley to Cardwell, Sept. 1, 1870, *ibid. Canada and the British Army*, 226–7.
[39]Cardwell to Kimberley, Dec. 6, 1870, Cardwell Papers, Box 5/31, and other letters in same box. [40]Kimberley to Gladstone, Dec. 9, 1870, *ibid.*
[41]*Canada and the British Army*, 252–3.

Confronted simultaneously with menaces in both Europe and North America, a situation whose potentialities their military resources were quite unequal to coping with, Gladstone and his colleagues came, in effect if not in form, to a decision to abandon Britain's political and military responsibilities in America, to withdraw from this continent to the utmost possible extent, and to concentrate their country's power at home, where it would be available to deal with European foes. The adoption of this policy was facilitated by the fact that earlier British administrations had encouraged the federation of British North America. Palmerston seems to have thought in terms of the new Dominion sharing Britain's North American responsibliities. Gladstone's Cabinet thought in terms of *transferring* those responsibilities to Canada, so far as she was able and willing to assume them—but, whether Canada assumed them or not, Britain clearly intended to get rid of them.

It seems evident that there was never a specific or formal decision in favour of this policy of abdication and withdrawal. It was never quite fully avowed by those who seem to have been most devoted to it. In 1869 Granville wrote to Cardwell on the necessity of making an early decision on what to do about the troops remaining in Canada. "I do not think this will be difficult," he wrote, "What will be more so is the language to be held in debate about our future relations with the Dominion. I do not think it would be wise to be abrupt on the subject."[42] There was always some opposition, in Parliament and in the country, to Gladstonian colonial policies, and it is even possible that too forthright a declaration of the view which Granville represented might have produced opposition within the Cabinet.

Finally, it must be added that the policy of withdrawal was never complete. In 1870–71 Britain got out of the interior of North America, but she did not get out of Nova Scotia. The Halifax base was evidently considered on balance a military asset rather than a liability, and there the British troops remained until well into the twentieth century. Also, the British Government never went so far as to declare that it would not defend Canada in case of war. On the contrary, the dispatch which early in 1870 announced the impending withdrawal of the troops took care to specify that the proposed arrangements "are contingent upon a time of peace, and are in no way intended to alter or diminish the obligations

[42]Granville to Cardwell, Sept. 9, 1869, Cardwell Papers, Box 5/28.

which exist on both sides in case of foreign war."[43] Those obligations could scarcely have been escaped without a formal separation; and however much some people might have welcomed this, Britain never got to the point of declaring herself independent of Canada. She did however effect, in the course of a few years, a complete revolution in her relations with North America. On one side, she settled, at heavy cost to herself and also to Canada, the issues outstanding between her and the United States, and thereby put an end to any immediate threat of an Anglo-American war. On the other, she suddenly withdrew from her traditional military responsibilities in the interior of this continent, thereby saving roughly a million pounds a year, facilitating the reform of her army, and materially strengthening her military position with respect to Europe. By 1872 it could almost be said that Great Britain had ceased to be a North American power; and it would seem that there were comparatively few Englishmen who regarded the change with any feeling except the deepest satisfaction.

[43]*Canada and the British Army*, 226–7. Britain also retained the small naval station at Esquimalt in British Columbia, but there was no army garrison there at this period.

Edward Cardwell and Confederation

P. B. WAITE

WITH THE CHEERFULNESS of a man whose responsibilities were now at an end Edward Cardwell, on July 7, 1866, wrote to Fenwick Williams in Nova Scotia. "My dear General,—I write you a few lines of farewell in my public character which came to a termination yesterday. Let us rejoice together in the success which has attended your Mission, and in the now, I trust, secure and certain union of the B.N.A. Provinces. I should indeed have liked to have introduced the Bill which is to clinch the nails,—but as fate has decided otherwise, I am about thoroughly to enjoy my holiday."[1] Fenwick Williams was plainly sorry to see Cardwell go. "I need not say," he replied, "that duties under you have been rendered as pleasant and satisfactory as any I *ever* passed in my long and chequered career: and to you (after all) will accrue the honor of our Confederation...."[2]

The honour of Confederation has accrued rather to the Earl of Carnarvon, Cardwell's successor, and for reasons that are obvious if not necessarily sufficient. Yet Cardwell's role deserves study. Confederation had been before the Colonial Office for several years; by and large it was thought unrealistic, being doubtless premature, perhaps even chimerical; and while it will not do to underrate that judgment, Cardwell had other considerations in mind. It is only an exaggeration to say that he reversed what had been a standing Colonial Office policy. What he did was to alter, rather abruptly, the relative importance of Confederation, and to impose his view upon rather more conservative permanent officials. He also succeeded in

[1] New Brunswick Museum, Fenwick Williams Papers, Cardwell to Williams, July 7, 1866 (private). Lt.-Gen. Sir William Fenwick Williams (1800–83) had been Officer Commanding in British North America, 1859–65. In the autumn of 1865 he was made Lieutenant Governor of Nova Scotia, a post which he held until 1867.
[2] Public Record Office (P.R.O.), Cardwell Papers, Williams to Cardwell, July 19, 1866.

Reprinted from *Canadian Historical Review*, XLIII (1), March, 1962

persuading his colleagues that Confederation was a means by which Great Britain could decently get rid of the petty concerns of five, possibly seven (with Rupert's Land eight), colonies in North America. At the same time, by throwing more of the responsibilities for their defence upon the colonies themselves, Confederation might help to resolve one or two peculiarly intractable problems of defence. That Confederation was achieved at all was due in part to Cardwell's energy and perseverance; and when he left the Colonial Office for good, it was near to being realized and the principal features of its structure largely established.

Cardwell tackled Confederation with the same forcefulness—at times ruthlessness—that he was later to use in reforming the British army and in withdrawing the imperial legions from Canada. Cardwell could be very determined when there was an anomaly to be removed, an abuse to be stopped, and some new and systematic order of things put in their place. His union of the Horse Guards and the War Office, his abolition of the purchase of army commissions (for both of which he is best known in Great Britain), were products of the same logic as Confederation, or for that matter, as the shotgun union of British Columbia and Vancouver Island in 1866. His object was to clarify, to render order out of disorder, and, in the case of Confederation, to clear up the out-of-date book-keeping of the British government and some of its principal self-governing colonies.

Cardwell came by his business instincts naturally. He was born in Liverpool in 1813, where his father was a prominent merchant. There were also academic connections: his uncle was Camden Professor of Ancient History at Oxford, and young Edward's schooling gave evidence that if he had commercial prospects they were going to be subordinated, temporarily or otherwise as the case might be, to a thorough academic training He went to Winchester, took the Balliol prize, and went on to a bright career at Oxford, where, like his contemporary William Gladstone, he was awarded a double first. Cardwell was not, even at this time, showy; his brilliance was often concealed by his modesty of demeanour and his distrust of virtuosity.

He was in fact a Conservative, in politics and in habit, though it was characteristic of his political sensitiveness that coming from Lancashire, he became a free trade Conservative. He was early associated with Peel; the two found each other congenial company, and Cardwell's familiarity with business made him extremely useful. He became Peel's Secretary of the Treasury, and with his chief went down in the grand *débâcle* of June, 1846. He joined the Aberdeen ministry in 1852 as President of the Board of Trade, and when Aberdeen resigned in 1855, Cardwell went with him, despite, apparently, an overture from

Palmerston to become Chancellor of the Exchequer.[3] But Cardwell's career afterward was a reluctant drift toward the Liberals, and in 1859 he joined the Palmerston government as Secretary for Ireland.

Cardwell's Conservatism and free trade sympathies combined to give him a philosophy of politics (he would perhaps have deprecated the expression) not unlike later Republican business philosophy in the United States. He believed the state's function was that of guardian, to superintend, and to restrict only when restriction served commercial, hence national, advantage. Cardwell was sensitive to other interests but he was exceedingly cautious about introducing measures that would inhibit business enterprise. His Railway and Canal bill in 1854 illustrates his position. On the one hand there was a widespread public demand for railway regulation: on the other there were the railway companies which seemed to deserve the beneficence of the state. Cardwell was well aware of public opinion, but at the same time he had a lively realization of railway interests, particularly since he was a railway director himself. In this kind of struggle Cardwell usually gave way to the interests of his class, as the Railway and Canal Act showed.

The Colonial Office involved him in no such conflict. There public opinion combined with the interests of the commercial class to which he belonged. The prevalent colonial philosophy of the 1860's was informed by the attitude that while some of the colonies offered real commercial or military advantages, there were others which were inconvenient and expensive, and others still whose disadvantages were serious, imminent—and quite disturbing. In this last group were the British North American colonies, of whom Canada was head and front of the offending. Canada had in the past shown some reluctance to do what many critics in Great Britain believed was her simple duty of helping to defend herself; and one consolation became the hope that as a self-governing colony Canada would mature into an independent community. But neither Canada's dereliction of duty nor her ultimate independence seemed to warrant the present sacrifice of British treasure or blood. Some public men did not share this attitude about Canada, notably Palmerston, Russell, and to a degree Cardwell himself; but many of the leading journals, and politicians, some of them close to Palmerston's government, did share it, and they were both pessimistic and articulate.[4] Such a philosophy had been at times in the past

[3] A. B. Erickson, *Edward T. Cardwell: Peelite* (Philadelphia, 1959), 20.
[4] See C. A. Bodelsen, *Studies in Mid-Victorian Imperialism* (2nd edition, London, 1960), 37–59. A criticism of some of Bodelsen's views appears in J. S. Galbraith, "Myths of the 'Little England' Era," *American Historical Review*, LXVII, 1 (Oct., 1961), 34–48. Professor Galbraith goes so far as to say that "no responsible statesman during the 'Little England' era embraced the view that separation of the colonies from

warrant for polite indifference on the part of Colonial Secretaries to the unrewarding perplexities of colonial administration; but if Cardwell was lukewarm in his colonial enthusiasms, he was too able an administrator, and had too thorough a mind, to procrastinate or to make the Colonial Office a sinecure, despite some illustrious precedents for doing so. Because public and Parliament had often been indifferent to colonies and colonial questions, it did not follow that the colonies could be ignored or allowed to drift. The *Saturday Review* of April, 1864, when Cardwell's appointment as Colonial Secretary was announced, gave this opinion of him:

> Mr. Cardwell will probably never become a statesman of the highest rank, but it was absurd to condemn one of the most industrious and competent members of the cabinet to total idleness. . . . He will conduct the affairs of the colonies with businesslike punctuality, and with the fairness which may be expected from a dispassionate character and from a legal training. To general deliberations on domestic and foreign policy he will bring one of the clearest heads among the Ministers. . . .[5]

He was even better than that. He brought to bear upon the office not only his quick grasp of essentials and his tremendous application, but also the full force of his passion for neatness and system. He had in the Colonial Office no commercial interests to restrict him, no *bourgeois* sensibilities to impede him: on the contrary, those interests and sensibilities combined to make a coherent colonial policy both desirable and necessary.

Cardwell was far from subscribing to the doctrine of the separatists. He did not believe the colonies were millstones; nor did he think they were a useless expense. He thought that the tendency, already discernible, in the direction of self-government should be sustained and fostered, not only in the interest of Great Britain, but of the colonies themselves. It would relieve expense, no doubt, but it would also encourage colonial maturity. One detects in his speeches even a vestige of pride in the prospect of these young oaks growing up around the venerable tree. At Oxford in January, 1865—by then his constituency— Cardwell criticized the "lynx-eyed logicians" who perennially demonstrated "that a live colony is a dead loss. . . ." He was diffident (or

Britain was a desirable prospect" (p. 35). Cf., however, Earl Russell's opinion of the sentiments of "Derby and Dizzy," and of Stanley in respect of Canada (*infra*, 38) or Lord Granville's famous despatch to Sir John Young of June, 1869. Professor Galbraith would aver that Canada is, in some important respects, an exception to his general rule. For the economic aspect of the revisionist view see J. Gallagher and R. Robinson, "The Imperialism of Free Trade," *Economic History Review*, 2nd series, VI (Aug., 1953), 1–15.

[5]*Saturday Review*, April 9, 1864. "Total idleness" refers to the fact that Cardwell was Chancellor of the Duchy of Lancaster, 1861–4. This issue of the *Saturday Review* is also quoted in an excellent B. Litt. thesis for the University of Oxford in 1958, "Edward Cardwell at the Colonial Office: Some Aspects of His Policy and Ideas," by Miss G. J. Sellers. It is in the Rhodes House Library, Oxford.

logical) enough to remark that "we have nothing to answer that they can understand"; but at the same time he offered a tangible theory of imperial development. "It is given to other countries to be great and powerful Empires, but it has been given to England alone to be also the mother of great and free communities." The time may come, he went on, "when they will be both able and willing to repay the assistance and protection they have received from the Mother Country, and when England, speaking as the parent of those distant communities, may be glad to have her quiver full of them. . . ." The *Times* was sceptical, and described these sentiments as official "wafting amenities across the ocean, and soothing with soft words his rough and querulous clients. We put no great trust in 'the gratitude' of colonies. . . ."[6] It is probably fair to say that Cardwell did not put much trust in colonial gratitude either, but one wonders if he did not discern something more spacious than the narrow utilitarianism that had often informed the editorials in the *Times*. If he did, he kept the details to himself, and, so far as the self-governing colonies were concerned, let the general principle of colonial emancipation be his guide.

Some of the senior officials of the Colonial Office were more profoundly separatist in sympathy. Henry Taylor regarded the North American colonies as "a sort of *damnosa haereditas*" and often told the Duke of Newcastle so.[7] Sir Frederic Rogers, the Permanent Undersecretary, was of a similar mind, though he was more judicious, and he believed that British honour and self-respect demanded that colonies be kept until they themselves wanted to go. As for Confederation, few Colonial Office officials seem to have believed, before Cardwell actively took up the policy, that it might be a means in this direction. They had shown in the past some sympathy, but little positive energy for British North American union. The movement in North America had so far been ephemeral, and then the idea itself must have seemed rather impracticable. Cardwell's predecessor, the Duke of Newcastle, after a visit to North America in 1860, had actively preferred the straightforward and rational principle of uniting the three Maritime provinces. Thomas Elliott, the Assistant Under-secretary, who kept the affairs of the North American (and Mediterranean) colonies continuously under review, was, it is fair to say, generally opposed to Confederation, though aware of the advantages of a commercial union. Arthur Blackwood, the Chief Clerk, was more open and accommodating, though he too could be narrow-minded on occasion. This is not to suggest that the Colonial Office's senior servants were either short-sighted or

[6]*Times*, Jan. 7, 1865, reporting Cardwell's speech at Oxford, and editorial comment thereon.
[7]Taylor to the Duke of Newcastle, Feb. 26, 1864, in *Autobiography of Henry Taylor, 1800–1875* (2 vols. London, 1885), II, 234.

obscurantist; they had sound reasons for their views and Cardwell's triumph over them on the issue of Confederation was not so much that of right over wrong (however much Canadian historians are disposed to view it that way), as that of the supersession of one policy by another.[8]

At first Cardwell had pursued, with his accustomed energy, the Maritime union policy inherited from the Duke of Newcastle. Sir Richard MacDonnell, the new governor of Nova Scotia, arrived in Halifax on June 22, 1864, with instructions to do what he could to forward Maritime union. But there was not much that could be done, even by Cardwell and MacDonnell, for the Maritime union movement had largely evaporated. It was the Canadians with Confederation who provided the incentive for the Maritime union conference. MacDonnell then took the initiative in arranging it, though he was doubtful how far he was authorized to go in allowing Confederation as a subject even of informal discussion.[9] On MacDonnell's request for authority Charles Fortescue, the Parliamentary Under-secretary, reflecting perhaps the Government rather than the Colonial Office, minuted on August 4, 1864:

I would express no opinion as to the advisability or practicability of a union of all the B.N.A. Provinces but simply approve of Sir R. McD.'s answer to Lord Monck— and express a hope that the small union may not be imperilled or delayed by the discussion of a larger plan with which it is not inconsistent.

Cardwell, too, was cautious:

That he has acted quite rightly in appointing Delegates: and I concur with him in thinking that this [?] official mission must be limited to the Union of the Lower Provinces: that the wider question is one on which the views of the Ministers of Canada have not yet been officially made known to me: and on which I am not yet prepared to enter:—that I agree with Sir R.M. in the opinion he expresses that in proceeding with the Union of the Lower Provinces you will be throwing no impediment in the way of a wider Scheme. . . .[10]

---

[8]The role of the Colonial Office in Confederation has deservedly attracted Canadian historians. Chester Martin's "British Policy in Canadian Confederation," (*C.H.R.*, XIII, 1, March, 1932), showed the dramatic change in policy that took place in 1864 and demonstrated the forceful use of means that followed it. More recently J. A. Gibson's "Colonial Office View of Canadian Federation, 1856–1868," (*C.H.R.*, XXXV, 4, Dec., 1954), has explored the attitudes of Colonial Office officials and the relations of these attitudes to the policies of successive colonial secretaries. D. G. Creighton's *John A. Macdonald: The Young Politician* (Toronto, 1952) gives, inter alia, a perceptive account of Colonial Office policy at the time of Confederation.

[9]*Infra*, note 15.

[10]Minutes on C.O. 217, MacDonnell to Cardwell, July 18, 1864. Chester Martin interprets Cardwell's remarks as a refusal to consider Confederation. ("British Policy in Canadian Confederation," 9). Creighton's view in *Macdonald*, 360–2, tends in the opposite direction. It would seem from the context that Cardwell had not yet made up his mind. Cardwell's views were incorporated in C.O. 218, Cardwell to MacDonnell, Aug. 9, 1864.

Cardwell was also considering the question of North American defence. A note to Gladstone just a week before illustrates Cardwell's practical realism in sorting out that problem. "If our troops were (as I wish they were) elsewhere than in Canada, I would say to Canada 'no troops of ours shall go to you till you have built suitable fortifications':—but our troops *are* there, and I submit we are reduced to this dilemma, viz. 1. Withdraw them or 2. Take immediate measures to put them into a defensible position."[11] Two weeks afterward Gladstone reminded him of the problem. "I hope you read the Times of Saturday [August 13] on Canada defences."[12] Cardwell probably had. He was not one to neglect the press; indeed, he was sometimes too ready to defer to other opinions, whether in the papers or in the House of Commons. And if he was reading the *Saturday Review* (which he probably was, for it was at this time Peelite in sympathy), he would have been aware already that the "Canadian crisis," as the *Review* called it, offered broad opportunities for constructive solutions to some pressing imperial problems.[13] It was not long before Cardwell's mind had fastened on this point: that the broad union suggested by Confederation and the problem of defence might well be related, and that if the one were effected the other might be solved.

While preparations for Charlottetown were afoot, and the Conference itself convened, Cardwell was probably digesting the despatches that bore on the question. He was kept well informed of proceedings both before and after Charlottetown. The visit of some hundred Canadian newspapermen and parliamentarians to Saint John, Fredericton, and Halifax in mid-August MacDonnell considered as having been intended to influence the meetings at Charlottetown; and, he added "I cannot but be sensible that a better spirit, a wish for more united action and a desire to merge small politics in larger and more generous views is thereby engendered."[14] On September 15 he sent in

[11]Gladstone Papers, British Museum, Add. MSS 44118, Cardwell to Gladstone, July 27, 1864.
[12]Letterbook, Gladstone Papers, Add. MSS 44534, Gladstone to Cardwell, Aug. 16, 1864. Gladstone's reference to the *Times* was to a letter from "A Canadian Volunteer," dated Hamilton, C.W., July 22, 1864, and published in the *Times* on Aug. 13. It was a damning indictment of Canadian defences. ". . . the defences of Canada consist of 25,000 half-drilled volunteers, scattered over half a continent from Gastra [sic] to Sarnia —no Militia, no commissariat, no medical department, no depots of arms or supplies, not rifles enough in the province to arm a regiment, except what belongs to the Imperial Government; not material for a solitary gunboat, nor the armament for one if launched; a loyal people, who would fight to the last . . . but who are cursed by the imbecility or fear of the Government, and whose patriotism is damped by a Legislature many of whose members openly assert that as Canada has no voice in making a quarrel with her neighbour, if England wants to fight, she must pay; while other[s] hold this doctrine, and publish it—that the best armament for Canada is no armament at all."
[13]E.g., *Saturday Review*, July 16, 1864.
[14]C.O. 217, MacDonnell to Cardwell, Aug. 18, 1864.

his report of the Conference, and asked permission to send delegates to Quebec. Upon the receipt of this despatch Arthur Blackwood sensibly concluded, on September 27, "I think it wd. be very advisable to withdraw from the injunction laid upon the N.A. Governors by the Duke of Newcastle. This federation movement is getting beyond the scope of Secretaries of State; and it is of no use to impose instructions if you can't well enforce them."[15] The next day Cardwell added, "I have received from Ld. Monck an intimation that he is about to communicate with me on this subject and since [?] time is important I have no hesitation in giving him [Sir Richard MacDonnell] the required permission."[16]

Cardwell by this time had been virtually won over to Confederation. And he had received a good deal of information about it already, not so much from Monck who was behind with his despatches, but from Arthur Gordon of New Brunswick who, on September 12, sent a long despatch on the proposals emanating from the Charlottetown Conference.[17] This despatch reveals much about that Conference. Gordon's criticisms were not without point, but Cardwell was convinced that, whatever were the objections to federation, the principle of union was sound and that the dangers of the former might well be risked in the hope of effecting the latter. Further, it was a movement concerted with the utmost determination by the Canadians, and one which he—and apparently very soon his colleagues—could safely support. Here Cardwell's private correspondence is helpful, and it also shows Cardwell at his best, tirelessly dealing with the importunities of Gordon and the refractoriness of New Brunswick politics. "I have read with much interest your despatch [of Sept. 12] on the subject of Federation," Cardwell wrote to Gordon on October 1; "Monck assures me that there is no idea of that feeble Legislature wh. you so justly object to: that they wish a strong central Legislature with subordinate Municipal Institutions."[18] Two weeks later Cardwell again emphasized this point, replying to another long despatch that Gordon had sent on September 22. Gordon's account had been, Cardwell said, "much less sanguine

[15]Blackwood's Minute of Sept. 27, on C.O. 217, MacDonnell to Cardwell, Sept. 15, 1864. The injunction referred to was probably that of Newcastle's confidential circular despatch of Jan. 27, 1860, which required the North American governors to report to the Colonial Secretary before authorizing delegates to discuss British North American union. Blackwood presumably considered that this instruction was not contravened by Newcastle's despatch of July 6, 1862, which was used by Canada as authority for the Quebec Conference. The fact that MacDonnell wrote home for authorization to appoint delegates to the Charlottetown Conference would suggest that MacDonnell agreed with Blackwood's interpretation. See also W. M. Whitelaw, *The Maritimes and Canada before Confederation* (Toronto, 1934), 217–18.
[16]Cardwell's Minute of Sept. 28, on C.O. 217, MacDonnell to Cardwell, Sept. 15, 1864.
[17]C.O. 188, Gordon to Cardwell, Sept. 12, 1864 (confidential).
[18]Cardwell Papers, Cardwell to Gordon, Oct. 1, 1864 (private).

than Monck's; and this, I think was to be expected. The bold, ambitious, leaders of public opinion in Canada are more likely to work for a complete fusion wh. would extend their powers—than are the ministry and parliament-men of New Brunswick whose occupation would in that case be ended—Meanwhile we all agree in favouring a complete fusion, not a federation."[19]

By this time Cardwell was fully engaged in the ramifications of Confederation in consultation with some of his colleagues, notably Gladstone. Gladstone's aim was, as he put it to Cardwell, "to shift the centre of responsibility" from Britain to Canada. "It is for them chiefly and primarily to judge as to everything which appertains to [their welfare?]: and my belief is that when they have assumed this duty, everything else will fall into its place. . . ."[20] Cardwell agreed. He expected "practical and creditable suggestions from the Can. ministry"; the danger to be apprehended was that the small provinces would insist upon federation. Cardwell, like many British North Americans, was possessed of the conviction that the United States had got into civil war partly because of the federal principle; and since the whole question of union was now assuming such cardinal importance, "I think we should be justified in exerting a good deal of firmness in supporting the sound policy of Upper Canada against the unsound policy of the Lower Provinces."[21] Cardwell's analysis of the position of the British North American provinces was not altogether inaccurate, and his conclusion was certainly established; and it was soon brought to bear on the results of the Quebec Conference forthcoming from Canada.

Late in November the text of the Quebec Resolutions and the covering despatches of Lord Monck were received. These went at once to the Foreign Office printers and were circulated to the cabinet on November 25. There was not much doubt about what cabinet reaction would be. Cardwell's opinions were warrant enough. "I think I may safely assure you," he told Gordon, "that they are one and all most anxious to promote the end in view, that they will allow no obstacles to prevent it, if those obstacles can be surmounted; and that if there are provisions which they do not entirely approve, they will be very slow to consider these provisions as rising to the magnitude of insurmountable obstacles."[22] Clumsily put, no doubt, but the intention was clear: Gordon's elaborate despatches were largely a waste of time. Learned and critical they certainly were, but they left the British government unmoved. What they did do was to confirm Cardwell in

[19]*Ibid.*, Cardwell to Gordon, Oct. 14, 1864.
[20]Letterbook, Gladstone Papers, Add. MSS 44534, Gladstone to Cardwell, Oct. 25, 1864.
[21]Gladstone Papers, Add. MSS 44118, Cardwell to Gladstone, Oct. 27, 1864.
[22]Cardwell Papers, Cardwell to Gordon, Nov. 26, 1864.

what he had been led by MacDonnell of Nova Scotia to expect: resistance to union by the Maritime provinces. MacDonnell thought Tupper and his friends could still carry union, but only by a *coup de main* which would cause immense trouble. "Therefore," MacDonnell wrote, "I should insist on dissolving and appealling to the country on the great question of union."[23] Cardwell did not agree. "I do not think you ought to insist on dissolving. . . ."[24]

Cardwell's determination and the Government's support of him was embodied in the famous despatch of December 3, 1864. This despatch gave out the unmistakable diapason of decision. There were a few reservations, but they were placed there by the Government, as George Brown explained, "to save themselves in the House of Commons in the event of attack."[25] Cardwell was careful in such matters. He thought it was easier to keep out of trouble than to get out of it, and he had a sharp eye for what would go in the House.[26] The broad principle remained: the Quebec Resolutions, being "the deliberate judgement of those best qualified to decide," and with evident precautions to secure central supremacy, were received by the British government with "the most cordial satisfaction." Cardwell himself had no doubts about the import of his despatch. ". . . my official despatch," he wrote Gordon, "will show you that Her Majesty's Government wish you to give to the whole [scheme] all the support and assistance in your power."[27]

George Brown who had arrived in London on December 2, the day before the despatch was sent, may have been of some influence. The morning and afternoon of December 3 he spent at the Colonial Office, and he received a very solicitous welcome.[28] Brown was delighted; nothing could be more gratifying to him than the reception the British government accorded the Confederation proposals. The resulting despatch was, he said, the strongest that had ever gone to a British colony.[29] The Colonial Office continued to encourage him; he wrote his wife at 6 P.M. Friday, December 9, that he had gone down to the

[23]C.O. 217, MacDonnell to Cardwell, Nov. 24, 1864 (confidential). This despatch was written in MacDonnell's hand, and he said no copy of the despatch would be kept in Nova Scotia.
[24]C.O. 217, draft despatch of Dec. 8, 1864 (confidential).
[25]Brown to Macdonald, Dec. 22, 1864 (private and confidential), in J. Pope, *Memoirs of Sir John Alexander Macdonald* (Toronto, [1930]), 289–90.
[26]G. E. Marindin, ed., *Letters of Frederic [Rogers], Lord Blachford* (London, 1896), 226. Miss G. J. Sellers, "Cardwell at the Colonial Office," 46, quotes a letter out of the Parker Papers from Lord Blachford to Lady Cardwell, Sept. 10, 1886, which is to much the same effect.
[27]C.O. 189, Cardwell to Gordon, Dec. 10, 1864 (confidential).
[28]Brown Papers, Public Archives of Canada (P.A.C.), George Brown to Anne Brown, Dec. 3, 1864.
[29]*Ibid.*, Dec. 5, 1864.

Colonial Office at 2 P.M. and had been kept there talking ever since.[30] On Saturday, December 17, Cardwell took him down to spend the weekend with Palmerston at Broadlands near the New Forest.[31] Well might Brown write Macdonald, "Our scheme has given prodigious satisfaction here. The Ministry, the Conservatives, and the Manchester men are all delighted with it, and everything Canadian has gone up in public estimation immensely."[32] The *Times* had published the Quebec Resolutions on November 24, and followed this, while Brown was in London, with a tribute to "the ability with which on the whole that principle [federation] has been worked out."[33] The weekend Brown went down to Broadlands, the *Saturday Review* wrote, "It would thus seem that, in future, the vast territory of British North America may be viewed as the seat of a genuine national existence."[34] And while the *Saturday Review* was less willing than the *Times* or the *Edinburgh Review* immediately to conclude that independence was in sight, it saw British North American union "as a means of softening the inevitable shock" of independence when it did come. "Some day or other the time of parting must come, when a great nation will be able to run alone, and will not wish to accept its rulers from an island three thousand miles away."[35] As for the British reaction, wrote the *Saturday Review*, Confederation had received the fullest co-operation from the Government, and "no one can doubt that it will be met in the same spirit by the Houses of Parliament."[36] By February, 1865, it was hoping that the next mail would bring news that Confederation was complete so far as the colonies could make it, "and that nothing remains but for the British Parliament to give its final sanction. . . ."[37]

It was not to be quite that simple. Prince Edward Island was already making it obvious that it had no intention of accepting Confederation. The recalcitrance of the island colony was regarded in London with some vexation. Cardwell decided that pressure would have to be

[30]*Ibid.*, Dec. 9, 1864.
[31]*Ibid.*, Dec. 16, 1864. See also *infra*, 30. Note also the following from Frances Monck's diary, January 19, 1865: "Mr. Brown dined [here at Spencer Wood yesterday]; he is just come from London, and looks quite happy; he says he was received with open arms in England, was asked about, and treated very grandly. He was invited to Broadlands, and Lord Pam said, 'Brown, will you take a walk? You don't mind snow, do you?' He [Brown] says there is great excitement about confederation in London. He was enchanted with his visit." Frances E. O. Monck, *My Canadian Leaves: An Account of a Visit to Canada 1864–1865* (London, 1891), 294.
[32]Brown to Macdonald, Dec. 22, 1864 (private and confidential), in Pope, *Memoirs of Macdonald*, 289–90.
[33]*Times*, Dec. 13, 1864. It had doubts, however, about the division of powers.
[34]*Saturday Review*, Dec. 17, 1864.
[35]*Ibid.*
[36]*Ibid.*, Jan. 14, 1865.
[37]*Ibid.*, Feb. 11, 1865.

applied. He wrote to Dundas on February 19, 1865, that the "position of Prince Edward Island, in common with that of all the North American Provinces, has now become such that Parliament could not be expected long to continue paying out of the Taxes of this Country the salary of the Lieutenant Governor . . . if the Union does not take place, it will be . . . necessary within a very short time to provide for the salary of the Lieutenant Governor out of the Revenues of the Colony."[38] This unhappy exigency was not finally effected until 1869, when at last a reluctant Island Assembly provided £1400 a year.[39] Two months later, in April, 1865, Cardwell returned more forcefully to his theme, and with a new variation:

> . . . they [your Legislature] evince in their Address a consciousness of obligation incumbent upon themselves, which I must say, plainly, and with regret, they have not shown any sufficient disposition to fulfil in the measures which you have reported to me,—coupled with a rejection of a scheme approved by Her Majesty's Government for this, among other reasons, that it was intended to provide for the easier and more effectual defence of all the British North American Provinces.
> You will bring this Despatch under the consideration of your Responsible Advisers.[40]

The same kind of pressure, although less of it, was also being applied in Newfoundland. Anthony Musgrave, the new Lieutenant Governor, had been, like Shea, Tupper, and Tilley, sanguine of success. Charles Fortescue noted on the back of Musgrave's hopeful despatch of December 27, 1864: "This looks well. I think the Lt. Govr. might be told—confidentially—that Mr. Cardwell had no doubt . . . that it wd. be desirable that he should promote that object [Confederation] by any means within his power—and, if possible, procure the settlement of the question without the delay of a general election." The resulting draft despatch of January 24, 1865, was marked "confidential," but Cardwell had little patience with confidential despatches when it was desirable that the weight of the British government's opinion be felt. He crossed out the "confidential," and added "You will hear from the Gov. Genl. what measures are being taken in the other Provinces for obtaining the decision of the respective Legislatures. In the absence of any serious reason to the contrary, I think it most desirable to obtain this decision without delay."[41]

There were already too many delays. Even Cardwell became a little impatient with the turn of events in New Brunswick, where Tilley was

[38]C.O. 227, Cardwell to Dundas, Feb. 18, 1865.
[39]F. MacKinnon, *The Government of Prince Edward Island* (Toronto, 1951), 86–7.
[40]C.O. 227, Cardwell to Dundas, April 28, 1865.
[41]C.O. 194, Musgrave to Cardwell, Dec. 27, 1864; minutes by Fortescue and Cardwell; draft despatch of Jan. 24, 1865. An election was due for the Newfoundland Assembly by the autumn of 1865.

extremely reluctant to bring Confederation into the existing legislature and was not very happy about an immediate dissolution.[42] If Gordon was the cause of the impasse in New Brunswick, Gordon could go elsewhere. Gordon admitted his own "apparent *cantankerousness*"[43] and was prepared to go. Early in March, 1865, Cardwell offered him Hong Kong at £5000, a considerable increase over what he was getting in New Brunswick; Gordon at first accepted, but later, after Tilley's defeat, remained.[44]

Nova Scotia posed less complicated by scarcely less difficult problems. It has often been said, by Tupper not least, that the defeat of Confederation in New Brunswick in 1865 finished it for the time being in Nova Scotia. So it did. But its existence was precarious even before the unhappy news from over the Bay of Fundy. MacDonnell wrote in mid-February, "I regard the adoption of the scheme by Nova Scotia during the current year as a result on which it would be unwise for Her Majesty's Government to calculate." And he was sure that imperial pressure would not help. Indeed, such was the present temper of Nova Scotia, said MacDonnell, that "the least semblance of dictation would be most impolitic and would utterly defeat its intended object."[45] MacDonnell was personally opposed to the form Confederation took, unhappy about the way it was handled by the Canadians, and not unsympathetic to the position taken by the Nova Scotian anti-Confederates. Despite this bias, his despatches were accurate and shrewd, and they described, though perhaps too forthrightly, the general feeling in Nova Scotia on the Confederation issue. In the end MacDonnell was "promoted" to Hong Kong in the autumn of 1865, after being in Nova Scotia just a year and a half.

By the spring of 1865 there were vital questions facing Cardwell, indeed the British government as a whole, in North American affairs. Relations with the United States in the past six months had grown noticeably more strained. The St. Albans Raid of October 19, 1864, had been bad enough; the dismissal of the raiders by a Montreal magistrate in mid-December was much worse, and it produced a violent reaction in the United States—in Congress, in the State Department, and a vociferous clamour in the Northern newspapers.[46] The possibility had to be faced that the dark clouds meant a storm of some proportions,

---

[42]Cardwell Papers, Cardwell to Gordon, Jan. 21, 1865; Gordon to Cardwell, Feb. 8, 1865.
[43]*Ibid.*, Gordon to Cardwell, Dec. 19, 1865. (Gordon's italics.)
[44]J. K. Chapman, "The Career of Arthur Hamilton Gordon, 1st Lord Stanmore, to 1875," Ph.D. thesis, University of London, 1954, 61.
[45]C.O. 217, Macdonnell to Cardwell, Feb. 15, 1865 (confidential).
[46]See R. W. Winks, *Canada and the United States: The Civil War Years* (Baltimore, 1960), 295–320.

and the question that British statesmen found acutely difficult to answer was what is to be done with Canada? The facts are well known. Britain had about 10,000 troops in British North America, in Halifax, Fredericton, San Juan Island, and most important of all, in Quebec and Montreal. The crucial province was Canada, whose long frontier with the United States made her nearly indefensible. Indefensible or not, Canada was garrisoned with British troops. Were these to be risked in war without the support of adequate fixed defences? And if there were to be permanent defensive works, who was to pay for them? Canada had already evinced in 1862 a lamentable reluctance to appropriate even half a million dollars for militia. In 1864 Colonel Jervois suggested that some £1,754,000 would be needed to build defences at Kingston, Montreal, and Quebec. The Canadian ministry in 1864 were in a better position to do something positive; the government was stronger and the threat was more obvious. It agreed to pay for a quarter of the permanent works and to spend a million dollars for militia, provided Britain would pay for armaments and for the defence works at Quebec.[47] Armed with that, and the Quebec Resolutions, Brown had gone to London in November, 1864.

The tension in British-American relations evoked all the varying philosophies of colonial disintegration in Great Britain. Confederation was in these circumstances a positive boon. It would simplify; it would make at least five colonies into one; best of all, it would throw upon British North Americans more of the responsibility for looking after themselves, and perhaps even allow British troops to be withdrawn from what many in England felt was an untenable position. This attitude was particularly to be observed in the *Edinburgh Review*. In the *Times*, however, it became gradually modified. John Delane, the editor of the *Times*, was a close friend of Palmerston, and though Lord Russell and the *Times* were not very amiable and Gladstone was cool, Palmerston was the Prime Minister and Cardwell was a man who watched both the Prime Minister and the influential papers. With the arrival of Brown in December, Delane was subject to some influence from Palmerston to at least inform his comments with first-hand information. On December 14, 1864, Palmerston wrote to Delane, "We are expecting the Cardwells and Mr. Brown, the Canadian. . . . If you should be free for a day or two, and would meet the Cardwells and Brown, we should be very glad to see you."[48] It is not known whether Delane went down to Broadlands then or not; but it is evident from

[47]Creighton, *Macdonald*, 386–7; C. P. Stacey, *Canada and the British Army* (London, 1936), 165–8.
[48]Palmerston to Delane, Dec. 14, 1864, in A. I. Dasent, *John Thaddeus Delane, Editor of The Times, His Life and Correspondence* (2 vols., London, 1908), II, 135.

the *Times* in 1865 that it was becoming more sympathetic to the Canadians than it had been. It admitted that it was difficult for Britain to meet the loyalty evident in British North America with an equally generous spirit of chivalrous protection; but so long as British North Americans were prepared to match British efforts with their own, "it would be no less blindness to our coarsest interests than it would be derogation of our national grandeur to leave any one of them a prey to the spoiler."[49]

The *Times* believed there was a clear connection between defence and Confederation. The readiness of the colonies to defend themselves must be "gathered not from words but from deeds; and the first practical proof they can offer is Union, or Confederation. . . . we venture to say that if Nova Scotia and New Brunswick seriously intend to be loyal, they ought to act accordingly, and declare for Confederation. . . . Independence is the only hope of the Colonists; independence in its present form, or, if it must be at some distant day, formal, literal, and absolute self-government. For the present there is only one question, and only one way of answering it—Confederation, or not?"[50] And two weeks later, when the news of the defeat of Confederation in New Brunswick arrived, the *Times* was sharp: "We cannot put any force upon a dissentient population, but it will be open to us to observe that the contribution made from the Imperial treasury may be regulated by our own conceptions of true colonial interests."[51] In April it *was* prepared to put force upon dissentient populations. "If, in short, these colonies ever wish us to defend their whole soil, they must combine in a general organization. . . . the House of Commons ought to have the courage, if necessary, to enforce it upon the colonies."[52] In June, 1865, when Delane went so far as to ask Robert Lowe to write an article supporting the work of "Cartier and Co.," Lowe rebelled. He was writing about 150 articles a year for the *Times*, but he was not going to "chop around" like this, and he at least did not believe in forcing the Maritime colonies to join Confederation.[53] On this issue the *Times* separated from Lowe, and its editorial of June 20, 1865, duly praised Confederation and urged the British government to use its influence to obtain it.

Thus it did not require the arrival of the four leading Canadian ministers at the end of April, 1865, to persuade Cardwell that action was desirable. It was abundantly clear from the *Times*, and from

[49]*Times*, Jan. 7, 1865.
[50]*Ibid.*, March 7, 1865.
[51]*Ibid.*, March 21, 1865.
[52]*Ibid.*, April 12, 1865.
[53]Lowe to [G. W. Dasent, Assistant Editor ?], n.d., in *History of The Times* (5 vols., London, 1939–52), II, 131–2.

Parliament, that the cheapest defence was Confederation. Gladstone had been particularly unhappy even with the £50,000 that the Government had appropriated for the Quebec defences,[54] and the cabinet as a whole appear to have felt that, while some gesture was necessary, it would be far better to have a British North American union that would coalesce colonial efforts. So the bearers of the good tidings of Confederation were wined and dined for a month and a half. Brown, Macdonald, Cartier, and Galt attended the Derby; they were feted at West End dinners; Cartier gave a major speech at Fishmonger's Hall; Macdonald was given a D.C.L. at Oxford; Galt and Brown breakfasted at least one morning with Gladstone at Carlton House Terrace.[55] In the meantime the British government worked hard to get something definite in the way of agreement on defence; but after six weeks of what Gladstone called "long and wearying discussions"[56] not much was agreed on except Confederation, and preliminary arrangements about fortifications and Rupert's Land. Gladstone was firmly of the opinion that the United States would have more than enough to do to control the South and would not be too concerned with Canada; delay over defence expenditures could do little harm. The Canadians seemed altogether too impatient and alarmist to Gladstone.[57] But their views were given substantial consideration by the British government; as Gladstone remarked, the Canadians were treated "as *usually* in the attitude of an independent Power," as far as defence was concerned.[58]

Out of these discussions came the powerful and dramatic despatch of June 24, 1865. It reflected the determination both of Cardwell and of the Canadians. It was sent to all four Maritime colonies, with minor additions, *mutatis mutandis*, for each, and it produced a lively reaction in all of them. The despatch has been cited often enough and perhaps one sentence will suffice: "the Colonies must recognize a right and even acknowledge an obligation incumbent on the Home Government to urge with earnestness and just authority the measures which they consider to be most expedient. . . ." It produced a tart and forthright answer from New Brunswick (the Minute of July 12), and it led to J. C. Pope's "no terms" resolutions in Prince Edward Island in 1866.[59] In Newfoundland the anti-Confederate St. John's *Patriot* praised the

[54]Another £150,000 was promised in the succeeding three years.
[55]Letterbook, Gladstone Papers, Add. MSS 44535, Gladstone to Brown, May 25, 1865. For other details about the Canadian visit to London see Creighton, *Macdonald*, 412–17.
[56]Gladstone Papers, Add. MSS 44320, Gladstone to Gordon, July 11, 1865.
[57]*Ibid.*, Add. MSS 44118, Gladstone to Cardwell, May 23, 1865 (private).
[58]*Ibid.*, Add. MSS 44320, Gladstone to Gordon, July 11, 1865 (Gladstone's italics).
[59]D. C. Harvey, "Confederation in Prince Edward Island," *Canadian Historical Review*, XIV, 2 (June, 1933), 149.

New Brunswick Minute as "a State Paper calculated to immortalize its authors, as containing the whole text of Responsible Government. . . ."[60] The despatch of June 24, 1865, was nearly minatory; and by joining patriotism to support of Confederation, it made the position of the anti-Confederates, particularly with the advent of Fenians, rather uncomfortable. British orders for Confederation had not much effect in Prince Edward Island and Newoundland, where shots "direct from the Imperial foundry," as one paper called the despatches,[61] had long been familiar in the struggles of Prince Edward Island with the land proprietors and of Newfoundland over the French Shore. But in New Brunswick, despite the biting remarks of the Minute of Council, the despatch had some effect, and, as in Nova Scotia, the results were more impressive as time went on.

A. J. Smith, the Premier of New Brunswick, was at the time in London, and there had a frank interview with Cardwell. It was made perfectly clear to Smith that the British government intended to have Confederation in some form; Smith, faced with this, seemed ready to resist.[62] William Annand of Nova Scotia was also in London, and received (and probably gave) much the same impression as Smith. Leonard Tilley arrived in London in July, followed by George Dundas, the Lieutenant Governor of Prince Edward Island, and finally by Arthur Gordon. With the general election in July, Cardwell was having a busy summer. A letter to Russell early in September, 1865, reveals very well Cardwell's line of attack. He sent Russell a long letter from Joseph Howe, and enclosed another from Lord Monck. Monck's was particularly important: it suggested that changes in the Quebec Resolutions might be acceptable to, or even suggested by Canada. Cardwell continued:

I had scarcely received Monck's letter, when A. Gordon, the Governor of N. Brunswick came in. He said that such a proposal from Canada would relieve him of his difficulties personally; and though some of his Ministers would resign, he thought the best of them would remain to carry Resolutions for Union on such a basis: viz. on the basis of permitting the Imperial Government to improve the programme of Quebec, by making the Union more complete. . . . By this mail I will urge upon Monck to obtain from his Ministry some formal sanction of such a proceeding. He will leave Quebec soon after receiving my letter, and will be here about October 10. In the meantime I have desired [?] A. Gordon to remain at least till after I have seen Monck.[63]

[60]St. John's *Patriot*, Sept. 23, 1865.
[61]St. John's *Morning Chronicle*, Dec. 20, 1865.
[62]P.R.O., Russell Papers, Cardwell to Russell, Aug. 15, 1865. This letter is quoted in part by Creighton in *Macdonald*, 423.
[63]Monck did not see Cardwell until October 20, 1865. Gordon arrived back in Saint John, New Brunswick, on October 28, so that their meeting was probably impossible. Gordon went to see Monck at Montreal, February 22–25, 1866.

I will communicate again with Howe. I suppose "quorum pars magna fui" is a considerable maxim with him: and even in his declamatory epistle favouring separate governments, he seems to leave a door open for suggesting Legislative Union.[64]

Here probably was the origin of the change from the Quebec scheme to one made under the "arbitrament"—the word appears frequently in 1866—of the imperial government. It was known in French Canada as "l'arbitrage impérial," and it was a touchy issue. Nevertheless this new elasticity, so justifiably suspect by the French Canadians, was essential for the adhesion both of New Brunswick and Nova Scotia. It was used both by Gordon in his negotiations with Smith, and by Fenwick Williams, the new Lieutenant-Governor of Nova Scotia, in his negotiations with William Annand.[65] With a new governor in Nova Scotia, Gordon back in New Brunswick, Dundas returned to Prince Edward Island, Musgrave apparently well in control in Newfoundland, and, early in February, 1866, Monck at last in Quebec, the stage was set for the final and most climactic act of the Confederation play.

Cardwell had left nothing undone that could be done to ensure success. Fenwick Williams in Nova Scotia asked for, and got, power to create additional legislative councillors should it be necessary to swamp the Nova Scotian upper house. This power was a highly dangerous commodity; if used too soon, Cardwell warned, it would be far more damaging than helpful.[66] As Cardwell properly observed, "You cannot be too *secret* in respect to this document, until you shall be obliged to use it,—which I hope you will not."[67] As it turned out, it was unnecessary. When, on April 16, 1866, Confederation came to a vote in the Legislative Council of Nova Scotia, it passed 13–5.[68]

Cardwell anticipated that all colonial legislative action on Confederation would be completed by the middle of April, 1866, and that the colonial delegates would be in London by the end of the month. He relied upon Gordon's optimistic accounts of progress in New Brunswick. But Gordon had been too confident. The fascinating story of Gordon's adventures in New Brunswick in 1866 is not the immediate concern here; but the result of the delay in New Brunswick threw all

[64]Russell Papers, Cardwell to Russell, Sept. 7, 1865. Howe was in London about this time. There is a copy of his letter to Cardwell, dated Sept., 1865, in the P.A.C., Howe Papers.

[65]Annand recounts his role, Halifax *Morning Chronicle*, March 2, March 23, 1869. See also P. B. Waite, *The Life and Times of Confederation, 1864–1867* (Toronto, 1962), 225.

[66]Fenwick Williams Papers, Cardwell to Williams, Feb. 3, 1866.

[67]*Ibid.*, Cardwell to Williams, March 17, 1866. (The italics are probably Cardwell's, although Williams often seems to have been in the habit of underlining important words in Cardwell's letters.) Cf. also C.O. 218, Cardwell to Williams, March 17, 1866 (confidential).

[68]Nova Scotia, Legislative Council, *Journals*, 1866, 45.

imperial, Nova Scotian, and Canadian arrangements into confusion. It was June 21, 1866, by the time new elections had been held in New Brunswick and a new Assembly convened to consider Confederation. Williams in Nova Scotia expressed the hope to Cardwell that they would make "short work of it." (They did.) Prince Edward Island, Williams added, ought to be ashamed of itself for resisting this long. But, with the troops there to deal with the Tenant League trouble, manipulation of the circumstances was possible. "You can," said Williams amiably, "by a hint at the withdrawal of these men [the troops] get what is required: as I have been in their Island and personally know their public men, I feel sure I do not miscalculate the tension required to snap their thread of sand."[69] Cardwell took this up with Dundas on July 7, 1866.[70] That was the day after Cardwell had given up the seals of office.

The Russell government had resigned. The death of Palmerston in October, 1865, had put Lord Russell at the helm (and nearly put Cardwell in the War Office). On June 27, 1866, Russell resigned after a defeat in the Commons of his Reform bill; and on July 6 Cardwell turned over the Colonial Office to the Earl of Carnarvon, of the incoming Derby ministry.

Cardwell had carefully briefed Carnarvon on Confederation, but it soon became apparent that Cardwell could not go on holiday just yet. What was needed was Cardwell's support, and that of his colleagues, for the immediate introduction into Parliament of the British North America bill. The delegates from Nova Scotia, New Brunswick, and Canada were now expected within three weeks. The British Columbia bill, uniting the colonies of Vancouver Island and British Columbia, brought into Parliament in June by Cardwell, was passed late in July, receiving royal assent on August 6[71]; eastern British North America was to be united at the same time. Carnarvon developed the idea of settling the main features of the eastern union by bill, leaving the controversial sections for further discussion and eventual implementation by Order in Council. On July 14, 1866, Cardwell, Russell, and some other members of the late Government met and agreed to give the Derby administration all assistance possible to carry Confederation. They had, however, considerable doubts about important sections of the bill being decided by Order in Council.[72] Carnarvon hesitated.

[69]Cardwell Papers, Williams to Cardwell, June 21, 1866 (private).
[70]*Ibid.*, Cardwell to Dundas, July 7, 1866 (private) (copy).
[71]The British Columbia bill was brought into Parliament by Cardwell and read for the first time June 11, 1866. Owing to the change of government, it did not receive its second reading until July 16, its third on July 20. It went through all stages in the House of Lords in a week, July 23–30. There were no debates in either House.
[72]Cardwell Papers, Cardwell to Carnarvon, July 14, 1866.

Should the project be abandoned? But it appeared that Lord Russell was "most anxious that the Confederation scheme should be ratified this year by Parlt." And, Cardwell added, "I need scarcely say that I am equally so. . . ."[73] Carnarvon then set the scheme in motion, his foremost object being, as he said, "to strengthen, as far as is practicable, the central government. . . ."[74] Cardwell could approve of this; but, he told Carnarvon, the point of cardinal importance was whether the bill was acceptable to the delegates. "Now the Canadian Parlt. has, I think you will find, proceeded upon the understanding that the Quebec Resolutions constitute the scheme: while the two Lower Provinces proceeded on the understanding that there will be a closer union than the Quebec Resolutions wd: create."[75] Cardwell insisted that unless these disparities were carefully reconciled a disagreeable wrangle might follow.

Saturday morning, July 21, Cardwell went to the Colonial Office at Lord Carnarvon's request to discuss the question. Carnarvon had the printed outline of a bill before him and asked Cardwell if Lord Russell and his colleagues could agree to it. But despite Carnarvon's obvious desire for categorical assurances Cardwell would not commit himself just yet. He was clearly uncomfortable in these personal negotiations and was unwilling to go very far beyond the reach of pen and paper. Indeed the very existence of the records of the transaction is evidence of Cardwell's caution. It was not in fact a very pleasant interview, but Cardwell did agree that every means should be used to get the bill passed now, "even if it were necessary to keep Parliament together a little longer in order to do so."[76] Cardwell was away for the weekend, and on his return to his house in Eaton Square, on Tuesday, July 24, he found a note from Carnarvon enclosing the printed draft of the British North America bill.[77] Carnarvon had already submitted it to cabinet and it had been approved, subject to the further approval of the delegates when they arrived.

As finally printed, the bill is dated July 21, 1866. It is not necessary to quote this document in full, but it is useful to comment on it, particularly in those respects wherein it differed from the Quebec Resolutions that preceded it and the British North America Act of 1867 that followed it.

[73]*Ibid.*, Cardwell to Carnarvon, July 19, 1866.
[74]*Ibid.*, Carnarvon to Cardwell, July 19, 1866 (confidential). Cf., however, Carnarvon's remarks in Parliament in 1867, *infra*, 39.
[75]Cardwell Papers, Cardwell to Carnarvon, July 20, 1866.
[76]Cardwell wrote out a long memorandum of his interview with Carnarvon, doubtless for the information of his colleagues.
[77]Carnarvon to Cardwell, probably July 23, 1866. It is dated July 20, but as Cardwell himself pointed out, this was presumably by mistake.

There were 22 clauses subsumed under seven heads. The first six heads were concerned mainly with what might be legislated at once: the seventh outlined the principal items to be passed by Order in Council. The heads were as follows:

I. Union
II. Legislation
III. Judicature
IV. Military
V. Seat of government
VI. Provincial governments and legislation
VII. Arrangements consequent on union

Under "II. Legislation" (Clause 8) lay the general grant of power to the central government. It was given without any of the examples of Section 29 of the Quebec Resolutions, or of those that "for greater certainty" were given in Section 91 of the British North America Act. "Subject to the provisions of this Act, it shall be lawful for Her Majesty, her heirs and successors, with the advice of the two Houses of Parliament of the United Province [of British North America], to make laws for the peace, order and good government of the United Province and of the several Provinces." Under "VI. Provincial Governments and Legislation" (Clause 19) was the power of the Lieutenant Governor "with the advice and consent of the Provincial Council" to make "Ordinances in relation to matters of provincial interest, coming within the classes of subjects to be specified in this behalf by Order in Council." Unless otherwise indicated such Ordinances were to be lawful "as long and as far only as they are not repugnant to any Act of Parliament of the United Province."[78]

There is nowhere a reference to any specific powers for the central government, either in the bill or in the items reserved for Order in Council. It seems probable that in 1866 "peace, order and good government" was intended to stand on its own sufficient legs. The phrase was to apply not only to the United Province as a whole, but specifically also to the separate provinces. It seems clear that the Colonial Office, besides following the Quebec Resolutions, was also acting under the impress of the New Zealand Act of 1852. Sir Frederic Rogers considered the New Zealand Act a worthwhile, though perhaps unsuccessful, effort to strike a mean between legislative and federal union.[79] Thus the "Provincial Council" referred to under head vi prob-

[78]There is a copy of the printed bill in the Cardwell Papers.
[79]Sir Frederic Rogers has an interesting Minute on this subject dated Oct. 17 [1865], which is in C.O. 60, Despatches from British Columbia. It is quoted in Waite, *Confederation, 1864–1867*, 326.

ably meant not an executive council in the usual sense, but a body more analogous to the provincial councils of New Zealand. The "Ordinances" that such a Council was to pass were a strong indication that it was the New Zealand example that Carnarvon, or Rogers, had in mind.

Upon receipt of this draft bill Cardwell at once wrote to Russell at Richmond. The sections of the bill to be settled by Order in Council were, Cardwell noted, very considerable, and it might well be doubted whether the House would accept the bill in that form, even if recommended both by Government and Opposition. Possibly more might be put into legislation. But in Cardwell's view there was a greater difficulty that still remained, which Lord Carnarvon had not dealt with: Lord Palmerston's government, and hence Lord Russell's, was pledged to propose three guarantees for British North America, covering loans for the Intercolonial Railway, fortifications, and the purchase of the Hudson's Bay Company's rights, in all a total of nearly £5 million. Gladstone attached great importance to these considerations (as Gladstone would) because of the impropriety of asking the House "to enter into any implied liability at this late and exhausted period of the Session." But that the issue was vital Cardwell had no doubt, especially the £3 million guarantee for the Intercolonial Railway. "N. Brunswick would scarcely have accepted Confederation without the Railway,—or Nova Scotia either. The question is so important that I will endeavour to see you by driving over to Richmond tomorrow afternoon."[80] It was decided that individual members of the Opposition should stand by their pledges, though Russell was willing to support a bill without guarantees if that would be acceptable.[81] But he had little confidence in the Derby government when it came to colonies, whatever he may have thought about Carnarvon. "I suppose Derby and Dizzy do not in the least care whether they preserve Canada to the Empire or not, and that Stanley will be glad to give it up."[82]

At this point, however, all haste came suddenly to an end. That same day, Saturday, July 28, 1866, Carnarvon wrote to Cardwell:

I have this morning received the news that the N. American steamer is in with the delegates from N. Scotia and N. Brunswick alone. Neither the Can. delegates nor Ld. Monck have come nor is there any certain news of the day when they may be expected. Under these circumstances it is clear that any legislation for this Session must be abandoned: but I give it up with regret for I see how many uncertainties and difficulties are ahead.[83]

---

[80]Cardwell Papers, Cardwell to Russell, July 24, 1866 (copy).
[81]*Ibid.*, Russell to Cardwell, July 25, 1866.
[82]*Ibid.*, Russell to Cardwell, July 28, 1866.
[83]*Ibid.*, Carnarvon to Cardwell, July 28, 1866.

And the Canadians did not arrive until four months later.[84] Long before that time Cardwell, and Gladstone, were holidaying in Italy.

In the London Conference Carnarvon was forced to give up his aim of strengthening the central government. The French Canadians were determined to hold to the Quebec scheme as nearly as they could; and the provincial power in the final British North America bill resembled much more the Quebec Resolutions than the 1866 draft. In his speech in the House of Lords, February 19, 1867, Carnarvon made a virtue of necessity. "We have thought it desirable," he said, "to reserve to the local Legislature as ample a measure as possible of local action and self-government, of municipal liberty and freedom...."[85] But Cardwell, for his part, regretted these concessions. "I must candidly confess," he said in the House of Commons nine days later, "that I should have liked to see a clause, such as there was in the New Zealand Act, giving greater controlling power to the central Government."[86]

A few months later there was an amusing reminder of Canadian affairs in Cardwell's correspondence: a letter from an unknighted and irritated George Cartier, on the Knighthood of the Bath he did not get. Cardwell could now afford to be jocular. "It seems," he wrote to Gladstone, "the Shower Bath has not had the refreshing effect intended,–the string has been clumsily pulled and dissatisfaction takes the place of gratitude."[87]

Cardwell had a civil servant's temperament and a statesman's mind. He saw things that needed to be done, and, if possible, would make order out of chaos; and if he worked under a chief who conceded something to his abilities and supported him in the House of Commons, Cardwell could, and did, achieve much. He was a pertinacious man; he set about his business with both discipline and diligence. Yet he was by no means a plodder; he was quick to grasp the nub of a problem. And if he sometimes preferred a logical to a practicable solution, that was perhaps the defect of his virtues. He was remarkably patient; he answered Gordon's importunities with the most disarming geniality, though that may have been out of loyalty to the memory of Lord Aberdeen, Gordon's father. Few Colonial Secretaries of his time were more accessible.

Cardwell probably disliked the hurly-burly of politics, preferring

[84]For explanations of the Canadian action see Pope, *Memoirs of Macdonald*, 315–27; Creighton, *Macdonald*, 443–7; Waite, *Confederation, 1864–1867*, 284.
[85]Great Britain, Parliament, *Debates on the Confederation Bill* . . . (London, 1867), 3.
[86]*Ibid.*, 21.
[87]Gladstone Papers, Add. MSS 44118, Cardwell to Gladstone, Aug. 1, 1867.

administration; he had little taste for, or joy from, the clash of ideas and tempers in the House of Commons. He could also be mightily determined when seized of the vital importance of a measure. Especially was this true if he thought he had Parliament behind him. He never doubted it was desirable to amalgamate Vancouver Island and British Columbia, in spite of the manifest reluctance of the British Columbians and not a few cries of woe from Vancouver Island. He never doubted, once having made up his mind, that Confederation was a good thing. In his view the more centralized it could be the better; but, unlike Gordon and MacDonnell, he did not believe it was bad because it was not sufficiently centralized, or because it was not a legislative union. He probably recognized that other fulminations of Gordon and MacDonnell were true: that the Canadians were using Confederation to relieve themselves of their embarrassments; that Canadian politicians never looked at things but from a Canadian point of view. It was true, but it was politics; especially was it true of the inglorious savagery of colonial politics. Cardwell put these considerations aside. He probably felt that the selfishness of Canadian purposes need not affect their value. Indeed, the driving power of the Canadians could be harnessed and used for imperial advantage; hence Cardwell's despatches represented Canadian determination as well as his own. But he overestimated the power both of despatches and Canadians. Cardwell had something of the blindness of administrators: he sometimes failed to distinguish a plausible from a substantial result.[88] Three thousand miles of ocean did not make it any easier. Confederation was one thing viewed from London, quite another in British North America. Doubtless Cardwell understood that it was of no use for imperial despatches to command a union unless there existed forces in North America capable of realizing it; here the purposiveness of the Canadians, the ambitions of Maritime politicians, and the optimism of some of the governors made it difficult for Cardwell to fully assess local conditions even were he disposed to do so—which he was not. A. J. Smith and William Annand spoke their mind to him, and so also did Howe; but Cardwell tended to dismiss such views as merely refractory opposition to the achievement of a great design. With Cardwell the means subserved, all too obviously, the end in view. Oddly enough for an efficient administrator, he was basically a diffident man; his ruthlessness is explained by a superbly logical mind which swung easily and noiselessly from premise to conclusion. It is also explained by the fact that his Confederation policy proceeded under an impressive display of support from the leading papers and from Parliament.

Whether Cardwell had any higher sense of the destiny of empire

[88]Marindin, ed., *Letters of Frederic [Rogers]*, 226.

both Miss Sellers and Professor Erickson have doubted.[89] There is some reason to believe, however, the sentiments in his Oxford speech of January, 1865, and his House of Commons utterances in 1867, and they expressed a more generous spirit and a more spacious logic than what might have been expected from the hard-headed *bourgeois* intellectual from Liverpool. The *Saturday Review*, welcoming the new Dominion of Canada, said there were abundant indications that the old free trade theory of empire would be replaced "by the sounder theory of a real absorption into a common federation with the whole Empire...."[90] Cardwell did not go so far as to express such views. But he believed that the self-governing colonies should be just that: what more than self-governing they could be he was too practical to say. At the same time he was convinced, with Sir Frederic Rogers, that to turn them out into the world against their will was a derogation of duty and of national honour.

For the good and the bad in the achievement of Confederation Cardwell has not perhaps been given his full due. The enthusiastic support of Canada by the Colonial Office, the overturn of the New Brunswick government, the coercion of Nova Scotia, were all part of the same policy; and if this policy failed to work in Newfoundland and Prince Edward Island it was not from any lack of effort by Cardwell. And his determination was as manifest on the west coast as it was on the east. Whatever Carnarvon's contribution in getting Confederation through its final stages, the bulk of the work was already done. It was Cardwell who was responsible for the weight of the British government behind Confederation, Cardwell who patiently deployed his governors and urged them on with his incisive directives, and it was only an accident of fate that prevented him—thorough workman that he was—from finally "clinching the nails."

[89]Sellers, "Cardwell at the Colonial Office," 301; Erickson, *Cardwell*, 101.
[90]*Saturday Review*, April 20, 1867.

The Quebec Bishops and Confederation

WALTER ULLMANN

RELATIVELY LITTLE IS KNOWN about the attitude of the Quebec bishops towards Confederation. What information exists deals largely with the hierarchy's position towards an already enacted British North America Act. What remains to be elucidated are the ideas of the bishops on the desirability of a union of the British North American colonies. There is something enigmatic in the attitude of the Quebec bishops towards Confederation. During all the lengthy negotiations for Canadian union the hierarchy played a relatively passive role. Such a position can be understood in a context of shifting emphasis of political activities from Quebec to the new federal capital of Ottawa, but it certainly does not explain the real or apparent lack of interest of the bishops in the very question of transfer of powers. The reasons for this must be found elsewhere.

Various explanations have been offered for the absence of a definite attitude on the part of the Quebec bishops towards Confederation, the most common being that Confederation was essentially a political question and as such beyond the sphere of proper interest for the clergy. Certainly, Confederation was first and foremost political in character, but with equal certainty it had far reaching implications with respect to the preservation of Quebec's French and Catholic character. Regarding the political question of the Fenian raids, an issue almost contemporary with Confederation and one which had no direct bearing on matters concerning the Catholic faith, the bishops left no doubt where they stood. Their numerous pastoral letters and circulars[1] show clearly that when confronted by an American challenge the bishops' desire to maintain the British connection overrode what-

[1] The bishops of Quebec and Montreal were particularly outspoken on the subject.

Reprinted from *Canadian Historical Review*, XLIV (3), September, 1963

ever other reservations they might have had about British rule. Their position was equally unequivocal on the question of seigneurial tenure. Their indifferent attitude towards Confederation contrasts strangely with their frequent and explicit pronouncements on other issues of a purely political character.

A second major explanation interprets the relative silence of the bishops as a tacit approval of Confederation. This argument was used by the Conservative press at the time:

Ainsi donc, il n'y a pas de malentendu, et que le peuple l'apprenne dès l'aujourd'hui: *que nos évêques sont en faveur de la confédération et que le silence des évêques et du clergé est une approbation tacite du PROJET DE CONFEDERATION*. La Minerve, Le Courier du Canada et Le Courier de Saint-Hyacinthe se sont exprimés à peu près dans le même sens, ce sont les organes du clergé, et voici Le Journal des Trois-Rivières, immédiatement sous la surveillance des hautes autorités religieuses, qui est plus explicite.

Voilà donc un fait historique bien établi si ces journaux restent sans contradictions.[2]

Why did the bishops express their concurrence and approval by the indirect method of remaining silent, as had been suggested by the editor of *Le Journal des Trois-Rivières*? Was not Confederation essentially a project of the Conservative party, the party which had always enjoyed the bishops' support? Nothing would have been easier for the hierarchy than to approve *viva voce* a project of the political party of its choice; contrariwise, it would have been rather difficult to disapprove openly and by so doing admit the existence of a conflict of opinion between the Conservative party and the Roman Catholic hierarchy of Quebec on the subject of Confederation. While the editorial opinion of *Le Journal des Trois-Rivières* expressed wishful thinking rather than harsh political realities, *La Minerve* carried such hopes still further when its editor claimed Confederation to be "l'œuvre tacite du clergé" and held the clergy responsible for its future effects on French Canada.[3]

Lastly, an attempt has been made to construe the approval expressed by the bishops, once the British North America Act had been placed on the statute books, as an indication of the hierarchy's sympathy for Confederation.[4] Such a view overlooks the fact that the Catholic Church habitually upheld legislation once it was enacted. The question, of course, is not whether the bishops' silence might be interpreted as ideological concurrence with the British North America Act, or whether their approval of an already existing piece of legislation might be taken as approval or consent. What is of interest is what they

[2]*Le Journal des Trois-Rivières* 10 fév. 1867; see also *La Minerve*, 13 fév. 1867.
[3]*La Minerve*, 13 fév. 1867.
[4]Léon Pouliot, S.J., "Monseigneur Bourget et la Confédération," *Société Canadienne d'Histoire de l'Eglise Catholique, Rapport* (1959), 4.

thought of Confederation when the project was first conceived and was actually in the making and how much they did to promote it or to oppose it. Of the five bishops of the ecclesiastical province of Quebec, only one is known to have considered the issue of Confederation in a wider context, in a framework transcending the limits of strictly religious interest. The others simply followed a cautious, routine procedure, although an occasional pronounced view on the question can be discovered. All things considered, the bishops did not speak with their customary authority.

At the time of Confederation, two men stood out among the Quebec hierarchy, Mgr Ignace Bourget, the Bishop of Montreal, and Mgr Louis-François Laflèche, the coadjutor of Three Rivers. It was to them, rather than to their metropolitan, the Archbishop of Quebec, that the remaining members of the episcopate looked for leadership and guidance. They had good reason to do so since both Bourget and Laflèche were known for their pronounced views on most major questions of the day. The Bishop of Montreal, a man in his sixties and titular head of the diocese for some twenty-five years, had seldom failed to make his voice heard on any issue affecting the status and welfare of his flock. It happened that precisely at the time of Confederation, Bishop Bourget was in the midst of two heated controversies, the one concerning the ill-fated *Institut Canadien*, the other the division of his own cathedral parish of Notre Dame. Laflèche, Bourget's junior by almost twenty years and his great admirer, had not as yet reached episcopal rank but was by that time well on his way to a prominent career in the Quebec hierarchy. Vicar general of the see of Three Rivers since the early 1860's and coadjutor to the ailing Bishop Cooke since 1867, Laflèche had long since been the *deus ex machina* of the diocese. Among the episcopate Bourget and Laflèche were politically by far the most astute and it was to be expected that at least one of them would emerge spokesman for the hierarchy on questions connected with Confederation. Such a course of events was anticipated, since the metropolitan see of Quebec was at first in the hands of the ailing Archbishop Turgeon, who died in 1867, and then occupied at the very time of Confederation by Mgr Baillargeon as administrator. The see of St. Hyacinthe had as its head Mgr Charles Larocque, much of whose clerical and intellectual formation had been acquired at the Montreal bishopric. Finally, Mgr Jean Langevin, the Bishop of Rimouski, had only taken possession of his see two months before Confederation was achieved.

Yet more than all these external circumstances, the dominant personalities of Bourget and Laflèche were responsible for their emergence as natural leaders among the hierarchy in questions relating to

Confederation. Zealous, resourceful, gifted with magnetic appeal, and venerated by a large following of priests and laymen, both bishops were noted for a long and impressive record of distinguished service to their faith. Bishop Bourget's refusal to commit himself must have disappointed the Quebec episcopate. The reasons for his stubborn position are almost entirely a matter of conjecture. Laflèche, however, made a notable attempt to analyse the whole question and actually issued one of the rare explicit statements on Confederation among those made by the Quebec bishops. To understand at least part of the reasoning behind the actions of the two men, one must look briefly into their pasts and into their intellectual backgrounds.

Few figures in Quebec's history, where politics are so intermingled with religion, have raised as much controversy as the second bishop of Montreal. Born of poor parentage in 1799, Ignace Bourget distinguished himself at an early age by his zeal and piety. Ordained at twenty-two, he almost immediately became permanently attached to the Montreal diocese where Bishop Lartigue soon recognized the unusual skills of the young priest. For the born administrator it was fortunate to be at the centre of affairs. Gradually Bourget became Lartigue's secretary and eventually emerged as the bishop's right hand. No one was surprised when upon the death of his ordinary in 1840 Ignace Bourget succeeded to the see of Montreal.[5] Whatever the verdict of history on Bourget, even his staunchest opponents cannot deny the lasting and in many respects highly admirable legacy which he left to his diocese during his thirty-six-year tenure as second bishop of Montreal. The introduction of some religious orders to Canada, the foundation of others, the erection of hospitals and asylums, and a host of other charitable works are but some of Bishop Bourget's lasting monuments. They all speak eloquently for the bishop's excellent administration. It is, however, far more difficult to draw equally unequivocal conclusions about Bourget's politico-religious views and about his outlook on the world in general.

Ignace Bourget was a thorough conservative—a product of pre-1789 social thought. Although an exemplary student and seminarian, he never attempted to experience the excitement of intellectual discovery that comes with questioning of one's intimate environment. Nor did the bishop ever display any deep interest in intellectual life. He was entirely devoted to the interests of the Church as he understood them. An untiring worker, accustomed to strict hierarchical authority, Bishop Bourget was the living example of the benevolent yet ultra-conservative and paternalistic churchman. In an age of vast and inescapable

[5]L. Pouliot, S.J., *Monseigneur Bourget et son temps* (Montréal, 1956), I. Most of the data on Bourget used in this article stem from this source of information.

change, with one current of thought rapidly following another, Bourget remained a pillar of the old eighteenth-century order.

Louis-François Laflèche was a man of different outlook, although hardly less strong in his commitment to the old order. Despite this attachment, Laflèche displayed striking intellectual curiosity. Much better educated than Bourget and obviously a man of wide reading, Laflèche seemed more at home in the world of affairs than did the saintly Bishop Bourget whose piety bordered on mysticism. The onetime missionary in the Red River region found time to learn the Montagnais language and, upon his return to the East in 1856, taught philosophy at the seminary of Nicolet, his alma mater.[6] It was there, through the Abbé L.-E. Bois, that he had become aware of the unsatisfactory quality of scientific education in Quebec and partly for this reason the Nicolet Seminary acquired a first-class scientific library. Given the nature of scientific thought in the positivistic 1850's and 1860's, it can readily be seen that Laflèche was not one to allow his conservatism to limit his intellectual awareness of current trends. An active collaborator of Le Journal des Trois-Rivières, an ardent nationalist, and a staunch supporter of the ideas of Louis Veuillot whom he admired,[7] Laflèche accordingly defined his views on the proper place of religion in politics. According to him French Canadians possessed all the elements of nationhood in their common language, their common faith, customs, and institutions. Like any other nation, they had been given a providential mission: the safeguarding of Catholicism in the New World. Laflèche considered the role of the priest in society and in politics fully justified, since the latter derived his authority directly from God. Liberalism which committed the error of building a society on a purely secular basis was wrong. Finally, not only revelation, but reason and history as well, had proven that politics was indeed a proper field of religious influence.[8]

These views were not entirely novel; still, Laflèche's clear and straightforward mode of thought and expression shed much light on his personality. Of the two, Laflèche was easily the more original thinker, even though Bourget's seniority, his greater experience in administrative matters, and his immense popularity made him appear stronger. Not until 1876, when the ailing Bishop Bourget resigned his episcopal charge, did Laflèche emerge as the acknowledged leader of

[6]A. Dugré, S.J. Monseigneur Laflèche (Montréal, n.d. [probably 1924]), 4–6 (printed pamphlet)
[7]Letter of Mgr Albert Tessier to author, October 12, 1960.
[8]L.-F. Laflèche, Quelques Considérations sur les Rapports de la Société Civile avec la Religion et la Famille (Trois-Rivières, 1866); first published as a series of articles in Le Journal des Trois-Rivières, 1866. See also R. Rumilly, Monseigneur Laflèche et son temps (Montréal, 1938), 26–7.

Quebec ultramontanism. In view of all this, then, as well as of Laflèche's greater legal abilities, it is not surprising that Laflèche, rather than Bourget, was the first among the bishops to venture an opinion on the delicate question of Confederation.

To do so, Laflèche did not have to be prodded. Although he never pretended to have studied the various drafts of the Confederation proposals at great length, he clearly considered them more than a simple piece of legislation and foresaw the full implications of so radical a change in the structure of Canadian government. As early as 1864, in a letter to Boucher de Niverville, member of Parliament for Pointe-du-Lac, Mgr Laflèche wrote:

Le projet de Confédération est tellement vaste et complexe en lui-même et dans ses détails qu'il est bien difficile de l'aborder sans en avoir auparavant fait une étude spéciale; et c'est que je n'ai point fait. Cependant je vous dirai en peu de mots la manière dont je forme mon opinion relativement à ce projet d'une importance si grande pour notre avenir.[9]

After this frank admission of not having given the Confederation proposals any particularly detailed attention, Laflèche nevertheless proceeded with a perceptive analysis of the present state and future prospects of French-Canadian affairs.

J'ai d'abord considéré que notre pays se trouve en présence de telles difficultés que la législation est à peu près complètement paralisée [sic] depuis trois ans et que les partis politiques sont presque sur le pied de deux camps ennemis en face et prêts à en venir en mains. Or un tel état de choses ne saurait durer sans amener les conséquences les plus désastreuses pour nous surtout, Bas-Canadiens; et autant qu'on peut le prévoir, finir par la guerre civile ou la domination du Haut-Canada dans l'Union Législative....[10]

Considering the complexity of the political situation, the Vicar General could see a possible solution; what is more, he had the courage to propose it openly. Other leading French Çanadians must have held similar views, but few of them dared to state them with equal candour: "... Donc, il faut un remède à un mal si grave. Quel est-il? Le rappel de l'Union pur et simple est impossible. La prépondérance pour le Haut-Canada dans l'union législative, c'est notre déchéance, et l'anéantissement de nos institutions et de notre nationalité. Il ne reste donc que la Confédération qui nous offre réellement une planche de salut."[11] To Laflèche, Confederation constituted this platform of salvation. It might not be the ideal proposal but, all circumstances considered, it certainly was practical and expedient. He thus evaluated the proposed

[9]Archives du Séminaire des Trois-Rivières, Correspondance Laflèche, Laflèche to Boucher de Niverville, 2 mars 1864.
[10]Ibid.
[11]Ibid.

union of the British North American provinces: "Autant que j'ai pu comprendre après une lecture attentive, le projet qui en a été dressé à Québec par les premiers hommes de notre pays, je me suis convaincu plus en plus que c'est là vraiment le moyen pratique le plus avantageux que nous ayons de sortir de nos difficultés."[12]

It might be said that Laflèche was merely a political realist. The existing state of affairs no longer seemed tenable to him; changes were bound to come. Were French Canadians simply to be overtaken by them, were they going to be overrun by history, or were they to take an intelligent and active interest in their political future? Such, to him, was the primary question. Whatever other deficiencies the proposed scheme of Confederation may have had, they all were secondary to the opportunities which it offered French Canadians. To Laflèche, Confederation was both the most practical and the most advantageous solution to all the difficulties of his compatriots. His evaluation of Confederation showed a clear understanding of the basic Anglo-French problem, a keen grasp of political realities as well as the ability to combine lofty principles with the actual possibilities of down-to-earth politics. It showed further that Laflèche's love and devotion for his own people did not involve him in any utopian blindness. Staunch defender of things French and Catholic though he always was, he also found it possible to preach peace and harmony between French and English Canadians:

Nous devons donc accepter cet état de choses avec confiance, et traiter ces nouveaux compatriotes [the English] avec toute la bienveillance qu'ils ont droit d'attendre de nous. Nous isoler systématiquement serait un Malheur et pour nous et pour eux; ce serait jeter une division regrettable entre ceux que Dieu a appelé à vivre sous un même ciel, à vivre en frères, puisqu'il les a mis sous la tutelle d'une commune mère-patrie.[13]

In short, Laflèche correctly conceived that this was not the time for entrenchment behind a nationalist wall. Only flexibility and willingness to compromise and to make the best of the situation could bring happy results for the French Canadians.

Mgr Laflèche contributed more than any member of the Quebec hierarchy to the success of Confederation, a fact both he and his associates fully realized. A mere three days after the official proclamation of the British North America Act, the Abbé Luc Desilets, a priest of the Three Rivers diocese and later its vicar general,[14] reminded George-Etienne Cartier of his debt to the Bishop of Three Rivers and

[12]*Ibid.*
[13]L.-F. Laflèche, *Le Patriotisme* (n.p., n.d.), 14 (printed pamphlet).
[14]In later years, Luc Desilets became one of Bishop Laflèche's staunchest supporters in all major politico-religious questions of the day. Like his ordinary, Vicar General Desilets was one of the pillars of Quebec ultramontanism.

THE QUEBEC BISHOPS AND CONFEDERATION 55

to Mgr Laflèche, and of the aid which Cartier received from there for his project of Confederation. Requesting Cartier's support for the political aims of a certain Dr. Bourgeois, who was upheld by Bishop Cooke in his campaign for the Nicolet seat in the new federal parliament, the Abbé Desilets stated quite bluntly:

Quant à moi, j'ai la ferme confiance que vous tiendrez tout le compte que mérite la recommendation de Sa Grandeur et que vous ne lui ferez pas la peine d'un désappointment, quand Elle a pris si généreusement l'initiative de la défense publique de la Confédération. Je sais d'ailleurs que vous accordez volontiers à l'Eglise du Canada sa part légitime d'influence; et que vous n'ignorez pas que Mgr Laflèche est un des plus grands leviers de la puissance ecclésiastique du pays dans les affaires sociales, dont il est bon de se ménager le concours.[15]

The reference to the ever increasing importance of the future Bishop of Three Rivers was no vain boast. For the next three decades Mgr Laflèche was a power whom politicians in Quebec could ill afford to ignore.

In view of such keen interest in Confederation on the part of Mgr Laflèche, Bishop Bourget's lukewarm attitude towards the project comes as a surprise. On major questions of policy, Bourget and Laflèche had nearly always agreed. Almost singlehandedly they upheld the ultramontane position, long after it had become anachronistic even in Quebec. Seldom has there been greater kinship of mind and heart. Yet on Confederation the two men seemed to have had quite different views. Although neither considered Confederation the ideal solution for the existing state of affairs, Laflèche compromised on the issue of Confederation while the Bishop of Montreal remained inflexible.

Perhaps the earliest opinion on Confederation by the Bishop of Montreal, indirect though it might be, is to be found in a letter of Fr. M.-J.-O. Paré, the bishop's secretary, in which Paré replied to some accusations voiced against the bishop in the anti-Confederationist *Presse*. Paré protested a statement of the editor who had used some remarks of a certain parish priest of the Montreal diocese in his favour. On behalf of Bishop Bourget, Paré censored the priest for having violated the principle of clerical non-intervention in politics, but in so doing, made it clear that while the priest was being called to order, the reprimand must not be interpreted as an opinion of the bishop on the merits of the Confederation question.[16] From Rome, in May 1865, Bourget confided to his Vicar General that he was there, among other

[15] Archives de la Province de Québec, Collection Chapais, Desilets to Cartier, 4 juillet 1867.
[16] *La Minerve*, 12 juillet 1864. R.P. Pouliot's notes on this particular article evaluate it in the following terms: "Mgr Bourget ne se prononce pas sur le mérite de la question [Confederation]; il blâme la conduite de ce prêtre." The name of the parish or of the priest are not given in *La Minerve*'s account, nor could R.P. Pouliot reveal his identity. He merely refers to him as "un curé de campagne."

reasons, to seek instructions for Catholic legislators in the matter of Confederation and codification of laws which was to be debated the following July. The Bishop expressed the desire for a solid study of these questions and suggested to Truteau that such an inquiry into the nature of the whole matter be undertaken without delay.[17] Shortly after Bourget reiterated his stand and stated that religion was vitally interested in these subjects and that it was an error to assume that religion had nothing to do with the constitution and the government of a civil society.[18]

Some three months earlier, however, Vicar General Truteau, who had received the news that Cartier claimed to have the support of the hierarchy in his project of Confederation, disavowed any such approval on the part of his ordinary and reaffirmed Bourget's strict policy of non-intervention. Writing to Vicar General Cazeau of Quebec, Truteau stated:

M. Cartier, m'a-t'on dit (car je n'ai pas eu le temps de voir cela par moi-même sur les journaux) aurait dit, en pleine Chambre, que les plus hauts dignitaires des Eglises de chaque diocèse du Canada étaient en faveur de la Confédération. Je ne sais ce que les autres évêques pensent là-dessus; mais quant à Mgr de Montréal, je suis positif à dire qu'il n'a pas voulu se prononcer jusqu'ici sur cette question. Avant de partir pour Rome [14 novembre 1864], il disait qu'il aimait mieux attendre avant de prendre aucun parti là-dessus.[19]

Cartier, who had indeed claimed that "those of the clergy who are high in authority, as well as those in humbler position, have declared for Confederation"[20] was now being reprimanded by the high Church authorities. The Vicar General of Quebec took immediate action to bring the opinions of his ordinary about Confederation into proper focus. He thus explained the basis for Cartier's assertion to Truteau:

En effet, Mgr de Tloa [Baillargeon] lui [Cartier] a exprimé, ainsi qu'au premier ministre, Sir E.-P. Taché, que sans être enthousiasmé pour la Confédération, il s'y resignait plutôt qu'à la Représentation basée sur la population, qui devenait inévitable. La même chose lui a été dite par Mgr Lynch, Ev. de Toronto, et il croit que Mgr le G.-V. Raymond, de St.-Hyacinthe, lui a parlé dans le même sens.[21]

This sheds much light on the position taken in Quebec and St. Hyacinthe towards Confederation. Of greater importance still is the

[17]Archives de l'Archevêché de Montréal, Lettres Bourget, Bourget to Truteau, 3 mai 1865.
[18]Ibid., Bourget to Truteau, 1865. The exact date is illegible, but it is obviously some days later.
[19]Ibid., Truteau to Cazeau, 20 fév. 1865.
[20]Canada, Legislature, *Parliamentary Debates on the Subject of Confederation of the British North American Provinces* (Quebec, 1865), 62.
[21]Archives de l'Archevêché de Québec, Registre des Lettres, Cazeau to Truteau, 26 fév. 1865.

following comment obviously referring primarily to the Bishop of Montreal:

Quant aux autres chefs ecclésiastiques de la Province qui n'ont pas émis d'opinion, il [Cartier] a sans doute regardé leur silence comme un acquiescement, et il a cru *avec raison* que, s'ils avaient été opposés au projet, ils n'auraient pas manqué de le proclamer d'une manière quelconque. Voilà sur quoi M. Cartier s'est fondé pour faire l'assertion qu'on lui reproche. . . .[22]

From 1866 to 1867 *La Minerve*, the official mouthpiece of the Conservative party, published numerous articles in favour of Confederation and repeatedly printed verbatim pronouncements of various prelates (even from outside the Province of Quebec) endorsing the project. However, the attempts of the editor to associate Mgr Bourget with the various endorsements are not too convincing.

Eventually Bishop Bourget's position towards Confederation became the subject of an animated debate between Conservatives and Liberals, the former insisting on his approval and support of the scheme, the latter asserting his opposition to it. The issue centred on two questions. Was the bishop's supposed opposition to Confederation simply a form of revenge against its chief architect, George-Etienne Cartier, whose stiff resistance the Bishop had encountered during his struggle for the division of the Montreal cathedral parish? Or was it primarily ideological, not motivated by any political considerations but simply a manifestation of the bishop's fear for the faith of Catholics under the new constitution?

Cartier was the chief advocate of the Sulpicians in the parish question. He was more than that—he was also their disciple and great admirer. Thus his advocacy of the case of his former teachers was of more than academic interest to him; it was an act of conviction as well. To his intellectual and legal skill Cartier now added his own sentiments and his deep personal affection for the Sulpicians. Since 1861, when the issue first arose, Bishop Bourget and Cartier had been feuding. It would be unrealistic, under the circumstances, to expect an entirely neutral attitude towards Confederation on the part of the Bishop. Yet, in spite of being a militant authoritarian, there is no basis on which to argue that Bourget would have permitted an issue of personal prestige to influence a decision of momentous politico-religious significance.

To minimize the impression of any friction between the eminent leader of the Conservative party in Quebec and the Bishop of Montreal, *La Minerve*[23] attempted to shift the emphasis of the whole question to Rome. In an article dealing specifically with the subject of clerical approval of Confederation, the government-inspired paper

[22]*Ibid.*, my own emphasis.
[23]*La Minerve*, 30 mai 1866.

declared editorially that Cartier already had obtained approval of his project by the Sovereign Pontiff. This was a questionable assertion, since no such approval had ever been given.[24] What actually did happen was a simple pronouncement on the question by two ranking churchmen in which they approved of Confederation in principle and, in particular, of its marriage and divorce clauses. It would seem rather obvious, however, that such an opinion, no matter how eminent the station of its proponents, did not necessarily mean approval of Confederation by the Holy See itself.[25] In a letter published in *La Minerve*[26] Hector Fabre,[27] Montreal correspondent of *Le Canadien* and brother of Canon Fabre[28] of the Montreal bishopric, challenged both the acceptance of Confederation by the Sovereign Pontiff and the Pope's explicit approval of the new civil code and a number of paragraphs relating to marriage.[29] *La Minerve* avoided the issue and replied by accusing Fabre of an attempt to make political capital of his personal connections with the Montreal chancery and simply reiterated its previous stand.[30]

Léon Pouliot, S.J., the most recent biographer of Bishop Bourget and his great admirer, does not deny that Mgr Bourget did indeed oppose Confederation. He admits the possibility of Hector Fabre's having certain confidential information from his brother who, in turn, was likely to be familiar with the opinions of his ordinary. R.P. Pouliot cautions, however, that it would be incorrect to make final comments on Bishop Bourget's position towards Confederation on the basis of this single incident. He does indeed believe that Bourget was opposed to Confederation and thinks himself justified in attributing the bishop's misgivings about the scheme to fear about the future of the Church; to Pouliot's knowledge, however, no document supporting this suggestion can be traced. In his annotations on the Fabre-*Minerve* controversy, he simply states: "Jusqu'ici (3 décembre 1956), je ne connais aucun texte ni aucun geste de Mgr Bourget qui permet d'affirmer qu'il était, avant l'événement, pour ou contre le projet de confédération.[31]

Only one more explicit document of Bourget's antedates the actual proclamation of the British North America Act: his circular to the

[24]Cardinal Ballerini and Dr. de Angelis, a noted Roman theologian, had indeed approved the project in principle.
[25]It should be noted though that Bishop Bourget himself, in his recollections of his voyage to Rome in 1864–5, did mention some sort of general approval of Confederation by Pius IX.
[26]*La Minerve*, 2 juin 1866.
[27]Hector Fabre was both a Liberal and a liberal but not a radical.
[28]Later archbishop of Montreal, successor to Bourget.
[29]*La Minerve*, 2 juin 1860; also private notes of R.P. Pouliot on the subject.
[30]*Ibid.*
[31]Notes of R.P. Pouliot and interview with him (Montreal, March, 1959).

clergy of May 23, 1867. All other references to the Bishop's views on the subject postdate the event. Despite this, they shed much light on Bourget's views and are in many ways more illuminating than the essentially formalistic documentation of pre-Confederation days.

In the official circular to his clergy, preceding Confederation by a bare five weeks and, therefore, most certainly not imagined to influence seriously the already approved new constitution, the word Confederation is not even mentioned. In essence, the circular is simply a piece of pastoral guidance, a routine letter sent to the *curés* prior to each federal or provincial election exhorting the priests to ensure that the faithful fulfil their duty of electors in an orderly and dignified fashion. This practice, itself mentioned in the circular, goes back to the Second Provincial Council of Quebec. Consequently, there is no ground whatsoever for assuming that the bishop intended the circular to become anything but an appeal for proper and lawful elections.[32] The bishop's pastoral letter of July 25, while making specific mention of Confederation, can, by its very date, no longer be construed as an attempt by Bourget to swing public opinion for or against Confederation. The document is simply a pastoral exhortation to accept the new *status quo*, an appeal to respect and to recognize the new state of affairs, and nothing more. It urged French Canadians to respect Confederation in the same spirit as once they had accepted the lawfully established authority of the kings of France—"Aujourd'hui elle accepte sans réplique le Gouvernement fédéral, parce qu'il émane de la même Autorité (légitime)."[33] The very titles of both documents prohibit any other interpretation.

Although not always explicit and, like the pastoral letter, of an *ex posteriori* nature, easily the most significant evidence of Bourget's real thoughts about Confederation is an exchange of letters between him and the Bishop of St. Hyacinthe, Charles Larocque. Whatever the technical defects of this documentation, its content is revealing and provides considerable evidence for the view that the Bishop of Montreal quite obviously did not agree with the rest of the Quebec hierarchy on the subject of Confederation. Such a contention can definitely be supported by the following words of Larocque to Bourget:

Votre Grandeur ne peut ignorer avec quelle mauvaise foi les *libéraux avancés* ont exploité la prétendue division qui selon eux existait entre Votre Grandeur et les autres Evêques du Bas-Canada, au sujet des événements et des faits politiques du

---

[32]*Mandements, Lettres Pastorales, Circulaires et autres documents publiés dans le diocèse de Montréal* (Montréal, 1887), V, 212–14, circular of Bishop Bourget, 25 mai 1867.
[33]*Ibid.*, V, 236–44, pastoral of Bishop Bourget, 25 juillet 1867.

jour, et de la manière de les juger et de les apprécier. Il est évident par tout que ces fidèles imitateurs de leurs frères d'Europe ont dit et écrit dernièrement, qu'ils veulent se tenir pour appuyés par l'opinion de Votre Grandeur qui selon eux serait opposé à la Confédération, et aurait vu sans peine le triomphe de leur parti aux dernières élections....[34]

It is hardly to be expected that Bishop Bourget would have desired a Liberal victory in any electoral contest, no matter how unsatisfactory certain parts of the Conservative platform might have been. Yet there must have been enough reason for Bishop Larocque to mention such a possibility of misrepresentation of his Montreal colleague; and evidently information of sufficient weight must have reached the Bishop of St. Hyacinthe to prompt him to act. It may well be, as it appears from the letter, that Larocque personally was convinced of Bourget's support of Confederation, but he most definitely seemed dissatisfied with the manner and the wording of both Bourget's circular letter and the pastoral which the Bishop of Montreal had issued at the occasion of British North American union.

Si j'avais pu avoir le moindre doute relativement à votre manière de voir dans ces importantes questions, ce que vous me disiez ainsi qu'à Mgr Laflèche, mercredi dernier, au couvent de Berthier,[35] aurait été bien plus peu suffisant pour m'enlever jusqu'à l'ombre du doute. Je demeure plus que jamais convaincu que si vos deux lettres circulaires n'ont pas été plus explicites, les circonstances seules dans lesquels vous vous trouviez placé, vous ont empêché d'entrer dans des détails analogues à ceux dans lesquels vos frères Evêques ont cru bon d'entrer.[36]

Just what these particular circumstances of Bishop Bourget were does not appear evident from the context of the letter. Was Larocque referring to Bourget's dispute with Cartier or were there other reasons for the enigmatic attitude of the Montreal bishop towards Confederation? Whatever the answer, one thing emerges quite clearly from Larocque's letter:

Il n'en est cependant pas moins vrai que nos ennemis communs continuent à faire du mal, en argumentant de cette prétendue division ou différence d'opinion, pour arriver à prouver que le droit est pour eux et que les Evêques qui ont condamné plus ou moins directement leurs faits et gestes politiques, ont eu tort de le faire, et sont condamnés par le silence que vous avez gardé, prétendent-ils, relativement aux sujets abordés par les Mandemens [sic] ou Lettres Pastorales.[37]

And Larocque concludes with an outright demand for an open and public statement by Bourget regarding Confederation:

[34]Archives de l'Evêché de St.-Hyacinthe, Correspondance Mgr Charles Larocque, Larocque to Bourget, 12 oct. 1867.
[35]No record of the Berthier conversation could be traced.
[36]Correspondance Mgr Charles Larocque, Larocque to Bourget, 12 oct. 1867.
[37]Ibid.

En présence d'un si dommageable état de choses, Votre Grandeur, ne faussait-Elle pas se prononcer, ne devrait-Elle pas même le faire assez ouvertement et publiquement pour faire cesser le scandale mené par la malice et la mauvaise foi sur la vue [?] des faibles?—Votre Grandeur voudra bien me permettre de Lui dire que le désir que je Lui exprime n'est point particulier au pauvre évêque de St-Hyacinthe.—Mais qu'en Lui adressant la présente lettre, j'agis en conformité à l'opinion de quelques autres évêques, et de plusiers prêtres des mieux pensans [sic] et des plus distingués. Je prie Votre Grandeur de me pardonner la liberté que j'ai prise de lui faire cette demande ou suggestion; et de me croire. . . .[38]

It took courage for Biship Larocque to write in such frank language to his one-time superior. However, as Larocque himself stated, he was by no means alone in criticizing Bourget. Obviously the situation had by now become so serious and the consequences of the lack of unanimity among the episcopate on the question of Confederation now appeared so grave, that some, if not all of the Quebec hierarchy, had delegated Larocque to approach Bourget on that subject. The letter made it quite clear that among the episcopate Bourget's stand had never been doubted—at any rate, Larocque so assured Bourget—but that the veiled and non-committal wording of both pastoral and circular was an open invitation to misinterpretation by any political enemy. Under these circumstances one might go as far as to question the validity of the mollifying passages of the letter and explain them as little more than mere courtesy. The fundamental question remained: why did the Bishop of Montreal, always known as a man of rather pronounced and uncompromising views, not come forward with a clear and positive statement about Confederation; why did he have to be prodded by his colleagues to clarify his previous pronouncements on the issue?

In his answer to Larocque, Bourget did not come any closer to the problem; in fact he avoided it. It may well be, as he asserted in his reply, that he thought he had given Confederation sufficient support in his pastoral letter and in his circular to the clergy; he was genuinely convinced that he had done his share. But he categorically refused to go beyond any statement of a general nature or beyond the evasive assertion that he was, now and always, a staunch supporter of the established government.[39] He seemed quite satisfied with the manner in which he had proceeded and thus concluded his reply to Bishop Larocque:

Un de nos chauds conservateurs, qui est membre des deux Chambres, fédérale et locale,[40] disait, dans une certaine réunion, que l'Evêque de Montréal, dans

---

[38]Ibid.
[39]Lettres Bourget, Bourget to Larocque, 15 oct. 1867.
[40]Hector Langevin?

ses lettres sur la Confédération, avait pris une position qui lui permettait de défendre ses principes, sous n'importe quelle Administration, pourvu qu'elle soit vraiement constitutionelle. Placé sur ce terrain, je me crois bien solidement appuyé, pour défendre les vrais principes, contre les doctrines du *Pays* et de *l'Union nationale*. . . .[41]

The issue, of course, was not the defence of Bishop Bourget's principles but his inability or rather his unwillingness to clarify his previously tepid approval of Confederation. What Larocque, and the other members of the hierarchy on whose behalf he spoke, requested Bourget to do was not simply to declare his open allegiance to and loyal co-operation with the new order of things. What they had hoped for was more in the nature of an authoritative statement. Such a pronouncement, issued in good time before the proclamation of the British North America Act, explaining the whole issue of Confederation and giving the bishop's explicit approval of it, would have left no room for anyone to question his position. Instead, Mgr Bourget refrained from an outright commitment to Confederation and continued to avoid the issue with a number of general and rather peripheral clarifications.

Bishop Larocque was in a delicate position. Although Bourget's equal in the Quebec hierarchy, he clearly lacked the long experience and immense prestige of Bourget and certainly must have found it difficult to admonish his former superior. On the other hand, he felt compelled to speak up and to warn his colleague of the consequences resulting from Bourget's ambiguity on the question of Confederation. It is obvious that Larocque did not intend to influence Bourget's stand on the question but merely asked him to clarify his position in order to forestall any misinterpretation:

Je me suis bien mal exprimé si ma lettre a pu vous faire croire que je vous demandais de vous prononcer plus explicitement que vous l'avez fait sur la question de la Confédération. Mon intention était de vous dire ce que Votre Grandeur ne peut pas ignorer; que l'on n'a pas encore cessé de dire qu'il y a de division dans la manière de voir sur autres Evêques dans leurs Mandemens [sic]. Je crois que vous avez sincèrement accepté la Confédération.—Aussi, ce n'est nullement làdessus que je croyais qu'il eut été à propos de vous prononcer ouvertement; mais sur la prétendue division que je viens de signaler à Votre Grandeur; et dont la mauvaise foi se sent encore à l'heure qu'il est pour mettre les Evêques en contradiction, et ruiner ainsi l'autorité de leur parole. . . .[42]

Bourget had two possible alternatives if he chose to clarify his position and in so doing to silence the opposition. He could either issue a new and explicit statement on the whole Confederation issue or, if he preferred, adhere to his previous two pronouncements on the question, simply making it known that a different and less pronounced

[41]Lettres Bourget, Bourget to Larocque, 15 oct. 1867.
[42]Correspondance Mgr Charles Larocque, Larocque to Bourget, 16 oct. 1867.

wording was not intended to detract from his positive stand towards Confederation. The Bishop of Montreal refused to do either; he not only refused to modify his position, he also did not think it necessary to explain such refusal at any great length. In vain did his colleagues and the Bishop of St. Hyacinthe, their spokesman, attempt to change his mind:

Je ne puis, malgré toute bienveillance de votre lettre, changer de conviction et m'empêcher de croire, qu'il résulte de là un très grand mal; et je ne suis pas seul à le croire. Il me semblait que Votre Grandeur eut pu *facilement trouver* le moyen et l'occasion de protester contre cette prétendue division ou contradiction, sans entrer dans plus de détails que vous n'avez fait sur la question de la Confédération elle-même. Quelques mots, quelques paroles que vous eussiez pu faire publiquement entendre, à telle occasion et sous telle forme qu'il vous eut semblé bon, eussent suffi pour imposer silence à ceux qui accusent avec tant de persistance et avec aussi mauvaises connaissances les Evêques de différer de doctrine ou d'opinion....[43]

Larocque, apologizing to his one-time ordinary for the liberty he had taken in offering Bourget advice, felt nevertheless justified in having done so. He concluded bluntly, "... et mon opinion est que la division qu'on nous importe, fait un mal uncalculable.[44]

Nor did George-Etienne Cartier gain any deeper insight into Bourget's mind when, early in 1867, he sent him a draft of the proposed British North America Act. Politely but curtly the bishop replied:

Je reçois à l'instant la copie du *British North America Bill* que vous avez eu la bonté de m'adresser et je m'empresse de vous présenter mes sincères remerciements pour votre bienveillante attention.

Je comprends vivement que ce *Bill* intéresse à un haut degré notre pays, qui, après toutes les phases d'administration par lesquelles il lui a fallu passer depuis un certain nombre d'années, a grand besoin de se fixer sur des bases stables et durables.

Il serait superflu de vous dire que le clergé tout en se mettant en dehors de toutes luttes de partis politiques, n'en est pas moins attaché au pays qui l'a vu naître, et qui l'aime, comme un bon enfant aime sa mère, et cet amour est d'autant plus ardent, qu'il lui est inspiré par la religion....[45]

The wisdom of Bourget's attempt to use this occasion for an official statement of his position can be debated. After all, Cartier quite obviously had presented Bourget with an accomplished fact rather than having invited him to participate in the genesis of the bill. Still, would this not have been a unique occasion for Bourget to speak his mind, to tell Cartier, privately if need be, what he really thought of Confederation? Bourget had fought back from positions of much

[43]*Ibid.*, my own emphasis.
[44]*Ibid.*
[45]Public Archives of Canada, Cartier Papers, Bourget to Cartier, 11 mars 1867.

greater disadvantage[46]—why did he refuse to avail himself of the opportunity? His silence at this crucial moment defies explanation. The contention that Bourget's reply to Cartier "was one in terms so cordial as to warrant the assumption that it was through him that they [the bishops] had kept in touch with all the proceedings of Confederation"[47] can be substantiated neither by the letter itself nor by the context in which it was written.

There is yet one more argument to be considered—the contention that peculiar circumstances, the whole atmosphere of Montreal, had forced Bishop Bourget to steer a course somewhat different from his colleagues.[48] Montreal, the traditional centre of French-Canadian liberalism and *Rougisme*, was also the chief rallying point of the opponents of Confederation. At first three newspapers, the *rouge* organ, *Le Pays*, *L'Ordre*, and the English Catholic *True Witness* opposed the project. When Confederation was given royal sanction, *L'Ordre* and the *True Witness* changed their line of argument in favour of federal union. The *volte-face* is attributed to Bourget's influence on these two papers—"il faut voir là, nous n'en doutons pas, l'influence personnelle de Mgr Bourget sur la direction de ces journaux."[49] There is no doubt about Bourget's voice in the direction of these papers. But it is because this is so that one is bound to ask why Bishop Bourget held back until March, 1867, the date of the Queen's approval of the British North America Act, to have his press change their line of argument. What would seem important then is not that Bourget fell into line "après ce geste décisif"[50] (the royal sanction of Confederation), but why he did not oppose British North American union out of his own conviction while it was still permitted "s'y opposer sans encourir la note d'infidélité ou de désobéissance à l'autorité légitime."[51] Had he influenced the editorials of both *L'Ordre* and the *True Witness* prior to that time, it could be argued that he had thrown his influence and prestige behind Confederation. Having done so only after royal sanction, we cannot give him such credit, but merely can state that he had followed the traditional line of conduct of the Church. And there had never been any question about that.

For that matter, *Le Journal des Trois-Rivières* and *Le Courier de Saint-Hyacinthe* were as much, if not more, influenced by their respective ordinaries who obviously saw to it that Confederation would

[46]The Laval-Victoria university quarrel is a particularly good example of this.
[47]F. J. Wilson, "Roman Catholics and the Confederation Movement," M.A. thesis, Queen's University, 1936, 30.
[48]Pouliot, "Monseigneur Bourget et la Confédération," 41.
[49]*Ibid.*
[50]*Ibid.*, 34.
[51]*Ibid.*

get support long before March, 1867. Why did Bishop Bourget not do likewise with the press under his control? This is the primary question, for it is this immediate pre-Confederation period with which we are concerned. The firmness of the bishop's doctrine, his respect for and obedience to the law of the land were never issues. Nor is it to be assumed that Bourget remained aloof from Confederation simply to square old accounts with Cartier. The best argument against such a hypothesis is the simple fact that at the time of the actual division of the Montreal cathedral parish, Confederation seemed to have been accepted so generally that even as powerful a voice as Bishop Bourget's could hardly have influenced it to any great extent.

On the other hand, there is ample evidence to substantiate Bourget's fear of dissent. Bishop Bourget did not wish to go on record as an opponent of Confederation, but he also did not wish to go beyond a certain point in approving it for the simple reason that he had serious doubts about the implications of Confederation for the future of Catholicism in Canada. Clearly the bishop had reasons for his reserve. He had spoken up before and would have done so again had he considered it appropriate. This time he must have seen that his protest would not have been of much avail, that his open disavowal of Confederation would only have caused a split in the Quebec hierarchy, and most probably a serious division of opinion within French Canada. Such consequences he was not prepared to risk; but neither was he willing to endorse a project which he thought detrimental to the faith.

Under normal circumstances the Archbishop of Quebec, the metropolitan of the whole ecclesiastical province, would undoubtedly have taken the initiative in expressing the position of the hierarchy as a whole towards Confederation. However, at the time when Confederation was the topic of the day in Canadian politics, the archepiscopal see of Quebec was vacant. The archdiocese was administered by Mgr C.-F. Baillargeon, titular bishop of Tloa. Junior in rank to most of his colleagues and perhaps self-conscious about his own provisional status, Bishop Baillargeon preferred a non-committal role to that of an active participant. In the absence of a strong lead given by the titular metropolitan, the matter was allowed to drift and eventually become one of personalities.

Once again, Bishop Laflèche, the coadjutor of Three Rivers, provided some lead and direction. He pointed out to Baillargeon the advisability of some concerted pronouncement on the part of the bishops.[52] The latter semed to have acted on this suggestion and communicated its contents to his suffragan bishops, who in turn issued

[52]Léo Bérubé, vice-archivist of the archdiocesian archives of Rimouski to author, October 8, 1960. Father Bérubé does not give the exact date of his sources; in his letter he merely affirms that all his contentions are based on correspondence in the archives of

pastoral letters in support of Confederation.[53] In his own pastoral Baillargeon remarked that Confederation was brought about by trusted and experienced men and while at one time it might have been quite proper to discuss its merits and defects, this was no longer so. As the future law of Canada, it had to be obeyed, for anything but obedience would be a revolt against the divine order and against God: "Résister à sa volonté; ce serait marcher à l'anarchie, à la trahison, à la révolte et à tous les maux qui en sont la suite."[54]

Like Bourget, Baillargeon carefully abstained from any judgment on the merits of Confederation proper and limited his comments to a rather general approval of the inevitable. As early as 1865 his Grand Vicar thus summed up Baillargeon's true feelings about the issue:

Donc, qu'il soit bien entendu que, si nous admettons le projet de Confédération, ce n'est pas que nous soyons épris d'une grande amour pour cette nouvelle forme de gouvernement mais c'est qu'ayant à choisir entre deux maux inévitables, la confédération, ou la représentation basée sur la population, nous préférons le premier, qui est à coup sûr le moins dangereux pour ce qui nous est cher.[55]

Only one other source for Baillargeon's views is available. There is a reference to a meeting on October 9, 1867, in which Baillargeon approved of Bourget's conduct, with specific reference to the Montreal bishop's pastoral urging the faithful to participate in the forthcoming elections.[56] Bourget now could (and did) use this exchange of views between himself and Baillargeon to back up his own position. It would appear, then, that Mgr Baillargeon was virtually uncommitted in the Bourget-Larocque dispute and simply tried to stay aloof from the whole argument as best as he could. Larocque, for his part, quite naturally wished to have the Quebec bishop's approval of his action since he sought Bishop Baillargeon's consent prior to the issuing of his own pastoral letter on Confederation. On June 13, 1867, he informed Grand Vicar Cazeau of Quebec that the draft of his pastoral dealing with that subject was ready. He withheld publication pending Baillargeon's consent since he was concerned that his observations would not differ too much from those of the Archbishop of Quebec.[57] La-

---

the Archdiocese of Rimouski. However, Bérubé's testimony is clearly supported by a letter of Bishop Langevin (Rimouski) to Bishop Larocque (St. Hyacinthe); see Correspondance Mgr Charles Larocque, Langevin to Larocque, 25 mai 1867.

[53]A.-X. Bernard, éd., *Mandements des Evêques de Saint-Hyacinthe* (Montréal, 1889), II, 421-37; also *Mandements des Evêques de Rimouski* (n.p., n.d.), pastoral of Bishop Langevin, 13 juin 1867; also *Mandements des Evêques des Trois-Rivières* (n.p., n.d.), pastoral of Bishop Cooke, 12 juin 1867.

[54]H. Têtu and C.-O. Gagnon, éds., *Mandements, Lettres Pastorales et Circulaires des Evêques de Québec* (Québec, 1888), IV, 579.

[55]Registre des Lettres, Cazeau to Truteau, 26 fév. 1865.

[56]Archives de l'Archevêché de Rimouski, Correspondance Mgr Langevin, Langevin to Larocque, 25 mai 1867.

[57]*Ibid.*, Larocque to Cazeau, 13 juin 1867.

rocque seemed rather impressed with the already published pastoral of the Bishop of Three Rivers which appeared to him "vraiment un document bien digne et bien fait."[58] He informed Cazeau that his own pastoral coincided in principle with that of the Bishop of Three Rivers and asked whether "quelque chose du même genre" was contemplated in Quebec.[59]

Bishop Larocque, while trying to associate himself with the general point of view of the metropolitan see, had no desire whatsoever to do likewise in respect to Bishop Bourget. His own pastoral is the best proof for his independent point of view:

Et d'abord, Nous vous le disons sans hésiter, N.T.C.F., l'union de ces provinces dans laquelle il est généralement admis que les autres provinces britanniques entreront bientôt, est un fait d'une portée immense, puisqu'il est évident qu'il nous a cheminé à prendre tôt ou tard notre rang parmi les nations de la terre, et, sous ce rapport, un fruit sans pareil dans les annales de notre histoire.[60]

There is a striking difference between this cheerful and optimistic pronouncement of the Bishop of St. Hyacinthe and the correct, yet resigned, tone of Bishop Bourget. Larocque was well aware of this and so was Bishop Langevin of Rimouski. They both tried, at the eleventh hour, to bring about a change in Bourget's position. Langevin, attempting to make use of Larocque's acqaintance with Bourget, requested the latter to convince the Bishop of Montreal of the necessity for a concerted action of the whole hierarchy.[61] Larocque tried, but obviously to no avail. Disappointed, he reported to Langevin:

J'ai vu Mgr L'Evêque de Montréal vendredi dernier. Je me suis fait un devoir de lui communiquer les deux questions sur lesquelles Votre Grandeur me priait en sa lettre du 25 dernier d'attirer son attention.—Sur la première de ces questions (confédération), j'ai eu la réponse à laquelle je m'attendais. Car déjà j'ai eu la permission de prendre communication du document que l'ev. de Montréal faisait imprimer dans le moment sur le sujet même. Ce Document est tout simplement une Lettre Circulaire en laquelle le vénérable Prélat donne à son Clergé des avis sur la conduite à tenir en vue des élections prochaines, recommandant neutralité et abstention, et soumission aux lois et à la constitution, *mais sans dire un mot en faveur du nouvel ordre de choses, le mot de Confédération ne se trouvant même pas dans la lettre.* Les Curés devront instruire leurs peuples d'après ces avis et ces idées. Mais la parole de L'Evêque ne se fait point directement entendre aux fidèles. C'est là tout ce que fit Sa Grandeur sur le sujet. . . .[62]

After this straightforward appraisal of Bourget's position towards Confederation by one of his episcopal colleagues there seems little use in

[58]*Ibid.* [59]*Ibid.*
[60]Bernard, éd., *Mandements des Evêques de Saint-Hyacinthe* II, 422–3, pastoral of Bishop Larocque, 18 juin 1867.
[61]Correspondance Mgr Langevin, Langevin to Larocque, 25 mai 1867.
[62]Correspondance Mgr Charles Larocque, Larocque to Langevin, 4 juin 1867. (My italics.)

commenting on his stand any further. The difference of opinion on the subject between him and the rest of the hierarchy appears to be established beyond any doubt.

The views of Bishops Cooke and Langevin remain to be considered. Mgr Thomas Cooke was bishop of Three Rivers at the time of Confederation but by that time was already severely incapacitated by illness. Thus his role in the whole Confederation project is negligible compared to that taken by his vicar general and successor to the see, Mgr Louis-François Laflèche. The official pastoral of the Three Rivers diocese, signed by Cooke, but obviously composed by Laflèche, re-stated in realistic terms Laflèche's original attitude.[63]

Bishop Jean Langevin of Rimouski, the newest member of the Quebec hierarchy and the brother of Hector, fully acquiesced in Laflèche's proposal for concerted action by the bishops and, after previous consultation with Mgr Baillargeon and Bishops Horan of Kingston and Farrell of Hamilton,[64] issued the desired pastoral. Reminding the faithful that the bishop of Canada had never failed to give guidance to them at times of momentous importance and further that the flock never had reason to regret the heeding of such advice, he made it clear to them that once again they were faced with a momentous historical event. The new constitution about to be proclaimed, the bishop pointed out, was the product of long and mature deliberations and was necessary to break the complete deadlock in the machinery of government. Hence, as Catholics, "vous la respecterez donc, Nos Chers Frères, cette nouvelle Constitution, qui vous est donné, comme expression de la volonté suprême du Législateur, de l'autorité légitime, et par conséquent, par celle de Dieu même."[65] The document concluded with a warning against the advocates of annexation (a common but certainly not meaningless exhortation at the time) which, in the bishop's view, would definitely lead to "la ruine de notre peuple, la perte de nos mœurs, de nos coutumes, de notre langue, l'anéantissement de notre nationalité."[66] Only in the very last sentence of Langevin's pastoral, as an indication of the bishop's genuine sympathy for Confederation, did he order the singing of "une grande messe solennelle" in all churches of his diocese to celebrate the event.[67]

This seemingly routine gesture nevertheless contrasted strangely with the attitude of Bishop Bourget. The Bishop of Montreal, asked by Father Aubry, the parish priest of St. Jean Dorchester, whether bells were to be rung in salute to the new constitution, received a

[63]*Mandements des Evêques des Trois-Rivières*, pastoral of Bishop Cooke, 12 juin 1867.
[64]Léo Bérubé to author, October 8, 1960.
[65]*Mandements des Evêques de Rimouski*, pastoral of Bishop Langevin, 13 juin 1867.
[66]*Ibid.*
[67]*Ibid.*

THE QUEBEC BISHOPS AND CONFEDERATION 69

uninterested reply, ". . . vous pouvez le faire, si cette demande a un caractère officiel. . . ."[68] It compared equally unfavourably with the festivities held in Three Rivers. There, as in Rimouski, a solemn high mass had been celebrated and church bells were ringing all over the city. In the afternoon a special cricket match had been staged on the St. Louis grounds, while bands played throughout the city which was illuminated by fireworks in the evening.[69] Unable to stem the tide of events, the Bishop of Montreal had apparently reconciled himself to the new order of things by March, 1867. At any rate, it would seem that he must have considered Confederation a *fait accompli* by that date. He thus commented to Mgr Guigues, the Bishop of Ottawa: ". . . Nous voici avec la Confédération; prions pour qu'elle nous amène la paix avec l'abondance de ses biens. . . ."[70]

The position of the hierarchy as a whole is difficult to appraise. Even Bishop Laflèche, by far the strongest supporter of Confederation, and the generally sympathetically disposed Bishop Larocque, had their reservations. Baillargeon and Langevin were lukewarm at best and their support of Confederation was more an acquiescence and an acknowledgement of the inevitable than a positive statement of approval. While Baillargeon and Langevin at least in public spoke out plainly in favour of Confederation, Bourget fought to the end, even over matters of terminology and semantics. Nevertheless, when the time came for the Quebec bishops to speak as a body, they closed ranks without further hesitation. It says much for their political acumen that at this important hour of French-Canadian history they found it possible to do so.

[68]Lettres Bourget, Bourget to Aubry, 27 juin 1867.
[69]*Le Journal des Trois-Rivières*, 2 juillet 1867.
[70]Lettres Bourget, Bourget to Guigues, 12 mars 1867.

The Basis and Persistence of Opposition to Confederation in New Brunswick

ALFRED G. BAILEY

RECENT research has done much to clarify the circumstances surrounding New Brunswick's entrance into Confederation. The crucial impact of British official importunity upon the sentiments of the people of the province, and the influence of Canadian campaign funds in the critical election of 1866 have been assigned their due weight as factors in inducing New Brunswick to accept the proposed change in the constitution of British North America. The use of the Fenian scare to impress upon the people the inadequacy of existing means of defence has received the attention which the importance of the subject warrants, and something of the effect of the failure to renew the Reciprocity Treaty has been noted. Yet there still remain certain aspects of the story which deserve a fuller treatment than they have hitherto received. Adequate consideration, for instance, has not yet been given to the causes for the rejection of the Quebec Resolutions in the New Brunswick election of March, 1865, or to the ensuing circumstances in the face of which the anti-Confederation cause gradually deteriorated to a point at which opposition became politically ineffective. This article attempts, therefore, to examine the grounds upon which opposition to union was based, and to describe how certain of those grounds became increasingly untenable throughout the year that followed the defeat of the Tilley government.

I

It is evident that in the early stages of the union movement there was a misapprehension of its significance, together with some degree of apathy, rather than a reasoned opposition. There was an inclination to regard Confederation "as intended to produce, by its agitation, some immediate effect on the condition of existing political parties rather than as designed to inaugurate a new constitutional system."[1] But apathy and a "willing ignorance" of the whole matter gave way to an increasing hostility throughout the autumn of 1864 on the part of influential sections of the press. Many, wrote one editor, as early as October 19, did not understand why the delegates who had gone to Charlottetown

[1] *Correspondence Respecting the Proposed Union of the British North American Provinces, etc. Presented to both Houses of Parliament by Command of Her Majesty, 8th Feb. 1867* (London, 1867), 85.

Reprinted from *Canadian Historical Review*, XXIII (4), December, 1942

to consider Maritime Union, were now at Quebec, having given the lesser question the slip. It was insinuated that they were carried captive by the Canadians who "have a definite purpose to effect, a pressing internal difficulty to overcome . . . and it is not to be wondered at that they should strain their views to effect a union with the Lower Provinces, that will give them peace within themselves, besides some considerable material advantages."[2] But it would "not be very gratifying . . . to see . . . a portion of the revenue of this Province drawn off to widen and deepen and extend Canada's magnificent canals, as the Toronto *Globe*, with scarce concealed exultation, says will be done. It would be a source of regret to many to see their roads, byeroads, bridges, and schools going down, down, down, while they see Canada growing great partly by aid of their money."

Money was a prominent feature of a long article carried by the *Headquarters* of Fredericton, on October 19. The assimilation of tariffs, it predicted, would mean the adoption of those of Canada. "Unless Canada consents to economize and curtail its expenses to a very considerable degree, which is not likely to happen, the Lower Provinces will have to raise their tariffs to that standard, as they will require a greater revenue to meet the expenses of government under the new confederation. It appears that they will have to make sacrifices and pay something handsome for the privilege of entering it, and seeing their representatives starring it in the Magnificent Parliament House, with its quadrangle, towers, and turrets at Ottawa." More than half the yearly expenditure of Canada had already been incurred. It must be clearly understood that none of this must be charged upon the revenue of the provinces, under the general government, but that it must be made a matter in which Canada alone would be liable.

Canada, however, was not the only villain in the piece. With some prescience the editor wrote, "The idea can hardly be ignored that this confederation business is more than a political move on the part of Canada—that the British government are at the bottom of it, and that the reversal of their colonial policy is not far distant."[3] British sentiments regarding defence were becoming known in the provinces, since the views of Englishmen were

[2]Fredericton *Headquarters*, Oct. 19, 1864.
[3]Compare Chester Martin, "British Policy in Canadian Confederation" (*Canadian Historical Review*, XIII, March, 1932, 3-19).

quoted at some length in the local papers.[4] It could not, however, yet be said positively that Britain would support Confederation on this ground. "In the uncertainty it would be a great relief to know positively what the British government expect the colonies to do." It would make "all the difference in the world" if it were known that the British government had expressed not merely approval, but desire.[5] The editor's remark requires qualification. A large body of opinion continued hostile, even after a year of constant appeal to "loyal" sentiments. In the meantime it was necessary to use other means to mitigate the hostility.[6]

It is safe to say that the larger part of the New Brunswick press looked unfavourably upon Confederation throughout the autumn of 1864 and the winter of 1865. The reception accorded to Tilley and Gray while campaigning in Saint John was reported as cold and critical. However, this attitude was attributed by one editor, who had not yet become irrevocably committed to the support of either faction, to the fact that Confederation was a new subject concerning which the audience had only half-formed opinions. Although Tilley "delivered himself with his usual facility and energy," the speeches were not calculated "to convince their judgement and arouse enthusiasm" for Confederation. The sceptical editor was puzzled by the peculiar state of opinion early in the campaign. Everyone, he reported, admitted that the union must take place sooner or later; nevertheless there was a disposition evident on the part of some persons "to put the matter off," and of others, "to make the road rough." Tilley had shown "what he thought the people would get by the scheme, but he did not clearly make out what they would have to pay for it." He had scouted the idea that higher taxes would be imposed, or that the Canadian tariff would be the standard of assimilation. But he failed to convince his opponents, and the lukewarm among his constituents, that the general government, with its railway obligations and its provincial subsidies, could be carried on without raising the imposts on dutiable articles coming into the provinces. "He said the Canadian tariff was not to be the standard, at one time, because the forty-seven Lower Province members ... would resist its imposition; at another he maintained that it was

[4]See for example the article by A. A. Bridgmen in the *Headquarters*, October 12, 1864.
[5]Fredericton *Headquarters*, Oct. 19, 1864.
[6]Public Archives of Canada, Macdonald Papers, Confederation Correspondence, VI, 43, Tilley to Macdonald, Nov. 23, 1864.

not in reality higher."[7] It was asserted that Tilley pitched his hopes too high and his figures too low. In truth, none knew what the project would cost. "For all the outcry against Mr. A. J. Smith's figures, he is as likely to be correct as any of them."[8]

Soon after the adjournment of the Quebec Conference it had become known that Albert J. Smith would lead the opposition. He and his associates, drawn largely from among the opponents of the Tilley government, soon had a numerous following with the aid of which they hoped "to alarm the people and carry the elections."[9] As public opinion warmed, the fight began to take on the aspect of a personal tilt between the two champions. The province became alive with public meetings as the leaders stumped the country proclaiming their respective faiths. Early in January, 1865, Tilley invaded Smith's home county of Westmorland.

> Then welcome be Samuel L's tongue to the shock,
> Though his figures be strong as the Westmorland rock,
> For woe to his figures and woe to his cause,
> When Alfred [Sic] the dauntless exposes his flaws

sang one anti-Confederationist. Borrowing epithets from the prize ring, Smith, with grandstand bravado, was hailed as "the Lion of Westmorland" and the "Douglas of Dorchester."[10]

Although the provincial intellect was no doubt titillated by such superficial chaff, it never lost sight of the real issues that beat with an ever insistent and fateful rhythm upon the public consciousness. Politicians, editors, farmers, manufacturers, and financiers, wrestled with the crucial problem of hard cash. What was Confederation to cost? Would it increase taxes? Would it stimulate business? Would it facilitate·trade, ensure the safety of New Brunswick and the Empire generally? How were the signs of the times to be read and interpreted?

Early in the campaign the Smith faction gained a powerful supporter in the person of William Needham of Fredericton, who, throughout the ensuing months, raked the Quebec scheme with his broadsides. Referring to the resolution concerning the development of the West, he asked what New Brunswick could do, with only fifteen members in a House of one hundred and ninety-four, to prevent the expenditure of any amount in such

[7]Fredericton *Headquarters*, Nov. 23, 1864.
[8]*Ibid.*, Dec. 7, and Dec. 21, 1864.
[9]Macdonald Papers, Confederation Correspondence, VI, 49, Fisher to Macdonald, Dec. 6, 1864.
[10]Fredericton *Headquarters*, Dec. 28, 1864.

undertakings.[11] And in addition to Canada's canals, the people of New Brunswick would "have to pay also for making a highway —a railroad—between Canada and the Pacific, a project on which old George Brown has breakfasted, dined, and supped for the last twenty years."[12] In the railways to the North-West the Maritime Provinces could have no present or future interest, but they would bring upon present or future generations large burdens of taxation.[13] It seemed clear to him that New Brunswick, with its small representation in the proposed federal Assembly, could not hope to block a large expenditure on public works from which the anti-unionists conceived she would derive no benefit.

If the development of the West were the price the Maritime Provinces would have to pay for securing the Intercolonial Railway, provided this railway were held out as a bait on the hook of Confederation, what constitutional guarantee was there that the railway would be built forthwith? This was, perhaps, a difficult question for Tilley to answer, even to his own satisfaction. On February 13, he placed the issue squarely before Macdonald:

We have always regarded it as the policy of the conference that the subsidy to the Local Governments and the building of the Intercolonial Railway would be secured to us by Imperial Act. The delegates from the Lower Provinces could never have consented to the union on any other terms, and so understanding it have represented it to our people. . . . It is said that you stated that there would be no Imperial Legislation on the subject of the Intercolonial. Now I can assure you that no delegate from this Province will consent to union unless we have this granted. And we will certainly fail in all our elections unless I have word . . . saying that this security will be given us. All will be lost without this; as it is, great alarm and anxiety has been created.[14]

Macdonald had stated publicly that an agreement to build a railway could not be a portion of a constitution. But a week later he telegraphed his assurance to Tilley that, as the railway was one of the conditions on which the constitution was adopted at Quebec, it would be inserted in the imperial Act giving legal effect to the union.[15] But in spite of Macdonald's assurance to Tilley, and Tilley's assurance to the electorate, that the railway would be provided for in the imperial statute, it was as yet by no means certain that the provision would be agreed to by the British

[11]*Ibid.*, Dec. 14, 1864.
[12]*Ibid.*
[13]*Ibid.*, Feb. 22, 1865.
[14]Macdonald Papers, Confederation Correspondence, VI, 61, Tilley to Macdonald, Feb. 13, 1865.
[15]*Ibid.*, Macdonald to Tilley, Feb. 20, 1865.

government. It was at least felt by Governor Gordon that the imperial government would incorporate in the Act only those provisions of a general constitutional nature, and that the details would be left to the good faith of the provinces themselves.[16] There is no doubt that the measure of uncertainty with regard to the railway contributed to the defeat of the unionists in March, 1865.

Even if the securing of the Intercolonial Railway appeared certain to some observers, the vaguest notions were entertained as to which sections of the province would benefit by the railway, since the route would be decided by the general legislature of the union. That the northern route would be chosen seemed probable, as it was favoured by half the members of the New Brunswick government, and by the whole of Nova Scotia. Moreover, it was in the interest of Canada East to have as much of the road as possible within its own territory, namely, by building it across the Gaspé highland from Rivière du Loup to the Baie des Chaleurs. It would serve the steam-mills of Buctouche, Richibucto, Miramichi, Bathurst, and Dalhousie, all of which shipped large quantities of deals and lumber to Canada, which would thus support them in pressing for the northern route.[17] No consistent statement could be secured from the government. Charles Fisher of Fredericton asserted that the road would pass north through the Saint John and Keswick valleys. Mitchell and Johnson, both of the North Shore, stated quite as definitely that their section would have it.

> Mr. Tilley, will you stop your puffing and blowing
> And tell us which way the railway is going?[18]

wailed an exasperated rhymster. How would Saint John benefit from a railway along the North Shore? asked Smith. Even if it were run up the Saint John River valley, the effect, he asserted, would be to cause a flow of the products of the up-river counties into Canada, instead of bringing them down to the provincial metropolis at the mouth.[19]

While the different sections fought over the railway route, speculation ran rife concerning the possible effects of Confederation upon the industrial structure of the province. The cleavage of opinion seems not to have followed either occupational or class

[16]*Correspondence Respecting the Proposed Union of the British North American Provinces*, Gordon to Cardwell, Feb. 27, 1865.
[17]Fredericton *Headquarters*, Feb. 1, 1865.
[18]*Ibid.*
[19]*Ibid.*, Feb. 8, 1865.

lines. The manufacturing interests were divided, some strongly favouring union. Having viewed it "in all its bearings" they felt satisfied that it would prove beneficial not only to domestic manufacturers, but to every other interest throughout the province. But dissenting voices were loud and long. In a measured oration delivered early in December, 1864, Needham asked how union would open up to the manufacturers of the province an immense market in Canada.

I ask you tanners, I ask you foundrymen, is it possible, is it likely that you will flood that country with your wares. If so, why is our Province flooded, our shops crammed with American goods! Look at it—where we have one foundry, one tannery, one distillery, they have thousands. After the Union you will be in a worse position than you are now; for you will . . . have the Canadians flooding you with goods also.[20]

According to this school of thought Canada would have no need for the manufactures of the Maritime Provinces, but would have no objection to flooding them with her goods. With arguments such as this one anti-Confederation editor wrote that Needham had "Knocked Fisher higher than a kite."

While the fight waxed hot over local issues a measure of attention was given to the imperial implications of the proposed change. The argument for Confederation as a means toward improved defence did not go unchallenged. It was publicly alleged that Canada was trying to get the Maritime Provinces into Confederation, to share the burden of her defence as agreed with the British government.[21] It was easy to prove, maintained one orator, that the mother country was determined to drive these colonies into some kind of union, and the ravings of those who were determined to resist it "might as well be addressed to the planet Saturn." The *Headquarters* expressed a forthright disbelief that the British government were determined to force the colonies into union.[22] Moreover, it was ridiculous to suppose that Confederation would put British North America into a better state of defence. With or without it, if there were an invasion, it would be as impossible for New Brunswick to resist as for a shad to walk up a bean-pole.[23]

When other arguments were deemed insufficient, high constitutional principle was invoked against the delegates who had

[20] *Ibid.*, Dec. 14, 1864.
[21] *Ibid.* Disapproval of Confederation as a defence measure was by no means unanimous. See *The Borderer and Westmorland and Cumberland Advertiser*, Sackville, N.B., Feb. 24, 1865.
[22] Fredericton *Headquarters*, Dec. 21, 1864.
[23] *Ibid.*, Jan. 18, 1865.

abandoned the legislative union of the Lower Provinces for the Quebec scheme without the consent of the legislatures to which they owed their appointments. It was denied that the Governor-General had called the Quebec Conference with the assent and approbation of the Queen. More probably, no one on the other side of the Atlantic had heard anything about it.[24] It was on the ground of the well-understood principle of responsible government, that Needham declared that the wish of the people should first have been heard through their representatives; that the Governor-General had had no right to call the Quebec Conference "there to sign and seal and deliver over to himself a protocol making a radical change in the constitution of the country, without going to the people and asking them whether they would have it or not."[25]

As early as the first week in December, 1864, A. J. Smith announced his objections to the Quebec scheme and foreshadowed the platform upon which his party would appeal to the electorate. The adoption of the Quebec plan could mean increased taxation; the loss to the province of political influence and status; the expenditure of vast sums on Canadian canals; the unfairness of eighty cents a head as a basis for taxation, since it would not be increased, whereas the revenue of the general government would be increased; and the unconstitutional behaviour of the delegates at Charlottetown and Quebec. Moreover, he asserted, the Intercolonial Railway would be "no great boon."[26]

In the light of the ubiquitous blasts of the anti-Confederation press, it is difficult to discover the basis for the Lieutenant-Governor's optimistic belief in the victory of the union party. According to his diagnosis, local interests and local partialities would decide the issue. Only in three constituencies, Saint John, York, and Westmorland, would Confederation affect the result. Fisher was less sanguine of immediate success. He recognized that a hard fight lay ahead. "Some of us may go down for a while in the operation but we will carry it finally," wrote Fisher to Macdonald early in the campaign.[27] If Governor Gordon remained unimpressed by the gathering clouds of opposition he might at least have received some intimation of the approaching débâcle from the defection of G. L. Hatheway, an influential

[24]*Ibid.*, Dec. 14, 1864.
[25]*Ibid.*
[26]*Ibid.*, Dec. 7, 1864.
[27]Macdonald Papers, Confederation Correspondence, VI, 49.

member of the government, who became no ineffectual agent in securing the defeat of his former colleagues.[28]

The desertion of Hatheway only served to increase the popular suspicion of the government that stemmed in part from the diatribes of the opposition leaders against the Quebec Resolutions; and these leaders themselves pursued a policy of opposition because they were identified or involved with certain interested groups who believed that the realization of cherished objectives would be baulked if the proposed union were accomplished. Prominent among these groups were the banking community of Saint John, the Roman Catholic church, and the mercantile element who were eager for more effective communication with the United States. The testimony of John Hamilton Gray, a defeated candidate, justifies the emphasis placed upon the crucial role of the bankers in the overthrow of the government. A week after the election Gray informed Macdonald that ". . . the banking interests united against us. They at present have a monopoly and their directors used their influence unsparingly. They dreaded the competition of Canadian banks coming here and the consequent destruction of that monopoly[29]—and many a businessman now in their power felt it not sage to hazard an active opposition to their influences."[30]

Equally decisive was the action of the Catholic section of the population. Fear of the Protestant influence of Canada West and especially of Grand Trunk control of the Intercolonial Railway were salient motives. Control of the projected railway, if it were secured by the Grand Trunk, would give that company a guiding hand in land settlement adjacent to the railway line. The Bishop of Saint John had for years taken a great interest in the settlement of his co-religionists on the wilderness land of New Brunswick.[31] But by far the strongest single element opposed to union with Canada was the business fraternity who

[28]*Correspondence Respecting the Proposed Union of the British North American Provinces*, Hatheway to the Lieutenant-Governor, enclosed with Gordon to Cardwell, Jan. 30, 1865. See also the *Headquarters*, March 8, 1865: "Mr. Hatheway has been mainly influential in bringing about the signal defeat that Mr. Tilley and his government have sustained on the question that they were forced to submit to the people." It was, however, an over-statement.

[29]Their fears were apparently justified. In the first Dominion Parliament it was necessary for Galt to explain: "The Bank of Montreal did the government business in the greater part of the Dominion, and it was natural that they should extend an agency of that institution to do the public business in the Maritime Provinces" (quoted in the Ottawa *Times*, Nov. 12, 1867).

[30]Macdonald Papers, Confederation Correspondence, VI, 68, J. H. Gray (N. B.) to Macdonald, March 13, 1865.

[31]*Ibid.*, VI, 95ff., Tilley to Galt, March, 1865.

had been endeavouring for a decade to integrate the commerce of the province more closely with that of the United States, and thus to make the most of New Brunswick's historic position as the north-eastern extension of the Atlantic geographic province.[32] Separated as New Brunswick was from Canada by the Appalachian barrier, trade with that province was negligible in comparison with her expanding commercial relations with the United States. It is, therefore, not to be wondered at, that the rival Intercolonial Railway, which was so closely associated with the Confederation movement, did not appeal to practical business leaders who were intent upon promoting the extension of New Brunswick's European and North American Railroad westward to the Maine border where it was to connect with the railway systems of New England. Such an alignment of forces proved too strong for the government to withstand, and it is by no means surprising that it suffered defeat at the polls on March 6, 1865.

II

On March 27, 1865, the Tilley government resigned from office and an anti-Confederation government was formed by Albert J. Smith and R. D. Wilmot. Prominent among its members were Timothy Warren Anglin, Irish editor of the Saint John *Freeman*, and G. L. Hatheway who had resigned from the Tilley government before the election as a protest against the Quebec Resolutions. The new government, with a large majority in the legislature, seemed in a strong position. None of the important men of the union party possessed seats in the new Assembly, although in the Legislative Council, Mitchell and Chandler were to continue ably to uphold the unionist point of view.

In the session which opened in March, 1865, no new position was taken up by either party, and the old arguments, already familiar on the hustings and in the press, were repeated on the floor of the House. Owing to the absence of Tilley, Fisher, and Gray, and because of the small number of unionist representatives, the new government and its supporters were able to present their case more forcefully than were their opponents. It was doubtless for this reason that the broad vision of a new British-American nation, which had found such conspicuous expression in the public addresses following the Charlottetown Conference, was now

[32]A. G. Bailey,."Railways and the Confederation Issue in New Brunswick, 1863-5" (*Canadian Historical Review*, XXI, Dec., 1940, 367-83). See also E. E. Chase, *Maine Railroads* (Portland, 1926).

totally absent. In its place was to be found, notably from the tongue of Smith himself, the expression of a fairly definite, if not intense, local feeling and of pride in the achievement of a self-government which he claimed had been violated by the delegates who had proceeded to Quebec to alter the constitution of the province and had exceeded their powers, in a way for which history provided no precedent.

These delegates who assembled on Prince Edward Island for a particular purpose, abandoned their business and arrogated to themselves powers that did not legitimately belong to them, and undertook to alter the institutions of the country and surrender the independence we have so long enjoyed. Is it not the duty of the Government to exercise their functions within the four corners of the Constitution? Is it not their duty to preserve inviolate the independence of the People?

It would, however, doubtless be an error to stress this element in the anti-Confederation point of view. More practical considerations continued to weigh heavily. Although one member waxed sentimental over the destruction of the link with England, which he envisaged if the Quebec Resolutions were adopted,[33] dollar-and-cent considerations received the greatest attention. There was no guarantee that Canada would keep faith in the matter of the Intercolonial Railway.[34] The Lower Provinces would be dragged in to bear their proportion of the expense of the great canal project of Canada West. "Canada has to borrow money to pay the interest on her own debts, and then wants to assume ours. It is like a bankrupt wanting to assume the debts of a rich man." So ran the argument, which Needham took up on the question of status. Powers of local government "would be confined to making laws to prevent cows from running on the commons, providing that sheep shall wear bells, and to issue tavern licenses."[35] "Forty-eight thousand men in this province have said we don't want Confederation, and that should be the end of it."

MacMillan, former member of the Tilley government, took up the cudgel for Confederation. "I do not believe," he said, "that to unite these British North American Colonies under one rule would be a political injury to them, neither do I believe the people of the country think so. I do not believe that the people are prepared to say that it will be commercially injurious to them to have a free intercourse in all articles and manufactures between the Provinces, setting aside the barriers of the Customs House."

[33]*New Brunswick, Debates of the Legislative Assembly*, May 31, 1865, 111.
[34]*Ibid.*, May 30, 1865, 110.
[35]*Ibid.*, 111.

He asserted, moreover, that provincial opinion was veering, and that another election would show two-thirds of the people of the province in favour of Confederation. Indeed, Tilley thought he observed some indication of a change of heart on the railway question. The state of the public revenue, and the prospect of a decrease during the ensuing year, together with the discount at which provincial debentures were being sold in the English market, would prevent any government from undertaking Western Extension as a government work. This fact was becoming recognized in the financial circles of Saint John, which "began to fear that they have not acted wisely, hence the reaction in Saint John on the confederation question."[36] Nevertheless the reply to the Speech from the Throne expressed "regret that existing laws preclude immediate action for the accomplishment of the extension of the European and North American Railroad westward from Saint John to the American border."[37] Realizing that to commit the province to carrying out Western Extension as a government work would prevent the raising of New Brunswick's share of the loan for the building of the Intercolonial Railway, Fisher declared his unequivocal opposition to the project, stating that it should be built by a private company.

An amendment was moved to the reply to the Speech from the Throne, embodying the view that the road should be built by private enterprise aided from public revenues, but it was defeated by a vote of twenty-nine to ten.[38] It was necessary "to act conjointly with the people of the United States, for they have to meet us at the boundary," declared Smith.[39] The road must be "a part of the great highway to the United States." J. W. Cudlip, diehard "Anti," voiced the view of the commercial interests of Saint John when he asserted that ". . . it was necessary to connect with the United States. It would then give the people who travelled and who had an eye to our resources, an inducement to come in and develop them, and would greatly further the trading influence and make American people come into the Province who never came before. The commerce between the Province and the United States had very greatly increased, and was increasing year by year." New Brunswick now received vast quantities of goods from the United States which formerly came

[36]Macdonald Papers, Confederation Correspondence, VI, 95, Tilley to Galt, March, 1865.
[37]*Ibid.*, 33.
[38]*New Brunswick, Journals of the Legislative Assembly*, 1865, 26-8.
[39]*New Brunswick, Debates of the Legislative Assembly*, May 26, 1865, 96.

from England. On June 6, Cudlip moved that the government should proceed with the construction of Western Extension as part of the European and North American Railroad, but that, as haste was essential, a private company should not be prevented from undertaking the work with the aid of the provincial subsidy of $10,000 a mile as provided by the Facility Bill of 1864.[40] The same provisions should apply to "Eastern Extension" from the Bend to Truro so as to link Nova Scotia with the United States. The unionists endeavoured to block the move on the ground of inexpediency. The province should not commit itself to such an outlay at a time when there was such a heavy drain on public finances and a large debt due to creditors in Great Britain. Nevertheless, Cudlip's resolution was carried by a vote of twenty-five to thirteen.

In spite of the seeming assurance with which the government proceeded with the legislative programme, it was not as strong as it appeared. The completeness of the late victory at the polls could not disguise the divergent interests and views among members of the Cabinet. To some extent the attrition suffered by the government throughout the ensuing year, stemmed from Cudlip's resolution concerning Western Extension, which did not exclude the building of the road by private enterprise. Anglin, who had stated on nomination day that "it must be built as a government work," continued to sit in the government. The opportunity was not to be missed, and he did not go untaunted by the unionist press.[41] Although he had declared that he would use his efforts to turn out any government which would not build Western Extension as a government work, the administration endorsed a grant to assist a private company in its construction, "and still Mr. Anglin is its apologist and tame public servant."[42] Although he continued to support the anti-Confederation cause, Anglin had resigned from the Cabinet before the issue was again joined at the polls.

III

In the meantime, while "interest" became divided on the question of railway policy and on other matters, the people of New Brunswick were to suffer no misapprehension concerning the path of "duty" as decreed by the Colonial Office. That the

[40] *New Brunswick, Journals of the Legislative Assembly*, June 6, 1865, 223.
[41] *Morning News*, Saint John, May 8, 1865.
[42] *True Humorist*, Saint John, May 26, 1865.

Canadians contributed in no small way to the formulation of the view held at the Colonial Office is so well known as to need no stressing. On the other hand, the reaction of New Brunswick opinion and policy to the course set for it by the British government is important to delineate, because it was conceived to be the task of imperial policy to modify this opinion so that it should harmonize with imperial interest.

The effect of the defeat on Canadian policy had been marked. In that province the Quebec Resolutions had carried in both Houses by majorities of three to one. Tilley's defeat had so frightened the legislature of Nova Scotia that Tupper forestalled a hostile vote only by side-tracking the discussion in favour of the question of Maritime Union. Drastic action to reverse the verdict in New Brunswick was the immediate concern of Macdonald and his associates. Three weeks after the defeat he wrote:

We now send four of our ministers to England to take stock ... with the British government to see what can be done. ... We intend also to arrange, if possible, the subject of defence. I do not despair of carrying out our great project sooner or later. I quite agree ... that the British Government will carry their point if they only adopt measures to that end, and we shall spare no pains to impress the necessity of such a course upon them with what success remains to be seen.[43]

In 1865 A. T. Galt stressed Confederation as a means to the continuance of the British connection when he declared that a decided expression of policy on the part of the British government would have "a most marked effect on the loyal and high-spirited people of the Maritime Provinces."[44] Accordingly "the strongest delegation which had ever left Canada," Galt, Macdonald, Brown, and Cartier, set out for England within a few weeks of Tilley's defeat to impress the Colonial Office with the dire necessity of reversing the verdict in New Brunswick.[45] Fisher, Tilley, and Tupper were parties to the plan, bluntly declaring that the actions of the Governors of New Brunswick and Nova Scotia had ensured the defeat of the measure.[46] On April 5, Fisher wrote to Macdonald that he was "satisfied if the press here learn that the British government are anxious for the union it will influence their mood." It would be well "if the dispatch indicating that opinion could be got out before the middle or latter end of May .... It is said our governor has resigned or intends to. I hope

[43]Macdonald Papers, Confederation Correspondence, VI, 66, Macdonald to Gray (P.E.I.), March 24, 1865.
[44]Martin, "British Policy in Canadian Confederation," 18.
[45]*Ibid.*, 11.
[46]*Ibid.*, 17.

it is true. . . . I know everyone that he might be supposed to have the least influence with, or associates with in any way, violently opposed Confederation, a state of things I cannot think could exist without his procurement in some way." Macdonald was admonished to be sure, if a new incumbent were appointed, "that he is honestly and faithfully at heart in earnest to carry confederation." With such a man acting "friendly and in earnest," Fisher believed it could be carried in three months after his arrival. "That is the tendency of the public mind."[47]

The New Brunswick press was not slow to grasp the implication of the Canadian plan. The public must "keep watch on this Canadian Mission."[48] Nevertheless the anti-Confederation press affirmed their belief that the British government had their interests at heart, and might at most persuade, but would not attempt to coerce, the province. "We do not think that there will be any attempt made to force any unpalatable measure upon this province, but there will be some pressure brought to bear. . . ." Doubtless, surmised the *Headquarters*, the thought was running in Macdonald's head that "it is intolerable that New Brunswick with its paltry 250,000 of a population should stand in the way of a great scheme that Canada with 2,500,000 is desirous of adopting, and no doubt if it is properly represented the Imperial government would see it in the same light, and 'reason with' this stubborn province." "It is evident," was the conclusion "that these Canadian politicians will have to be narrowly watched." In June the Montreal *Gazette* took it upon itself to lecture to the Maritime Provinces concerning their duty to the mother country and the Empire, exploiting the sentiment of loyalty so constantly protested in those provinces:

The Imperial Government . . . will not dictate to the Maritime Provinces what they shall do in matters of local legislation or concernment; but it can and we believe it will, say upon what terms the Imperial navy will protect their coasts and . . . garrison their towns. It is idle for them to conceal the fact from themselves—confederation or union of some sort is a condition of the continuance of British connection. They have to decide now at how much they esteem that connection . . . or whether . . . it is mere lip loyalty.[49]

Since the British government had already expressed its approval of Confederation on the ground of imperial defence, the reception of the Canadian delegation at the Colonial Office was

[47]Macdonald Papers, Confederation Correspondence, VI, Fisher to Macdonald, April 5, 1865.
[48]Fredericton *Headquarters*, March 22, 1865.
[49]Quoted in *The Borderer*, Sackville, N.B., June 16, 1865.

extremely cordial. Cartier pointed out that the British government could exercise a very great influence through the decided expression of its views, in order to reverse the verdict. Cardwell replied that the government would "use every proper means of influence to carry into effect without delay the proposed confederation." The attention of the Smith government was to be drawn to the intimate connection between the small population and the measures that would be necessary for the defence of the province. New Brunswick was to bear in mind that as a separate province it could make no adequate provision for its own defence and that it would therefore "rest in a very great degree upon the defence which may be provided for it by Great Britain." "It will consequently be likely to appear to your advisors," wrote Cardwell to the Governor on April 12, 1865, "reasonable and wise that, in examining the question of the proposed union, they should attach great weight to the views and wishes of this country...."[50] Gordon was to impress upon his legislature the concern felt in England for imperial defence. The publication in the *Royal Gazette* on July 15, of the Monck-Cardwell correspondence could have left no doubt in the minds of New Brunswickers concerning the wishes of the British government.

The fears expressed earlier in the year by the Fredericton *Headquarters* were now realized. Its readers had been warned that the Canadian mission to England would have to be watched narrowly, for they intended to steal a march on New Brunswick. "It is evident they have done so.... It is evident that the Home authorities have only looked at the grand outline ... from an Imperial point of view; they have not curiously examined the details, and how they were likely to affect most injuriously the interests of this small province ... the .negotiations were conducted as between the British Government and Canada alone. The conduct of Canada throughout has been most arrogant, irritating and insulting to this Province."[51] The scheme originated in the political necessities of Canada and "the Imperial approval was only an after-clap." And the Saint John *Evening Globe* asked:

How many English publicists have examined the features of that obnoxious scheme of confederation agreed upon at Quebec? ... How many of them know anything about the Northwest territory, about the enlargement of Canadian canals, or the building of Canadian fortifications, in so far as these matters affect us? How many of them know that our taxation will be double the moment we enter upon

---
[50]Macdonald Papers, Confederation Correspondence, VI, 117.
[51]Fredericton *Headquarters*, July 19, 1865; Sept. 6, 1865.

Confederation? How many of them know that the Canadians are a people with whom we have little or no trade; that they are a people for whom we have no more affection than we have for the people of . . . any other British Colony.[52]

The *Freeman* could not contain its indignation, "expressed with Fenian venom" at the British Colonial Secretary for acting as though union were a *fait accompli*.[53]

There is little doubt that when Smith and Allen set out to lay the "true" situation and feelings of New Brunswick before the Colonial Office, they had the support of the majority in their own province. The *Headquarters* expressed confidence that the British government would give their views every consideration. But in view of the strong representations of the Canadian delegation, with whom the British government was now publicly in accord, the hopes of the editor were far too sanguine. Nevertheless the mission bore strong views across the Atlantic. Cudlip had stated in the House that false statements were being circulated in England by the Canadian delegation to induce the imperial Parliament to legislate for New Brunswick in the matter of intercolonial union. "If there is anything of that kind in contemplation, they had better pause before they attempt it, for we would resist coercion whether it was brought against us directly or indirectly." He had then moved that the delegation be sent to England to make known the view of New Brunswick, that "the consummation of the said Scheme would prove politically, commercially, and financially disastrous to the best interests" of the province. The right of the people to decide all questions affecting their own local interests for the promotion of their prosperity and welfare issued from their right of internal self-government. Moreover the committee of the House had "reason to fear that Her Majesty's Government are but imperfectly aware of the true feelings of the people of this Province on the subject." The resolution had passed by a vote of twenty-nine to ten. The Governor had been asked to inform the Secretary of State "how entirely this scheme has been rejected by the people of this province." On July 15, Gordon had forwarded to Cardwell an enclosure from the Executive Council, giving as the reason for having repudiated Confederation that "they were unable to discover anything in it that gave promise of either moral or material advantage to the empire or themselves; or that it afforded a prospect of improved administration or increased prosperity." "To confer on this Province a right of

[52]*Evening Globe*, Saint John, Sept. 8, 1865.
[53]*Morning News*, Saint John, Nov. 13, 1865.

self-government would have been a mockery" if the wishes of the mother country were in all cases to be followed when they did not coincide with the views of "those on whom alone the responsibility of action in the Province falls." In spite of these representations, Cardwell informed the delegates that he "could give no countenance to any proposals which would tend to delay the confederation of all the Provinces . . . ." The failure of the anti-Confederation mission was hailed as another milestone on the road to ultimate triumph by the unionist press.

IV

Long before Cardwell's rebuff, the Smith government showed a certain lack of strength. It had difficulty in filling vacancies in a number of public offices. By April 5, it had not appointed a postmaster, solicitor-general, or any legislative councillor,[54] through fear, an opponent stated, of suffering reverses at the polls. Uncertainty over railway policy was partly the cause, and British pronouncements may have had some effect, although the anti-Confederation faction continued to believe that the British government would not use coercion. "Rather poor comfort," commented Fisher privately.[55] The hope was expressed by the supporters of union that the Canadians would use means to influence the Orangemen of the province to vote for Confederation by playing up "loyalty" and the British connection through the lodges. Roman Catholics appeared to be as strongly opposed as ever. There were about six hundred Catholic voters in York County, and Fisher despaired of getting more than twenty of them in his forthcoming election campaign. "I find them," he wrote, "still in a solid phalanx united against confederation, and I know that no argument but one from the church will reach them."

In spite of this opposition, the unionists continued to plan how they could capitalize upon the weakened position of Smith's government, which had refused A. R. Wetmore the attorney-generalship because this would have necessitated his risking re-election in Saint John. Smith decided to take that office himself, and the unionists believed that he would be returned without opposition as he had strong backing in his own county

[54]Macdonald Papers, Confederation Correspondence, VI, Fisher to Macdonald, April 5, 1865.
[55]*Ibid.* Fisher to Macdonald (confidential), Aug. 13, 1865.

of Westmorland. Tilley was confident of victory in Saint John when that riding should be opened.⁵⁶

It was in York County, however, that the most conspicuous battle was to be fought. Attorney-General Allen having been raised to the Bench, the constituency was opened. Both sides prepared to engage in a major offensive. Fisher, who was the most likely unionist candidate, feared that the government might bring forth a strong lumber merchant and spend an enormous amount of money. Fisher might raise the cry of Fenianism against his opponent and arouse the Orange lodges, with the connivance of the Canadians, but as to money, he stated bluntly to Macdonald, he did not have it to spend.⁵⁷ It was felt that Fisher could be returned with an expenditure of eight or ten thousand dollars, and the Canadian unionists were solicited to contribute to the common cause.

When Smith arrived in Fredericton after his unsuccessful mission to England, a party caucus was held to determine what should be done to fight the election in York County. Although it seemed evident that the Catholic bishop and his followers would continue to oppose Confederation, Anglin was distasteful to the majority of Protestants, particularly those of Loyalist descent and the immigrants from the north of Ireland. In order to meet this situation it was determined that John Pickard, a wealthy lumber merchant and an Orangeman, should run on the anti-Confederation ticket. A Catholic candidate was also presented on the same ticket with Pickard, but on nomination day he retired in favour of Pickard who thus perhaps secured the bulk of the Catholic vote although he himself was an Orangeman. Moreover, Pickard could afford to spend a considerable sum of money on the election, and was in a position to pay it if he were elected. Only an outlay on the part of the Canadians could meet competition of this kind, because although Fisher did not lack resources of his own, it was suspected that the Smith government would spend "any amount of money."⁵⁸

Fisher did not present himself as a candidate until a short time before nomination day, and many in the county did not know that he had decided to run until after he was nominated as Pickard's opponent. On nomination day Fisher branded the government with Fenianism "without much mercy," but was

⁵⁶*Ibid.*, Tilley to Macdonald, Sept. 13, 1865.
⁵⁷*Ibid.*, 138 ff., Fisher to Macdonald (confidential), Aug. 13, 1865.
⁵⁸*Ibid.*, 167 ff., Fisher to Macdonald, Nov. 11, 1865.

compelled to state that before Confederation was adopted it must again be submitted to the people at a general election. As the campaign proceeded the whole province became excited from one end to the other. Although Fisher never left his office until the polling day,[59] Pickard, Needham, and other anti-Confederation leaders scoured the country. A lot of young men, acting in Fisher's interest, followed them around to refute their statements. Orangemen and Loyalists were not unmoved by the intense British feeling created by Fisher, and, according to one account, "all sorts of intimidation forced many of the voters to change their tickets." It is uncertain as to what part Governor Gordon played in the election. Although officially committed by his instructions from the British government to support Confederation, his personal views may have remained unchanged. His gardener, coachman, and grocer, it was stated, voted against Fisher.

Fisher wrote jubilantly to Macdonald about his victory in York County and of the moral effect on public opinion throughout the province. But he politely reminded Macdonald of the day of reckoning. His expenditure had been large: "We look to you," he wrote, "to help us out of the scrape, for if every dollar is not paid it will kill us at the general election. If it is met fairly, we have a plain course open for confederation. . . . Do not allow us to want now or we are all gone together."[60] He represented the victory as the turning point in the great Confederation struggle. It had inspired Confederationists everywhere with visions of ultimate success. The jubilation was general in official circles, although Cardwell was disheartened by the unopposed return of Smith from Westmorland. On November 22, Lord Monck wrote to congratulate Macdonald and his colleagues on the return of Fisher for York County. "I think," he declared, "that this is the most important thing that has happened since the Quebec conference, and if followed up judiciously affords a good omen of success in our spring campaign."

There are, however, reasons for believing that the official optimism was unwarranted and that Fisher's election did not in fact represent a marked swing of opinion toward Confederation. Fisher's friends did their best to keep the issue out of the campaign, and he himself only succeeded in checkmating the anti-unionists by pledging himself to oppose Confederation if it were

[59]According to his own statement. See *ibid.*, 167 ff.
[60]*Ibid.*, 167 ff., Nov., 1865.

presented to the then existing legislature. Moreover, his supporters diverted attention from the real issues involved by invoking the red herring of Fenianism. "The Fisher party have worked the Fenian cry well, and it has been successful .... the absurd, and as it is now known, fearfully exaggerated telegrams about Fenian doings in Canada, were artfully taken advantage of to work upon the fears of the electors...." So ran the *Headquarters*' post mortem. Furthermore, the belief was publicly stated that "the Canadian government have largely aided their party here by hard cash...."

Similar means were employed by the "Antis," although the origin of the funds remains partly undisclosed. The Saint John *Telegraph* revealed one source of support when it denounced the Smith government "for giving a certain enterprising lumber operator [Alexander Gibson], who happens to be a very active Anti-confederate, ... the privilege of purchasing certain tracts of land." The sale was denounced as a political act and awoke an outcry from the unionist opposition. "Antis" countered with the assertion that the land, comprising two tracts of 4,903 and 10,000 acres in York County, was, in any case, unfit for settlement. Nevertheless the opportunity for sniping was not to be lost. The *True Humorist*, tireless ridiculer of "Anti" politicians, concocted for the occasion an imaginary conversation between members of the Smith government, in the course of which they referred to themselves as having swapped away "15,000 acres of the Public Lands to one man for a few hours strutting around the polls," and as having paid out "the public money drawn from the emaciated vaults of the People's Bank!" The government of 1862 refused to go beyond a mere survey when it found Gibson wanted 15,000 acres of prime land on the central route of the Intercolonial Railway—"That's true, and Gibson turned against the Government from that hour, and got nothing until we came in; and then we rescinded the order. How he used to dog me around till we rescinded the order."

The resignation of R. D. Wilmot from the Cabinet proved to be a more serious problem for the Smith government than the jibes of the *True Humorist*. Wilmot afterwards declared that the abrogation of the Reciprocity Treaty had converted him, and denied that he had changed his opinion while on a visit to Canada in reply to the insinuation that he had been "bought." Whatever may have been the reasons for Wilmot's change of front, the Governor planned to capitalize upon it as a means of driving

Smith from office, by retaining Wilmot whom Smith refused to meet at the council table. The Governor could not be blamed for the failure of the plan, although the unionists continued to suspect him for remaining "at heart opposed to union" when he appointed two inveterate "Antis" to the Bench to the neglect of Wilmot's claim. "Wilmot is a methodist," wrote Fisher on February 13, 1866, "and the methodists, baptists, and presbyterians feel especially insulted at this appointment. These denominations are four-fifths of the confederation party alone . . . . Anti newspapers publicly speak of the policy of delay as a means by which they intend to worry out Canada until the coalition fails."

There can be no doubt that the more earnestly the Governor promoted union, as the representative of the British government, the more the effort to exert influence became distasteful to numbers of persons in the province. The Canadians, it was averred, had "brought all the pressure they could to break down the opposition in New Brunswick . . . . They have induced Mr. Cardwell to write a series of irritating despatches by way of exercising upon New Brunswick what he calls the just authority of the Imperial Government, and they are now waiting anxiously to see if New Brunswick will break down under the pressure."

V

A review of evidence gleaned from the press and from the public and private pronouncements of political leaders reveals that the opposition to Confederation was based upon economic, political, and religious considerations. Moreover, certain elements of the population, such as the Roman Catholic, appear to have been opposed to union on any terms on the ground that it would be harmful to their interests. Into this category also a section of the manufacturing group would appear to fall. On the other hand, there were those who directed their attacks not against the principle of Confederation so much as against the specific terms of union which had been embodied in the Quebec Resolutions. These, they held, would mean increased taxes, higher tariffs, Canadian competition in the provincial market, and loss of local monopolies. Some did not stress the positive evils of Confederation so much as doubt the benefits that would accrue from it. The most influential representatives of the commercial interest, particularly in the southern part of the province, were intent upon pursuing a project of a different nature, that of fostering trade with the United States by linking New Brunswick's railway with the New England system, and this development they feared Confederation would impede.

It is clear, however, that throughout the year that followed the defeat of the Tilley government, new circumstances arose which rendered several of the grounds of opposition to union no longer tenable. The decline of provincial debentures in the English market and the probability of a decrease in the public revenue prevented the government from extending their railway westward from Saint John to the American border as a government work, and when the task of construction was offered to a private company, Anglin, who had been a tower of strength, resigned. When the government's inability to complete the railway was linked with the failure of the Reciprocity negotiations the prospect for increased trade with the United States dwindled, and Wilmot followed Anglin out of the councils of the government to become later a Father of Confederation.

By contrast with Wilmot, other leaders, like Cudlip, persisted in their opposition to Confederation either in the hope of a renewal of the Reciprocity negotiations and the successful completion of the railway, or in the belief that even without these advantages the interests with which they were identified would be better off under existing conditions than if the province were merged in a larger union. The latter continued to find support among the Roman Catholic element, for nothing seems to have occurred in the interval to alter the policy of the Church. Furthermore the Quebec Resolutions remained the basis for the proposed union and the objections which had been levelled against them in the previous year were still in 1866 regarded by many as valid. Such considerations help to explain in part the remarkable persistence of opposition in spite of loss of government personnel and support in the face of deteriorating conditions. In this connection it will be recalled that Smith still commanded a majority in the Legislative Assembly at the time of his forced resignation from the premiership in April, 1866. Up to that time neither he nor his "anti" majority appear to have been sufficiently impressed by the declared wishes of the British government to change their policy on the union question.

Space does not permit a full examination of the reaction of the province to British policy, nor of the complex attitude of Smith himself in the light of the altered circumstances. All that can be said here is that, although privately persuaded of the difficulty of following his original party line, and under constant pressure from the Governor to adopt a policy favourable to union, he continued to adhere publicly to his "anti" position. This divergence between private opinion and public profession prevented Smith from giving effective leadership to those forces which, in the early months of 1866, still continued to resist the union of the provinces. Smith's hesitating and uncertain course must therefore be added to those factors already considered as having weakened the anti-Confederation position during the period under consideration, and which prepared the way for the later intensification of the appeal to support union on the ground of loyalty to the British connection. This, conjoined with the exaggerated menace of Fenian invasion and the persuasive power of Canadian campaign funds, carried New Brunswick into Confederation.

Act or Pact? Another Look at Confederation*

G. F. G. STANLEY

I

There are probably few Canadian historians, and even fewer political scientists, who have not, at some time or another, taken a second glance at the British North America Act of 1867; few of them, too, who have not lectured to their students upon the facts underlying the federal union of which the Act is the legislative expression, and commented upon the nature and essence of Canadian federalism. It is because of the generality of interest in the British North America Act that I have yielded to the temptation, not to present to you, as my presidential address, a detailed paper upon some narrow aspect of the historical researches which have absorbed my time during the last two or three years, but to offer for your consideration a few general comments upon a subject which has both a wide and a topical interest at the present time. My approach is, of course, that of the historian. I am concerned, not with what our constitution is or ought to be — that I leave to my scientifically political brethren — but with how it became what it is.

To my mind the principal factor — I do not suggest it as the sole factor but as one of the most important — in determining the course of Canadian constitutional development, has been the existence, within Canada, of two competing ethnic, cultural groups. The Earl of Durham, in his famous *Report*, chose to refer to them as "two nations warring in the bosom of a single state". [1] Were he writing in today's idiom, he might have preferred to substitute the word "co-existing" for "warring". Certainly "warring" is too strong and too inaccurate a word to describe what has been simply the political struggle on the part of the English-speaking population for supremacy, and on the part of the French-speaking population for survival. This struggle has dominated the whole story of Canadian politics. It probably accounts for the prepossession of Canadian historians with political and constitutional history. The struggle is one which still continues, and the issues are still the same; supremacy as against survival, or to use the contemporary terms, centralization as against provincial autonomy.

---

* Although this paper was read partly in English and partly in French, it is printed here entirely in English.

[1] Sir Reginald Coupland, *The Durham Report, an abridged version with an introduction and notes* (Oxford, 1945), p. 15. For an unabridged edition see that published by Methuen & Co. Limited, London, 1902; or Sir Charles Lucas, *Lord Durham's Report on the Affairs of British North America*, Oxford, 1912, vol. II.

And yet, perhaps, if the word "warring" is unsuitable as a general description of Anglo-French relations within the bosom of this country, Canada, at times it has not been without some aptness; for the bitterness and misunderstandings which have frequently accompanied our relations have cut, on occasions, close to the bone. That civil strife in Canada has never degenerated into civil war has been due, in part at least, to the recognition by both peoples of the necessity of some *modus vivendi* and the recognition by each of the rights of the other. The recognition and definition of these rights is the basis of the entente, understanding, pact, compact, call it what you will, which is the foundation of our political unity. Without such an entente there would have been, and would be no Canada as we know it today. Much has been written, both in the French and English languages about this pact; some of it narrow and legalistic; more of it unhistorical; much of it purely polemical. If we attempt to look upon this pact or entente as a legal contract, freely entered into by two parties and intended by them to be legally enforceable in a court of law, our vision will be so limited as to be distorted; for a pact or compact is not a contract in the legal sense. It is a gentleman's agreement, an understanding based upon mutual consent, with a moral rather than a juridical sanction. The Anglo-French understanding which alone has made government possible within the boundaries of the larger Canada has become sanctified by time and continued acceptance, until today it is looked upon by many as a convention of our constitution. It is my immediate purpose, this evening, to trace for you the origin and growth of this convention, and to discuss some of its implications in the development of our constitution.

II

It was the cession of Canada to Great Britain in 1763, that initiated the problem of which our bi-racial pact in Canada became the ultimate solution. It brought within an English, Protestant empire, a French, Catholic colony. How the one could successfully incorporate the other was the question which confronted British statesmen following the Treaty of Paris. Previous experience with Acadia offered little in the way of guidance; the expulsion of the inhabitants of the new colony was neither a humane nor a politically satisfying solution. The easy answer seemed to be assimilation; the King's new subjects might even be induced to abandon their heretical ways before they were swamped by British immigration to Canada. Assimilation was the object and essence of the Proclamation issued on October 7, 1763, over the sign manual of George III. [2] It was also the object of the long commission and letter of instructions issued the first British Governor of Canada, James Murray. [3] But

---

[2] A. Shortt and A. G. Doughty, *Documents Relating to the Constitutional History of Canada, 1759-1791* (Ottawa, 1918) I, 163 ff.
[3] *Ibid.*, 173 ff, 181 ff.

assimilation, particularly a half-hearted assimilation, proved unsuccessful. Its one effect was to stiffen the heart and mind of the French-speaking population, and to give strength and cohesion to its determination to survive as a cultural and as a political group. Ten years of criminations and recriminations between the King's old and new subjects resulted in a victory for the latter. In 1774, the Quebec Act [4] definitely removed the anti-French, anti-Catholic bias of earlier policy. It cleared the way for French Canadians to accept government appointments; it guaranteed to the French those civil laws and religious privileges which, to this time, had either been denied, neglected, or merely tolerated. In brief, the Quebec Act placed the French Canadians, the King's new subjects, on a basis of political and religious equality with the English and Anglo-Americans, the so-called old subjects. The Act did not father the French fact in Canada; what it did do was to provide it with a juridical foundation. An English-Canadian historian, Professor A. L. Burt, has written "the Quebec Act embodied a new sovereign principle of the British Empire: the liberty of non-English peoples to be themselves"; [5] a French Canadian, Etienne Parent, has called the Act, "a true social contract between us and England... the consecration of our natural right". [6] The Quebec Act, it might be noted in passing, was never repealed by the British Parliament; some of its provisions have been nullified by subsequent legislation, but it still stands, honoured by French Canadians as the Magna Charta of their national rights and privileges.

From the standpoint of the French Canadians, the guarantees afforded by the Quebec Act had come none too soon. Within several shot-riddled years, the whole demographic premise upon which the British Government had made the concessions embodied in the Act, that of a continuing predominance of the French-speaking population, had been altered by the coming of the United Empire Loyalists. From one-twentieth of the total population, the English-speaking inhabitants of the old province of Quebec increased, in a few months, to one-seventh. Co-existence, or perhaps I should say co-habitation, became more difficult than ever. The constitution of 1774 became an anachronism. It brought neither understanding nor prosperity to the province. It was, in truth, satisfactory neither to the French nor to the English-speaking population; both of whom could unite their voices upon two demands only, political separation from each other and a greater share in the management of their own local affairs. The Loyalists had been accustomed to and demanded elective, representative institutions on the British parliamentary model; many French Canadians, imbued with the pro-English ideas of Voltaire and the Encyclo-

---

[4] *Ibid.*, 570 ff; 14 Geo. III, c. 83.

[5] A. L. Burt, *The Old Province of Quebec* (Toronto and Minneapolis, 1933) p. 200.

[6] Quoted in L. Groulx, *Histoire du Canada français depuis la découverte* (Montréal, 1952) III, 75.

paedists, or perhaps only with those of Pierre du Calvet, likewise demanded the political freedom denied them by the constitution of 1774. Some there were in London who wondered what the effect of the changes would be: some who argued that the establishment of a "separate and local" legislature "under any form or model which can be adopted for the purpose" would lead inevitably "to habitual Notions of a distinct interest", and "to the existence of a virtual independence" and then, "naturally to prepare the way for an entire separation, whenever other circumstances shall bring it forward". [7] But the British government believed that it knew what the situation required: the old province of Quebec should be divided into two new, separate and distinct provinces on an ethnic basis, with the Ottawa river as the line of division; and each province should be provided with a new constitution generally assimilated to that of Great Britain, including an elective assembly as well as appointed legislative and executive councils. On June 19, 1791, Canada's second constitution by British parliamentary enactment received the royal assent and became law. [8]

Few British politicians, or Anglo-Canadians for that matter, fully appreciated what impact the Constitutional Act would have upon the problem of reconciling the French and English-speaking inhabitants of the two Canadas. Grenville seems to have had some vague ideas when he wrote to Lord Dorchester, sending him a draft copy of the new constitution, that "a considerable degree of attention is due to the prejudices and habits of the French Inhabitants who compose so large a proportion of the community, and every degree of caution should be used to continue to them the enjoyment of those civil and religious rights which were secured to them by the Capitulation of the Province, or have since been granted by the liberal and enlightened spirit of the British Government". [9] So too did William Pitt, when he answered Fox's objections to dividing the old province, that any effort to unite the two peoples within a single political entity governed by a single legislature, would lead only to "a perpetual scene of factious discord". [10] But Grenville, when he wrote about the rights of the French Canadians, was thinking only of how the British Government might distract their attention away from what Frenchmen, and French women too, were doing and saying in the streets of the

[7] Shortt and Doughty, *Documents*, II, p. 983; Discussion of Petitions and Counter Petitions re Change of Government in Canada, enclosed in Grenville to Dorchester, Oct. 20, 1789.
[8] *Ibid.*, II, p. 1031 ff.
[9] *Ibid.*, II, p. 988; Grenville to Dorchester, Oct. 20, 1789.
[10] *The Annual Register or a View of the History, Politics and Literature for the Year 1791* (London, 1795), p. 111. Charles James Fox had criticized the proposed division of the old province on the grounds that "the French and English Canadians would be completely distinguished from each other. But he considered such a measure big with mischief; and maintained that the wisest policy would be to form the two descriptions of people into one body, and endeavour to annihilate all national distinctions". (*Annual Register*, 1791, 110).

Paris of the Revolution. And William Pitt beclouded his argument with Fox by talking airly and unrealistically about how the French Canadians, novices in the art of parliamentary government, would be so impressed with the success attending the working of the new English-type constitution in the neighbouring province, that they would strive to enjoy its fullest benefits by uniting with English-speaking Canada. Race, religion, laws and traditions would, one after the other, be discarded as Lower Canadians sought the Holy Grail of political success and economic prosperity. The very fact of splitting Quebec into two provinces, Upper and Lower Canada, of which Fox (and the English-speaking minority in Lower Canada) had complained, would, in the end, be the means of bringing about ultimate unity. Edmund Burke spoke in a similar vein. It was a strange kind of reasoning. Granting the sincerity of their convictions, one may only conclude that they were ignorant of Canada, that they had misread its history, and that they misunderstood the whole concept of nationality. [11]

Far from encouraging the French to abandon their own consciousness of identity, the effect of the Constitutional Act of 1791 was to give renewed vigour to the idea of French Canadian separateness. It provided the French fact with a geographical as well as a political buttress. If the Quebec Act of 1774 guaranteed the survival of the French Canadians, the Constitutional Act of 1791 guaranteed the survival of French Canada. The Act of 1791 was the logical, if not the inevitable sequel to the Act of 1774. It was, in the words of Canon Groulx, "a renewed consecration of the French fact in Canada." [12]

This is not the place to discuss the internal defects of the Constitution of 1791. They are familiar to every student of our history. And yet I wonder, sometimes, whether there has not been too much inclination on the part of Canadians to treat the Act of 1791 as a kind of constitutional whipping boy; whether in trying to be political scientists, we cease to be historians. Do we not sometimes fall into the error of confusing the regime with its institutions? Do we not, all too frequently, look upon the history of Canada in isolation, forgetting that these years are, at the same time, the years of Conservative ascendancy in Great Britain, the years of the anti-liberal restrictive legislation inspired by the excesses of the French Revolution? Is it wholly without significance, when considering the constitutional developments of Canada between 1791 and 1840, to recall that only three weeks before the passage of the Act the same British government which sponsored it issued the first of the decrees against sedition; and that in 1830, only seven years before blood was shed on the banks of the Richelieu, and near Gallow's Hill, the Duke of Welling-

---

[11] W. P. M. Kennedy, *The Constitution of Canada, 1534-1937, an introduction to its development, law and custom* (Oxford, 1938), p. 86.
[12] Groulx, *Histoire du Canada français*, III, 133.

ton had cried that he would never bring forward any measure of parliamentary reform, and that "as long as he held any station in the Government of the country, he should always feel it his duty to resist any such measure when proposed by others".[13] I do not mean to imply that the Constitution of 1791 was without fault. I simply suggest that, taking conditions as they were, there could be no answer during these years to the dilemma of how to reconcile imperial centralization and colonial autonomy. There could be no accommodation between a reactionary, metropolitan Toryism and a revolutionary provincial democracy, within the rigid framework of the constitution. Under other circumstances the Constitution of 1791 might have worked moderately well; under the circumstances such as they were, it collapsed in fire and bloodshed.

The immediate sequel to the rebellions in Upper and Lower Canada was the suppression of the ill-fated constitution and the appointment of a special commissioner, the Earl of Durham, to inquire into the political situation and make recommendations regarding "the Form and Administration of the Civil Government" to be granted to the two Canadas. In his Report, dated January 31, 1839, Durham exposed the weakness of the previous regime, and recommended the concession of effective self-government to the Canadians. But if Durham favoured self-government (or what is known in our history as responsible government) it was only for a government dominated by English-speaking people. Essentially an Imperialist and a centralizer, Durham was the effective advocate of the supremacy of things English. He toyed with the idea of a federal union of the British North American provinces, but cast it aside when he realized that it would inevitably give the French Canadians of Lower Canada control over their own local affairs; instead, he recommended that Upper and Lower Canada be joined together in an indissoluble union with one government and one legislature. "I believe", he wrote, "that tranquillity can only be restored by subjecting the Province to the vigorous rule of an English majority; and that the only efficacious government would be that formed by a legislative union".[14] It was the old policy of assimilation all over again.

In 1840 the British Parliament performed the marriage ceremony. The two Canadian provinces, dissimilar in numbers, as well as in origin, faith, language and tradition, were united by the Act of Union.[15] The new constitution did not, however, follow strictly to the letter the recommendations which Durham had penned the year before. The union was not a thorough-going, punitive, Anglicizing union such as the Earl had contemplated. The demographic situation would not permit it. The fact

[13] Quoted in J. A. R. Marriott, *England Since Waterloo* (London, 1936), p. 88.
[14] Coupland, *The Durham Report*, p. 161.
[15] W. P. M. Kennedy, *Documents of the Canadian Constitution, 1759-1915* (Toronto, 1918), pp. 536-550; 3 & 4 Victoria, c. 35.

was that the English-speaking populations of the two provinces combined did not enjoy what Durham mistakenly believed to be the case, "a clear English majority".[16] A legislative union pure and simple, instead of overwhelming the French Canadians, would have had the opposite result; it would have given them unquestioned control of the legislature of the united province, and this state of affairs, even though it might endure only a few years, was regarded as intolerable. The only way to defeat the French majority would be to crib, cabin and confine it to Lower Canada; and this could best be done by preserving as distinct, political entities the two provinces which it had been proposed to obliterate and by giving each of them equal representation in the new legislature. Since the English-speaking representatives from Upper Canada could always hope to find a few compatriots among the representatives of Lower Canada, together they would outnumber the delegates of French origin. The new constitution was thus, in effect, a vague, unintended, and undefined form of federalism, with the provinces of Upper and Lower Canada continuing in existence under the names of Canada West and Canada East, despite their union in one political entity called the Province of Canada. *Nil facit error nominis, cum de corpore constat*, the name does not affect the substance so long as its identity is manifest, is a maxim familiar to every lawyer.

But British policy in the end defeated itself. By denying French Canadians the temporary advantage of representation according to population, the British authorities not only strengthened French determination to hold securely every privilege gained in 1774 and 1791, they unwittingly provided them with the very means of holding these privileges, when as expected, the numbers of the French-speaking population fell below those of their English-speaking rivals. Equality of representation for the two provinces which were the political and geographical expressions of the two racial groups, was a sword which cut both ways.

The federal nature of the new constitution became more and more apparent as the years passed. Voting and acting as a political unit, the French Canadians were too large and too significant a *bloc* to be ignored. Government by one province alone, Canada West, was impossible; the collaboration of Canada East was not only desirable, it was a political necessity. And this collaboration could only be obtained upon French Canada's own terms. Sir Charles Bagot recognized this fact when, in 1842, he finally took Louis LaFontaine, the French Canadian leader, into his ministry along with his English-speaking colleague, Robert Baldwin. Sir Charles wrote to an infuriated Colonial Secretary in London:

> I knew... that I could not hope to succeed with the French Canadians as a Race... and not as a mere party in the House, unless I could secure the

[16] Coupland, *The Durham Report*, p. 161.

services of men who possessed their confidence, and who would bring to my assistance, not only their own talents, and some votes in the House of Assembly, but the goodwill and attachment of their race, and that I could not obtain such services unless I was willing to place the individuals in a position in my Council which would prevent them from feeling themselves a hopeless minority against a suspicious and adverse majority. [17]

Bagot congratulated himself that he had "satisfied" the French Canadians that the Union was "capable of being administered for their happiness and advantage, and have consequently disarmed their opposition to it". He had, however, done a great deal more. He had established the first of the dual ministries with their premiers and their attorneys-general from both Canada East and Canada West; he had pointed the way to the development of the principle of the double-majority; he had given official sanction to the federal idea implicit in the Act of 1840. The two old provinces of Upper and Lower Canada might have ceased to exist in law, but they did exist in fact and in practice, and continued to exist throughout the whole of the Union period. There was real truth in John A. Macdonald's statement in 1865, "although we now sit in one Parliament, supposed constitutionally to represent the people without regard to sections or localities, yet we know, as a matter of fact, that since the union in 1841, we have had a Federal Union". [18] There was a wide gap between intention and reality. In spite of Bagot's precedent, the original idea behind the Union died hard. Metcalfe tried to win French support by appealing not to a race but simply to individuals of French origin. He failed. In the end Lord Elgin gave the *coup de grâce* to Durham's policy of denationalization and assimilation. He reverted to Sir Charles Bagot's policy, and in so doing restored the principle that an Anglo-French entente or understanding was the *sine qua non* of the successful operation of the Canadian political system. It is a principle which has lasted to the present day. Not only did Lord Elgin recall Baldwin and LaFontaine to his ministry, he also set the seal of approval upon the bi-national character of the regime by obtaining from the British authorities the abrogation of Article XLI of the Act of Union declaring English to be the one language of official record. And then, at the opening of the legislative session in January 1849, he read the speech from the throne both in French and in English. [19]

The Union did not, however, enjoy a long or peaceful life. Fundamentally the explanation for its early demise is to be found in the internal contradiction upon which it was based, for it was neither frankly federal nor unequivocally unitary. The union, indeed, managed to survive its twenty-five harried years only by applying the principles of disunion.

[17] K. N. Bell and W. P. Morrell, *Select Documents on British Colonial Policy, 1830-1860* (Oxford, 1928), pp. 62-71: Bagot to Stanley, Sep. 26, 1842.
[18] *Parliamentary Debates on the Subject of the Confederation of the British North American Provinces* (Quebec, 1865), p. 30.
[19] Kennedy, *The Constitution of Canada*, p. 257.

The heavy hammer blows which finally brought about its end were those wielded by the French-baiting, Catholic-hating Clear Grits of Canada West and their francophobe journalist leader, George Brown. *No Popery* and *No French Domination* were the constant Grit refrain; to which was added, once Canada West had passed the neighbouring province in population, the more positive and more politically dangerous slogan, *Rep. by Pop*. Representation by population was a denial of the political understanding upon which LaFontaine and Canada East had agreed to collaborate with Baldwin and Canada West in the administration of the United Province. It meant the end of the principle of equality, the collapse of the federal concept, the exposure of Lower Canada to the rule of a hostile, alien majority, the overthrow of the entente which had alone made government possible. As the new slogan gained adherents so too did the idea that the premise upon which Anglo-French collaboration was based, namely the mutual acceptance of equality of status, was a vital and fundamental principle of the constitution; that it constituted, if not an unbreakable pact, at least a gentleman's agreement between the two racial groups which went to make up the population. In 1849 LaFontaine had replied to Papineau:

> It is on the basis of the principle of looking upon the Act of Union as a confederation of two provinces... that I hereby emphatically declare that never I will consent to one of the sections of the Province having, in this House, a greater number of members than the other, whatever the numbers of its population may be. [20]

Hincks, Cartier and Macdonald all spoke in a similar vein. In April 1861, during one of the periodic debates on representation by population, Macdonald uttered what may possibly be the first statement in English of what we today speak of as the Compact theory of Confederation, when he said "The Union was a distinct bargain, a solemn contract". [21] This was no slip of the tongue. In 1865, during the Confederation debates, he again referred to "The Treaty of Union" between Lower and Upper Canadians. [22]

III

There is no need for me to discuss the various factors leading to Confederation — the threat of American imperialism, the fear of the westward expansion of the United States, the necessity for improved railway communications, the political impasse in Canada; all of this is familiar

---

[20] Quoted in Groulx, *Histoire du Canada français*, IV, p. 21.
[21] *The Leader*, Toronto, April 30, 1861. *La Minerve* (April 25, 1861) praised Macdonald for his stand against *Rep* by *Pop*: "Soyons francs! est-ce qu'il ne faut pas un grand courage, une grande force d'âme et beaucoup d'honnêteté pour agir ainsi? Mettez donc cette conduite ferme et sincère en parallèle avec la lâche conduite d'un de ses adversaires, et dites où est l'homme d'état, où est l'allié naturel des Bas Canadiens?"
[22] *Confederation Debates*, p. 28.

ground to generations of Canadian students. Nor is it necessary for me to chronicle the erratic course of the ambulatory conference of 1864 or to follow its members, bottle by bottle, as they travelled through the Maritimes and Canada, dispensing good will and self-congratulatory speeches to all who were prepared to listen to them. However, I do wish to direct your attention, for a moment, to the fundamental problem which faced the delegates who met at Charlottetown and at Quebec, that of reconciling the conflicting interests of the two racial groups and of the conflicting principles of centralization and provincial autonomy. Broadly speaking — and there are, of course, exceptions to this general statement — the English-speaking representatives, pragmatists, suspicious of ideas and generalizations, preoccupied with economic and political interests and secure in their every increasing majority over the French Canadians, were disposed to favour a strong central government, if not actually a legislative union; the French Canadians, empiricists, uneasy, apprehensive, and deeply concerned with the survival of their culture, were by religion and by history in favour of a constitution which would, at the very least, secure them such guarantees as they had already extracted from the British government during the hundred years which had gone before. No French Canadian, intent upon preserving his national identity or bettering his political future could ever agree to a legislative union. Only federalism would permit the two, distinct, and separate, cultures to co-exist side by side within the bosom of a single state. Federalism, not a half-way, hesitant, ill-defined, semi-unitary federalism like that which had evolved out of the Act of Union, but an honest, whole-hearted, clearly-stated, precise federalism was the only solution acceptable to the French Canadian leaders. Thus, the one group was, at heart, for unity and fusion; the other for diversity and co-operation; the one was dominated by economic fact and the other, philosophical principle.

The fundamental opposition of these two divergent points of view does not, unfortunately, appear in the documentary fragments of the conferences which we possess; it does, however, emerge clearly in a letter written by Sir Arthur Gordon, Lieutenant-Governor of New Brunswick, following his visit to Charlottetown and his conversations with Cartier, Brown and Galt. In a lengthy despatch to the Colonial Office outlining the details of the union scheme as the Canadians had put it up to the Maritimers, Gordon wrote:

> With regard to the important question of the attributes to be assigned to the respective Legislatures and Governments, there was a very great divergence of opinion. The aim of Lower Canada is a local independence as complete as circumstances will permit, and the peculiarities of race, religion and habits which distinguish its people render their desire respectable and natural. [23]

[23] Public Archives of Canada, New Brunswick, C.O. 189, vol. 9: Gordon to Cardwell, confidential, Sep. 22, 1864. This letter is reproduced, in part, in W. F. O'Connor, *Report pursuant to Resolution of the Senate to the Honourable the Speaker*

It was at Quebec that the new constitution took form and shape. To the old capital of New France came delegates from the six provinces, the four seaboard provinces of Nova Scotia, Newfoundland, Prince Edward Island and New Brunswick, and the two provinces of Canada, which, if they did not have a juridical basis, had, at least, as I have pointed out, a factual foundation. This gathering at Quebec was the first and only constituent body in the whole of our constitutional history. All previous constitutions had been drafted, considered, and passed, by an outside authority; in 1864 the thirty-three representatives of the British North American provinces met, with the blessing and approval of the British Government, to do what had hitherto always been done for them.

The constitution which they adopted in the form of seventy-two Resolutions had already been prepared in draft form before the Canadian delegates had ever disembarked at Charlottetown. In many respects it bore a striking resemblance to an outline plan which had appeared over the name of Joseph Charles Taché in *Le Courrier du Canada* in 1857, and which had been published as a book in the following year.[24] In summary form, what the Quebec Conference decided was that the new union should be federal in character; that its central parliament should comprise two houses, the upper based on representation by provinces, and the lower upon representation by population; that the powers of the central government should be of a general character and those of the provincial legislatures of a local nature. These powers were carefully enumerated, but the legislative residuum was given to the central parliament. The French and English languages were to enjoy equal status in the central parliament and courts and in the legislature and courts of the province of Lower Canada.

Georges Cartier, generally, was satisfied with what had been achieved. He felt that even though he had been obliged to yield much to the demands of Macdonald and Brown and other advocates of a strong central government, he had, nevertheless, succeeded in preserving the rights and privileges of his own people and of the province in which they lived.[25] He

by the Parliamentary Counsel (Ottawa, 1939), Annex 2, pp. 84-6. Large sections of the original letter were, however, omitted in the printed version. The quotation given here is one of the omitted portions.
[24] J. G. Taché, *Des provinces de l'Amérique du Nord et d'une union fédérale* (Québec, 1858).
[25] "Objection had been taken to the scheme now under consideration, because of the words, 'new nationality'. Now, when we were united together, if union were attained, we would form a political nationality with which neither the national origin, nor the religion of any individual would interfere. It was lamented by some that we had this diversity of races, and hopes were expressed that this distinctive feature would cease. The idea of unity of races was utopian — it was impossible.... We could not do away with the distinctions of race. We could not legislate for the disappearance of the French Canadians from American soil, but British and French Canadians alike could appreciate and understand their position relative to each other". (Cartier, Feb. 7, 1865, *Confederation Debates*, p. 60). Subsequently, in answer to the criticisms of A. A. Dorion, Cartier said, "I have always had the

ACT OR PACT, ANOTHER LOOK AT CONFEDERATION 105

had, moreover, succeeded in maintaining the fundamental principle of the entente between the two racial groups in Canada, equality of race, equality of religion, equality of language, equality of laws. Even George Brown, the old francophobe, had gone as far as to admit to the Canadian legislature "whether we ask for parliamentary reform for Canada alone, or in union with the Maritime Provinces, the French Canadians must have their views consulted as well as us (*sic*). This scheme can be carried and no scheme can be that has not the support of both sections of the province." [26] The new constitution might not be designed to be the most efficient, but it would, at least, be just.

The next step was as easy as it was logical. Since both races were equal, a decision taken, an agreement arrived at by the equal partners on the fundamental character of the new constitution, could not be changed without the consent of each. It was, in fact a treaty, a compact binding upon both parties. This was a view which scarcely roused a dissenting voice in the Canada of 1865. Not one of the Canadians who fathered the resolutions at Quebec failed to stress the unalterable character of the agreement they had made. Macdonald said, "these resolutions were in the nature of a treaty, and if not adopted in their entirety, the proceedings would have to be commenced *de novo*". [27] McGee, in his high-pitched but not unmusical voice, cried:

> And that there may be no doubt about our position in regard to that document, we say, question it you may, reject it you may, or accept it you may, but alter it you may not. (Hear, hear.) It is beyond your power, or our power, to alter it. There is not a sentence — ay, or even a word — you can alter without desiring to throw out the document.... On this point, I repeat after all my hon. friends who have already spoken, for one party to alter a treaty is, of course, to destroy it. [28]

Taché, Cartier, McDougall, Brown, all of them described the Quebec Resolutions as a "treaty" or as a "pact", and argued for adoption without amendment. [29]

---

interests of Lower Canada at heart and have guarded them more seduously than the hon. member for Hochelaga and his partisans have ever done". (*Confederation Debates*, p. 714). Hector Langevin, the Solicitor-General, took the same view He said, "We are considering the establishment of a Confederacy — with a Central Parliament and local parliaments. The Central or Federal Parliament will have the control of all measures of a general character..., but all matters of local interest, all that relates to the affairs and rights of the different sections of the Confederacy, will be reserved for the control of the local parliaments.... It will be the duty of the Central Government to see that the country prospers, but it will not be its duty to attack our religion, our institutions, or our nationality, which... will be amply protected". (*Confederation Debates*, pp. 367-8. See also pp. 373, 392.)

[26] *Confederation Debates*, p. 87.
[27] *Ibid.*, p. 16. Macdonald repeated this idea several times throughout his speech; see pp. 31-2.
[28] *Ibid.*, p. 136.
[29] *Ibid.*, pp. 83, 88, 714, 720. See also Chapter II in Sir George Ross, *The Senate of Canada, its Constitution Powers and Duties Historically Considered* (Toronto 1914).

It is easy for the lawyer or the political scientist, three generations later, to reply that in 1865 there was no treaty really made at all, that the Compromise of Quebec could not possess the attributes of a treaty or of a legal contract. Nevertheless the historical fact remains that the men who used these terms were the men who drafted the Resolutions; they chose their words with deliberation; many of them were lawyers, they knew what they were saying. They were not, every one of them, trying to becloud the issue before the legislature or to confuse the legislators. I have found no evidence which would lead me to question their sincerity or to believe that they disbelieved their own assertions. In strict law it is probably true that the terms they used to describe the Quebec Resolutions were not all that could be desired in the way of legalistic exactitude; but to my mind these terms adequately expressed the ideas which the Fathers of the Confederate Resolutions wished to convey to their listeners and to posterity, for they spoke to both. The idea of a compact between races was not a new one in 1865; it had already become a vital thing in our history. It influenced both the political thinking and the political vocabulary of the day; and it was already on the way to become a tradition and a convention of our constitution.

The idea of a compact as I have outlined it was essentially, in its origin, a racial concept. But the meeting of the maritime delegates with those of Canada at Charlottetown and at Quebec introduced a new interpretation which has had mighty impact upon the course of our later history, namely, the idea of a compact between the politico-geographic areas which go to make up Canada. Even before the conferences it had become the common practice to identify the racial groups with the areas from which they came. When thinking of French Canadians or of Anglo-Canadians, it was all too simple to speak of them in geographical terms, as Lower Canada and Upper Canada. It was a confusion of mind and speech of which we in our own day and generation are all too frequently guilty. Almost without thought "Quebec" and "French Canadians", or "Ontario" and "Anglo-Canadians", become synonymous terms in the mouths of Canadians of both tongues. It is, of course a slipshod way of thinking as well as of speaking, for there are French Canadians in Ontario and English Canadians in Quebec; and in many ways it has been unfortunate, for it has limited to Quebec language rights which might, under happier circumstances, have been accorded French Canadians in other parts of the country. That English did not suffer the same fate in Quebec as did the French tongue in other provinces, was due in part to the effective role of English-speaking Quebeckers, like McGee and Galt, in the drafting of the federative act, as well as to a greater appreciation on the part of French Canadians of the need for toleration. However, the point which I really wish to make is this; once Canadians (as distinct from Maritimers) began to identify provinces with specific linguistic groups, the idea of a pact between races was transformed into the idea of a pact between provinces. And the Compromise of Quebec became a compact between the provinces which participated in the conference. I have no need to labour this point. It emerges in all clarity from a careful reading of the speeches to be found in the Confederation Debates of 1865.

However, the compact idea, was still, in 1865, peculiarly a Canadian one. It was not shared by the delegates of the several Maritime colonies who had journeyed to Quebec. From what I have seen of the debates in the legislatures and the speeches reported in the press of Nova Scotia and New Brunswick, the words so familiar in Canada, words like "pact", "treaty" or "compact" were rarely used in reference to what had been decided upon at Charlottetown or Quebec. There was never any idea in the minds of the Maritime representatives that the Seventy-Two Resolutions were sacrosanct. Thus, when Nova Scotia and New Brunswick resolved in 1866 to renew the negotiations for a federal union with Canada, they sent their representatives to London with full authority to make any changes and to conclude any new arrangement they might see fit. In the case of Nova Scotia, Sir Charles Tupper, an ardent exponent of federation on the basis of the Quebec Scheme, accepted without comment a proposal that the Quebec Resolutions should be abandoned and a new confederate agreement drawn up in conjunction with the other provinces concerned.[30] This distinction between the Canadian and Maritime approaches to the Quebec Resolutions was brought out when the Canadian and Maritime representatives met in conference in London in December 1866. Macdonald, Galt and McDougall, all agreed that the Canadians, at least, were bound to adhere to the details of the Quebec scheme. Jonathan McCully and J. W. Ritchie of Nova Scotia took the view that, as far as they as Nova Scotians were concerned, they were bound by nothing. Said John A. Macdonald in reply, "The Maritime delegates are differently situated from us. Our Legislature passed an address to the Queen praying for an Act of Union, on the basis of the Quebec Resolutions. We replied to enquiries in our last Session of Parliament that we did not feel at liberty ourselves to vary those resolutions".[31] W. P. Howland, another Canadian delegate, added, "We place ourselves in a false position in every departure from the Quebec scheme".[32]

In the end, the terms of the agreement drafted and adopted at the Westminster Palace Hotel in London in December 1866, were substantially those which had previously been discussed and accepted at Quebec. A great deal has, I know, been made of the London Resolutions as a new departure and as an effective denial of the idea of a binding pact having

---

[30] *Nova Scotia Parliamentary Debates, 1866. 3rd Session. 23rd Assembly.* See debate April 3, 1866. Quotations from these debates will be found in O'Connor, *Report,* Annex 2, pp. 67-71.
[31] Joseph Pope, *Confederation: being a series of hitherto unpublished documents bearing on the British North America Act* (Toronto, 1895), p. 121.
[32] *Ibid.,* p. 122.

been concluded at Quebec; but a detailed comparison of the two sets of resolutions reveals no really substantial points of difference. The outline is similar; the wording in many instances is unchanged. Such alterations as were made, appear to have been either of a minor nature intended to clarify an ambiguity or inserted to strengthen, rather than to weaken the bi-racial, bi-cultural aspect of the pact. Certainly the people of the day who were most concerned viewed the revised resolutions after this fashion. On January 5th, 1867 the editor of *The Morning Freeman* of St. John, N.B., wrote, "If the Quebec Scheme has been modified in any important particulars they are profoundly ignorant of what the modifications are". [33] Two months later he wrote again while the British North America Bill was before Parliament:

> We ask any reasonable, intelligent man of any party to take up that Bill, compare it with the original Quebec Scheme, and discover, if he can, anything that could possibly have occupied honest, earnest men, for even a week, no matter what the particular objections to the few changes that have been made.... Could not all these matters have been settled as well and as much to the satisfaction of the public by letter, at an expense of a few shillings postage... as by this large and most costly delegation? [34]

The London Resolutions of 1866 were, in a word, little if anything more than an edited version of the Quebec Resolutions of 1864; the contractual nature of the pact remained unaffected.

The British seemed to like the idea of a provincial compact. Both the Colonial Secretary, Lord Carnarvon and his undersecretary, the Honourable Charles Adderley, accepted it as an accurate description of what was intended and what was achieved. Mr. Adderley, who introduced the Bill based on the resolutions into the British House of Commons, urged upon the members, in words which might have come straight from the mouth of Macdonald or Cartier, that no change or alteration should be made in the terms of the Bill:

> The House may ask what occasion there can be for our interfering in a question of this description. It will, however, I think, be manifest, upon reflection, that, as the arrangement is a matter of mutual concession on the part of the Provinces, there must be some external authority to give sanction to the compact into which they have entered.... If, again, federation has in this case specially been a matter of most delicate mutual treaty and compact between the provinces — if it has been a matter of mutual concession and compromise — it is clearly necessary that there should be a third party *ab extra* to give sanction to the treaty made between them. Such seems to me to be the office we have to perform in regard to this Bill. [35]

Lord Carnarvon, in the House of Lords, said:

> the Quebec Resolutions, with some slight changes, form the basis of a measure that I have now the honour to submit to Parliament. To those resolutions

---

[33] *The Morning Freeman*, Saint John, N.B., Jan. 5, 1867.
[34] *Ibid.*, March 7, 1867.
[35] Quoted in O'Connor, *Report*, Annex 4, p. 149.

all the British Provinces in North America were, as I have said, consenting parties, and the measure founded upon them must be accepted as a treaty of union.[36]

Later in the same speech Carnarvon, after pointing out that a legislative union was "impracticable", because of Lower Canada's jealousy and pride in "her ancestral customs and traditions" and her willingness to enter Confederation "only upon the distinct understanding that she retains them", stated emphatically that the terms of the British North America Bill were "of the nature of a treaty of union, every single clause in which had been debated over and over again, and had been submitted to the closest scrutiny, and, in fact each of them represented a compromise between the different interests involved". "There might be alterations where they are not material", he continued, "and do not go to the essence of the measure.... But it will be my duty to resist the alteration of anything which is in the nature of a compromise between the Provinces, as an amendment of that nature, if carried, would be fatal to the measure." [37]

The legalist will, of course, reply that the intervention of the Colonial Office and the passing of the Bill as an Act of the British Parliament in effect destroyed the compactual — I prefer to avoid the word "contractual" with its juridical connotation — basis of the historical process of confederation. Perhaps it does; to the lawyer. But to the historian the simple fact remains that the officers of the Colonial Office accepted without question the assessment of the situation given them by the colonial delegates. To them the Bill was in the nature of a colonial treaty, even if such a treaty were not to be found in the classifications usually given in the text books of international law. In consequence they were prepared to leave the colonial delegates alone, to let them make their own arrangements, thresh out their own differences, draft their own agreement. Neither Lord Carnarvon nor the members of his office entered the negotiations or took part in them until the Quebec Resolutions had undergone the revision or editing to which I have referred. When they did, it was at the specific request of the delegates, with the object of acting in an advisory capacity only. Perhaps the British role is best expressed in the suggestion that the Colonial Secretary acted in the capacity of a notary reducing to proper legal terms an understanding already arrived at by the parties concerned. That certainly was the role in which Carnarvon saw himself. The British North America Act was, therefore, not the work of the British authorities, nor the expression of ideas of the British Colonial Office; it was, in essence, simply the recognition in law of the agreement arrived at originally in Quebec and clarified later in London, by the representatives of the provinces of Nova Scotia,

---

[36] Sir R. Herbert, *Speeches on Canadian Affairs by Henry Howard Molyneux, fourth Earl of Carnarvon* (London, 1902) p. 92.
[37] *Ibid.*, pp. 110, 130.

New Brunswick, and Canada with its two divisions, Canada East and Canada West.

The British North America Act passed through its necessary readings in the House of Commons and in the House of Lords without change or alteration; on March 28, 1867, it received the Royal Assent. By royal proclamation it came into effect on the first day of July following. The new constitution was, without question, a statute of the British Parliament, and as such possessed the attributes of an ordinary statute. But it was a statute distinctly unlike any other previously passed by the Parliament at Westminster. The Quebec Act of 1774, the Constitutional Act of 1791, the Act of Union of 1840, all of them had been devised, drafted, and enacted, without reference to the people of the provinces concerned. Individuals and groups of individuals had been consulted, it is true; but the work was done and the responsibility was taken by the Imperial authorities. The British North America Act, however, was, to all intents and purposes, the work of the several self-governing, quasi-sovereign colonies themselves. The Colonial Office did no more than put the words into proper form and the British Parliament no more than give them legislative sanction. The British North America Act was, therefore, to use the words of an early Canadian jurist, "a simple ratification by the Mother Country of the agreement entered into by the provinces, which in confirming its provisions rendered them obligatory by giving them the authority of an Imperial Act". [38]

IV

But the legal supplementing of the interprovincial pact, both by the Canadian and British governments, did not mean that the problems of the coexistence of the two contending races within the bosom of a single state had been solved. Agreement there could be on broad lines of how to divide authority between the central and provincial governments, but disagreement on the details of the division was inherent in the very nature of a federal constitution, and particularly in Canada where federal union in the mouth of a Lower Canadian usually meant "the independence of his Province from English and Protestant influences" [39] and in that of

---

[38] Hon. Justice T. J. J. Loranger, *Letters upon the Interpretation of the Federal Constitution known as the British North America Act 1867* (Quebec, 1884) p. 63.

[39] O'Connor, *Report*, Annex 2, p. 83: Gordon to Cardwell, Sep. 12, 1864. After visiting Charlottetown during the meeting of the provincial delegates and receiving daily reports from the New Brunswick delegation, Lieutenant-Governor Gordon wrote to the Colonial Secretary:
    A "Federal Union" in the mouth of a Lower Canadian usually means the independence of his Province from English and Protestant influences. In the mouth of an inhabitant of the Maritime Provinces it means the retention of the machinery of the existing local Executive Government, the expenditure within each Province of the revenue raised from it, except a quota to be paid towards Federal expenses, and the preservation of the existing Legislatures in their integrity, with the somewhat cumbrous addition of a central Parliament

ACT OR PACT, ANOTHER LOOK AT CONFEDERATION   111

the Upper Canadian, a preference for a strong central government.[40] Ministers and Prime Ministers might pay lip service to the doctrine of a Pact;[41] they might honestly believe in its validity; they could shelve but could not shed their centralizing proclivities. There was never any underhand conspiracy to destroy the Anglo-French entente: but there was an open-handed effort to add to the powers of the central government at the expense of those of the provinces. I need only mention the names of Macdonald, Mowat and Mercier to recall to mind the early trials of strength of the two opposing points of view. Fortunately the arbiter was there, the courts: the controversies which opposing points of view engendered were resolvable by due process of law. The powers of the federal parliament and those of the provincial legislatures had, in 1867, been carefully tabulated. All that was necessary was to apply the tabulation to each specific dispute.

Although Canadian judges were at first disposed to take the view that the British North America Act was something more than a simple British statute,[42] the judges of the Privy Council preferred to base their judgments upon the principle that the courts should always "treat the provisions of the Act ... by the same methods of construction and exposition which they apply to other statutes".[43] These rules or methods are well known: the meaning of a statute is primarily to be gathered from the words of the statute itself, and not from what the legislature may be supposed to have intended;[44] if the words of a statute are ambiguous, recourse must be had to the context and scheme of the Act;[45] if there are seemingly conflicting provisions in a statute, the conflicting provisions must be read together and, if possible, a reasonable reconciliation effected:[46] and, the "parliamentary history" of a statute may not be referred to for the purpose of explaining its meaning, although "historical knowledge" of the circumstances surrounding the passing thereof may, on occasions, be used as an aid in construing the statute.[47] This one con-

to which the consideration of some few topics of general interest is to be confided under restraints prompted by a jealous care for the maintenance of Provincial independence.
[40] *Confederation Debates*, p. 29.
[41] See, for instance, statements by Sir Wilfrid Laurier (*House of Commons Debates, Canada*, Jan. 28, 1907, p. 2199); Robert Borden (*Ibid.*, Jan. 28, 1907, p. 2199); Ernest Lapointe (*Ibid.*, Feb. 18, 1925, pp. 297-300); Arthur Meighen (*Ibid.*, Feb. 19, 1925, p. 335) and Richard B. Bennett (*Ibid.*, Feb. 24, 1930, p. 24).
[42] See Strong J. in *St. Catharines Milling and Lumber Co. v. The Queen* (1887), 13, S.C.R. p. 606. For a criticism of this point of view see W. H. P. Clement, *The Law of the Canadian Constitution* (Toronto, 1916), p. 364; and V. C. Macdonald "Constitutional Interpretation and Extrinsic Evidence" (*The Canadian Bar Review*, Feb. 1939, XVII, 2).
[43] *Bank of Toronto v. Lambe* (1887), 12 App. Cas., p. 579.
[44] *Brophy v. Attorney-General for Manitoba* (1895), A.C., p. 216.
[45] *Attorney-General for Ontario v. Attorney-General for Canada* (1912), A.C., p. 583.
[46] *Citizens Insurance Company of Canada, v. Parsons* (1881), 7 App. Cas., p. 109.
[47] *Edwards v. Attorney-General for Canada* (1930) A.C., p. 134.

cession to the historical approach did not, however, mean very much. Rarely, if ever, did references to the Quebec and London Resolutions ever have a controlling or determining effect upon the decisions handed down by the Judicial Committee of the Privy Council. Judges and lawyers are bound by precedent and rule; they cannot shake off the shackles of a rigid legalism to enjoy the freedom of historical speculation.

The remarkable thing is that the courts have, nevertheless, rarely misunderstood the meaning of the union. This is, indeed, a tribute to the skill with which the Resolutions of 1866 were transformed into legal parlance by the lawyers of the Colonial Office. And perhaps it is just as well that the lawyers have not been prepared to take readily to the historian's approach; for nothing could be more frustrating to the legal mind than the effort to determine the "intentions" of the Fathers of Confederation. Including, as they did, some Fathers favouring a unitary state and others aiming at a wide degree of provincial autonomy, to try to determine the common denominator of their joint intentions from their speeches and their public statements before and after 1867 would produce only a series of irreconcilable contradictions.[48] The one sure guide as to what the Fathers really agreed to agree upon, was the language of their resolutions, or better still, the language of the British North America Act itself. And in construing this Act in the way they have, the judges probably arrived at a more accurate interpretation than have the multitude of critics who have so emphatically disagreed with them.

There have been many and severe critics of the judgments laid down by the courts. Within the last twenty years in particular it has been the common sport of constitutional lawyers in Canada to criticize, cavil and poke fun at the *dicta* of the judges of the Privy Council and their decisions in Canadian cases. Canadian historians and political scientists have followed the legal party line with condemnations of "the judicial revolution" said to have been accomplished by Lord Watson and Lord Haldane, and the alleged willful nullification of the true intentions of the Fathers of Confederation.[49] The explanation of these attacks on the part of lawyers, professional and lay, court and class-room alike, may

---

[48] See, for instance, the conflicting points of view of Sir John A. Macdonald and Sir Oliver Mowat after Confederation, although both of them had been delegates to the Quebec Conference. It is equally difficult to reconcile some of the statements of men like Galt and Macdonald, who hoped that federal union might develop into a legislative union, and those of Cartier and Langevin who upheld provincial rights, all of whom were "Fathers of Confederation."
[49] The most complete criticism from a legal standpoint is to be found in O'Connor, *Report*. See also N. M. Rogers, "The Compact Theory of Confederation", (*Proceedings of the Canadian Political Science Association*, 1931), pp. 205-30; F. R. Scott, *Canada Today, a Study of her National Interests and National Policy* (Toronto, 1938) pp. 75-8; A. R. M. Lower, *Colony to Nation, a History of Canada* (Toronto, 1946) pp. 328-9. For views contrary to those of O'Connor, see V. E. Gray "The O'Connor Report on the British North America Act, 1867" (*The Canadian Bar Review*, May, 1939, XVII, 5, pp. 309-337).

be found in the impact of the Great Depression of the 1930's upon the economy of the country and the inability of governments, provincial and federal, to deal with it. It is natural for the human mind to seek simple solutions and to find scapegoats for their ills.[50] If, by the simple process of an Act of Parliament, full employment can be secured and that Act of Parliament is unconstitutional, then change the constitution and the problem is solved. No provincial jurisdiction, no acknowledged right or privilege, no historic pact should be allowed to stand in the way of such an easy solution for the economic problems of the day. Facts, not principles should be the decisive determinants of history. Unfortunately, however, neither the causes nor the solution of the Great Depression were as simple as all that. The economic crisis of the 1930's was the result of a multiplicity of factors, external as well as internal, and a change in the interpretation of the British North America Act or in the Act itself would have given rise to as many new problems as it might have solved of the old. In any event, it is no part of the task of the judges to try to make the constitution fit the constantly changing facts of economic and political history.

Here is the criticism in its simplest terms. Proceeding from the basic premise that the fundamental intentions of the Fathers of Confederation were to limit strictly the powers of the provincial legislatures and give the central government a real, effective, and dominating position in the federal scheme, the critics of the courts contend that the tabulated or enumerated powers given to the federal parliament by Section 91 are, in fact, not specially allocated powers, but rather illustrations of an overriding general jurisdiction embodied in the well-known words "And it shall be lawful for the Queen, by and with the Advice and Consent of the Senate and the House of Commons, to make Laws for the Peace, Order and Good Government of Canada...."[51] They argue that the enumerated powers which follow later in the wording of the same section are not in addition to this general power, but flow from it and are examples of it. The critics take the view that the courts, by attaching a "primacy" to the enumerated powers, have altered the balance of Sections 91 and 92, and have, in consequence, distorted the aims and objects of the founding fathers and given greater authority to the provincial legislators than it was ever intended that they should have. The cumulative effect of judicial decisions over the years has been to establish a union in which the sovereign provincial legislatures, in effect, possess a field of jurisdiction so great, and the federal parliament a field so restricted, as to alter the whole purpose of the original federative Act.

It is not for me, at this point, to discuss the syntax of the controversial sections of the British North America Act. As I said at the begin-

---

[50] L. Richer, *Notre Problème Politique* (Montreal, n.d.), pp. 20-1.
[51] O'Connor, *Report*, Annex 1, pp. 18-51.

ning, my approach is, of necessity, historical. And, the pre-parliamentary history of the Act appears to me to confirm the interpretation of the criticized rather than that of the critics. From the date of the publication of the first practical scheme of confederation, framers of federal constitutions in Canada have followed the procedure, not of enumerating only the subject matters upon which one party to the federation may legislate and giving all the rest (the residuum of powers) to the other, but rather of tabulating or enumerating the legislative powers of *both* parties. The scheme advanced by Joseph Charles Taché in 1857, upon which the later Canadian scheme is sometimes said to have been based, followed this course. Taché allocated to the federal parliament "Commerce, including laws of a purely commercial nature, such as laws relating to banks and other financial institutions, of a general character; moneys, weights and measures; customs duties, including the establishment of a uniform tariff and the collection of the revenues which it produces; large public works and navigation, such as canals, railways, telegraph lines, harbour works, coastal lighthouses; postal service as a whole both inside and outside the country; the organization of the militia as a whole; criminal justice including all offences beyond the level of the jurisdiction of police magistrates and justices of the peace". All the rest "dealing with civil laws, education, public welfare, the establishment of public lands, agriculture, police, urban and rural, highways, in fact everything relating to family life in each province, would remain under the exclusive control of the respective government of each province as an inherent right". [52] The draft scheme of 1864, presented by the Canadians to the Maritime delegates at Charlottetown, likewise included a series of enumerated powers to be allocated to the federal and provincial legislatures. According to this scheme the "Federal Legislature" was to be given "the control of — Trade, Currency, Banking, General Taxation, Interest and Usury Laws, Insolvency and Bankruptcy, Weights and Measures, Navigation of Rivers and Lakes, Lighthouses, Sea Fisheries. Patent and Copyright Laws, Telegraphs, Naturalization, Marriage and Divorce, Postal Service, Militia and Defence, Criminal Law, Intercolonial Works". The local legislatures were "to be entrusted with the care of — Education (with the exception of Universities), Inland Fisheries, Control of Public Lands, Immigration, Mines and Minerals, Prisons, Hospitals and Charities, Agriculture, Roads and Bridges, Registration of Titles, Municipal Laws". [53]

When the delegates finally convened at Quebec to settle the details of the federation which they had agreed upon at Charlottetown, these lists of items, were thoroughly discussed between the 21st and 25th of October. The simplest method of proceeding would have been, once it had been decided to concede the residuum of powers to the federal parlia-

---

[52] J. C. Taché, *op. cit.*, p. 148.
[53] Gordon to Cardwell, confidential, Sep. 22, 1864, (*cf. supra*, note 23).

ment, to define only those powers which would belong exclusively to the provinces. This course was, in fact, suggested. "Enumerate for Local Governments their powers, and give all the rest to General Government, but do not enumerate both", said J. M. Johnston of New Brunswick; William Henry of Nova Scotia echoed this view, "We should not define powers of General Legislature. I would ask Lower Canada not to fight for a shadow. Give a clause to give general powers (except such as given to Local Legislatures) to Federal Legislature. Anything beyond that is hampering the case with difficulties".[54] But the Conference did not agree. From Henry's remark we may infer that Cartier and his colleagues were determined to follow the plan of specifying in detail the powers of *both* the federal parliament and the provincial legislatures. Accordingly, sections 29 and 43 of the Quebec Resolutions contained an enumeration of the powers of each party to the federation. Section 29 read: "The General Parliament shall have power to make laws for the peace, welfare and good government of the Federated Provinces (saving the sovereignty of England), and especially laws respecting the following subjects", and then listed thirty-seven specific matters upon which the federal parliament would be free to legislate. Section 43 outlined eighteen matters over which the provinces would have exclusive jurisdiction, ending with what may be regarded as a provincial residuum of powers: "generally all matters of a private or local nature, not assigned to the General Parliament".[55] From the evidence afforded by Joseph Pope, it would appear that the delegates at no time seriously attempted to define the scope of the enumerated items or their possible overlapping, beyond George Brown's suggestion that "the courts of each Province should decide what is Local and what General Government jurisdiction, with appeal to the Appeal or Superior Court".[56] The same procedure was followed at London. Sections 28 and 41 of the London Resolutions are almost identical (with one or two small exceptions) with their counterparts in the resolutions of Quebec.

The evolution of these two sets of resolutions through the various drafts of the British North America Bill supports the view that the Fathers intended that primacy should attend the enumerated heads. Section 36 of the first "Rough Draft" of the Bill prepared by the Canadian and Maritime delegates themselves, read simply that "The Parliament shall have power to make laws respecting the following subjects" and then listed thirty-seven, one of which was the power to pass laws for "the peace, welfare and good government of the Confederation respecting all matters of a general character, not specially and exclusively herein reserved for

[54] Pope, *Confederation Documents*, p. 87.
[55] Copies of the Quebec and London Resolutions will be found in Pope, *Confederation Documents*, pp. 38-52, 98-110; in O'Connor, *Report*, Annex 4, pp. 49-66, and in *British North America Act and Amendments 1867-1948*, (Ottawa, 1948), pp. 39-58.
[56] Pope, *Confederation Documents*, p. 85.

the Legislatures [of the provinces]". [57] This was altered in the draft prepared by the Imperial Government's draftsman and dated January 23, 1867, which adopted a wording which, with only insignificant changes, was to be that of section 91 of the British North America Act. [58] Thus, only in the final stages, after the Imperial authorities had been invited to put the bill into final shape, were the introductory words of Section 91, as we know them, interpolated, apparently for the purpose of lessening the possibility of overlapping jurisdiction. The colonial delegates had believed the enumerated powers to be mutually exclusive; only agriculture and immigration, which had been included among the powers assigned to both federal and provincial legislatures, seemed to provide any real problems, and these were to be obviated by giving federal legislation in respect to these matters precedence over that of the provinces. While there is no documentary evidence directly bearing on this point, it seems more than likely that the British draftsman pointed out the possibility of further overlapping and therefore revised the first draft of the Bill in such a way as to ensure, syntactically, the unquestioned paramountcy of the enumerated federal powers, upon which the delegates, ever since 1864, had placed so much emphasis.

That some of these conclusions may appear to be based upon circumstantial historical evidence is a valid criticism; but historians, no more than lawyers, are not to be debarred from using circumstantial evidence. The majority of the problems of historical synthesis are really problems of probability.

V

But to return to the question of the Confederative pact. Despite the frequency with which Canadian political leaders have reiterated the existence of the pact, despite the legal support afforded the concept of the pact by the highest court of appeal — as late as the 1930's, the Privy Council referred to the British North America Act as a "contract", a "compact" and a "treaty" founded on the Quebec and London Resolutions [59] — the pact concept was never universally understood or wholly accepted by each and all of the provinces of Canada. Indeed the popularity of the pact idea seems to vary in some provinces in inverse ratio to their fiscal need. The concept of the pact was slow to be accepted in the Maritimes. In the early years after Confederation, there was still strong opposition to the very fact of union, and the pact upon which it was based was never very popular. In 1869 the Saint John *Morning Freeman* criticized the idea of a pact of confederation, denying that there

[57] *Ibid.*, pp. 130-2.
[58] *Ibid.*, pp. 152-4.
[59] *Attorney-General for Australia v. Colonial Sugar Co.* (1914) A.C., p. 253; *In re the Regulation and Control of Aeronautics in Canada* (1932) A.C., p. 70; *Attorney-General for Canada v. Attorney-General for Ontario and others* (1937) A.C., p. 351.

was any continuity between the pre- and post-confederation provinces.[60] From time to time, various provinces have supported the doctrine of the pact, including New Brunswick, Alberta and British Columbia; but their support has not been marked by unanimity or consistency. Only in Ontario and Quebec has the concept remained undiminished in strength and popularity, at least in political circles, if not always in legal and academic. The Ontario-Quebec axis has transcended both time and political parties. The original alliance of Mowat and Mercier, has carried on through that of Whitney and Gouin, Ferguson and Taschereau, and Drew and Duplessis. It has always been the principal buttress of provincial autonomy.

The explanation why the pact idea has remained most vigorous in the two central provinces is to be found in their history. We need only recall the point I have established earlier this evening, the fact that the pact was, in its origin, an entente between the two racial groups of Old Canada, between the two provinces which were each the focus of a distinctive culture. Only in the two provinces of Old Canada did the racial struggle play any real part in our history; only in the two provinces of Old Canada did this struggle have any real meaning. The Maritimers of 1864 were not concerned with racial problems; their interest in federal union was largely financial, in the recovery of a passing age of sea-going prosperity. The western provinces, with the exception of British Columbia which found its own version of a compact in the terms of union in 1871, were the offspring of the federal loins; their interest in federal union was in their maintenance and subsistence. But in Upper and Lower Canada federation was the solution of the politico-racial contest for supremacy and survival, which had marked their joint history since the day Vaudreuil and Amherst signed the Capitulation of Montreal. The concept of a pact of federation was thus peculiarly a Canadian one (I use Canadian in the sense in which it was used in 1864, and in which it is still used in some parts of the Maritimes today); it still remains peculiarly Canadian. Duality of culture as the central feature of the constitutional problem has a meaning and a reality to the people of the two provinces of Old Canada which it cannot have to those of the other provinces. That is why neither Ontario nor Quebec has departed in its provincial policy from the strict interpretation of the federal basis of the constitution, or from the concept of a federative pact. The identification of the racial pact, which was a very real thing in the 1850's and 1860's, with the compromise arrived at by the several provinces in 1864 and 1866, has tended to obscure the racial aspect of the bargain and to deprive it of some of its strength. The Canadian delegates to Quebec and London were thoroughly convinced that their bargain was a treaty or a pact; however, this conviction was always weaker among the Maritimers than

[60] *The Morning Freeman*, Saint John, N.B., Nov. 25, 1869.

among the Canadians, and especially the French Canadians, whose principal concern as a vital minority, has been and must be the survival of their culture and the pact which is the constitutional assurance of that survival.

It is the racial aspect of the pact of Confederation which gives the pact its historicity and confirms its continued usage. If the population of Canada were one in race, language, and religion, our federation would be marked by flexibility; amendment would be a comparatively easy matter where there was agreement upon fundamental issues. Since history has given us a dual culture, with its diversities of race and language, we must maintain a precarious balance between the two groups; and our constitution is rigid and inflexible. That is what I meant, when I said at the outset, that the historic pact of the Union has become, by acceptance and usage, a necessary convention of our constitution. It will continue to be such so long as the minority group retains its numbers and its will to survive.